The Origins of English Financi

The late seventeenth century was a crucial period in English financial history. A host of joint stock companies emerged, offering the opportunity for investment in projects ranging from the manufacture of paper to the search for sunken treasure. Driven by the demands of the Nine Years' War, the state also employed innovative tactics to attract money, its most famous scheme being the incorporation of the Bank of England. This is the first comprehensive study of the choices and actions of the investors who enthusiastically embraced London's new financial market. It high lights the interactions between public and private finance, looks at how information circulated around the market and was used by speculators and investors, and documents the establishment of the institutions   the Bank of England, the national debt and an active secondary market in that debt   on which England's financial system was built.

ANNE L. MURPHY is Lecturer in the Department of History, University of Hertfordshire.

Cambridge Studies in Economic History

Cambridge Studies in Economic History comprises stimulating and accessible economic history which actively builds bridges to other disciplines. Books in the series will illuminate why the issues they address are important and interesting, place their findings in a comparative context, and relate their research to wider debates and controversies. The series will combine innovative and exciting new research by younger researchers with new approaches to major issues by senior scholars. It will publish distinguished work regardless of chronological period or geographical location.

The Origins of English Financial Markets

Investment and Speculation before the South Sea Bubble

Anne L. Murphy

University of Hertfordshire

CAMBRIDGE
UNIVERSITY PRESS

CAMBRIDGE UNIVERSITY PRESS
Cambridge, New York, Melbourne, Madrid, Cape Town,
Singapore, São Paulo, Delhi, Mexico City

Cambridge University Press
The Edinburgh Building, Cambridge CB2 8RU, UK

Published in the United States of America by Cambridge University Press,
New York

www.cambridge.org
Information on this title: www.cambridge.org/9781107406209

First published 2009
First paperback edition 2012

A catalogue record for this publication is available from the British Library

ISBN 978-0-521-51994-6 Hardback
ISBN 978-1-107-40620-9 Paperback

Contents

Tables

Figures and illustrations

Acknowledgements

This book emerged out of work done for my PhD thesis. The thesis was supervised by Huw Bowen and it is to him that my thanks must go first and foremost. His advice, constructive criticism, careful reading of the various drafts of this work and patient support was invaluable. I would like to thank my two examiners, Julian Hoppit and Phil Cottrell for their insights and advice. Phil Cottrell also encouraged and guided the transition from thesis to book. His support and willingness to put up with my moaning was, and is, very much appreciated.

Much of the work on the thesis and the subsequent alterations that formed this book was financed by two awards from the Economic and Social Research Council (grant numbers PTA-030-2002-00367 and PTA-026-27-0997). I am grateful for the Council's support. I am grateful also to Michael Watson and others at Cambridge University Press for guiding me through the production process.

I have received valuable assistance from staff at the British Library, Public Record Office, Guildhall Library, London, Corporation of London Record Office, Goldsmith's Hall and the East Sussex Record Office, but particular thanks must go to Sarah Millard and Jenny Ulph at the Bank of England for all their help, their patience in dealing with my numerous requests and for their interest in the subject.

A special debt is also owed to Margaret Makepeace at the India Office. Her unfailing passion for the East India Company is infectious and her careful reading of previous drafts was much appreciated.

Preliminary versions of some of the work contained in this book was presented at meetings of the Economic History Society, at Venice International University summer schools and at conferences, workshops and seminars at the universities of Leicester, Cambridge and Oxford and at the Institute of Historical Research. I am indebted to the various participants at those meetings for their comments, advice and questions. I have also benefited from the encouragement, support and advice of Larry Neal, Bernard Attard, John Coffey, Regina Grafe, Paolo Malinima, Wolfgang Kaiser, Biagio Salvemini, Rosemary Sweet, Gary Shea, Natasha Glaisyer,

Stephen Quinn, Luciano Pezzolo, Mauro Carboni and D'Maris Coffman who also read and commented on parts of the final draft. Three anonymous readers offered additional guidance and suggested changes, for which I am grateful. Any and all remaining errors are mine alone.

Along the way life was made much easier by good-humoured colleagues and friends at the University of Leicester, in particular, Stephen Brearley, Claire Townsend, Jeanette Fowler, Matt Tompkins, Cheryl Bailey and especially Tim Davies who also read drafts of the work and offered useful suggestions for improvements. Support also came from colleagues at the University of Exeter, especially from Anna Green and Tim Cooper. Last, but certainly not least, special thanks must go to Phil, Michelle, Ellie and Beth who have offered a home away from home during very many research trips. For these and numerous other reasons this book is dedicated to them.

Dates and spelling

All dates given conform to the Julian calendar, which was in common use in England until 1752, and was until 1700 ten days, and after 1700 eleven days, behind the Gregorian calendar used in many European countries.

It should also be noted that before 1752 the year began on 25 March. For the purpose of this study, however, the year is held to run from January to December. Thus, a date noted by contemporaries as being in January 1697 is transcribed here as January 1698.

Quotations in the text conform to the spelling and punctuation used in the original sources.

Abbreviations

Add. MS	Additional Manuscript, British Library
BL	British Library
BoE	Bank of England
EIC	East India Company
ESRO	East Sussex Record Office
GLL	Guildhall Library, London
HBC	Hudson's Bay Company
IOR	India Office Records
JHC	*Journals of the House of Commons*
LMA	London Metropolitan Archives
NA, PRO	The National Archives, Public Record Office
RAC	Royal African Company

Introduction

The years between 1685 and 1695 witnessed a revolution in public and private finance in England. Around a hundred new joint-stock companies were established, offering investors the opportunity to commit their capital to projects ranging from the manufacture of paper and textiles to the hunt for sunken treasure ships. Public enthusiasm for those investment opportunities stimulated the growth of a surprisingly sophisticated market in equities and derivative instruments. England's new investors learned quickly how to use the market to enhance investment income and manage risk and, inevitably, a new class of speculators and stock-jobbers were able to create risk and take advantage of the market's flaws and inadequacies. Driven by the costs of the Nine Years' War (1689–97) to find new ways of raising funds and having observed the enthusiasm of investors in the stock market, the state also took advantage of the interest in high finance. Between 1693 and 1698 it raised £6,900,000 through the flotation of lottery schemes, the sale of life annuities, and the incorporation of the Bank of England and the New East India Company.

Typically, the optimism with which the new debt and equity markets were greeted did not last. Fears were soon being expressed that the financial system was dominated by stock-jobbers and speculators and that it would draw investment away from trade, the true backbone of the English economy. Those who were brave enough to risk their capital in the stock-market boom of the 1690s had their hopes of large profits dashed as companies were dragged down by inadequate capitalisation, technical incompetence, poor management and the strains of the war and the recoinage of 1696 to 1697. Unsurprisingly, a few investors even found they had put their funds into projects that were little more than chimeras created to defraud the naïve. The new national debt was equally precarious. It has been argued that, because the Glorious Revolution placed control of the country's finances firmly in government hands, the public creditors could feel confident of the security of their investment.[1] Perhaps

---

[1] Most notably in D. C. North and B. R. Weingast, 'Constitutions and Commitment: The Evolution of Institutions Governing Public Choice in Seventeenth Century England', *Journal of Economic History*, 49 (1989), 803 32.

they did initially but their confidence was misplaced. By 1696, with the war progressing badly, the economy under strain and the government's credit deteriorating, no money could be found to pay the interest on the new long-term public debts. Boom had turned to bust.

Yet, this was no false start to England's financial revolution. Many of the small joint-stock companies set up during the 1690s may have failed but the new and innovative methods of raising long-term public funds proved permanent, as did changes in investment habits. Moreover, the institutions created at this time – the Bank of England, the national debt and an active secondary market in that debt – survived, flourished and became the foundation of London's modern financial system. On those foundations Britain built the economic and financial stability that allowed it to outspend its enemies during the wars of the eighteenth century and emerge by 1815 as a dominant imperial and world power. Moreover, despite the emphasis that is generally placed on the country's industrial past, the financial sector of the British economy has, on balance, provided a far more diverse and enduring basis for its wealth and stability. Thus, the development of London's financial system is inextricably linked to the evolution of modern Britain.

In spite of their long-term significance, the financial innovations of the late seventeenth century have seldom been the topic of detailed study. Indeed, when economic historians have considered the early development of England's financial system they have generally done so from rather narrow perspectives. Hence, D. W. Jones focused chiefly on the contribution of merchant capital to the successful establishment of the public funds.[2] Gary De Krey and Bruce Carruthers concentrated on the political motives for investment and the way that political associations may have defined investment choices.[3] Articles by K. G. Davies, Christine MacLeod and Ann Carlos and others offer insightful studies of innovation in the stock market before 1720, but were necessarily limited in scope.[4] Only in the

---

[2] D. W. Jones, 'London Overseas Merchant Groups at the End of the Seventeenth Century and the Moves Against the East India Company', unpublished PhD thesis (Oxford University, 1970). See also D. W. Jones, *War and Economy in the Age of William III and Marlborough* (Oxford: Blackwell, 1988).

[3] G. S. De Krey, *A Fractured Society: The Politics of London in the First Age of Party, 1688 1715* (Oxford: Clarendon Press, 1985); B. G. Carruthers, *City of Capital, Politics and Markets in the English Financial Revolution* (Princeton University Press, 1996).

[4] K. G. Davies, 'Joint Stock Investment in the Later Seventeenth Century', *Economic History Review*, 4 (1952), 283 301; C. MacLeod, 'The 1690s Patents Boom: Invention or Stock Jobbing?', *Economic History Review*, 39 (1986), 549 71; A. M. Carlos and J. L. Van Stone, 'Stock Transfer Patterns in the Hudson's Bay Company: A Study of the English Capital Market in Operation, 1670 1730', *Business History*, 38 (1995), 15 39; A. M. Carlos, J. Key and J. L. Dupree, 'Learning and the Creation of Stock Market Institutions: Evidence from the Royal African and Hudson's Bay Companies, 1670 1700', *Journal of Economic History*, 58 (1998), 318 44.

work of W. R. Scott can we find a comprehensive account of the period before 1720 but Scott's purpose was to explain the workings and financial structure of British business not to provide an account of the functioning of the early stock market.[5] Moreover, it is often the case that the innovations of the 1690s are acknowledged only as an interesting prelude to what in many people's eyes was the defining event of the early development of England's financial system: the South Sea Bubble of 1720. The dominance of the Bubble is to some extent understandable. Depending on your point of view it either provides a timeless insight into the depths of human folly or an early test case for the argument that all financial markets are inherently efficient. But countless reams of paper have been expended on this topic without reaching any definite conclusions. Moreover, neglect of the earlier period and obsession with the Bubble has distorted our view of the course of England's financial revolution in several regards.

First, ignorance of the origins of the English financial markets has led to the assumption that developments in public finance were the driving force behind innovation. Richard Dale went so far as to suggest that the development of a market in government debt preceded the emergence of a market in corporate securities.[6] Even P. G. M. Dickson's commanding study of the financial revolution barely mentioned the developments that took place in the private equity market during the 1680s and 1690s.[7] And Dickson's lead has been followed by many subsequent historians of the financial revolution who have concentrated their attention on explaining the structure and management of the national debt and, with the exception of Roseveare, have tended to look forward from 1720 rather than back to the origins of the market.[8] Yet, by the time of the government's first experiment with long-term funding an extremely active and innovative stock market had already been established, a clear indication that the development of the public funds was led by innovation in the private market.[9]

---

[5] W. R. Scott, *The Constitution and Finance of English, Scottish and Irish Joint Stock Companies to 1720*, 3 vols. (London: Cambridge University Press, 1910 12).

[6] R. Dale, *The First Crash: Lessons from the South Sea Bubble* (Princeton University Press, 2004), p. 22.

[7] P. G. M. Dickson, *The Financial Revolution in England: A Study in the Development of Public Credit, 1688 1756* (London: Macmillan, 1967).

[8] H. Roseveare, *The Financial Revolution, 1660 1760* (Harlow: Longman, 1991); L. Neal, *The Rise of Financial Capitalism: International Capital Markets in the Age of Reason* (Cambridge University Press, 1990); J. Brewer, *The Sinews of Power: War, Money and the English State, 1688 1783* (London: Unwin Hyman, 1994).

[9] This has been shown to have been equally true of the Amsterdam market in which, as Gelderblom and Jonker argue, it was the trading of VOC (Verenigde Oostindische Compagnie) shares rather than government debt that provided the crucial breakthrough

Secondly, in the history of English financial innovation too much credit has been given to the influence of Dutch expertise. The notion that the secret for funding a modern state was brought to England 'in William III's baggage' is still common in spite of the work of Roseveare and others, which shows quite clearly the legacy of changes made to the country's financial system during the period between 1660 and 1688 and the limited impact of Dutch innovation on the English public funds.[10] The chapters that follow will reiterate the point that English endeavour deserves as much, if not greater, credit for the development of England's financial systems and will show that when domestic projectors needed inspiration they looked not only to the Netherlands but to a variety of European financial innovations.

Thirdly, our understanding of the mechanisms for creating trust in the public funds has been distorted by the assumption, expressed most prominently by North and Weingast, that the Glorious Revolution was the turning point in relations between the state and its creditors.[11] North and Weingast argued that it was the promises offered by a state, rather than a sovereign, debt that convinced people to invest in the new long-term debt instruments. Those promises, they suggest, were underpinned by the fact that interest and annuity payments were backed by the appropriation of tax revenue and guaranteed by Act of Parliament and made credible by institutions which ensured that Parliament had no incentive to behave like the sovereign and renege on its debt. North and Weingast's analysis has proved remarkably influential but they had a poor understanding of the early financial revolution.[12] The following chapters will

---

to an active secondary market. O. Gelderblom and J. Jonker, 'Completing a Financial Revolution: The Finance of the Dutch East India Trade and the Rise of the Amsterdam Capital Market, 1595 1612', *Journal of Economic History*, 64 (2004), 666.

[10] Roseveare, *The Financial Revolution*; H. Roseveare, *The Treasury: The Evolution of a British Institution* (London: Allen Lane, 1969); H. Roseveare, *The Treasury, 1660 1870: The Foundations of Control* (London: George Allen and Unwin, 1973); M. J. Braddick, *State Formation in Early Modern England c. 1550 1700* (Cambridge University Press, 2000); C. D. Chandaman, *The English Public Revenue, 1660 1688* (Oxford: Clarendon Press, 1975); J. K. Horsefield, *British Monetary Experiments, 1650 1710* (London: G. Bell and Sons, 1960); S. Quinn, 'Banking before the Bank: London's Unregulated Goldsmith Bankers, 1660 1694', unpublished PhD thesis (University of Illinois at Urbana Champaign, 1994). M. 't Hart, '"The Devil or the Dutch": Holland's Impact on the Financial Revolution in England, 1643 1694', *Parliaments, Estates and Representation*, 11 (1991), 39 52; D. D. Coffman, 'The Fiscal Revolution of the Interregnum: Excise Taxation in the British Isles, 1643 1663', unpublished PhD thesis (University of Pennsylvania, 2008).

[11] North and Weingast, 'Constitutions and Commitment'.

[12] As Sussman and Yafeh argue, the influence of North and Weingast's argument has extended far beyond the financial systems of early modern Britain. N. Sussman and Y. Yafeh, 'Institutional Reforms, Financial Development and Sovereign Debt: Britain, 1690 1790', *Journal of Economic History*, 66 (2006), 906 35. The supposed importance of

show that the financial promises of the post-Glorious Revolution government were no more credible than those of previous Stuart monarchs. Indeed, credible commitment was not offered from above by the institutions of government, it was demanded from below by those who invested in the public funds and it was supported by the creation of an active secondary market in government debt. As such, a far more pertinent analysis of the mechanisms for creating trust is offered by Carlos and Neal's recent article examining the reasons why the British financial sector was able to withstand the shock of the South Sea Bubble. They highlight the resilience and 'sheer vitality' of eighteenth-century English public finance in the years immediately after 1720 which they rightly attribute to the liquidity of the secondary market, the diversity of the customer base for the government's debt, and early modern investors' commitment to the new vehicles for saving created by the financial revolution.[13] But their arguments were made entirely with reference to the period after 1720. Looking back to the origins of the financial market would have revealed that those factors had been a generation in the making. To discover the origins of a liquid market in government debt and account for the trusting relationship that, in the face of numerous obstacles, developed between the state and the public creditors we must look to the events of the 1690s.

Lastly, our understanding of the behaviour of early modern investors has been distorted, most notably by the Bubble debate, which has focused chiefly on whether or not investors responded rationally to the opportunities offered by the South Sea scheme. Opinions range from Charles MacKay's assertion that during 1720 the 'public mind was in a state of unwholesome fermentation' to Garber's dismissal of the episode as speculators 'working on the basis of the best economic analysis available and pushing prices along by their changing view of market fundamentals'.[14] The former arguments tend to draw on anecdotal evidence rather than a comprehensive analysis of behaviour. The latter, although more considered and based on a closer examination of the evidence, tend to ignore the

the Glorious Revolution is also emphasised in analyses of the rise of London's modern financial systems. See G. Burn, *The Re emergence of Global Finance* (Basingstoke: Palgrave Macmillan, 2006), pp. 176 7.

[13] A. M. Carlos and L. Neal, 'The Micro Foundations of the Early London Capital Market: Bank of England Shareholders During and After the South Sea Bubble, 1720 1725', *Economic History Review*, 59 (2006), 498 538.

[14] C. Mackay, *Extraordinary Popular Delusions and the Madness of Crowds* (Ware: Wordsworth Reference, 1995), p. 71; P. Garber, *Famous First Bubbles: The Fundamentals of Early Manias* (Cambridge, Mass.: MIT Press, 2001), p. 122. For a variety of other opinions between those two extremes see J. Carswell, *The South Sea Bubble* (Stroud: Allan Sutton, 1993); E. Chancellor, *Devil Take the Hindmost: A History of Financial Speculation* (Basingstoke: Macmillan, 1999); Dale, *First Crash*; C. P. Kindleberger, *Manias, Panics and Crashes: A History of Financial Crises* (London: Macmillan, 1989); Neal, *Rise of Financial Capitalism*.

human face of the financial market. Instead, such studies examine the behaviour, and most particularly the rationality, of early investors through the action of equity and debt prices.[15] In studying these idealised markets historians and economists have added something to our knowledge of the way price mechanisms work but they leave us with a woefully inadequate understanding of the aims and actions of early modern investors. Many questions remain, therefore, about who invested in the early financial markets, how they came to learn about the opportunities being presented to them and the factors that governed their decision-making.

This gap in our knowledge has become more obvious in recent years as the scope of investigations into the nature of the financial markets and the actions of investors has been widened by behavioural theorists and economic sociologists. Their work has shown that people do not always behave in the ways predicted by economic models.[16] Individuals are affected by their environment and by the opinion of their fellows, they often are unable to assimilate and interpret information correctly, and they frequently allow emotion to dictate their choices. A full understanding of the nature of the financial markets cannot be reached without giving due consideration to these factors and this is especially true of London's first financial markets.

London's early investors did not operate in a vacuum. They were profoundly influenced by a society that was itself struggling to assimilate the many changes imposed by the development of public and private finance. The nature of London's financial markets was closely scrutinised, and hotly debated, by a variety of social and political commentators whose arguments had a powerful effect on the perception of investment. Contemporaries frequently questioned the value of the joint-stock company as a means of raising money to pursue trade and manufacturing. Speculators were characterised as dishonest and manipulative individuals acting without regard for the social disruption that resulted from their

---

[15] See, for example, Neal, *Rise of Financial Capitalism*; Garber, *Famous First Bubbles*; P. Mirowski, 'What Do Markets Do? Efficiency Tests of the Eighteenth Century London Stock Market', *Explorations in Economic History*, 24 (1987), 107 29; and more recently a study of irrational behaviour that offers a similarly restricted focus, R. S. Dale, J. E. V. Johnson and L. Tang, 'Financial Markets Can Go Mad: Evidence of Irrational Behaviour During the South Sea Bubble', *Economic History Review*, 58 (2005), 233 71.

[16] For an overview of these theoretical developments see G. Gigerenzer and R. Selten, eds., *Bounded Rationality: The Adaptive Toolbox* (Cambridge, Mass. and London: MIT Press, 2001); J. H. Kagel and A. E. Roth, *The Handbook of Experimental Economics* (Princeton University Press, 1995); H. Shefrin, *Beyond Greed and Fear: Understanding Behavioral Finance and the Psychology of Investing* (Boston, Mass.: Harvard Business School Press, 2000); A. Shleifer, *Inefficient Markets: An Introduction to Behavioural Finance* (Oxford University Press, 2000); N. J. Smelser and R. Swedberg, eds., *The Handbook of Economic Sociology* (Princeton University Press, 1994).

actions. And there was some antagonism between the landed and moneyed interests with many accusations of political manipulation being levelled against the great moneyed companies. In consequence, investing in the early modern financial market often was depicted as a dangerous and dishonest endeavour. Investors were warned to be cautious in their approach and to be suspicious of professional speculators and rumourmongers. Consideration must be given to how people would have reacted to a market that was viewed in such negative terms especially since this issue not only impacted upon the behaviour of investors but also affected the attitudes of those who sought to regulate and control the new financial markets.

Those who did use the market had to contend with its failings. Information gathering was difficult. Poor communications forced them into the City where they would have struggled to find pertinent information among rumour, opinion and gossip. The assessment of risk was hampered by the dearth of consistent financial information and the limited progress of the complex mathematical techniques that are required for analysis. Where risk could be fully identified, methods of controlling it were limited. Derivative instruments were available but difficult to use. The possibilities for arbitrage were limited by a number of factors including the illiquid nature of the market, the absence of effective substitutes, the potential for collusion between market leaders and high transaction costs. This study will suggest that these factors created an inherently flawed market, one that failed to provide fully for the needs of all investors.

However, the fact that the market survived such unstable beginnings must indicate the presence of a group of investors whose objectives lay beyond mere capital gains. The financial markets in the late seventeenth century are indeed notable because, for many investors, the pursuit of economic goals was accompanied by non-economic ones. For some shareholders, the ownership of stock brought economic or political power and influence that was unattainable through more conventional channels. For many investors, the dominant view of shareholding during the late seventeenth century was one in which shareholder and company had reciprocal rights and responsibilities. Loyalty was demanded on both sides. Thus, the ability to pursue the rational course, that of switching into a more profitable area of investment, was constrained not only by lack of information but also by a sense of loyalty and by the perceived advantages that joint-stock ownership afforded – voting rights, status and, to some extent, political and economic power. The stability that this gave to the larger joint-stock companies of the period formed the foundation for the long-term survival of the financial markets.

Clearly, therefore, to ignore the human face of London's early financial market is to give a misleading impression of its development, its failures and its triumphs. As a result, this book, although predominantly about the construction of a market and, in particular, the complementary development of private and public finance at the end of the seventeenth century, contends that markets are built on and by the people that inhabit them. The main focus of the following chapters, therefore, will be the projectors, brokers, stock-jobbers and investors who provided and utilised England's first financial market. The aim is to understand who those people were, how they came to learn about the opportunities being presented to them, and what were the factors that governed their decisions to commit their capital, and their trust, to the new financial market.

The book is organised into three parts. The first will focus on the emergence and early development of London's financial market. Chapter 1 will examine London's first stock-market boom. In doing so it will draw particularly on the ledgers of the broker Charles Blunt, which include a large number of brokerage accounts covering the years between 1692 and 1695, a key period in the development of the financial markets and one that has, until now, been inadequately explored. Just under 1,500 transactions are contained in these ledgers. They provide a snapshot of a market that was highly sophisticated, and enable a detailed reconstruction of the level and type of business undertaken by specific investors, and by the market as a whole. Chapter 2 will look specifically at the development of the public funds in the period between 1693 and 1698. It will detail the broad European origins of financial innovation and demonstrate that both in terms of development and ongoing survival the public funds owed much to the inventiveness and determination of English projectors and financiers.

The second part will ask what investors knew about the market and how they found the information on which they based their decisions. Using the wealth of published literature that debated issues raised by the development of the market, Chapter 3 will examine how representations of the market were constructed and question the impact this had on investors and on those who sought to regulate the market. Chapter 4 will give attention to the type of printed market information made available in newspapers and market guides, and will attempt to understand how, and to what extent, such information was used by investors. Chapter 5 will reconstruct verbal networks of information in order to understand how those networks functioned and how they defined the investment choices made by individuals.

The final part of this book considers the aims and actions of the first investors in England's financial market. It draws on personal ledgers and account books, in addition to a database of more than 22,000 financial transactions created from information contained in the surviving transfer books,[17] subscription books and stock ledgers of the main joint-stock companies of the period. Chapter 6 will consider how the innovations of the 1690s functioned to extend the scope of the financial market and entice new investors to commit their capital. Chapter 7 will examine the actions of stock-jobbers. It will argue that although stock-jobbers certainly had the power to manipulate the prices of the smaller joint-stocks, their influence did not extend to the larger companies of the period. One of the factors that limited the power of the stock-jobbers was the presence of many risk-averse or inactive investors in England's first financial market. Chapter 8 will examine the aims, choices and behaviour of those investors.

---

[17] Transfer books, as the name suggests, were kept as a record of stock transfers and, although the transaction price was not recorded, they do contain a range of information including the names of the buyer and seller, the amount and the date of transaction. In many cases the occupation and addresses of both buyer and seller were listed. If either individual was absent at the time of the transaction, details would also be given of the person acting with power of attorney. On occasion other personal details were also recorded.

1   London's first stock-market boom

In June 1687, Captain William Phips sailed into London carrying a haul of Spanish treasure salvaged from a ship that had sunk off the coast of Hispaniola in the West Indies in 1641. The treasure, which chiefly consisted of silver, was valued at more than £200,000. At the time this was an astonishing sum and Phips was greeted as a returning hero.[1] Besides his share of the haul, which amounted to £11,000, Phips received a knighthood and was made provost marshal of New England. Phips's backers, among them Christopher Monck, the second Duke of Albemarle, were paid a dividend of just over £5,000 for every £100 invested.[2] Albemarle received an impressive £43,000, much of which went to pay the spendthrift duke's enormous debts.[3]

The incredible profits made by the adventurers ensured that Phips's triumphant return became the most talked-about event of the moment. John Evelyn wrote in his diary:

There was about this time brought into the Downes, a Vast treasure which after 45 years being sunk in a Spanish Galioon ... was now weighed up, by certaine Gentlemen & others, who were [at] the Charge of Divers &c: to the suddaine enriching of them, beyond all expectation: The Duke of Albemarles share came

---

[1] The contemporary account of Phips's life was C. Mather, *Pietas in Patriam: The Life of His Excellency Sir William Phips* (London, 1697) and the most recent and most comprehensive account of his adventure, P. Earle, *The Wreck of the Almiranta: Sir William Phips and the Search for the Hispaniola Treasure* (London: Macmillan, 1979). Other notable accounts include V. F. Barnes, 'The Rise of William Phips', *New England Quarterly*, 1 (1928), 271 94; C. H. Karraker, 'Spanish Treasure, Casual Revenue of the Crown', *Journal of Modern History*, 5 (1933), 301 18; R. H. George, 'The Treasure Trove of William Phips', *New England Quarterly*, 6 (1933), 294 318.

[2] The investors were Monck, Lord Falkland, Sir James Hayes, Sir John Narborough, Francis Nicholson, Isaac Foxcroft and John Smith, a London merchant. They agreed to share the treasure in proportion to their subscriptions after one tenth had been offered to the Crown and Phips had been awarded one sixteenth.

[3] For details of Albemarle's colourful life see E. F. Ward, *Christopher Monck, the Duke of Albemarle* (London: John Murray, 1915).

(tis believed) to 50000, & some private Gent: who adventured but 100 pounds & little more, to ten [thousand].[4]

A correspondent of John Ellis alluded to the great public interest in the adventure. 'Mountains are made of the matter', he wrote, 'but it is certainly a very considerable thing.'[5] The news also spread quickly throughout the country and around Europe. The Tuscan envoy wrote to his masters in Florence: '[t]he money fished up has caused great excitement and has awakened the spirit of many to engage in similar enterprises, which were previously thought impossible'.[6]

The envoy was correct in his assessment. In the years that followed a number of joint-stock companies were set up to fish for wrecks. Some were inspired by reports of other sunken treasure troves. Thomas Neale, a prolific projector, set up a joint-stock company in March 1691 to recover silver from a ship lost off Broadhaven in Ireland.[7] Other companies were inspired by technological innovations. In July 1691, John Overing applied for a patent on a diving suit that gave 'liberty for a man to see, walk, and work for a considerable time many fathoms under water'.[8] Having been granted his patent, Overing handed over his invention to a joint-stock company. In this way, according to the anonymous author of *Angliae Tutamen*, 'Projects, like Parents, beget their like, and multiply wonderfully, Projects upon Projects'.[9] For that observer, the great profits made by Phips and his backers provided the immediate catalyst for the stock-market boom of the 1690s.

The origins of the stock-market boom

Although Phips's adventure offers a pleasingly romantic beginning to London's first stock-market boom, as an explanation for the rise of financial capitalism it is not satisfactory. Even contemporary writers recognised that a variety of other short- and long-term factors contributed to the creation of an economic and social environment in which the

---

[4] J. Evelyn, *The Diary of John Evelyn*, edited by E. S. De Beer, 6 vols. (Oxford: Clarendon Press, 1955), vol. IV, p. 552. Narcissus Luttrell also noted the rich rewards paid to the adventurers in his diary: N. Luttrell, *A Brief Historical Relation of State Affairs from September 1678 to April 1714*, 6 vols. (Oxford University Press, 1857), vol. I, p. 407.
[5] G. Ellis, ed., *The Ellis Correspondence: Letters Written During the Years 1686, 1687, 1688, and addressed to John Ellis, Esq.*, 2 vols. (London, 1829), vol. I, pp. 296 7.
[6] Quoted in Earle, *Wreck of the Almiranta*, p. 191.
[7] For details of Neale's life and projects, see J. H. Thomas, 'Thomas Neale, a Seventeenth Century Projector', unpublished PhD thesis (University of Southampton, 1979); Scott, *Constitution and Finance*, vol. II, p. 488.
[8] Quoted in Scott, *Constitution and Finance*, vol. II, p. 488.
[9] Anon., *Angliae Tutamen: or the Safety of England* (London, 1695), p. 23.

financial market could thrive. Most notably, John Houghton, writing in 1694, argued:

a great many *Stocks* have arisen since this War with *France*; for Trade being obstructed at Sea, few that had Money were willing it should lie idle, and a great many that wanted Employments studied how to dispose of their Money, that they might be able to command it whensoever they had occasion.[10]

Similarly, Samuel Jeake, a merchant from the Sussex town of Rye, recorded in his diary the effect war had on his business. At first, as the prospect of war with France became ever more certain, his 'Trade of negotiating Bills of Exchange ... decreased & the war coming on [he] gave it over'. By 1694 Jeake was complaining that the war had spoiled all his trade '& I making but 5 per cent of my money at Interest upon Mortgages and Bonds, upon which I could but barely maintain my family'.[11] These factors led him to investment in the public funds. Historians have found evidence to support Jeake's complaints. In particular, D. W. Jones's exploration of the activities of merchants during the Nine Years' War has shown that for those merchants whose trade was most severely affected by the conflict, notably those active in the wine trade and those trading in the western Mediterranean, investment in the joint-stock companies of the period supplied employment for their redundant trading capital.[12]

The prospect of capital gains and the ease with which shares could be liquidated made them an ideal investment for merchants and they did show considerable enthusiasm for the new financial opportunities, becoming significant investors and speculators, as well as taking on the broking and market-making functions that were necessary to support stock-market liquidity. However, the link between idle merchant capital and talent and the evolution of the stock market, although important, was not necessarily as strong as Houghton and Jones asserted. It will be shown below that the investment opportunities of the 1690s ultimately attracted the talents of a broad range of individuals. Equally, historians agree that even without the constraints war put on overseas trade, investment capital was abundant during the late seventeenth century.[13]

---

[10] Houghton, *A Collection for Improvement of Husbandry and Trade*, 15 Jun. 1694.
[11] M. Hunter and A. Gregory, eds., *An Astrological Diary of the Seventeenth Century: Samuel Jeake of Rye, 1652 1699* (Oxford University Press, 1988), pp. 195, 233.
[12] Jones, *War and Economy*, pp. 249 50.
[13] In particular, see P. Deane, 'Capital Formation in Britain before the Railway Age', *Economic Development and Cultural Change*, 9 (1961), 356; Dickson, *Financial Revolution*, p. 301; Jones, *War and Economy*, p. 278.

By 1688 England was already a wealthy country. The post-Restoration period had seen significant improvements in all aspects of the English economy. Agricultural production had benefited from a continuous process of land reclamation, enclosure and advances in fertilisation and feeding practices.[14] Trade saw the greatest advances. Supported by Charles II's navigation policies, an increase in colonisation and the growth of domestic demand, trade to Asia and the Americas increased and the period between 1660 and 1688 witnessed the rapid and revolutionary growth of the re-export trade.[15] The 1680s, in particular, saw both a 'marvellous bounty' from the land and a significant increase in foreign trade.[16] Even industry, although still very much in its infancy, reaped the rewards of an increasingly affluent population, growing domestic demand, some technological innovation and, most notably, the growth in foreign markets.

Equally notable was the change in attitudes towards wealth and consumption which stemmed in great part from the moral relaxation associated with the reign of Charles II and the increasing secularisation of late seventeenth-century society.[17] For some contemporaries such changes generated fear. They worried particularly about religious and moral decline.[18] In a sermon preached in 1691 it was argued that 'Where Men are no more restrained by the principles of Religion ... Nature must break out, and undisciplined Appetites and Passions must work the Dissolution of Society and Government.'[19] Those appetites and passions seemed to manifest themselves not only in dissolute behaviour but also in the increasing pursuit of luxury, which undermined moral values and contributed to the erosion of social hierarchies as emulative consumption led to the 'mistress and her maid' desiring the same goods

---

[14] G. Holmes, *The Making of a Great Power: Late Stuart and Early Georgian Britain, 1660 1722* (London and New York: Longman, 1993), p. 49. Holmes also notes the importance of the Royal Society, which, from 1660, played an active role in disseminating information about improvements in agricultural techniques and practices.

[15] R. Davis, 'English Foreign Trade, 1660 1700', *Economic History Review*, 7 (1954), 162.

[16] Holmes, *Making of a Great Power*, p. 49.

[17] P. Earle, 'Economy of London, 1660 1730', in P. O'Brien, D. Keene, M 't Hart and H. van der Wee, eds., *Urban Achievement in Early Modern Europe* (Cambridge University Press, 2004), p. 91.

[18] For details of the consequent debate and attempts to bring about moral reform see D. W. R. Bahlman, *The Moral Revolution of 1688* (New Haven: Yale University Press 1957).

[19] G. Burnet, 'A sermon preached at Whitehall, before the king and queen, on the 29th of April, 1691', in G. Burnet, *A Third Collection of Several Tracts and Discourses Written in the Years 1690 to 1703* (London, 1703), quoted in J. Hoppit, *A Land of Liberty? England, 1689 1727* (Oxford: Clarendon Press, 2000), p. 238.

and wearing the same clothes.[20] More perceptive writers recognised the increased desire for consumer goods as a spur to economic activity and especially to trade. As Nicholas Barbon wrote, 'It is not Necessity ... but ... the wants of the Mind, Fashion, and the desire of Novelties, and Things Scarce, that causeth Trade.'[21] From the perspective of this study, it is clear that the 'wants of the mind' ensured not only a growth in trade but also that many people were keen to embrace the money-making opportunities that seemed to be offered by joint-stock investment.

Economic progress was supported by the emergence of what might be termed a financial services industry. Growing prosperity and the desire to protect and conserve wealth stimulated a rise in the business of insurance.[22] Fire and marine insurance were particular growth areas, the first a perceived necessity in the wake of the Great Fire of 1666 and the latter encouraged by the revolution in overseas trade. The speculative boom of the 1690s also saw the founding of businesses offering life insurance. The first of those was Richard Carter's Friendly Society for Widows established in 1696 to offer protection to wives against the economic hardship that often resulted from the death of their husbands.[23] The spread of the insurance business represented not only an important aspect of the development of finance capitalism, and one which served to underpin commercial confidence and preserve wealth, but also a growing sense in English society that the hazards of life and commerce could be converted into calculable, manageable risks.[24]

Equally, there emerged a class of men whose business it was to aid the flow and define the direction of capital. Scriveners, for example, began to play an increasing role in the land market and in servicing the financial needs of landowners. They also provided some banking functions for their customers, in addition to those services that might today be offered by solicitors, accountants, and stockbrokers.[25] And, as Stephen Quinn shows, more specialised financial services were provided by a growing network of goldsmith-bankers who, in addition to their traditional activities, provided many of the facilities we would associate with a modern bank.[26] This network not only reduced transaction costs, and created

---

[20] Hoppit, *Land of Liberty?*, p. 317.

[21] N. Barbon, *A Discourse of Trade* (London, 1690) quoted in Hoppit, *Land of Liberty?*, p. 316.

[22] G. Clark, *Betting on Lives: The Culture of Life Insurance in England, 1695 1775* (Manchester University Press, 1999), p. 2.

[23] Ibid., p. 73.   [24] Ibid., pp. 1 3.

[25] D. C. Coleman, 'London Scriveners and the Estate Market in the Later Seventeenth Century', *Economic History Review*, 4 (1951), p. 229.

[26] Quinn, 'Banking before the Bank', p. 2. See also W. R. Bisschop, *The Rise of the London Money Market, 1640 1826* (London: Cass, 1968).

networks of information of which private customers could take advantage, it also helped to increase money supply, and thus the capital available for investment, as bankers' notes and receipts circulated, as loans in excess of deposits could be made and as incomes were swelled by interest payments.[27]

Importantly for the development of the financial market, much of this progress was centred on London, which was by far the most populous city in Britain. It was also the dominant port for both overseas and coastal trade, the chief centre for industry and, by the end of the 1680s, London was reaping the benefits of the rapid expansion of mercantile activity. It also attracted migrants both from within the British Isles and, importantly, from Europe, making the city a 'truly cosmopolitan community' where the ideas and capital of recent migrants would support economic development.[28] By the start of the Nine Years' War, therefore, London was a fertile environment for the growth of an active financial market. What it lacked was not capital or skills but investment opportunities.

Although by 1688 the English joint-stock company already had a long history,[29] only a few companies existed before the Glorious Revolution and, for the most part, their capitalisation was low and their shareholders were few. The Hudson's Bay Company, for example, began its life in 1668 with £10,500 in capital and only eighteen shareholders.[30] Even the East India Company, which operated with a far larger capital, had only 511 shareholders by 1688.[31] The rewards for those few were great, especially during the 1680s. It was during this period that the East India Company paid dividends of 25 per cent, and in 1689, 50 per cent. The Hudson's Bay Company also paid a 50 per cent dividend several times during the 1680s. Even the Royal African Company paid dividends of

[27] Earle, 'Economy of London', p. 92.
[28] Ibid., p. 85.
[29] For histories of the most important English joint stock companies see, K. N. Chaudhuri, *The English East India Company: The Study of an Early Joint Stock Company, 1600 1640* (London: Cass, 1965); K. N. Chaudhuri, *The Trading World of Asia and the English East India Company, 1660 1760* (Cambridge University Press, 1978); J. Keay, *The Honourable Company: A History of the English East India Company* (London: HarperCollins, 1991); J. H. Clapham, *The Bank of England: A History*, 2 vols. (London: Cambridge University Press, 1945); K. G. Davies, *The Royal African Company* (London: Longmans, 1957); E. E. Rich, *The Hudson's Bay Company* (London: The Hudson's Bay Record Society, 1961); T. S. Willan, *The Early History of the Russia Company, 1553 1603* (Manchester University Press, 1956) and for an overview of the development of the English joint stock company see G. Cawston and A. H. Keane, *The Early Chartered Companies (AD 1296 1858)* (London: Edward Arnold, 1896); P. Griffiths, *A Licence to Trade: The History of the English Chartered Companies* (London: E. Benn, 1974); Scott, *Constitution and Finance*.
[30] Scott, *Constitution and Finance*, vol. III, pp. 472 3.
[31] India Office Records, Old East India Company, List of holders of stock, L/AG/1/10/2.

Table 1.1 *Annual averages of transactions in East India, Royal African and Hudson's Bay Company shares, 1661–1689*

	East India Company		Royal African Company		Hudson's Bay Company	
	Average number of transactions	Total value to nearest £100	Average number of transactions	Total value to nearest £100	Average number of transactions	Total value to nearest £100
1661 63	44	18,900				
1664 66	57	23,900				
1667 69	71	32,100				
1670 72	126	47,000				
1673 75	152	53,800	39	16,700	7	1,800
1676 78	131	55,400	41	16,200	6	1,800
1679 81	172	68,100	40	13,700	10	4,200
1682 84	780	268,300	67	16,400	29	4,550
1685 87	537	191,000	77	16,200	22	3,000
1688 89	655	238,000	91	23,400	23	2,700

Sources: P. Lougheed, 'The East India Company in English Domestic Politics, 1657 1688', unpublished PhD thesis (Oxford University, 1980) cited in Carruthers, *City of Capital*, p. 167; Carlos *et al.*, 'Learning and Stock Market Institutions', 326, 337.

10.5 per cent.[32] In consequence, interest in the opportunities offered by overseas trade increased considerably and, as can be seen in Table 1.1, there was a slow but steady growth in share trading.

Yet, although the stock market was expanding, it remained very difficult to find opportunities for joint-stock investment. Shares still changed hands infrequently and even bond issuances were invariably over-subscribed. Indeed, when John Verney was asked in 1676 by his father's friend Vere Gawdy to 'Remember the East India for I long to have £800 placed there', Verney was forced to reply that there was 'no hope ... they having more [capital] than they know what to do with'.[33] The complaint that the East India Company's restricted capital and monopoly trading rights privileged the few and excluded many more who desired a share in the very considerable profits that could be gained from trade with the East was heard very often during the 1670s and 1680s.

While the advent of the Nine Years' War cannot provide a complete explanation for the rise of the market, there can be no question that it did

[32] Scott, *Constitution and Finance*, vol. II, pp. 179, 237, 34.
[33] Quoted in S. E. Whyman, *Sociability and Power in Late Stuart England: The Cultural Worlds of the Verneys, 1660 1720* (Oxford University Press, 1999), p. 75.

Table 1.2 *Annual total of patents enrolled, 1680–1709*

Year	No. of patents	Year	No. of patents	Year	No. of patents
1680	0	1690	3	1700	2
1681	6	1691	20	1701	1
1682	8	1692	23	1702	1
1683	7	1693	19	1703	0
1684	13	1694	11	1704	5
1685	5	1695	9	1705	1
1686	3	1696	5	1706	4
1687	6	1697	3	1707	3
1688	4	1698	7	1708	2
1689	1	1699	5	1709	3
Totals	53		105		22

Source: C. MacLeod, *Inventing the Industrial Revolution: The English Patent System, 1660–1800* (Cambridge University Press, 1988), p. 150.

much to create new opportunities for investment. Indeed, many projects proposed during the early 1690s aimed to derive an advantage from the requirements of war. Hence in the years following 1689 there was a flood of applications for patents covering new types of weapons, methods of manufacturing gunpowder and saltpetre and the development of metal alloys suitable for ordnance.[34] Also a number of new industries were established to take advantage of the restrictions war placed on imported goods. William Stout, a Lancastrian grocer, recorded in his diary that the interruption of French imports 'put us upon the silk, linen, paper and many other of their manufactorys, to the enriching of the nation'.[35]

Yet, just as the capital that funded these innovations was not solely a product of the constraints of war, so an increase in the establishment of new projects was observable before 1689. As may be seen in Table 1.2, the peak of patenting activity occurred between 1691 and 1694 but there had also been a significant level of activity during the 1680s. Of course, patenting activity cannot necessarily be equated with technological progress. MacLeod makes the point that patents were used for a variety of reasons not connected with innovation. Some were used to secure licences for banking or lottery projects. Developers of watermills used patents to override objections about the diversion of water supply and many other projectors used patents to evade the regulation of an established

[34] MacLeod, '1690s Patents Boom', 558.   [35] Quoted ibid.

monopoly or guild.[36] Nevertheless, the figures do indicate a marked increase in entrepreneurial endeavour that predates the Nine Years' War.

Equally indicative of a longer heritage of innovation was the contribution of the Huguenot refugees who fled to England throughout the seventeenth century, but most particularly after the revocation of the Edict of Nantes in 1685. The refugees brought with them 'important increments of industrial knowledge as well as capital, credit and enterprise'.[37] The Royal Lustring Company, incorporated in 1692, was established by a group of prominent Huguenot refugees. According to Gwynn the company claimed, within a few years of its inception, to be employing 670 looms in London and a further 98 in Ipswich.[38] Huguenot contributions in terms of technical and entrepreneurial skill can also be found in other joint-stock companies of the period, notably the Company of White Paper Makers in England (hereafter referred to as the White Paper Company), which was founded in 1685 by John Briscoe with 'the assistance of some Frenchmen, who instructed him in the secrets of the trade'.[39] The King's and Queen's Corporation for the Linen Manufacture in England (hereafter referred to as the Linen Company) was also founded by Huguenot refugees for the exploitation of French methods of manufacturing fine white linen.[40]

The Nine Years' War, therefore, encouraged innovation and created opportunities for investment and speculation but it also interacted with factors that were already poised to stimulate the creation of an active capital market. It is clear that perceptions of the potential rewards of joint-stock investment were also being formed prior to the Glorious Revolution. In particular, the large and regular dividends paid by the trading companies during the 1670s and 1680s had taught investors that

---

[36] Ibid., 555.
[37] D. C. Coleman, *The Economy of England, 1450 1750* (Oxford University Press, 1977), p. 156.
[38] R. D. Gwynn, *Huguenot Heritage: The History and Contribution of the Huguenots in Britain* (London: Routledge and Kegan Paul, 1985), pp. 67 8.
[39] Scott, *Constitution and Finance*, vol. III, p. 64.
[40] For further on the Huguenot contribution to the various industries of the period see J. W. Thompson, 'Some Economic Factors in the Revocation of the Edict of Nantes', *The American Historical Review*, 14 (1908), 38 50; W. C. Scoville, 'The Huguenots and the Diffusion of Technology', *Journal of Political Economy*, 60 (1952), 294 311; P. Thornton and N. Rothstein, 'The Importance of Huguenots in the London Silk Industry', *Proceedings of the Huguenot Society of London*, vol. XX (1958 64), pp. 60 88; A. Plummer, *The London Weavers' Company 1600 1970* (London: Routledge and Kegan Paul, 1972). However, while Scott asserts that the ultimate importance of the influx of skilled Huguenot workers can scarcely be overrated, it should be noted that Holmes argues that their contribution was less significant and that many of the developments in the textile and other industries of this period were the product of domestic enterprise. Scott, *Constitution and Finance*, vol. I, p. 313; Holmes, *Making of a Great Power*, p. 54.

the potential rewards were great and this message was reinforced by the dividend paid to Captain Phips's backers. Having taken note of these lessons, many people were more than ready to invest in the new joint-stock companies that emerged during the late 1680s and early 1690s.

The extent of London's first stock market

Between 1685 and 1695 many projectors sought to raise capital through joint-stock funding. Their projects ranged from the wreck-diving companies mentioned above, to companies for the manufacture of paper, glass and textiles, mining enterprises, metal works, insurance companies and banks.[41] Any attempt to define the precise nature of investors' interest in those companies is, however, constrained by the fact that although a majority of the transfer books and stock ledgers of the main joint-stock companies survive, those of the smaller enterprises that existed during this time have for the most part been lost. Additionally, the transactions registered in the surviving transfer books and stock ledgers were only those where a physical exchange of stock took place. Other sources reveal the existence of a highly sophisticated and entirely unregulated market in what would today be described as derivative products.[42] Time bargains, puts and refusals – futures and options in modern parlance – were regularly traded in the London market from at least as early as 1691. The nature of those transactions, particularly those that expired unexercised or culminated in a cash settlement rather than a physical settlement, meant that there would have been no immediate need to register anything other than the original bargain and no necessity to retain this agreement once the exercise date was passed.

Given the dearth of surviving data, the ledgers of the broker Charles Blunt provide a unique, if only partial, insight into activity in the shares and derivatives of the joint-stock companies that emerged during the early 1690s.[43] Blunt was an upholsterer who turned to stockbroking in 1692. The precise reasons why he chose to neglect a thriving business to become involved in the financial market are not known but it is probable that, like many others, he was attracted by the prospect of easy profits. It is also

---

[41] Histories of many of the minor joint stock companies established prior to 1720 can be found in Scott, *Constitution and Finance.*

[42] Official regulation of the market was limited and difficult to enforce. However, while stock transfers fell under the control of the companies themselves, derivative products could not be policed in this way. Unregulated in this sense, therefore, indicates that control of such trading was beyond the reach even of the companies themselves. The issue of market regulation will be discussed further in Chapter 2.

[43] NA, PRO, Papers of Charles Blunt, C114/165.

likely that Charles was influenced in his decision by his cousin John Blunt. John, most famous as the chief architect of the South Sea Bubble, was a scrivener in the early 1690s and already an active speculator. He was to become cousin Charles's best customer.

Between 1692 and 1695, Charles Blunt acted as broker for more than 150 individuals and kept the transfer books for one company, Estcourt's Lead Mine, which was in business between 1693 and 1695. It is impossible to ascertain the proportion of the market formed by Blunt's clients so using his ledgers to estimate the volume of trade on London's first stock market is problematic. Nevertheless, we do know that there were a number of such brokers operating during the early 1690s, perhaps as many as thirty, thus Blunt's business did not dominate the market. We also know that brokers did not generally specialise in a particular company or instrument. In fact, in 1708 the brokers licensed by the City who were operating in joint-stocks and government securities not only traded in a broad spectrum of financial instruments but also found it necessary to be involved in other kinds of transactions in order to make ends meet.[44] Given the diversity of the transactions in Blunt's ledgers and the fact that he continued to pursue his upholstery business even at the height of his success, we may conclude that he too did not specialise in any particular company or instrument and that his business was broadly representative of London's early stock market. Thus, although Blunt's ledgers do not cover the entire period under consideration, as can be seen in Table 1.3, they do give an interesting insight into the volume of trade in shares and derivatives in the 1690s and allow us to draw cautious conclusions about the extent of London's first stock market.

Scott estimated that around 100 new English joint-stock companies were established between 1688 and 1695,[45] but the evidence presented in Blunt's ledgers shows that the market was not as extensive as might have been expected in an environment where so many companies existed. Blunt's clients traded in only twenty-three different companies. Nor is this finding necessarily a reflection of the limitations of Blunt's business. The activity recorded in the ledgers shows a marked similarity to the price lists published during 1692 in John Houghton's *Collection for Improvement of Husbandry and Trade*. Houghton's list of tradable securities included only eight companies when publication commenced in March 1692.[46]

44 Anon., *Reasons Humbly Offered Against Altering the Act for Restraining the Number of Brokers* (1708).

45 Scott, *Constitution and Finance*, vol. I, p. 327.

46 J. Houghton, *Collection for Improvement*, 30 Mar. 1692. In 1694 Houghton expanded his list of stocks to encompass approximately sixty companies, yet he did not provide prices for many of the smaller companies indicating that turnover in those enterprises remained low.

Table 1.3 *Annual number of stock and derivative transactions conducted by Charles Blunt's clients, 1692–1695*

Company	1692		1693		1694		1695	
	Stock	Derivatives	Stock	Derivatives	Stock	Derivatives	Stock	Derivatives
Royal African Company	27	11	9	1	2	1	1	0
Bank of England	–	–	–	–	1	0	3	11
Blue Paper Company	5	1	11	3	0	0	0	0
Carving	0	0	1	0	0	0	0	0
Company of Copper Miners	3	1	15	5	11	7	0	0
East India Company	29	22	14	26	3	14	0	0
Engine	0	0	2	0	0	0	0	0
Jersey Linen Company	5	2	3	0	2	0	0	0
Glass-Maker's Company	104	26	53	75	13	10	0	0
Glass Bottle Company	0	0	0	0	1	0	0	0
Hudson's Bay Company	3	0	0	0	0	0	0	0
Irish Paper Company	0	0	4	3	1	0	0	0
Estcourt's Lead Mine	–	–	73	94	7	13	0	0
Linen Company	302	124	95	70	19	2	0	0
Royal Lustring Company	0	0	1	1	0	0	0	0
Million Bank	–	–	–	–	–	–	3	2
Orphan's Bank	–	–	–	–	–	–	0	3
White Paper Company	28	10	36	33	3	0	0	3
Pennsylvania	0	0	1	0	0	0	0	0
Saltpetre	0	0	2	1	0	0	0	0

Table 1.3 (cont.)

Company	1692		1693		1694		1695	
	Stock	Derivatives	Stock	Derivatives	Stock	Derivatives	Stock	Derivatives
Tap	0	0	6	2	0	0	0	0
Venetian Steel Company	0	0	0	0	1	0	0	0
Water Company	–	–	–	–	17	2	7	0
Totals	506	197	326	314	81	49	7	16

Source: NA, PRO C114/165. In approximately one-third of the transactions recorded in his ledgers Blunt acted as broker for both the purchaser and seller of the stock or derivative. For the purposes of this table the two sides of the transaction are counted as one trade.

Blunt used short forms to record the details of his clients' trades; thus, not all of the unfamiliar companies listed above can be easily identified. The ones that can be readily identified are: the Blue Paper Company, the Company of the Copper Miners of England, the Company of the Royal Corporation of London for carrying on the Linen and Paper Manufacture within the Islands of Jersey and Guernsey, the Company of Glass-Makers of London, the Glass Bottle Company, the Irish Paper Company, Estcourt's Lead Mine, the King's and Queen's Corporation for the Linen Manufacture in England, the Orphan's Bank, the Royal Lustring Company of England, the Company of White Paper Makers of England, the Company for making Salpetre in England and the Venetian Steel Company. For the most part the histories of those companies can be found in Scott, Constitution and Finance. Those that cannot be readily identified are Carving, Tap, Pennsylvania, Engine (which probably referred to Captain Poyntz's engine for draining lands) and Water (possibly Marchmont's Waterworks).

Table 1.4 *Annual number of stock transfers in the main trading companies, 1688–1698*

Year	EIC*	RAC	HBC
1688	624	101	25
1689		82	26
1690		39	50
1691	3,139	930	149
1692		491	109
1693		391	85
1694	2,426	207	57
1695		194	54
1696		129	22
1697		195	19
1698	1,158	734	12

Sources: IOR, L/AG/1/10/2, fos. 199 204; IOR, Old East India Company, Transfer Books, L/AG/14/3/2 4; NA, PRO, Royal African Company, Transfer Books, Stock Journals and Stock Ledgers, T70/187 9; NA, PRO, Hudson's Bay Company, Transfer Books, BH 1/465, A 43/1 2.

*Few East India Company transfer books survive from this period and those records encompass no complete years. Thus, the above figures have been calculated by taking an average of the trades conducted in the known periods and multiplying them by 240 the average number of trading days in a year. In 1691, therefore, 1,086 trades were conducted between 4 June and 19 September on 83 trading days an average of 13.08 per day. Multiplying this figure by 240 trading days gives an estimated total for that year of 3,139 trades.

The eight, which were the East India, Royal African, Hudson's Bay, Linen, Glass-Maker's and White Paper Companies, the Company of Copper Miners and a wreck-diving company corresponded closely to those companies most actively traded by Blunt's clients.[47] Therefore, it would seem that those companies formed the core of the stock market during the early 1690s.

Blunt's ledgers also give us an insight into the volume of share trading at this time. A comparison of the number of transactions conducted by Blunt's clients with the number of transfers of stock of the main trading companies of the period (presented in Table 1.4) demonstrates that Blunt's business encompassed only a very small proportion of the activity

[47] The wreck diving company was not specified by Houghton but has been identified by Parkinson as the Company for Recovering Treasure from Wrecks off Broadhaven. G. Parkinson, 'The London Stock Market in the 1690s', unpublished MPhil dissertation (University of Cambridge, 2006), p. 35.

in the East India and Royal African Companies. Since Blunt was not a specialist, it may be inferred that there was, in the market as a whole, a very considerable turnover of stock in the White Paper and Glass-Maker's Company and, most particularly, in the Linen Company. This assumption is confirmed by the history of the companies presented by Scott and also by the author of *Angliae Tutamen* who noted particularly that the Linen Company attracted a great deal of speculative interest.[48]

The smaller companies listed in Blunt's ledgers undoubtedly commanded far less general interest although, as will be seen below, they were not immune from the attentions of speculators. A more or less complete trading history survives for Estcourt's Lead Mine that demonstrates the level of activity in the smaller joint-stock companies. In 1693, its first year of existence, there were only 99 share transactions, in 1694 there were 105 transactions, and in 1695 there were only 30.[49] In spite of the fact that Charles Blunt kept the Company's transfer book, his brokerage business did not command a monopoly of the trade, thus the number of time bargains and options traded on Estcourt's Lead Mine stock cannot be established accurately. However, from the evidence presented in Table 1.3, it may be suggested that the number of derivatives traded was similar to, or slightly greater than, the number of share transactions conducted. There were, therefore, approximately 200 trades per year in the shares and derivatives of Estcourt's Lead Mine. Since Estcourt's Lead Mine was more representative of the joint-stock companies of the period than the Linen Company or East India Company, it must be assumed that although the boom of the early 1690s extended the scope of the investment market it still offered opportunities to few investors.

Derivatives trading in the 1690s

The most important insights to be gleaned from Blunt's ledgers concern the volume, structure and purpose of derivatives trading in the early modern period. Between 1692 and 1695 Blunt's clients traded 576 derivatives – the majority of those being stock options. That sum represented just over 39 per cent of all transactions recorded by the broker. This implies that at the height of the stock-market boom – the period between 1691 and the end of 1693 – several thousand derivatives were transacted each year against a variety of different joint-stock companies.

---

[48] Scott, *Constitution and Finance*, vol. III, pp. 67 70, 110 13, 90 1; Anon., *Angliae Tutamen*, p. 24.
[49] NA, PRO, C114/165.

That the stock market of the 1690s supported an active trade in derivatives should not be seen as surprising. Throughout the seventeenth century and probably before, options had been used in Europe to speculate in commodities, particularly those that experienced wide price fluctuations, such as corn, salt, herrings and, of course, tulips.[50] Gerald Malynes, writing in the 1620s, had introduced options to an English readership stating that they were 'commodious when a mans money is not so readie, to buy much, and to make a great imployment with little money, which happeneth upon some soden advice many times unexpected'.[51] Although not so widely used in London as on the Continent, English merchants would certainly have known about such instruments and probably used them to speculate in commodities. Malynes himself claimed to have made money in corn and salt.[52] And what was commonplace in the trading of commodities was easily transferable to the trading of equities and debt.

The nature of the London stock options market certainly indicates that participants were taking advantage of prior knowledge and experience. Blunt's ledgers show that the market was simple in structure and the instruments used were highly standardised, a feature which undoubtedly made it easier to match clients' needs under what were often illiquid trading conditions.[53] However, as may be seen in Figure 1.1, these simple trading structures were supported by very detailed pre-printed contracts which showed a focused understanding of the practical risks involved in the trading of options. Notably, the contracts were very specific about issues that might have led to disagreements between buyers and sellers, for example, the transfers of funds, the allocation of potential dividend payments and the means of informing the option seller of intention to exercise.[54]

[50] Tulip bulbs became objects of particularly heavy speculation in the Netherlands between 1634 and 1637. For details of this episode see Garber, *Famous First Bubbles*; A. Goldgar, *Tulipmania: Money, Honor and Knowledge in the Dutch Golden Age* (Chicago and London: University of Chicago Press, 2007); Mackay, *Extraordinary Popular Delusions*.

[51] G. Malynes, *Consuetudo, Vel Lex Mercatoria* (London, 1622), p. 203.

[52] Ibid. For further details of the use of options in the Amsterdam market see V. Barbour, *Capitalism in Amsterdam in the Seventeenth Century* (Ann Arbor: University of Michigan Press, 1950), p. 74; O. Gelderblom and J. Jonker, 'Amsterdam as the Cradle of Modern Futures Trading and Options Trading, 1550 1650', in W. M. Goetzmann and K. G. Rouwenhorst, eds., *The Origins of Value: The Financial Innovations that Created Modern Capital Markets* (Oxford University Press, 2005). And for a broader history of trading in derivatives see E. J. Swan, *Building the Global Market: A 4000 Year History of Derivatives* (London: Kluwer Law International, 2000).

[53] The call options recorded, for example, were chiefly of six month duration and struck at the money (meaning that the strike price of the option the price at which the trade would be executed, if exercised was the same as the current market price of the stock).

[54] For an analysis of the history of derivatives markets with particular regard to the regulation and legal history of the instruments see Swan, *Building the Global Market*.

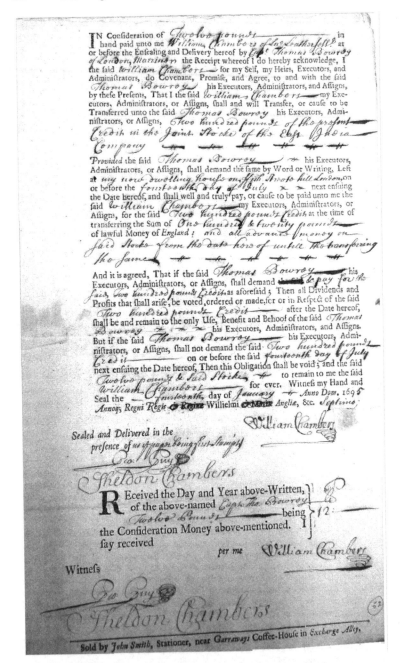

1.1 Example of a standard printed options contract
Source: Guildhall Library, Papers of Thomas Bowrey, MS 3041/9.
Reproduced by permission of Guildhall Library, City of London
Corporation.

The pricing of the options during the 1690s also indicates the application of experience. At this time there was no formula for calculating the cost of an option, prices would have been arrived at by educated guesswork and haggling between buyer and seller. But analysis of the options in Blunt's ledgers shows that pricing was consistent, responsive to changing risk environments and that it took account of the factors that are used by modern traders to calculate value.[55] This indicates that the criteria used to determine price were understood and agreed upon by the majority of participants in the market.[56] At the very least, therefore, investors in London's first stock market had paid close attention to the lessons offered by Malynes. But in all probability many were merely transferring experience honed in the trading of commodities to the new stock market.

It is, of course, impossible to discover the motives of individual investors from the details preserved in Blunt's papers, but trades recorded in the ledgers, supported by commentaries in the contemporary published literature, strongly indicate that options were used first and foremost for the management of risk. Indeed, because purchasers of options have the right to walk away from a trade without penalty thus limiting their losses, early modern writers often equated the purchase of an option with insurance. Joseph de la Vega, for example, described options as 'ropes which secure the vessel against shipwreck and anchors which resist the storm'.[57] This characteristic was undoubtedly valued both by speculators and risk-averse investors.

John Houghton, for example, argued that options could be used to manage the risks of investment in new and untried enterprises. He stated this as one of the advantages of purchasing puts in combination with an existing shareholding and suggested that 'By this means many are incouraged to come into new Stocks, the success whereof is very uncertain'.[58] Equally, investors might have chosen to use calls to create a position in a new stocks without the risks associated with the purchase of shares. Blunt's ledgers contain trades that appear to be calls on the subscription to the Orphans' Bank, established in 1695. The details recorded in the ledger are sparse but it is possible that the calls were the equivalent of

[55] These factors are defined in the modern market as the length of time to the expiry of the option, the relationship between the current price of the stock and the price at which the option is struck and the volatility of the underlying stock.
[56] For a more detailed discussion of the pricing of early modern options see A. L. Murphy, 'Trading Options before Black Scholes: A Study of the Market in Late Seventeenth Century London', Economic History Review 62, S1 (2009), 8 30.
[57] J. de la Vega, Confusion de Confusiones (Boston, Mass.: Baker Library, 1957), p. 7.
[58] Thus the put would provide protection against a fall in the value of the shares. Houghton, Collection for Improvement, 6 Jul. 1694.

warrants, giving investors the right, but not the obligation, to subscribe to the newly issued stock at a certain price.[59] In the modern stock market, warrants are often used as 'sweeteners' to entice participation in an uncertain new issue.

Trades recorded in Blunt's ledgers indicate that similar strategies were used to manage the risks of investment in established joint-stock companies. In December 1692, for example, Sir Thomas Estcourt, one of the most celebrated speculators of the age, purchased 500 Royal African Company stock. An unprotected purchase would have been a risky strategy since at this time the Royal African Company was suffering due to wartime losses and a political environment that threatened its monopoly.[60] Perhaps understanding the risks, Estcourt also purchased a put on 500 Royal African Company stock at a price of five guineas per 100 shares. Thus, he was protected against falls in the value of the stock but retained the right to participate in future rallies.[61]

Another risk-management strategy that was common to Blunt's clients was the liquidation of a physical position in stock and its replacement with the purchase of calls. In June 1693, for example, Thomas Cross sold five shares in the Royal Lustring Company to Gabriel Glover, a linen draper, and at the same time purchased a six-month call of five shares at a cost of four guineas per share, plus total brokerage charges of £5.[62] Thus, Cross eliminated his physical position in Royal Lustring stock but retained the right to participate in further price rises without risk of significant loss if the share price fell. Such a transaction would have been a logical choice for investors who anticipated increased risks in the future but did not wish to abandon completely their position in a particular stock.

While the purchasers of options limit their losses, sellers, for a fee or premium, must be prepared to deliver or accept shares at off-market prices at the buyer's pleasure. An example will serve to illustrate the risks of this strategy. In November 1693 John Haddon sold a six-month call on five Copper Company shares to Benjamin Collyer at a strike rate of £10 for a fee of 2 guineas per share.[63] Had the share price risen

[59] See for example NA, PRO, C114/165, Account of Samuel Cudworth, 1695.
[60] For further on the difficulties facing the Royal African Company during the early 1690s see Davies, *Royal African Company*.
[61] In effect, therefore, Estcourt had created a call. NA, PRO, C114/165, Account of Sir Thomas Estcourt, 1692. For further on the relationships between puts and calls and their implications for trading strategies see R. S. Johnson and C. Giaccotto, *Options and Futures: Concepts, Strategies and Applications* (Minneapolis: West Pub. Co., 1995), pp. 51 100.
[62] NA, PRO, C114/165, Account of Thomas Cross, 2 Jun. 1693.
[63] Ibid., Account of Thomas Haddon, 9 Nov. 1693.

to £20 and Collyer exercised the option, Haddon would have been obliged to deliver shares at £10, thus incurring a £10 per share loss with only a small premium to offset that loss. Had the share price risen to £100 before Collyer exercised his option, Haddon still would have been obliged to deliver shares at £10 and accept the corresponding loss.

The Black-Scholes model, developed in the early 1970s, now allows the risks of selling options to be managed, although by no means eliminated.[64] However, during the late seventeenth century, the hedging choices available to the sellers of options were limited to two: creating a complete hedge (thus the sale of a call on 100 shares would be covered by the purchase of 100 shares) or leaving the position open. It was understood by early modern investors that neither action gave the seller effective cover. John Houghton, who assumed that option sellers would automatically completely hedge their positions, explained the problems, noting that the seller 'has his Share in his own Hand for his security ... he cannot without Hazard part with them the mean time, tho' they should fall lower, unless he will run the hazard of buying again at any rate if they should be demanded; by which many have been caught, and paid dear for'.[65] However, as Houghton was quick to acknowledge, employing such a hedge exposed the option seller to losses if the market did move lower. '[I]n plain English, [the buyer] gives Three Guinea's [the premium] for all the profits if they should rise, [the seller] for Three Guinea's runs the hazard of all the loss if they should fall.'[66]

In spite of the difficulties of managing a short option position, there were reasons to sell. Options could, of course, be sold for purely speculative purposes. Most notably, given the strong association between options and insurance, it may be argued that while the purchaser of an option sought the advantage of such insurance, the seller predicted that either the anticipated future event would not occur or, if it did,

---

[64] The Black Scholes model provides a systematic means of option valuation and a method managing the resulting risk. The search for a model to manage option risk had been a long one. Indeed, modern attempts by academics to develop a method of determining and controlling option risk can be traced back to the work of Louis Bachelier. His dissertation, written in 1901 and entitled 'The Theory of Speculation', outlined the use of Brownian motion to model options on French government bonds. Bachelier's dissertation is reprinted in P. H. Cootner, ed., *The Random Character of Stock Market Prices* (Cambridge, Mass.: MIT Press, 2000), pp. 18 92. Black and Scholes's findings were first published in 1973 in the *Journal of Political Economy*. This paper appeared almost simultaneously with one by Robert Merton, which proposed some useful extensions to the Black Scholes model. F. Black and M. S. Scholes, 'The Pricing of Options and Corporate Liabilities', *Journal of Political Economy*, 81 (1973), 637 54. R. C. Merton, 'Theory of Rational Option Pricing', *The Bell Journal of Economics and Management Science*, 4 (1973), 141 83.

[65] Houghton, *Collection for Improvement*, 22 Jun. 1694.   [66] Ibid.

the sum received in premium would be more than sufficient to cover the resulting losses. Another reason often cited by contemporaries was that selling options offered some investors the opportunity of taking a position in the stock market without initial outlay. It was alleged that many who could not have afforded to invest in shares used the options market in this way.[67]

Options could also be sold as part of a profit-taking strategy. For example, John Houghton purchased Estcourt's Lead Mine shares at a price of £10 in February 1693. In October 1693 he could have sold the shares at £17, yielding £7 per share profit. Instead, he sold a call on Estcourt's Lead Mine shares at £17 for a price of around 4 guineas per share. As a result of this combination of trades, as long as prices remained above £12, Houghton's profit was secure, but limited. Nevertheless, as with all trade combinations that contain a short option, some risks remained. Had prices dropped back to £10 a share, for example, the profit on Houghton's shares would have disappeared, but he would have retained the 4 guineas received in premium. Had prices dropped to £5 per share, Houghton would have still retained the premium received on his call, but would also have incurred a £5 per share loss on his physical stock, thus creating an overall loss on the combined trades. Houghton's strategy, therefore, while yielding a limited profit in a rising market, did involve retaining some residual exposure to a falling market.

As their varied use suggests, derivatives were not just being traded by speculators, they could also be used to good effect by the ordinary investor. Yet, despite the versatility of these products for hedging and manipulating risk, they were not suitable for all. The market may have been standardised but options were still quite complicated instruments. Their value was dependent upon variable factors meaning that negotiation of option price required an intimate knowledge of the market or the willingness to purchase the advice of a broker or other agent. Furthermore, it was the option purchaser's obligation to inform the seller of intent to exercise the option either 'personally by Word of Mouth ... or by a Note in Writing' and if exercise was not completed before the expiry date of the option, then the contract would be void.[68] Thus, maintaining an option position required both seller and purchaser to keep a very close eye on the progress of the market, something that would not have been possible for all investors at this time.

---

[67] See, for example, D. Defoe, *The Villainy of Stock Jobbers Detected* (London, 1701), p. 26.
[68] Houghton, *Collection for Improvement*, 29 Jun. 1694.

The ending of the stock-market boom

Charles Blunt's ledgers show a market of some depth where a few companies attracted very significant levels of interest from investors and speculators and where trade in derivatives was commonplace and served both the risk-seeking and the risk-averse. But this was still a market that lacked breadth. While the number of companies established at this time make it clear that many projectors successfully raised capital through what we might now term an initial public offering, subsequently very few of those company stocks were actively traded. The capitalisation of most companies remained very low and in consequence they attracted relatively few shareholders, especially when compared to the new instruments of the public debt. Most importantly, as its rapid decline was to prove, London's first stock market was inherently vulnerable.

By the end of 1693 many recently established joint-stock companies were in trouble. Some, due to poor management or technical incompetence, were the architects of their own downfall. The Linen Company was a case in point. According to Charles Howard, neither of the two founders, Nicholas Dupin and Henry Million, had any 'new invention or mysteries' nor did they have the technical know-how necessary to work with flax. Both were also guilty of gross financial mismanagement.[69] Since Charles Howard was in dispute with the Company, the details of his evidence must be regarded with some caution but the Board of Trade set up in 1696 to investigate the state of the English economy did offer some corroboration of his statements. The Board also found that the Linen Company's own manufacturing had ground to a halt by 1696 and it had been reduced to buying in the linen it offered for sale.[70]

Contemporary observers also argued that, given investors' thirst for capital gains, the utility of many enterprises was a secondary concern to the potential rewards that could be gained from a rise in share prices. Daniel Defoe famously lost money invested in John Williams's wreck-diving enterprise when Williams, who claimed to be an engineer skilled in recovering wrecks, made no attempt to use his skills and ultimately just absconded with his investors' funds.[71] Those who satirised the newly established market also pointed to the seeming absurdity of some

[69] MacLeod, '1690s Patents Boom', 564.
[70] 'The Commissioners of Trade and Plantations Report on the State of Trade, 1697', in J. Thirsk and J.P. Cooper, eds., Seventeenth Century Economic Documents (Oxford: Clarendon Press, 1972), p. 576.
[71] MacLeod, '1690s Patents Boom', 563.

projects. In Shadwell's play *The Volunteers*, first performed in 1693, characters discussed a patent for a mousetrap 'that will invite all Mice in, nay Rats too, whether they will or no; a whole share before the Patent, is fifteen Pound; after the Patent, they will not take sixty'. Another projector undertook 'to kill all the Fleas, in all the Families in England, provided he hath a Patent, and that none may kill a Flea by himself'.[72]

We should, however, be wary of dismissing all the companies established during the stock-market boom as empty enterprises designed to defraud naïve investors. Schemes that seem fanciful to modern eyes were often based on solid foundations and sought to fill the genuine needs and desires of business and consumers.[73] John Lofting's Sucking-Worm Engine, for example, was regarded by John Houghton as indisputably useful not only for quenching fires but also for draining lands.[74] The Blue Paper Company also provided a sought-after product. It arose out of a patent granted in 1691, the paper in question being wallpaper decorated 'with all sorts of figures and colours by several engines made of brass'. Shares in this company performed weakly, but the business itself seems to have flourished. In 1692 sales were sufficient to justify the opening of a large warehouse and a number of agencies. Over the following ten years advertisements for the product continued to appear and, thus, Scott concluded that business did well throughout the fourteen-year period for which the patent was granted.[75]

Equally, some managers recognised the inadequacy of their technical knowledge and sought to improve their skills. Thomas Neale's brass-making enterprise, for instance, which was in a 'ruinous condition' in 1695, employed George Ball to train the workmen and improve the quality of the goods produced. Ball apparently succeeded in his task since in 1697 John Houghton praised the productivity of the enterprise, estimating that the works produced around 80 tons of copper a year.[76] Clearly, therefore, some companies continued to be successful even though their shares were no longer actively traded on the stock market.

Of those companies that did fail, managerial dishonesty or incompetence was not always the cause. The companies established during the late 1680s and early 1690s faced a difficult birth. They existed in a political

[72] T. Shadwell, *Epsom Wells, and, The Volunteers, or, The Stock Jobbers*, edited by D. M. Walmsley (Boston: D.C. Heath and Co., 1930), pp. 272 3.

[73] Davies also asserted that most of the patents issued in the late seventeenth century were intended as serious contributions to industrial development. Davies, 'Investment in the Later Seventeenth Century', 283.

[74] Houghton, *Collection for Improvement*, 20 Jul. 1694.

[75] Scott, *Constitution and Finance*, vol. III, pp. 71 2.

[76] MacLeod, '1690s Patents Boom', 565.

environment that did not always offer protection to emerging businesses. Some had to contend with hostility from existing industries. The English woollen industry was particularly aggressive in protecting its business against rival textile manufacturers. Equally, although the Nine Years' War was initially a boost to the domestic economy, the strains of conflict soon began to tell. Indeed, Scott attributed the decline of the stock market to the negative effects of the war on the economy. He cited accumulating losses in shipping and the constriction of trade, and the dislocation of credit that resulted from increased remittances abroad to fund the war effort coupled with the poor state of the English coin and consequent recoinage of 1696 and 1697.[77]

Contemporaries offered a more straightforward reason for the demise of the stock market. They blamed stock-jobbers and speculators whose actions destabilised the market and distracted managers from the pursuit of their business.[78] The details and veracity of such accusations will be examined in later chapters but at this point it is important to note that for all the sophistication evident in London's first financial market, the distinction between speculation and investment was not always easily made. As Kavanagh argues, the emergence of the stock market had raised questions about the nature of economic activity and in particular had undermined the belief that the rewards gained by thrift and hard work could not be replicated by the operation of pure chance.[79] Phips's adventure exemplified this idea by putting vast wealth into the hands of idle speculators. Many of London's first investors rejoiced in this notion. As one fictional stock-jobber proclaimed, 'Hang *Trade*, all *Trade* is an Ass to *Stock*, there's more to be got by Stock in a Week, or sometimes in a Day then by any other Business that he ever was acquainted with in a Year.'[80]

Moreover, the close association between gambling and investment was constantly reinforced at this time. Because risk was ever-present, methods of utilising and controlling it were varied and often involved actions that would today be classified as gambling. Merchants, inspired

---

[77] Scott, *Constitution and Finance*, vol. I, pp. 347 9. For a more detailed examination of these factors see Jones, *War and Economy*.

[78] Stock jobbing ostensibly referred to the practice of buying and selling stock in order to make profits from the price differential between bid and offered rates or through short term position taking. Nevertheless, the term was also used during this period to refer to any type of activity in the financial market including the purchase and sale of short term government debt and Bank of England notes. In general the term was used pejoratively.

[79] T. M. Kavanagh, *Enlightenment and the Shadows of Chance: The Novel and the Culture of Gambling in Eighteenth Century France* (Baltimore and London: Johns Hopkins University Press, 1993), p. 85.

[80] Anon., *Plain Dealing: in a Dialogue between Mr. Johnson and Mr. Wary* (London, 1691), p. 2.

by pragmatism rather than patriotism, took out wagers on the progress of the Nine Years' War to hedge investments in overseas trade. This practice was sufficiently troublesome for the City of London authorities to take action against it. In 1692 they moved to try and prevent the placing of wagers, particularly those that bet upon the failure of the military campaign. This practice the City defined as 'evill', 'false and scandalous', and likely to 'discourage their Majesties Subjects in their due allegiances'. But it was clearly widespread by this point because the City ordered that 200 copies of its threat to prosecute wrongdoers be posted about the Exchange and in other places around the City.[81]

The state also reinforced the connections between gambling and investment when it floated the Million Adventure lottery in early 1694. The lottery was structured to appeal to a wide range of investors. It offered 100,000 tickets for sale at the relatively small cost of £10 each and unlike other lotteries, all non-prize-winning, or blank, tickets entitled the holder to a modest but reasonable return on their investment of £1 per year until 1710, making the Million Adventure a secure investment for the cautious and inexperienced public creditor. However, the lottery also offered 2,500 generous prizes, the highest being worth £1,000 per year for sixteen years; the lowest yielded £10 per year. Thus, it was clearly designed to appeal also to the speculative instincts of early modern investors. In this respect it proved to be a great success. It raised £1,000,000 in public funds and provided the opportunity for tens of thousands of investors to share in the excitement and potential of the financial market.

The Million Adventure inspired dozens of private projectors to float their own lottery schemes and although financial historians have seldom considered lotteries to be part of the financial revolution, contemporaries were in no doubt about the similarities between the aims and actions of those who played the lotteries and those who invested in joint-stocks.[82] The author of *Angliae Tutamen*, for example, argued that there was a strong association between joint-stock enterprises, the Bank

[81] London Metropolitan Archives, Repertories of the Court of Aldermen, COL/CA/01/01/101, fos. 50 1.

[82] A number of rather dated examinations of lottery schemes do exist. See J. Ashton, *A History of the English Lotteries* (London: Leadenhall Press, 1893); J. Cohen, 'The Element of Lottery in British Government Bonds, 1694 1919', *Economica*, 20 (1953), 237 46 and R. D. Richards, 'The Lottery in the History of English Government Finance', *Economic History*, 3 (1934 37), 57 76. The most comprehensive work on the subject remains C. L. Ewen, *Lotteries and Sweepstakes: An Historical, Legal and Ethical Survey of their Introduction, Suppression and Re establishment in the British Isles* (London: Heath Cranton, 1932) and for a more recent analysis see A. L. Murphy, 'Lotteries in the 1690s: Investment or Gamble?', *Financial History Review*, 12 (2005), 227 46.

of England and the many lottery schemes that were floated during the 1690s.[83] Other commentators noted that there was little difference between gambling and stock-jobbing or suggested that there was no distinction to be made between investing in overseas trade, speculating in stocks and playing the lotteries.[84] T. Saunders even asked, who were the greater fools? 'London Rack [wreck]-adventurers who seek for a Needle in a Bottle of Hay ... or we Lottery-Adventurers that are sure of the Needle, and that some of the Adventurers must find it'.[85]

Thus, the dominant contemporary perception of England's early financial revolution was that it presented opportunities for gambling and speculation rather than sober investment. And, while it is unlikely that many people gave over their businesses to speculate in the financial market, it does seem probable that the perception that vast riches could be obtained for little trouble encouraged individuals, for the first time, to consider investment in joint-stock companies. Moreover, given the environment, it was perhaps inevitable that London's first stock market would not sustain investors' interest once expectations of great wealth began to disappear and when an alternative source of high and seemingly guaranteed returns was offered in the shape of the new public funds.

The argument that investment in private enterprise was crowded out by the returns offered by government debt is sometimes applied to the later eighteenth century.[86] But the evidence presented in Table 1.3, and depicted more clearly in Figure 1.2, also suggests a link between the emergence of the public funds in 1693 and early 1694 and a declining interest in private enterprise. This analysis is supported by Christine MacLeod's study of the number of patents enrolled during this time, which, as can be seen in Table 1.2, indicates that the peak of interest in private schemes was between 1691 and 1694.

Of course, crowding out was not solely responsible for the destruction of London's first stock-market boom. For the reasons stated above, the stock market was already in decline by the time the public funds

[83] Anon., *Angliae Tutamen*, passim.
[84] Anon., *Plain Dealing*, p. 2; T. Saunders, *Fortunatus's Looking Glass, or an Essay Upon Lotteries* (London, 1699), p. 1.
[85] Saunders, *Fortunatus's Looking Glass*, p. 4.
[86] See, for example, J. G. Williamson, 'Why was British Growth So Slow During the Industrial Revolution?', *Journal of Economic History*, 44 (1984), 687 712; C. E. Heim and P. Mirowski, 'Interest Rates and Crowding Out During Britain's Industrial Revolution', *Journal of Economic History*, 47 (1987), 117 39; P. Temin, and H. J. Voth, 'Credit Rationing and Crowding Out during the Industrial Revolution: Evidence from Hoare's Bank, 1702 1862', *Explorations in Economic History*, 42 (2005), 325 48.

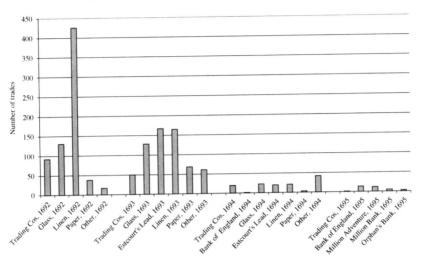

1.2 Blunt's ledgers, total trading volume, 1692 1695
Source: NA, PRO, C114/165.

emerged. But the funds offered high and seemingly guaranteed returns. Moreover, they were backed by the appropriation of tax revenue and supposedly guaranteed by Act of Parliament. Indeed, the Act of Parliament that provided for the incorporation of the Bank of England was, according to contemporary commentators, specifically designed to encourage investors. One pamphleteer noted that the 'Recompenses and Advantages proposed in the Act ... were framed on purpose to convince every Man it was his private Interest to serve the Publick ... and to encourage the advancing of Money, upon the Credit and Reputation of that Act.'[87]

The validity of these promises will be questioned in the next chapter. It will be shown that the Glorious Revolution may have allowed Parliament to gain control of the nation's finances but it did not immediately endow it with the knowledge and experience to deal with the country's finances, nor was parliamentary control a magic formula for dealing with a lengthy and expensive war. Nevertheless, when faced with the choice between uncertain and disappointing returns from the private equity market and as yet untarnished promises from Parliament many investors quickly switched allegiances. Thus, the emergence of the national debt helped to bring London's first stock-market boom to an end.

[87] Anon., *Reasons for Encouraging the Bank of England* (London, 1695), p. 3.

Summary

In 1688 London was already a wealthy city. It had a vibrant economy supported by unprecedented growth in mercantile activity. It attracted the experience, skills and capital of foreign migrants, supported a nascent industrial base, and was home to an expanding financial elite. Even prior to the Glorious Revolution these factors had helped to create a strong demand for investment opportunities. Thus, while Phips's adventure and the Nine Years' War were the catalysts for the rapid growth of a trade in equities, there is no question that these factors interacted with others that were already poised to support the emergence of a financial market.

Yet, while up to a hundred new joint-stock companies were established between 1685 and 1695, we should not overestimate the extent of stock-market activity. Certainly there was a core of companies whose shares attracted significant speculative interest and the widespread use of derivative instruments does indicate a level of sophistication that belies the market's immaturity. But this was still a market that lacked breadth and consequently provided opportunities for relatively few investors. Nor should we overestimate the broader economic value of the new joint-stock companies. Brian Parsons has estimated the market value of all English joint-stock companies in 1695 at just under £4 million. This amount represented a mere 1–2 per cent of the estimated total wealth of England at that time and the figures require further qualification.[88] In fact, much of the £4 million of Parsons's estimate derives from Bank of England stock, valued at £1,044,000, and East India Company stock and bonds, valued at £1,708,657. Of the remaining companies, as we have seen, few offered good long-term prospects. Some lacked the technical skills required to make their businesses work, a few were mere frauds and many failed to survive the economic crises of the mid-1690s and the emergence of the public funds. Thus, although the corporate sector of the economy should not be described as negligible, it cannot be claimed that it constituted a vital element of England's wealth during the late seventeenth century.

Nor should we delude ourselves about what investors hoped to gain from their involvement in joint-stock investment. The dominant learning experience, reinforced by the financial market's strong association with gambling, was how to speculate. Indeed, although it can be argued that England's financial revolution was born of economic necessity and the

---

[88] B. Parsons, 'The Behaviour of Prices on the London Stock Market in the Early Eighteenth Century', unpublished PhD thesis (University of Chicago, 1974), pp. 23, 30.

exigencies of war, it was the prospect of gaining a large fortune that encouraged many to involve themselves in the stock-market boom of the 1690s. This had important consequences for the progress of the financial revolution. First, the speculative elements that dominated during those early years raised many questions among those who looked at the new financial market with concern, seeing in it the potential for price instability and social disruption. Secondly, it is clear that many investors had unrealistic expectations of their investments and were thus vulnerable to disappointment. This tended to make for instability as investors moved rapidly from one opportunity to the next. It also, in the short term at least, privileged the instruments of the public debt, which seemed to offer guaranteed high returns to investors.

2   The rise of the public funds

One of the most important consequences of the Glorious Revolution was that it brought to the English throne a king whose prime concern was the struggle against Louis XIV, and who considered that England, as a Protestant nation, had an obligation to become involved in that struggle. Consequently, in May 1689 William III took England into a European coalition against France, thus beginning the Nine Years' War.[1] But, as Charles Davenant complained, war was a costly affair and much changed from

> the time of our Forefathers; when in a hasty Expedition and a pitch'd Field, the Matter was decided by Courage ... now the whole Art of War is in a manner reduced to Money ... the Prince, who can best find Money to feed, cloath, and pay his Army, not he that has the most valiant Troops, is surest of Success and Conquest.[2]

The Nine Years' War resulted in a rise in English public expenditure from under £2 million per annum in 1688 to between £5 and £6 million per annum in the years from 1689 to 1702.[3] Similarly, revenue from taxation grew substantially over this period. According to Brewer, average tax revenues during the Nine Years' War were £3.64 million per annum, almost double the revenues obtained prior to 1688.[4] But, endless increases in the tax burden were undesirable for a new and uncertain regime and the war was unprecedentedly costly. Consequently, expenditure quickly outstripped income.

The new regime's first resort was to short-term borrowing and it was reasonably successful at raising funds by this means. Between 1688 and

---

[1] Sometimes referred to as King William's War, the War of the League of Augsburg or, occasionally, the War of the Grand Alliance.
[2] C. Davenant, *An Essay upon Ways and Means of Supplying the War* (London, 1695), pp. 26 7.
[3] Dickson, *Financial Revolution*, p. 46. For an overview of the changes to the taxation system introduced during the 1690s see Brewer, *Sinews of Power*, pp. 95 101; C. Brooks, 'Public Finance and Political Stability: The Administration of the Land Tax, 1688 1720', *Historical Journal*, 17 (1974), 281 300.
[4] Brewer, *Sinews of Power*, p. 89.

1697 the Exchequer received more than £32 million in short-term loans at interest rates of between 5 and 8 per cent.[5] But by 1693 the government's credit was deteriorating. Lenders became reluctant to commit any more capital to a regime mired in a difficult war and clearly in financial difficulties. Attempts to pay the most pressing of the state's debts with tallies instead of cash failed when the government's creditors found they could raise no money on the tallies in the secondary market.[6] In May of 1693, for example, the City of London's gunmakers complained that the tallies with which they had been paid were worthless. And in September 1693 the Commissioners for Sick and Wounded Seamen reported that government credit was very bad in the Medway towns of Rochester and Chatham. Weakened credit led to deterioration in the terms offered by those still willing to lend short-term funds and significantly affected the value of remittances abroad to pay the troops.[7] What was needed, therefore, was a means of raising substantial amounts of money immediately and funding it, through taxation, over the long term.[8]

Parliament first contemplated raising money through long-term borrowing in January 1692, when one of the proposals considered was a scheme put forward by William Paterson and Michael Godfrey for raising £1 million on 'bills of property' at a yearly rent.[9] But, at that time, agreement could not be reached and the idea of long-term borrowing was not returned to until the end of the year. In December 1692 Parliament accepted a scheme, again probably devised by William Paterson, for the raising of money through a tontine loan.

The terms of the tontine were quite complex. Contributors were placed in groups and paid interest pro rata and tax-free during their lifetime or the lifetime of a nominee. As each contributor or nominee died, the funds would be shared among fewer and fewer until only seven people were left in each group. After that, the interest would abate

---

[5] Dickson, *Financial Revolution*, pp. 343 4.
[6] Tallies referred to the government's short term securities. They encompassed the traditional wooden laths issued by the Exchequer as receipts for short term loans and by government departments as payments for goods and services (the wooden sticks were cut with notches to represent the amount owed in pounds, shillings and pence and split down the middle to form foil and counterfoil of the receipt) and also the newer printed Treasury Order first introduced during the 1660s.
[7] Dickson, *Financial Revolution*, pp. 343 5. Dickson provides numerous other examples that confirm the government's deteriorating creditworthiness.
[8] Quinn also argues that difficulties in raising short term funds spurred innovations in public finance. See S. Quinn, 'Tallies or Reserves? Sir Francis Child's Balance Between Capital Reserves and Extending Credit to the Crown, 1685 1695', *Business and Economic History*, 23 (1994), 41.
[9] Dickson, *Financial Revolution*, p. 51.

with each death. Long-lived participants, or those who chose their nominees well, could expect a very good return on their money.[10] Nevertheless, there must have been some doubts about English investors' willingness to accept the scheme. The Act, which received royal assent in January 1693, provided for £1 million to be raised through the tontine, but also had a clause that allowed funds to be raised through the sale of single life annuities at 14 per cent if the tontine was not taken up. As it turned out, the tontine was indeed too complex for the inexperienced English investor; it raised only £108,100. The life annuities were more to people's tastes and it was their sale that made the loan up to the £1,000,000 provided for.[11]

Capitalising on this initial slow but steady success, the Treasury expanded its fund-raising activities during 1694. As Table 2.1 shows, an additional £300,000 was generated through the sale of life annuities and a further £1 million came into the public coffers through the Million Adventure Lottery. The lottery, which was very successful, offered 100,000 tickets for sale at the relatively small cost of £10 each and promised 2,500 generous prizes. Also in 1694 came the most important of the government's new fund-raising schemes. Following yet another scheme put forward by William Paterson and Michael Godfrey, the Bank of England was established. The Bank was required to lend £1,200,000 to the government for the purpose of 'carrying on the War against France' in return for annual payments of £100,000, a sum which represented interest at 8 per cent and an additional administration fee of £4,000 per annum.[12] The sum of £1,200,000 was to be raised by a subscription that was open to all, 'Natives and Foreigners, Bodies Politick and Corporate'.[13] It was greeted with much enthusiasm and the subscription books, which opened on 21 June 1694, were filled by 2 July.[14]

The Bank of England followed its initial £1,200,000 loan with a number of others during 1695 and 1696. But by early 1697 the Bank's directors were declaring themselves unable to lend further funds, having already given an additional '£800,000 and upwards upon Tallys on Parliamentary Funds, severall of which have been deficient, and none

---

[10] The last annuitant died in 1783 while receiving payments of over £1,000 on his original £100 investment. C. Wilson, *England's Apprenticeship, 1603 1763* (London: Longman, 1971), p. 218.

[11] Dickson, *Financial Revolution*, p. 53.

[12] Cited in J. Giuseppi, *The Bank of England: A History from its Foundation in 1694* (London: Evans Bros., 1966), p. 10.

[13] Ibid., p. 12.

[14] Bank of England Archives, List of the original subscribers to the Bank of England, 1694, M1/1.

Table 2.1 *Government long-term borrowing, 1693–1698*

Date of royal assent to Loan Act	Amount raised £	Interest %	Loan details
26 January 1693	108,100	10 until midsummer 1700, then 7	Tontine loan
26 January 1693	773,394	14	Sale of single life annuities
8 February 1694	118,506	14	Sale of single life annuities
23 March 1694	1,000,000	14	Million Adventure lottery
24 April 1694	1,200,000	8	Lent by subscribers who were to be incorporated as the Bank of England.
24 April 1694	300,000	10, 12 and 14	Sale of annuities for one, two and three lives.
16 April 1697	1,400,000	6.3	Malt Lottery. When the lottery failed the government issued the tickets as cash.
5 July 1698	2,000,000	8	Lent by subscribers who were to be incorporated as the New East India Company.
Total	6,900,000		

Source: Dickson, *Financial Revolution*, pp. 48 9.

yet paid'.[15] The Bank's unwillingness to keep lending short term to the government led to another attempt to raise long-term funds. In April 1697 the Malt Lottery was floated. It offered 140,000 £10 tickets for sale. But the prizes were less generous than those offered by the earlier Million Lottery and by 1697 the government's credit was very poor indeed, so few of the tickets were sold. The £1,400,000 anticipated from the Malt Lottery was only realised when the Treasury issued the unsold tickets as cash.[16]

The last long-term borrowing scheme of this period was more successful. Coming after the end of the Nine Years' War and as the culmination of a long drawn-out political battle between the East India Company and its rivals, in July 1698 the New East India Company was incorporated. Its charter was secured by the promise of a £2,000,000 loan to the government at 8 per cent.

[15] Bank of England Archives, Minutes of the General Court of Proprietors, 1694 1702, G7/1, 4 Jan. 1697.
[16] Dickson, *Financial Revolution*, pp. 47 9.

Overall, between 1693 and 1698 only £6,900,000 was raised through long-term funding, an insignificant sum when set against a total government expenditure of £72m.[17] Furthermore, the schemes were very costly. Although the legal maximum rate of interest during the 1690s was 6 per cent, Parliament was not bound by its own laws and its need was such that it was forced to pay higher rates. It paid 8 per cent interest to the Bank of England and the New East India Company, and the costs of the lotteries and annuities ranged between 6.3 and 14 per cent.[18] The lottery and annuity funds were also expensive to administer and, since they were held by a large and diverse group of creditors, it proved difficult to renegotiate their terms and conditions. Yet, the impact of those novel methods of fund raising was considerable for both state and investors. They marked the establishment of a debt deliberately created to be funded in the long term, thus laying the foundations for the evolution of an effective and efficient system of state finance. The debt created during the 1690s had, for the first time in England, a broad popular appeal. Indeed, the Million Adventure attracted funds from investors from all walks of life. The creation of a long-term national debt also marked the beginning of a new relationship between the state and the public. Finally, as Carruthers noted and contemporaries well understood, for the sovereign, debt is not just about raising capital, debt also has the power to create allies since creditors, having an interest in the ability of sovereigns to repay their debts, also have an interest in the survival of their regime.[19]

This chapter will detail the initial appeal and subsequent failures of the new funds and explain how the trust of the public creditors was maintained in spite of the deterioration of the government's credit and the cessation of interest and annuities payments during the period from 1695 to 1698. First, however, it will examine the origins of the innovations that attracted the public's capital.

The path of financial innovation

The assumption that innovation in English public finance was derived from methods used by the Dutch and brought to England by William III's

---

[17] Funds to cover the remaining government expenditure continued to be raised through taxation and short term borrowing, the majority coming through taxation with Customs yielding £13.2 m, Excise, £13.6 m and the new Land Tax, £19.2 m in the period up to 1702. Dickson, *Financial Revolution*, pp. 47 9.
[18] Ibid., pp. 48 9.   [19] Carruthers, *City of Capital*, p. 4.

advisors is common but misleading.[20] Certainly, the English regarded
the Dutch economy with envy and much effort was expended in attempts
to identify the factors that made it so vital. Josiah Child, in his *Discourse
of Trade* published in 1690, pointed to good laws, a multitude of
people, efficiency in production, most notably in the fishing and ship-
building industries, and low interest rates.[21] But English admiration for
the Dutch economy was long-standing and, as Child's concerns show,
broadly based. And when it came to public finances, other European
experiences were just as likely to arouse interest. Indeed, one pamphleteer, writing in the 1650s, recommended the ancient Roman model of
managing state finance.[22] Those with an interest in more recent experience particularly admired improvements to French public finance.
Davenant traced their progress from 'the Duke of Sully, a frugal Man,
who, by natural Wisdom and meer Honesty, brought the Revenue out
of infinite Debts into such a flourishing condition' to Richelieu who
'accustom'd the French to ... Zeal, Diligence and Honesty' and Colbert
who, through the encouragement of trade and manufacturing, brought
what Sully had started to 'perfection'.[23]

Moreover, as the preceding chapter has shown, the English did not
lack the skills necessary to implement change, nor did they lack the
ingenuity needed for effective innovation. Indeed, England's own project to reform public finances extended back to the Restoration, if not
farther.[24] Arguably, changes in tax raising and collection instigated
during the Civil War and Interregnum had begun the process of placing
the nation's finances on a surer footing. The introduction of the excise
in 1643 created a secure basis for borrowing and over the long term
provided an increasing proportion of total revenues.[25] In the period
between 1660 and 1685, these improvements were built on as the

---

[20] See, for example, J. D. Tracy, *A Financial Revolution in the Habsburg Netherlands: Renten
and Renteniers in the County of Holland, 1515 1565* (Berkeley: University of California
Press, 1985), p. 213; Dickson, *Financial Revolution*, p. 26.

[21] J. Child, *A Discourse of Trade* (London, 1690). For a more complete analysis of how
English writers viewed the state of the economy see L. Magnusson, *Mercantilism: The
Shaping of an Economic Language* (London and New York: Routledge, 1994).

[22] Coffman, 'Fiscal Revolution', p. 65.

[23] Davenant, *Ways and Means*, pp. 8 9.

[24] For analysis of the early management of English public finance see S. B. Baxter, *The
Development of the Treasury, 1660 1702* (London: Longmans, 1957); Braddick, *State
Formation*; Chandaman, *English Public Revenue*; Horsefield, *British Monetary Experiments*;
Roseveare, *The Treasury*.

[25] Dickson, *Financial Revolution*, p. 42; Braddick, *State Formation*, p. 255. Although Dickson
argues that the introduction of the excise was based on Dutch precedents, 't Hart shows
quite convincingly that if there was Dutch influence, it was indirect. 't Hart, '"The Devil
or the Dutch"', 43. See also Coffman, 'Fiscal Revolution'.

abandonment of tax farming allowed for greater centralisation and more efficient administration.[26] Equally, the Treasury underwent a series of reforms that by 1702 had transformed it into a professional body of civil servants.[27] Some of the financial innovations of the Restoration also laid the groundwork for the developments of the post-Glorious Revolution period. The introduction by Sir George Downing of Treasury orders, essentially promises-to-pay when tax revenues became available, was an important step forward. The Treasury Orders were the forerunner of the Exchequer Bill and could be sold or transferred by endorsement, thus they were legally negotiable, unlike most other credit instruments of the time.[28] Another notable innovation was the introduction of payment of short-term loans in strict order. This was done by issuing a numbered repayment order along with the traditional tally or new Treasury Order, which offered an indication of when the debt would be repaid. Eventually, the proposed repayment schedule was backed by the appropriation of a specific tax revenue, thus significantly enhancing the credibility of the debt.[29]

Although often ignored by historians, it is also important to acknowledge the interaction between public and private finance in the period after the Restoration. As Quinn shows, goldsmith-bankers by branching out into tax collection and funding short-term debt, providing intermediation for international credit and bullion movements, and encouraging the circulation of paper money, integrated London's financial and monetary institutions and built a framework on which later institutions, like the Bank of England, were built.[30] The above-mentioned changes may not have fully equipped the state to deal with the expense and difficulties of the Nine Years' War, but they did begin the transformation of a royal debt into a public debt.[31] And they prove Roseveare's assertion that the English financial revolution could be claimed as the legacy of Charles II rather than that of William III.[32]

Of course, the Nine Years' War made the task of modernising and improving state finance more urgent. It also stimulated the ingenuity of the public. Recognising the pressures of war, projectors and would-be economic advisors offered the government a steady stream of opinion and novel fund-raising schemes. Some presented detailed critiques of the government's management of the public purse. Charles Davenant

---

[26] P. K. O'Brien and P. A. Hunt, 'The Rise of a Fiscal State in England, 1485 1815', in R. Bonney, ed., *The Rise of the Fiscal State in Europe, c. 1200 1815* (Oxford University Press, 1999), p. 60.
[27] Roseveare, *Treasury, 1660 1870*, p. 18.   [28] Ibid., p. 24.
[29] Braddick, *State Formation*, p. 258.   [30] Quinn, 'Banking before the Bank', p. 2.
[31] Braddick, *State Formation*, p. 264.   [32] Roseveare, *Financial Revolution*, p. 26.

published a 160-page pamphlet specifying the *Ways and Means of Supplying the War*, which rejected the government's experiments with long-term debt as being detrimental to trade and recommended an overhaul of the tax system that would place increased emphasis on the excise and an 'Impartial Land-Tax ... [being the form] most Agreeable to the Ancient Constitution of this Kingdom'.[33] Davenant's concerns were common. John Briscoe also criticised the new public funds as being detrimental to trade and injurious to the nobility, and he too proposed a revision of the tax system.[34]

Others eschewed overt criticism of the government and focused on practical solutions to aid the public finances, with many offering new and more 'effective' methods of taxation. One suggested the entire population of England should be taxed at a rate of a farthing a day, with 'the richer sort of People paying for the Poor in each Parish' in order to raise a total of £6,000,000 for the war effort.[35] Other projectors sought to tax usurers, wearers of broad cloth, the ownership of horses and even the ownership of graven images and 'pictures, or likeness of such things as God hath forbidden to be made'.[36] John Kynvin offered a scheme for the raising of a tax on parchment and paper and, because he had knowledge of how a similar duty was collected in Spain, he petitioned the Treasury Board to be allowed to manage its collection.[37] The coinage particularly exercised the ingenuity of many concerned citizens. Various proposals were made, including one that suggested a lottery in which tickets would be given to those who subscribed plate that could be coined into new money, and another that laid out a strategy for the gradual lowering of the value of guineas in order to encourage the circulation of coin.[38]

It would be quite wrong to argue that English projectors did not borrow from Dutch innovations but, as John Kynvin's adoption of a Spanish tax suggests, they also drew inspiration from a variety of European precedents. This was especially true of the long-term funding expedients adopted by the government during the 1690s. The tontine

---

[33] Davenant, *Ways and Means*, pp. 42 4, 117.
[34] J. Briscoe, *A Discourse on the Late Funds of the Million Act, Lottery Act, and the Bank of England* (London, 1694).
[35] Anon., *Proposals Humbly Offered ... for the Raising of Six Millions of Pounds Sterling* (London, 1696?).
[36] Anon., *A Way to Catch the Usurer* (London, 1689); Anon., *A Proposal Humbly Offer'd ... to raise Two Hundred Thousand Pounds per Annum* (London, 1696?); James, Lord Mordington, B. Whitelocke and R. Cotton, *A Proposal Humbly Offered ... For Raising a Considerable Sum of Mony Yearly* (1696?); R. Vaughan, *For the Perusal of all and every of You* (London, 1695).
[37] Dickson, *Financial Revolution*, p. 52.
[38] Anon., *A Proposal for the Speedy Procuring a Sufficient Quantity of Plate* (London, 1695?); Anon., *A Plain and Easie Way to Reduce Guineas* (London, 1695?).

loan, for example, was the invention of Lorenzo Tonti, an expatriate Neopolitan banker who proposed the scheme to Cardinal Mazarin of France in 1652.[39] Tontines were certainly used in the Netherlands as a form of speculative life cover by private investors and for the raising of municipal finance.[40] But they were also used by the French crown for the first time in 1689 and, interestingly, a tontine scheme had been proposed by the City of London as early as 1674.[41]

The use of life annuities certainly owed something to Dutch innovation but 't Hart notes that the Dutch did not typically use life annuities for fund-raising purposes during the later seventeenth century, having already discovered them to be too expensive and inefficient.[42] If England's financial revolution was solely the product of Dutch ingenuity, we might ask why this lesson was ignored.

Similarly, 't Hart notes that Dutch influence on the structure of the Bank of England was limited.[43] The Bank of Amsterdam was clearly not a model for the Bank of England since the former was first and foremost a commercial bank. It did not lend directly to the Hague government, nor did it issue notes.[44] Indeed, the fact that the Bank of England became an issuing bank distinguished it from all previous European public banks, except the Bank of Sweden.[45]

The Bank of England was created principally to lend to the state. Certainly, those who had written throughout the late seventeenth century in favour of the creation of a public bank did point to the need to regulate and stimulate the increasingly complex English economy, bring down the rate of interest and increase the availability of capital, advantages they perceived had been conferred by such banks not only on Amsterdam but also on Venice and Genoa.[46] But the Bank of England's commercial role was not specified in its charter and had it become

---

[39] D. R. Weir, 'Tontines, Public Finance, and Revolution in France and England, 1688 1789', *Journal of Economic History*, 49 (1989), 102.
[40] Dickson, *Financial Revolution*, p. 41.
[41] Weir, 'Tontines', 105; Dickson, *Financial Revolution*, p. 41.
[42] 't Hart, '"The Devil or the Dutch"', 50 1.   [43] Ibid.   [44] Ibid., 42.
[45] A. Andréadès, *A History of the Bank of England, 1640 1903*, 4th edn (London: Cass, 1966), p. 82. Fratianni and Spinelli also draw comparisons between the Bank of England and the Venetian Banco Giro. M. Fratianni and F. Spinelli, 'Italian City States and Financial Evolution', *European Review of Economic History*, 10 (2006), 272.
[46] Acres asserts that a scheme for a public bank was referred to a Committee of Parliament in 1658, and various schemes were discussed during the reign of Charles II. W. M. Acres, *The Bank of England from Within, 1694 1900* (London: Bank of England, 1931). In this period, schemes generally met with the objection that such a bank might allow the king to raise money without the consent of Parliament. A concern that was still current in 1694; the Bank of England was forbidden to lend to the king without the consent of Parliament.

merely an investment trust managing the state's debt, that would not have violated any early expectations of its contribution to the English economy. Equally, the structure of the loan advanced by the Bank of England had its precedents in English public finance, rather than Dutch. As Dickson notes, Customs and Excise commissioners had been advancing money on anticipated revenue long before the Glorious Revolution.[47] The timing of the Bank of England's establishment was certainly an accident of King William's war,[48] but the idea and the structure of the Bank were not direct Dutch imports.

The New East India Company was established in 1698 along similar lines to the Bank of England and was quite clearly the product of a very protracted political argument between those who controlled trade to the East and those who wanted a share in the business. In fact by 1698 the government, with or without the advantage of any number of Dutch or any other financial innovations, had very few places to turn. War had devastated the public finances, the purses of the investing public were all but exhausted and the government had already imposed too far on the goodwill of the Bank of England. The only option was to ignore the East India Company's monopoly and sell the potentially lucrative trade to the East to the highest bidder. The East India Company, although weakened by the war, did offer the government £700,000 at a rate of 4 per cent in an effort to retain their monopoly. But such was the need, that a rival bid at twice the rate of interest but for a far greater capital sum was accepted.[49] Thus, the New East India Company was established and the £2,000,000 capital raised from the sale of its shares helped to restore the public finances. Although the funds from the New East India Company went some way towards alleviating the state's financial difficulties, it did not resolve the battle over trade to the East. The Old East India Company continued to exist and continued to trade. Moreover, its superior experience and organisation proved more than a match for its rival. The result was the slow deterioration of the New Company and, in 1709, a union between the two companies was formally effected.

Perhaps the most innovative of the state's new fund-raising schemes was the Million Adventure lottery and it is worth exploring its evolution in some detail. Here too, ideas emerged from a very broad European heritage. The first European lottery can be traced back to Burgundy in 1420 and during the sixteenth century state lotteries were held in

[47] Dickson, *Financial Revolution*, p. 342.   [48] Clapham, *Bank of England*, vol. I, p. 1.
[49] For further details see Scott, *Constitution and Finance*, vol. II, pp. 163 7.

Germany, France and Florence.[50] Moreover, an English state lottery was held in 1567/68 to raise money for the improvement of the Cinque Ports. At ten shillings each, tickets were expensive and the lottery did not prove especially popular.[51] In the Netherlands lotteries were not generally used for raising public funds until the early eighteenth century. Apparently, seventeenth-century Dutch oligarchs disliked the idea of marrying state finance with speculation.[52] However, lotteries were used in the Netherlands and throughout Europe by merchants and retailers for the disposal of goods, and often for charitable purposes. Again the English were familiar with the use of lotteries for the latter purpose since after the Restoration they were used to raise money for the relief of 'many poor Cavaliers'.[53]

In fact, during the reign of Charles II there were regular private lotteries in England and by 1688 the business was subject to a monopoly that was rented at £4,200 each year indicating that lotteries had become both popular and profitable.[54] There is, however, little to suggest that the monopoly holders recognised or exploited the public enthusiasm for money-making schemes that emerged during the stock-market boom of the early 1690s or that they made any attempt to adapt their schemes for the purpose of raising public funds. Thus, the emergence of rivals for the business was inevitable.

The most prominent of those rivals was Thomas Neale, Groom Porter to their Majesties. As Groom Porter, Neale was responsible for gaming within the royal households but had no control over lotteries. As early as 1683 he was arguing that this situation was damaging to the Groom Porter's office, and petitioning Charles II to either suppress all lotteries, or bring them under the Groom Porter's purview.[55] Nothing was achieved by this petition but by 1693 a changing economic climate meant that the monopoly could no longer be enforced, opening the way for others to promote lotteries.[56]

---

[50] G. Reith, *The Age of Chance: Gambling in Western Culture* (London and New York: Routledge, 1999), p. 55.
[51] Ewen, *Lotteries and Sweepstakes*, p. 25.   [52] 't Hart, '"The Devil or the Dutch"', 50.
[53] S. Schama, *The Embarrassment of Riches: An Interpretation of Dutch Culture in the Golden Age* (London: Collins, 1987), pp. 307 9; Reith, *Age of Chance*, p. 55; Anon., *The Arraignment, Trial, and Condemnation of Squire Lottery, Alias Royal Oak Lottery* (London, 1699), p. 10.
[54] Ewen, *Lotteries and Sweepstakes*, p. 123.
[55] Thomas, 'Thomas Neale', p. 271.
[56] The farmers of the Royal Oak Lotteries made several attempts to preserve their monopoly in the following years and in October 1694 an advertisement was taken in the *London Gazette* to 'desire [that] all Civil Magestrates ... forthwith effectually sup press, and punish ... all such as shall so presume to Erect Use or Exercise any such Lotteries and Inventions without the License of the said Farmers'. *London Gazette*, 18 22 Oct. 1694.

Neale's first offering was a private rather than a state lottery. It was held in 1693 and was based on a Venetian project of the previous year.[57] It was the success of this private scheme that encouraged the government to believe Neale's assertion that lotteries could be adapted to the purpose of raising public funds. Indeed, Neale's scheme for the Million Adventure was an ideal vehicle for mobilising the capital of the investing public and it showed a shrewd understanding of the financial problems facing the state. Notably, in order to attract funds from sections of the population who could not afford to invest in annuities or the Bank of England, tickets were priced at just £10.[58] Neale also understood that government could not be seen to be encouraging people to fritter their money away on games of chance. The Million Adventure, therefore, guaranteed a return to all participants. Those with prize-winning tickets could expect to receive between £10 and £1,000 per year for sixteen years. All others were entitled to a modest but reasonable return on their investment of £1 per year until 1710. Thus, although the capital would not be returned, there would be no losers in the Million Lottery. That way Neale could argue the state's lottery could not be subject to the same strictures as other lotteries which 'tak[e] away Money, and los[e] it quite from Servants, and such as have but a little'.[59]

More than any other of the innovations of the 1690s, the Million Adventure demonstrates how financial innovation spread between the private and the public sector. In creating his schemes Thomas Neale borrowed ideas from already existing English private lotteries and foreign schemes that he may simply have heard about or indeed may have played. English names have been found on European lottery lists from as far back as the mid-fifteenth century.[60] Once Neale's circumvention of the existing monopoly had opened up the English market, he was joined by dozens of projectors all eager to promote their own innovations. In addition to various projects offered for the government's use, dozens of private lotteries were floated.[61]

The ingenuity of their projectors is demonstrated by the variety of prizes offered. Apart from lotteries that paid out in cash, there were schemes that offered prizes in the form of land, property, consumer

[57] Ibid., 31 Aug. 4 Sep. 1693.
[58] T. Neale, *A Profitable Adventure to the Fortunate* (London, 1693).
[59] Ibid.   [60] Ewen, *Lotteries and Sweepstakes*, p. 25.
[61] Proposals offered to the government included a project offering 20,000 tickets at £50 each offering annuities as prizes and to be funded out of a duty on liquor and a project to sell 1,000,000 tickets at £2 each with prizes to be paid for out of a tax on all subjects over the age of 16. L. G. and F. P., *Project for the Ready Raising of a Million* (London, 1694); Anon., *A Proposal for Raising Two Millions of Money* (London, 1695).

goods and shares. The 'Royal Academies' Lottery even offered as its prize a four-year course of lessons in a subject of the winner's choice.[62] And the *Gentleman's Journal*, rather tongue in cheek, suggested a lottery of 'Maids and Batchelors', in which 50,000 men and the same number of women would commit a guinea each to fund dowries for the lucky few. It was reckoned a sure incentive for those poor women who found 'their Vertue and their Beauty too weak allurements to attract the hard hearted men of this age'.[63]

Equally important as an indicator of the vibrancy of English innovation during the late seventeenth century was the inventiveness of the schemes themselves. Novel machines were created to mix the tickets prior to the lottery draw. The organisers of the Honourable Undertaking designed a glass cube suspended on two poles. The cube could be rotated to ensure that the tickets were properly mixed and was made of glass to guard against fraud. Those interested could view models of the cubes at Mr Conly's, Queens Head Tavern, Temple Bar or at the Free School at St Mary Ax.[64] Projectors also used random number generators to choose winners. The Ludus Mathematicus generated winning numbers by drawing five numbered wooden squares from a globe. The globe contained five of each number from 0 to 9, thus the highest number that could be generated was 99,999. The promoters apparently claimed that their system meant that no 'Fallacy [could] be imposed on the Adventurers'. However, as Thomas Saunders pointed out, very few people could grasp the concept well enough to understand it, while the printed numbers, being large enough to be seen by the audience when they were drawn, were also large enough to be seen, and selected, by the drawer.[65]

It is also possible to see the consequences of the Europe-wide intellectual debate about the nature of probability manifested in the lottery schemes created by English projectors.[66] The application of sound mathematical principles to the organisation of schemes and the purchase of lottery tickets was particularly noticed by Samuel Pepys, who wrote to Isaac Newton commenting that the lotteries had:

[62] Houghton, *Collection for Improvement*, 22 Feb. 1695.

[63] *The Gentleman's Journal or the Monthly Miscellany*, April 1694, p. 82.

[64] Anon., *The Honourable Undertaking; or Five Hundred Pounds for One Shilling* (London, 1698).

[65] Saunders, *Fortunatus's Looking Glass*, p. 17.

[66] For an analysis of the development of the concept of probability in Europe see I. Hacking, *The Emergence of Probability: A Philosophical Study of Early Ideas about Probability, Induction and Statistical Inference* (Cambridge University Press, 1975); G. Gigerenzer *et al.*, *The Empire of Chance: How Probability Changed Science and Everyday Life* (Cambridge University Press, 1989).

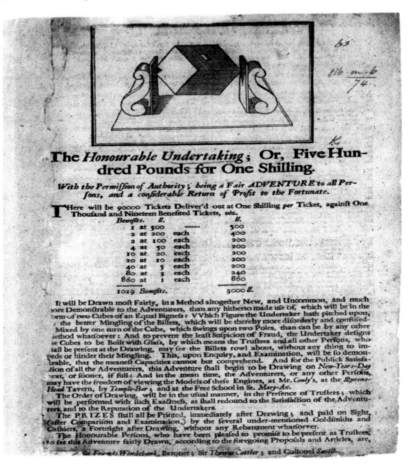

The *Honourable Undertaking*; Or, Five Hundred Pounds for One Shilling.

With the Permiſſion of Authority; being a Fair ADVENTURE to all Perſons, and a conſiderable Return of Profit to the Fortunate.

There will be 90000 Tickets Deliver'd out at One Shilling per Ticket, againſt One Thouſand and Nineteen Benefited Tickets, *&c.*

Benefits.	ll.			ll.
1 at	500	—		500
2 at	200	each		400
3 at	100	each		300
4 at	50	each		200
10 at	20	each		200
20 at	10	each		200
40 at	5	each		200
80 at	3	each		240
860 at	1	each		860
1019 *Benefits.*				3000 *ll.*

It will be Drawn moſt Fairly, in a Method altogether New, and Uncommon, and much more Demonſtrable to the Adventurers, than any hitherto made uſe of, which will be in the form of two Cubes of an Equal Bigneſs: VVhich Figure the Undertaker hath pitched upon, the better Mingling of the Billets, which will be thereby more diſorderly and confuſed: Mixed by one turn of the Cube, which Swings upon two Poles, than can be by any other method whatſoever: And to prevent the leaſt Suſpicion of Fraud, the Undertaker deſigns the Cubes to be Built with Glaſs, by which means the Truſtees and all other Perſons, who ſhall be preſent at the Drawing, may ſee the Billets rowl about, without any thing to impede or hinder their Mingling. This, upon Enquiry, and Examination, will be ſo demonſtrable, that the meaneſt Capacities cannot but comprehend. And for the Publick Satisfaction of all the Adventurers, this Adventure ſhall begin to be Drawing on New-Years-Day next, or ſooner, if full: And in the mean time, the Adventurers, or any other Perſons, may have the freedom of viewing the Models of theſe Engines, at Mr. *Cauly's*, at the *Queens Head* Tavern, by *Temple-Bar*; and at the Free School in St. *Mary-Ax.*
The Order of Drawing, will be in the uſual manner, in the Preſence of Truſtees; which will be performed with ſuch Exactneſs, as ſhall redound to the Satisfaction of the Adventurers, and to the Reputation of the Undertakers.
The PRIZES ſhall all be Printed, immediately after Drawing; and paid on Sight, (after Compariſon and Examination,) by the ſeveral under-mentioned Goldſmiths and Caſhiers, a Fortnight after Drawing, without any Rebatement whatſoever.
The Honourable Perſons, who have been pleaſed to promiſe to be preſent as Truſtees, to ſee this Adventure fairly Drawn, according to the foregoing Propoſals and Articles, are,
Sir Francis Winchcomb, Baronet; *Sir Thomas Cutler*; and Collonel *Smith*.

2.1 Broadside advertising the Honourable Undertaking lottery. Reproduced by permission of the British Library.

almost extinguised for some time at all places of publick conversation in this towne, especially among men of numbers, every other talk but what relates to the doctrine of determining between the true proportions of the hazards incident to this or that given chance or lot.[67]

In practical terms this debate allowed projectors to devise complex schemes to either charm or confuse potential players. The 'Unparallel'd Adventure', for example, was based on a complex mathematical formula. The draw was designed so that out of the 21,000 tickets entered, only

---

[67] Pepys to Newton 22 Nov. 1693 quoted in Thomas, 'Thomas Neale', p. 272.

3,000 would actually be drawn and each of them would win a prize of at least £5, but then the remaining tickets in that series of seven would be designated blank; thus if the number six were drawn, then numbers one to five and seven would automatically be removed from the draw. That way if an adventurer bought seven tickets in a numerical series, at a cost of £7, he would be guaranteed a minimum £5 return.[68]

From a distance it is easy to admire the determination and ingenuity of early modern financial innovators but they were not so well regarded by contemporaries who considered projectors to be self-interested, if not utterly dishonest. In some respects their views were justified. Thomas Neale, for example, was the epitome of the devious projector.[69] He was an inveterate gambler and risk-taker who unquestionably exploited the state's need in order to promote his own financial gain. Indeed, Neale's eulogist was not unjustified in his assertion that Neale had turned England into a nation of gamblers:

> Mourn all ye Sons and Daughters of the Lott,
> Who crowd'd up *Mercers Hall*, now He is *Not*,
> Who influenc'd every Gaming School about Him,
> Nor cou'd you get one Happy Chance without him.[70]

Yet, as Dickson pointed out, revenue departments that were too inexperienced to offer the guidance they were able to provide by the mid-eighteenth century were more than willing to accept the ideas of private individuals.[71] Moreover, many projectors offered schemes that were well researched and fit for purpose. And, in spite of public opinion of Thomas Neale and the genuine concern about the social impact of gambling, the Million Adventure was of immense value to the government because it created a means of mobilising the capital of the small investor. It was a lesson copied by successive English governments and lotteries were not abandoned as a means of raising public funds until the early nineteenth century.[72]

The initial appeal and subsequent failures of the public funds

The attraction of the new public debt lay partly in its novelty and, of course, in the returns offered by a government desperate for funds and

---

[68] *Athenian Mercury*, 23 Mar. 1695; 12 Feb. 1695.   [69] Thomas, 'Thomas Neale'.

[70] Anon., *An Elegaick Essay upon the Decease of the Groom Porter and the Lotteries* (London, 1700), p. 5.

[71] Dickson, *Financial Revolution*, p. 52.

[72] J. Raven, 'The Abolition of the English State Lotteries', *Historical Journal*, 34 (1991), 371 89.

able to pay interest over the legal maximum rate of 6 per cent. But the factor that really set the public funds apart from other investment opportunities of the time was that interest and annuity payments were backed by the appropriation of tax revenue and guaranteed by Act of Parliament. As North and Weingast argue, it was the very fact that investors were committing to a national rather than a sovereign or a private debt that encouraged them to believe their capital would be safe and interest payments assured.[73] For North and Weingast, the faith of the public creditors was entirely justified. They argue that Parliament's assumption of control over the nation's finances after the Glorious Revolution removed the arbitrary powers of the sovereign to appropriate funds or renege on debts.[74] This was because Parliament was prevented from replacing the sovereign and engaging in similarly 'irresponsible' behaviour by the development of institutions that acted as a check on government.[75] Equally, the handling of much of the government's debt by the Bank of England meant that the Bank in effect became an overseer and enforcer of the government's promises. North and Weingast suggest that the Bank 'must have instantly stopped payment if it had ceased to receive interest on the sum which it had advanced to the government'.[76] And, as Weingast elaborated in a later article, the concentration of loan decisions in the hands of the Bank of England created a check on potentially profligate behaviour and provided a strong voice for the community of public creditors.[77]

---

[73] North and Weingast, 'Constitutions and Commitment'. For further discussion of the issues raised by North and Weingast see F. Capie, 'The Origins and Development of Stable Fiscal and Monetary Institutions in England', in M. D. Bordo and R. Cortes Conde, eds., *Transferring Wealth and Power from the Old to the New World: Monetary and Fiscal Institutions in the 17th through the 19th Centuries* (Cambridge University Press, 2001), pp. 19 58; M. Levi, *Of Rule and Revenue* (Berkeley and London: University of California Press, 1988); J. Wells and D. Wills, 'Revolution, Restoration, and Debt Repudiation: The Jacobite Threat to England's Institutions and Economic Growth', *Journal of Economic History*, 60 (2000), 418 41; and for a discussion of the impact of parliamentary supremacy on economic behaviour in the early modern period see R. B. Ekelund and R. D. Tollison, *Politicized Economies: Monarchy, Monopoly and Mercantilism* (College Station Texas: Texas A&M University Press, 1997).
[74] For details of the financial settlement imposed on William III after the Glorious Revolution see C. Roberts, 'The Constitutional Significance of the Financial Settlement of 1690', *Historical Journal*, 20 (1977), 59 76.
[75] North and Weingast, 'Constitutions and Commitment', 804.
[76] T. B. Macaulay, *The History of England from the Accession of James the Second*, 8 vols. (London: Dent, 1915), vol. V, p. 2438 quoted in ibid., 821.
[77] B. R. Weingast, 'The Political Foundations of Limited Government: Parliament and Sovereign Debt in 17th and 18th Century England', in J. Droback and J. Nye, eds., *The Frontiers of the New Institutional Economics* (San Diego and London: Academic Press, 1997), p. 231.

In some respects North and Weingast present a convincing argument. It is certain that the financial integrity of the previous Stuart monarchs had been tainted by their use of monopoly grants and other forms of expropriation of wealth, and especially damaged by the Stop of the Exchequer in 1672.[78] The Stop was a suspension of payments on Charles II's debt rather than an outright repudiation, but some goldsmith bankers who had lent money to the Crown were ruined, as were their creditors. Thus, it remained prominent in the collective memory and left a legacy of suspicion among potential investors.[79] There can also be no doubt that public creditors recognised the difference between a sovereign and a national debt.[80] Indeed, for many people investment in the public funds was a political act in support of the post-Glorious Revolution regime and thus a conscious acceptance of a new relationship between Parliament and monarch. Yet, North and Weingast do not present a complete story.[81]

While Parliament might have gained power over the nation's finances, it had not yet learned responsibility or self-discipline, nor did it have any experience of large-scale finance.[82] As a result, misjudgements and errors abounded. There was an initial unwillingness to impose new taxes for more than limited periods of time, meaning the early years of the war were funded by a proliferation of small short-term loans that

---

[78] North and Weingast, 'Constitutions and Commitment', 811.

[79] For further discussion of the Stop see J.K. Horsefield, 'The Stop of the Exchequer Revisited', *Economic History Review*, 35 (1982), 511 28. For an analysis of its effects on property rights see Carruthers, *City of Capital*, pp. 122 7.

[80] Dickson, *Financial Revolution*, p. 50.

[81] While this study challenges North and Weingast's argument with regard to the early English public debt, their arguments have been challenged on a number of other counts. Gregory Clark, for example, has used data on the return on capital and land prices to demonstrate that secure private property rights existed in England from at least as early as 1600. G. Clark, 'The Political Foundations of Modern Economic Growth, 1540 1800', *Journal of Interdisciplinary History*, 25 (1996), 564 5. Carruthers too has argued that property rights were not materially affected by the Glorious Revolution. In particular, he notes that the assignability of public debt had been in place since the late Middle Ages. Carruthers also notes that it was the free assignability of debt that created the trust between debtor and creditor because it did not 'permanently bind two individuals ... [and] the role of creditor could be passed from one person to the next'. Carruthers, *City of Capital*, p. 135. For further challenges to North and Weingast's views see S. Quinn, 'The Glorious Revolution's Effect on English Private Finance: A Microhistory, 1680 1705', *Journal of Economic History*, 61 (2001), 593 615; D. Stasavage, 'Credible Commitment in Early Modern Europe: North and Weingast Revisited', *Journal of Law, Economics and Organization*, 18 (2002), 155 86; N. Sussman and Y. Yafeh, 'Institutional Reforms, Financial Development and Sovereign Debt: Britain, 1690 1790', *Journal of Economic History*, 66 (2006), 906 35.

[82] Dickson, *Financial Revolution*, p. 47; D. Stasavage, 'Partisan Politics and Public Debt: The Importance of the "Whig Supremacy" for Britain's Financial Revolution', *European Review of Economic History*, 11 (2007), 123 53.

proved difficult to manage and were backed by taxes that were likely to expire before the loan was repaid.[83] When long-term funding was introduced, the schemes chosen, although innovative, proved to be expensive, complicated and difficult to administer. Most importantly, the funding of both short- and long-term debt was hindered by the fact that new taxes seldom yielded expected revenues. In great part this was due to a lack of time and facilities to make a systematic study of patterns of consumption and thus arrive at clear estimates of prospective yields. But equally, there was a marked tendency among projectors and political arithmeticians to be overly optimistic in their estimates and a rather misguided willingness on the part of Parliament to accept those over-optimistic calculations.[84] In consequence, according to Dickson's figures, by 1697 there was a deficiency of more than £5 million in the taxes appropriated to cover both short- and long-term debts.[85] Looking back from 1710 Daniel Defoe identified those deficiencies as having resulted in the reduction of 'Tallies on those Funds to intollerable, unheard of Discounts, to the Ruin of all that we called Credit'.[86]

Parliament's inexperience was compounded by pre-existing economic problems, most notably, the dreadful state of the English coin which, by the 1690s, was heavily clipped. Clippers removed small amounts of metal from the unmilled coin and then passed the coin back into circulation where, although it had declined in weight it continued to circulate at its face value. Although within the domestic economy the coin functioned well as a token currency, the necessity of making large remittances of bullion abroad to fund the war effort led to an increasing loss of public confidence.[87] After long and divisive discussions about the best course of action, in 1696 the decision was taken to recall and remint all English coin.[88] Although necessary, the recoinage was highly disruptive. It led to a severe shortage of circulating credit and precipitated what has been described by D. W. Jones as the gravest economic crisis of the century.[89]

---

[83] Dickson, *Financial Revolution*, p. 348.   [84] Ibid., p. 349.   [85] Ibid., p. 354.

[86] D. Defoe, *An Essay upon Publick Credit* (London, 1710), pp. 17 18.

[87] Jones estimates that after April 1692 foreign remittances on government account averaged £16,000 per week, a sum that continued to rise until 1695. In total more than £8.5 m was remitted abroad between 1688 and 1697. D. W. Jones, 'London Merchants and the Crisis of the 1690s', in P. Clark and P. Slack, eds., *Crisis and Order in English Towns, 1500 1700* (London: Routledge, 1972), pp. 316 17.

[88] For further on the recoinage see Horsefield, *British Monetary Experiments*; M. H. Li, *The Great Recoinage of 1696 9* (London: Weidenfeld and Nicolson, 1963).

[89] D. W. Jones, 'Defending the Revolution: The Economics, Logistics, and Finance of England's War Effort, 1688 1712', in D. Hoak and M. Feingold, eds., *The World of William and Mary: Anglo Dutch Perspectives on the Revolution of 1688 89* (Stanford University Press, 1996), p. 61.

And blame for the crisis was laid very firmly at Parliament's door. In his anonymously published pamphlet *Account of the Proceedings in the House of Commons*, Samuel Grascome alluded to 'very great Anger against the Parliament' having been aroused by the privations of the recoinage.[90]

As the cost of the war spiralled and the military situation abroad and the economic situation at home became more uncertain, Parliament descended deeper into financial trouble. On the death of the Duchess of Modena in late 1695 the Treasury was forced to confess that there was not even enough money to provide the king with a 'mourning coach or mourning for a footman to waite on him'.[91] And by 1696 there was no money to pay the public creditors. Benefit payments on government annuities and on Million Adventure tickets ceased, and interest due to the Bank of England went unpaid.

An attempt to head off financial disaster provided a further example of Parliament's inability to manage the nation's finances. In 1696, Parliament, willing to pursue any avenue that might generate additional funds, encouraged a rival to the Bank of England. The Land Bank was to lend the government £2,564,000, raised from subscribers in specie.[92] But, although it commanded support from across the political spectrum, the Land Bank scheme had two flaws that ensured its rapid failure. First, it sought to raise subscriptions in specie at a time when coin was scarce because of the recoinage. Second, presumably in order to ensure that the new project was not overtaken by its rival, anyone with any connection to the Bank of England was prevented from investing in the Land Bank. This dramatically reduced the fund of capital from which the Land Bank could draw subscriptions. Ultimately, only £7,100 was subscribed to the project, of which only a quarter was paid in.[93]

Although with hindsight it is easy to disregard this challenge to the Bank of England's position, the Bank of England's directors and shareholders took the threat very seriously. The General Court of the Bank's Proprietors was called together on 10 February 1696 'upon the Rumour Spread of Erecting another Bank [and the directors sought the Court's advice] concerning what was fitt for the Corporation to doe for their owne safety in their present Circumstances'.[94] Protests were lodged and an attempt made to offer the government further funds in order to

---

[90] [S. Grascome], *An Account of the Proceedings in the House of Commons in Relation to the Recoining the Clipp'd Money* (London, 1696).
[91] Quoted in Dickson, *Financial Revolution*, p. 345.
[92] D. Rubini, 'Politics and the Battle for the Banks, 1688–1697', *English Historical Review*, 85 (1970), 699.
[93] Ibid., p. 709.   [94] Bank Archives, G7/1, 10 Feb. 1696.

frustrate the need for the Land Bank, but these overtures were rejected. Thus, the Bank of England was placed in an isolated and vulnerable position from which it was rescued by the failure of its rival, rather than by the support of its friends in Parliament.

By 1696, therefore, faith in Parliament's ability to honour its financial commitments was not substantially increased, as North and Weingast argue, but significantly eroded. Nor could creditors be sure that interest payments would resume in the future. Indeed, a series of incidents, including the death of Mary II in December 1694 which, in some people's eyes, diminished the legitimacy of the monarchy, and the discovery of a plot to assassinate William in 1696, pointed to the growing political risks of investing in William III's regime. In addition to political problems at home, the military campaign during 1696 was not successful and the defection of Savoy in August of that year further weakened the allies' position. As the public creditors undoubtedly recognised, defeat for William would have meant the return of James II with no guarantees that the restored monarch would honour the financial commitments of the previous regime. In consequence, even though investors perceived support of the war effort to be a patriotic duty, Parliament's ability to raise funds in both the short- and long-term money market was severely reduced.[95] The failure of the Malt Lottery in early 1697 offers a potent demonstration of the suspicion with which government debt was regarded during those dark days. Of 140,000 tickets offered for sale, only 1,763 were sold.[96] The government recognised that much of the fault was theirs. As Charles Montagu, the Chancellor of the Exchequer, wrote to William Blathwayt: 'I was always fearfull of the success of a new Lottery when the old Tickets were not pay'd but wee must make the best wee can of it.'[97]

What saved the public finances?

It was the liquidity provided by the financial market that had grown up to support the transfer of shares in private companies rather than action taken by the government that served to support the public funds in the short term. It is especially notable that a secondary market in Million Adventure tickets developed very rapidly. In fact, even prior to the lottery draw, which took place in November 1694, there were

[95] North and Weingast, 'Constitutions and Commitment', 805.
[96] Dickson, *Financial Revolution*, p. 49.
[97] BL, Add. MS 34,355, Earl of Halifax's Letters on the Land Banks and Finance, 1696 1697, fo. 27.

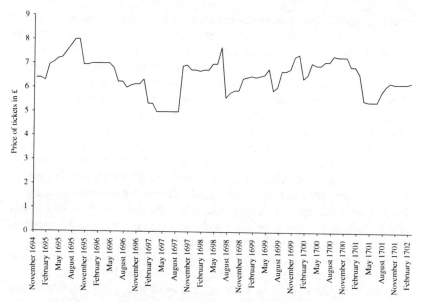

2.2 Price of blank tickets in the Million Adventure, 1694 1702
Source: Houghton, *Collection for Improvement*.

indications that it would be possible to trade the tickets once their value was assigned. Between May and October 1694 blank tickets, which yielded an annuity of £1 a year for sixteen years, were being quoted in John Houghton's *Collection for Improvement* at £7.[98] Thus, the secondary market emerged spontaneously, initially to provide an opportunity for disappointed adventurers who did not want to wait for sixteen years to realise their investment. When the government began to fail to keep up the payments on the tickets, the market became of central importance because it meant that investors who had lost faith in the public funds were not obliged to remain bound to the government.

It is impossible to trace the full extent of the secondary market but, as may be seen in Figure 2.2, Houghton provided continuous prices for blank tickets up until 1702. The price variations seen here indicate significant activity.

Moreover, it was not just whole tickets that could be exchanged in the secondary market. Investors were also offered the opportunity to

[98] Houghton, *Collection for Improvement*, 18 May 26 Oct. 1694.

exchange individual interest payments. This was possible because Million Adventure tickets incorporated a series of coupons that had to be cut off and presented at the Exchequer in order to claim each interest payment. It was, therefore, a simple thing to clip the coupon and present it to a third party in exchange for a discounted cash payment. Frederick Herne, for example, was able to sell one future interest payment on his lottery tickets for a sum of 17s in the pound, thus satisfying an immediate need for money, but retaining the right to participate fully in future payments.[99] Thomas Neale, never one to allow a money-spinning opportunity to pass him by, also offered holders of Million Adventure tickets the chance to enter their holdings for a 'second drawing' of the lottery. In essence, what Neale offered was a restructuring of the payment schedule which would allow holders of both blank and benefit tickets to exchange their right to annual annuities for upfront lump sums, at a healthy discount of course.[100]

Ostensibly, life annuities were less flexible because, even when transferred, payments continued to be made on the life of the original nominee and thus proof was always required that the person was still living.[101] Because it was almost impossible to ascertain the health of the nominee, it was also rather difficult to assign value to the annuity. Nevertheless, it was still possible to alienate annuities and, as Samuel Jeake informed his wife in 1697, investors were even able to exchange lottery tickets for government annuities which paid '14% ... *if* [author's italics] ye security continue'.[102]

Investors in the Bank of England also found that, despite falling share prices and the cessation of dividends in 1696, Bank stock remained liquid. And it was easy and convenient to transfer shares. Although both parties to the transfer had to present themselves or send their attorneys to represent them at the Bank, the transfer process was simple, fast, reliable and relatively cheap.[103] In addition, the transfer office was highly accessible. The Bank's directors stipulated that office hours should be between eight and five each day, except Sundays and those holy days already observed at the Custom House, the Excise Office and

[99] Guildhall Library, London, Herne Family Papers, MS 6372, ii, fo. 12.

[100] T. Neale, *The Second Drawing of the Blank Tickets of the Million Adventure* (London, 1695).

[101] Dickson, *Financial Revolution*, p. 458.

[102] East Sussex Record Office, Frewen Family Archives, Papers of Samuel Jeake, the younger, FRE 5330.

[103] Transfers were subject to a stamp duty of 6d from mid 1694 and the Bank of England charged an administration fee of 5s for each transaction. This was to be paid by the seller as a contribution towards 'the bearing & defraying the charge of Books Accountants Law=duty & other like expences'. Bank Archives, G7/1, 15 Dec. 1694.

among the goldsmiths.[104] This meant that although transfer books were also closed during periods when elections to the Court of Directors were taking place and when the dividends were being calculated, there remained over 240 days in each year on which investors could be sure of being able to conduct their transactions.

As Figures 2.3 and 2.4 demonstrate, apart from a small downturn in 1696, turnover of stock increased steadily between 1694 and 1700. Those needing to liquidate their shares would, therefore, have encountered few difficulties.

Those who were unwilling or unable to alienate their holdings in government debt did not merely accept the failings of the early financial revolution. They acted both to call the government to account and, when necessary, in defence of their property rights. In particular, a strident pamphlet campaign sought to remind the government of the promises made in the Acts of Parliament that had created the public funds. One pamphleteer asked the government to remember that the Acts had been presented to investors as 'a true Prospect of the Advantages [they] were to enjoy' and had offered 'Certainty and Assurance' about the returns offered.[105] Another detailed the interest payments outstanding on Million Adventure tickets and reminded the government that 'the Credit and Honour of the Nation, and of Parliamentary Funds [were] concerned in the due Payment of these Lottery Tickets'.[106] Critics also warned that, like any private individual, Parliament's creditworthiness would be undermined if promises were not kept. Hence one writer cautioned that 'taking away, changing or altering any Parliamentary Funds without ... free and voluntary Consent, will render them precarious and uncertain, and by a natural consequence destroy their Credit and Esteem'.[107] He went on to assert that ill-using the public creditors would create long-term distrust. Indeed, 'all Publick-spiritedness will infallibly vanish at the remembrance of the Ingratitude shewed'.[108]

[104] Bank of England Archives, Minutes of the Court of Directors, G4/1, 22 23 Aug. 1694. The holy days observed seem to have been the main ones of the Christian calendar, Christmas, Easter, Pentecost and Whitsun. The market also observed some national holidays, such as the King's birthday on 4 November and the anniversary of the death of Charles I on 30 January.
[105] Anon., *Reasons for Encouraging the Bank*, p. 3.
[106] Anon., *The Case of the Adventurers in the Million Lottery, Humbly Offer'd to the Consideration of the Honourable House of Commons* (London, 1697).
[107] Anon., *A Letter to a Friend concerning Credit, and how it may be restor'd to the Bank of England* (London, 1697), p. 2.
[108] Ibid., p. 7.

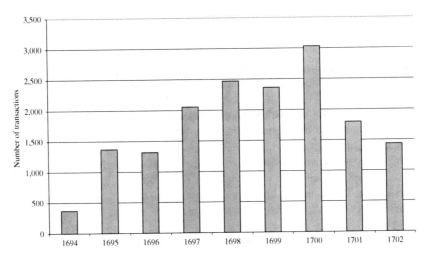

2.3 Annual number of transfers of Bank stock, 1694 1702[a]
Source: Bank of England Archives, Transfer Books, 1694 1702, AC28/
32233; AC28/1513 22.
[a] For a detailed breakdown of activity in Bank of England shares see
Appendix 3.

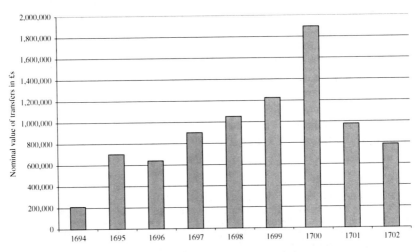

2.4 Value of transfers of Bank stock, 1694 1702
Source: Bank Archives, AC28/32233; AC28/1513 22.

With regard to the position of the Bank of England, direct comparisons were drawn with private bankers. It was argued that for a private banker to be trusted, 'Men believe that such a Banker hath a good Foundation, is a careful, cautious, and honest Man; that he hath an Estate to satisfy every Creditor, and will not dispose or alienate any part of it ... that [he] doth not launch out his money in many Foreign Adventures, or on doubtful Projects, or uncertain Funds.' The only way that the Bank of England could establish such a reputation, the author continued, was through the support of Parliament which was after all responsible for the funds that maintained the Bank.[109]

Although pamphlets and broadsides offer the clearest insight into the arguments used against the government, the debate was not just carried on in print. Disillusioned and angry public creditors met to discuss the state of the public finances. Samuel Jeake's papers record his attendance at meetings of the holders of Million Lottery tickets in 1696. He also attended many of the Bank of England's General Courts, which, during the mid-1690s, were constantly occupied with framing responses to the government's demands for additional funds. And Jeake's letters imply that General Courts were preceded by well-attended meetings and discussions with other shareholders.[110] Moreover, the public creditors were not content just to debate the government's shortcomings; they were also willing to take action to protect their investments and to punish the failures of the financial revolution.

Of course, one of the most powerful actions a group can take against government is the withdrawal of its support.[111] As noted above, the failure of the Malt Lottery was a powerful expression of the public's discontent and it shows very clearly how quickly the entire edifice of public credit might have collapsed. Similar action was taken by the holders of Bank stock in early 1697. At that time, having failed to raise funds through the Land Bank, the government asked the Bank of England to lend £2,564,000 and, in addition, to accept 8 per cent interest to engraft all parliamentary tallies onto its capital.[112] The shareholders, having lost patience with the government's schemes, declined to lend the £2.5 million noting that the government had failed to honour its previous obligations and that as a consequence the Bank

---

[109] Ibid., p. 1. [110] ESRO, Jeake Papers, passim.

[111] B. R. Weingast, 'The Economic Role of Political Institutions: Market Preserving Federalism and Economic Development', *Journal of Law, Economics and Organization*, 11 (1995), 26.

[112] Bank Archives, G7/1, 2 Jan. 1697.

'cannot at present raise the Sume of £2564000 ... apprehending, that in their present circumstances, should they undertake to raise so great a Sume, the Government would be disappointed'.[113] On the question of the engraftment of the short-term debt, however, the shareholders were more accommodating. Probably some saw the need to make recompense after refusing to fund the initial loan, but more importantly many shareholders held tallies and it is likely that they were quite keen to exchange debt dependent on degraded government credit for the slightly less tarnished guarantees offered by ownership of Bank shares.

Moreover, the shareholders rather shrewdly took the opportunity to attach a number of demands to their agreement to engraft the short-term debt. The conditions started with an understandable demand that the interest and principal would be repaid on time in future, and included requests for the extension of the Bank's charter, for an agreement that the Bank should be exempted from taxation, and for measures to be passed to prevent the counterfeiting of the Bank's notes.[114] Another of the most notable demands was that 'no other Bank, or any Constitution whatever in the nature of a Bank, be Erected or Established, permitted or allowed, within this Kingdome, during the continuance of the Bank of England'.[115] It was a measure of the government's financial desperation and a testament to the growing power of the Bank of England that most of these demands were met.

Conclusion

Of course, had the government's financial position continued to deteriorate, direct action would merely have put off the inevitable. Ultimately, therefore, the government's experiments with long-term funding were saved only by the ending of the Nine Years' War in September 1697. Although the Treaty of Ryswick benefited William III more than Louis XIV, it was not a decisive victory and it led to an uneasy peace. But the ending of the war did relieve the immediate burden of heavy expenditure and gave Parliament the time to restore the nation's finances and regain the confidence of the public creditors. By 1698 annuity and interest payments had recommenced and the Bank of England's share price was

---

[113]   Ibid., 4 Jan. 1697.
[114]   The process of negotiation that accompanied this and the eight further Bank charter renewals between 1697 and 1844 is detailed in J. L. Broz and R. S. Grossman, 'Paying for Privilege: The Political Economy of Bank of England Charters, 1694 1844', *Explorations in Economic History*, 41 (2004), 48 72.
[115]   Bank Archives, G7/1, 4 Jan. 1697.

moving steadily upwards from a low of 51 in 1697 to a high of 148 in March 1700.[116] Yet, this most forceful demonstration of the faith of investors remained an expression of trust in the financial market, rather than in Parliament, and it is to the questions of how that market was constructed and how it functioned that the following chapters turn.

[116] Houghton, *Collection for Improvement*, 5 Feb. 1697; 1 Mar. 1700.

3   The contemporary debate

Activities that supported economic development were highly regarded in late seventeenth-century England. Lewes Roberts went so far as to define commerce as 'an Art or Science invented by ingenious Mankind'.[1] Yet the financial market was widely reviled. Many contemporaries believed that instead of facilitating economic progress and directing idle capital towards deserving projects, trading in financial instruments merely encouraged speculation, which turned honest men away from commerce and consequently retarded trade and industry. Equally concerning were the links between finance and politics. The East India Company's attempted manipulation of the political system during the 1690s brought this issue to the forefront of public opinion but it was the creation of a direct link between the country's government and the moneyed men through the establishment of the public funds that caused the greatest concern. These issues were widely discussed but, as this chapter will emphasise, should not be seen merely as matters of public interest. The debate that surrounded the financial market constituted an important source of information for those considering investment in debt or equities and therefore must have influenced decision-making. The war of words also had practical consequences for investors. The value of shares was compromised by attacks on the monopolies of some companies and attempts to regulate the market constituted a threat to liquidity and to the legality of some investment instruments.

The perceived dangers of stock-jobbing

In 1697 Daniel Defoe observed that 'past Ages have never come up to the degree of Projecting and Inventing ... which we see this Age arriv'd to'.[2]

---

[1] L. Roberts, *The Merchants Map of Commerce: wherein the Universal Manner and Matter of Trade is Compendiously Handled* (London, 1676), p. 6.
[2] D. Defoe, *An Essay Upon Projects* (London, 1697), pp. 1 2.

While Defoe was ambivalent about the value of many of those projects, others argued that the 'projecting age' was of potential benefit to the English economy. One author asserted, 'Searching Mines, Improving Lands, Exercising Manufactures, Forreign and Domestick Traffick, are Noble Enterprises, which denote a private Man publick spirited: by these the Poor are imploy'd, the Revenues increased, the Honour and Reputation of the Nation's inhanc'd.'[3] Reflecting the mercantilist ideals that influenced many writers at this time, projects that increased domestic production and reduced the need for expensive imports were especially encouraged.[4] John Houghton concluded, 'our Windows and Looking Glasses ... much outdo what was done before by our selves or Neighbours', '[t]he *Japan* is brought to that perfection that it not only out-does all that is made in *India*, but vies for its Lacquer with the Japan Lacquer itself' and '[t]he *Lutestring* is a Trade we wanted very much, and tis gotten to such a height, that the Proprietors talk of out doing any of the rest'.[5]

Houghton also argued in favour of the use of the joint-stock company to fund such ventures. In particular he questioned 'who will have a Share, if to save his *Life*, *Estate* or *Freedom*, he might not part with it'?[6] In other words, without the liquidity offered by the financial market, few would have been willing to make the investment necessary to capitalise new enterprises. Moreover, Houghton cautiously suggested that in spite of the problems caused by speculation, joint-stock companies were

---

[3] Anon., *Plain Dealing*, pp. 6 7.
[4] The chief concern of such writers was the balance of trade. It was postulated at this time that the world's resources being finite, any country that imported more than it could export must be ruined by the export of bullion to pay for its goods just 'as a private person must be, who every year spends more than the Income of his Estate'. Davenant, *Ways and Means*, p. 21. Nevertheless, historians continue to question the extent to which mercantilist ideals impacted upon economic behaviour. For an overview of the chief arguments see J. O. Appleby, *Economic Thought and Ideology in Seventeenth Century England* (Princeton University Press, 1978); D. C. Coleman, 'Mercantilism Revisited', *Historical Journal*, 23 (1980), 773 91; A. Finkelstein, *Harmony and the Balance: An Intellectual History of Seventeenth Century English Economic Thought* (Ann Arbor: University of Michigan Press, 2000).
[5] Houghton, *Collection for Improvement*, 20 Jul. 1694. The Patentees for Lacquering after the manner of Japan established their company in 1693. In 1696 the Company advertised a variety of items of furniture for sale including cabinets, looking glasses and tea tables. Nevertheless, Scott was of the opinion that Houghton's enthusiasm for the project was not entirely justified. The Royal Lustring Company, more popularly known as the Lutestring Company, was established in 1688 for the manufacture of fine black silk referred to as lustring because of a manufacturing technique that imparted a shine or gloss to the material. This Company was far more successful, in the short term at least. It is probable that business ceased with the ending of their charter in 1713, probably as a result of opposition from the weavers. Scott, *Constitution and Finance*, vol. III, pp. 119, 73 89.
[6] Houghton, *Collection for Improvement*, 25 Jun. 1697.

effective in raising capital for the pursuit of industry. In May 1696 he noted with reference to the glass trade that 'what e'er may be said against *Stock-Jobbing*, yet it has been the Means to raise great Summs of Money to improve this Art'.[7] He made a similar defence of the copper industry suggesting that

whether People have or have not thriven by Stocks, 'tis a plain Case that *England* has and particularly by the *Copper Stocks*; for *Dockwra's* stock alone produces, as I am inform'd about 80 Tun a Year; and the rest, it's probable as much, both about 160 Tun, which at 100 *l.* the Tun (and sometimes it has been sold at 120 *l.*) amounts to 16000 *l.* the Year, which must hinder the Importation of so much, and at 10 *l.* the Year a Head, finds Livelihoods for 1600 Persons, beside what the turning it into *Brass*, the making of *Battry*, *Wire*, *Pins* and other Manufacture Causes.[8]

Yet, critics of the financial market rejected the notion that speculation was a mere inconvenience that could be offset by the benefits that manufacturing brought to the domestic economy. Their views were coloured by existing attitudes towards those who speculated in foodstuffs and who, it was alleged with some justification, cared little for the disruption and hardship they caused so long as they could make a profit. Equally, it was thought that those who speculated in financial instruments sought to profit from the misfortunes of others. Their actions created nothing that was of value to the economy, on the contrary they resulted in anomalous prices and deceitful modes of transacting.[9]

Stock-jobbing also acted to the detriment of the economy because it turned men away from honest and beneficial trades. In one satirical pamphlet a concerned citizen recalled a conversation with a neighbour who asked why he should 'stand pilling straws or thrumming caps behind the Counter, [when] ... besides *East India*, *Affrica*, and *Hudson's Bay Stock* there was now ... almost a hundred other *Stocks* for which either *Patents* [were] granted or procuring' and to which his capital could more profitably be committed.[10] That such individuals might turn away from their occupations to speculate in stock was a great concern since the neglect of trade and commerce had a deleterious effect on the wealth of the kingdom.[11] This caused particular unease after the establishment of the public funds, which, as Charles Davenant alleged, were

[7] Ibid., 2 May 1696.   [8] Ibid., 25 Jun. 1697.

[9] S. Banner, *Anglo American Securities Regulation: Cultural and Political Roots, 1690 1860* (Cambridge University Press, 1998), p. 19.

[10] Anon., *Plain Dealing*, p. 2.

[11] See, for example, Anon., *A Proposal for Putting some Stop to the Extravagant Humour of Stock Jobbing* (London, 1697); J. Briscoe, *An Explanatory Dialogue of a Late Treatise intituled, A Discourse on the Late Funds* (London, 1694), pp. 25 6.

so Inviting, and of such infinite Profit, that few are now willing to let out their money to traders at 6 *per Cent.* as formerly; so that all merchants, who subsist by Credit, must in time give over, and they being the greatest part, and, perhaps, the most Industrious, any Man may judge what damage this will be to the Kingdom.[12]

This was not an unreasonable fear. The impact of the emergence of the public funds on trade cannot adequately be measured but, as one Member of Parliament complained in 1702, it is probable that some merchants found 'a better return between the Exchequer and the Exchange than [they made] by running a hazard to the Indies'.[13]

There was no sense that stock-jobbing brought any value to the economy because it was presumed that whatever was made by one person was lost by another.[14] Furthermore, the pursuit of wealth that would necessitate a loss to another individual was unquestionably immoral.[15] Even those on the periphery of the financial market had cause for concern over this issue. The purchasers of lottery tickets were warned by the *Athenian Mercury* that they endangered their souls. To stake one's own money in order to win another man's was sinful, and the expectation of gain pointed to covetousness and the idolisation of money.[16] The prospect of gain was also believed to encourage deceit. Stock-jobbers, it was alleged, spread rumours and misinformation in order to manipulate prices to their own advantage. Indeed, Defoe characterised stock-jobbing as

a compleat System of Knavery ...'tis a Trade found in Fraud, born of Deceit, and nourished by Trick, Cheat, Wheedle, Forgeries, Falshoods and all sorts of Delusions; Coining false News, this way good, that way bad; whispering imaginary Terrors, Frights, Hopes, Expectations, and then preying upon the Weakness of those, whose Imaginations they have wrought upon, whom they have either elevated or depress'd.[17]

[12] Davenant, *Ways and Means*, p. 44; See also Briscoe, *Discourse on the Late Funds*. In particular the Bank was singled out as being a danger to trade. The author of *Angliae Tutamen* suggested that the Bank had 'given a mighty damp to Commerce'. Another anonymous pamphleteer asked, 'what must the Trade of England dwindle and sink into, when so much of the Stock and Cash of the Nation ... comes to be withdrawn from it, and committed to the Husbandry of a Bank?' Anon., *Angliae Tutamen*, p. 6; Anon., *Some Considerations Offered against the Continuance of the Bank of England, In a Letter to a Member of the present Parliament* (London, 1694), p. 7.

[13] Cited in W. A. Speck, 'Conflict in Society', in G. Holmes, ed., *Britain after the Glorious Revolution, 1689 1714* (London: Macmillan, 1969), p. 141.

[14] Anon., *Plain Dealing*, pp. 6 7.

[15] For a further discussion of this issue with reference to the financial market in Amsterdam see N. De Marchi and P. Harrison, 'Trading "in the Wind" and with Guile: The Troublesome Matter of the Short Selling of Shares in Seventeenth Century Holland', in N. De Marchi and M. Morgan, eds., *Higgling: Transactors and their Markets in the History of Economics* (Durham, N.C. and London: Duke University Press, 1994), pp. 47 65.

[16] *Athenian Mercury*, 16 Dec. 1693.

[17] D. Defoe, *The Anatomy of Exchange Alley* (London, 1719), pp. 3 4.

Other writers suggested that stock-jobbers used complex strategies to control the market in certain stocks. The unexplained and seemingly mysterious movements of the market were often attributed to the 'necessity some are under of Buying or Selling to answer *Pollicies* and *Contracts* they are unwittingly drawn into by subtil and designing Men'.[18]

Stock-jobbers were also accused of establishing joint-stock companies not because they intended to pursue a business but in order to sell off the shares at inflated values to 'ignorant men, drawn in by the reputation, falsely raised and artfully spread, concerning the thriving state of their stock'.[19] This was dishonest in itself but was made more problematic by the structure of management within joint-stock companies during this period. The governors and directors of all joint-stock companies were drawn from a pool of prominent shareholders. In fact, a minimum shareholding was required before a governorship or directorship could be taken up. To allow or even encourage a company's stock to fall into the hands of the inexperienced and naïve investor or avaricious stock-jobber was therefore to condemn it to be managed by individuals who knew nothing of the trade or industry that their company pursued and who would inevitably cause the business to fail.[20]

Devious stock-jobbers also had the power to destroy thriving companies. The report of the new Board of Trade set up in 1696 to examine the state of the English economy referred to both linen and paper manufacture as being industries hindered by stock-jobbing. The Board found that

the linen manufacture in this kingdom hath made [no] great progress of late. The stock subscribed for that purpose was soon diverted by a stockjobbing trade, and thereby all the Corporation disabled to promote it ... they have not any looms ... what linens they sell at their sale are only such as they buy of weavers in Yorkshire, Durham and Lancashire.[21]

The paper industry, although it was described as a 'very useful manufacture', was similarly hindered 'by the perversion of the stock subscribed for that purpose into a stock-jobbing trade'.[22] Even when the commissioners identified an industry that required greater capital, such as the fishing industry, they remained cautious about recommending joint-stock financing. The commissioners asserted that the fishing industry was destined to remain inadequately funded 'till a common stock can be

---

[18] Anon., *Plain Dealing*, p. 3. Houghton also described such practices. Houghton, *Collection for Improvement*, 13 Jul. 1694.
[19] *Journals of the House of Commons*, vol. XI, p. 595.   [20] Anon., *Plain Dealing*, p. 8.
[21] 'Commissioners of Trade and Plantations Report', p. 576.
[22] Ibid.

raised, and a Company erected, upon such Terms, as may secure the Management of it from the destructive shuffling of the stock-jobber'.[23]

It is, of course, worth questioning the extent to which stock-jobbers deserved their reputation. Certainly they were obvious targets for the critics of the new financial market. They drew attention to themselves with their loud talk and rowdy behaviour. The City found them to be a physical nuisance. Contemporaries bemoaned the fact that 'our *Royal Exchange*, the most renowned in the Universe for its Structure, and the daily Concourse of Merchants there, in the exercise of their noble and laudable Professions, [had] become a *Theatre* for such vile Practices'.[24] Even when they left the Exchange in the mid-1690s, stock-jobbers and brokers continued to disrupt City life.[25] An order dated October 1700 stated,

That by the daily Resort and Standing of Brokers and Stock Jobbers in [Exchange Alley], not only the Common Passage to and from the *Royal Exchange* is greatly obstructed, but Incouragement is given by the tumultuary Concourse of People attending the said Brokers, to Pick Pockets, Shop Lifters, and other Idle and Disorderly People to mix among them.[26]

This order makes it clear that not only were the stock-jobbers and brokers a nuisance but that they were also counted among the lowest elements of London society.

Equally, evidence of market manipulation and attempted manipulation will be presented below. Indeed, the limited capitalisation of many of the smaller companies of the period meant that they were dangerously exposed to concerted attacks on their share price. Yet, the influence of stock-jobbers was not all-encompassing. The establishment of any new enterprise during a time of great economic and political uncertainty carries numerous risks. Chapter 1 showed that companies set up during the early 1690s failed for numerous reasons unconnected with speculation. The condemnation of stock-jobbers was therefore based on a superficial understanding of the causes of failure among the new businesses set up during this period.

[23] Quoted in E. V. Morgan and W. A. Thomas, *The Stock Exchange: Its History and Functions* (London: Elek, 1969), p. 23.

[24] Anon., *Plain Dealing*, p. 5.

[25] The precise reasons for their departure are unclear. John Francis suggested that the brokers left of their own accord having been annoyed by objections to their presence, while Scott suggests that they were expelled. J. Francis, *Chronicles and Characters of the Stock Exchange* (London: Hindsight, 2001), p. 10; Scott, *Constitution and Finance*, vol. I, p. 360.

[26] Mayor Levett, Jovis Decimo die Octobris, 1700, *Annoq. Regni Regis Willielmi Tertii Angliae, &c.* [Order that none of the Exchange Brokers do for the future agitate any business in open Alley, 10 October 1700] (London, 1700).

Nevertheless, although the precise complaints raised by contemporary critics may not have been entirely justified, the arguments offered did reflect genuine concerns. They also constituted the dominant view of the market and thus inevitably impacted upon the actions of investors. Naturally, for some, the notion that the market would reward deception was an encouragement to take deceitful actions. Others may have had greater concern for their souls. As will be seen in the next chapter, some investors certainly harboured concerns about the morality of their actions with regard to the new financial market. Perhaps most tellingly the stock market initially attracted the capital of only a very few investors. There were many reasons for this but it is reasonable to suggest that some were deterred by the seeming dangers of the new investment opportunities and the apparent difficulties of negotiating with duplicitous brokers and stock-jobbers.

Hostility towards joint-stock companies

The contemporary debate on the nature of the new financial system not only impacted upon the choices of investors but also upon the value of their investments. The criticism that was directed against stock-jobbers was inevitably extended to the form of economic organisation that made their speculative actions possible. Specifically, this meant that the joint-stock company was regarded with notable hostility by many commentators who considered that this method of funding potentially useful projects also harboured the means of their destruction. Moreover, because joint-stock companies were not regarded as valuable additions to the English economy, the industries funded by the smaller companies that emerged during the early 1690s were often afforded little protection or encouragement from the state. Thus, the White Paper Company was badly affected by the imposition of high taxes on its products and the English Linen Company was offered little protection from the hostility of the woollen manufacturers and was adversely affected by the government's decision to encourage the Irish linen industry.[27] This prejudice was also reflected in the debate surrounding the management of overseas trade.

Foreign trade, however, was a far more conspicuous element of the English economy than domestic manufacturing. It required a great deal of investment and in return yielded great profits. The wealth of London's merchant families was well known and the changes wrought

---

[27] Scott, *Constitution and Finance*, vol. III, pp. 69, 94 5, 97.

within society by overseas trade were widely appreciated. With regard to
the East India Company, for example, Lawson noted that people from
all levels of society came to know of the Company's influence on their
lives particularly in respect to diet and clothing and, for Londoners, in
the buildings they saw around them.[28] It is also certain that although
modern analyses can demonstrate that foreign trade played a relatively
small part in the English economy of the 1690s, it was not understood to
be so by contemporaries.[29] Until the 1690s regular statistics were not
recorded and thus the value of foreign trade could not be measured
accurately. As such, contemporaries did not view trade as a proportion
of the total economy but rather they judged it by the contribution it made
to the country's wealth and strength relative to other countries.[30]
Consequently, trade assumed an exaggerated importance in the eyes of
many observers and the actions of the trading companies were closely
scrutinised and often criticised. The East India Company, in particular,
aroused strong opposition from three sources.

Opposition came firstly from those who felt that the Company was
failing the English economy. Importantly, the East India Company
violated mercantilist theories of the balance of trade by exporting
bullion in order to pay for manufactured foreign goods.[31] The
Company's claim that profits from the re-export trade balanced the
outflow of bullion was often disregarded and, of course, offered little
comfort to those domestic manufacturers who found their own exports
superseded by foreign goods. Indeed, domestic producers saw their
interests being damaged in markets at home and abroad. The most
vocal of them were the woollen manufacturers who mounted a consistent campaign against the supposed destruction of their markets by
imports of Indian textiles. Their dislike of the Company spilled over
into violence on at least one occasion during the 1690s. In January
1697 East India House was beset by a 'rabble of Weavers'. Their attack
caused great consternation and led to a considerable expenditure on
additional security measures and compensation for those unfortunates
who had been attacked by the mob. This included the sum of three
guineas paid to James Field, an officer in the 'Poultrey Countrey',

[28] P. Lawson, *The East India Company: A History* (London and New York: Longman, 1993),
p. 60.
[29] Coleman, 'Mercantilism Revisited', 782.   [30] Ibid.
[31] J. Cary, *An Essay On The State Of England In Relation to its Trade, its Poor, and its Taxes*
(Bristol, 1695), pp. 51 2. See also G. L. Cherry, 'The Development of the English Free
Trade Movement in Parliament, 1689 1702', *Journal of Modern History*, 25 (1953),
104 6.

'who was knockt down, by the Rabble, and lost his Hat and Halbeard'![32] Public and political sympathies, however, were not on the side of the Company and the insistent lobbying of the weavers led to legislation in 1700 and 1720 that prohibited the import of many types of Indian fabrics.[33]

Secondly, the East India Company's monopoly was much resented. Monopoly in the late seventeenth century was still regarded as a product of the royal prerogative, thus it was associated with the undermining of the liberty of both Parliament and the subject.[34] Other critics cited the perceived cost of monopoly to the ordinary consumer. One pamphleteer explained that allowing the East India Company a monopoly on trade to the East was akin to

granting them a Power to tax the Nation, when and to what degree they please, one hundred tun of *Pepper* or a hundred Bails of *Muslins* arrive, which being (and there's always one thing or another) wanting, they take Advantage of the Nation's Necessity, and prise them accordingly, whereas were the Goods fairly exposed at the Candle in reasonable Lots, the Company would have a sufficient Profit, we should all that are Buyers partake of the Trade, and the Publick would be served at easier Rates.[35]

Equally, the East India Company's monopoly was challenged by private merchants who were prevented from taking advantage of opportunities for trade to the East and who particularly resented their exclusion from the fast-growing re-export trade in Asian and other tropical imports.[36]

The question of why the East India Company and, to a lesser extent the other trading companies, continued to arouse such passionate opposition from private traders in the midst of a war that had served to cripple foreign trade is a complex one. In part, it can be answered by Chaudhuri's assertion that the East India trade had a 'different cost-benefit yardstick' than other commercial ventures.[37] In particular, the trade had an extended time-horizon and thus the immediate difficulties suffered during wartime were offset by its perceived long-term potential. But perhaps

---

[32] IOR, East India Company, Court Books, B/41, 22 Jan. 1697.

[33] Jones, 'London Overseas Merchant Groups', p. 266.

[34] T. Keirn, 'Monopoly, Economic Thought, and the Royal African Company', in J. Brewer and S. Staves, eds., *Early Modern Conceptions of Property* (London: Routledge, 1995), p. 433. See also D. W. Stump, 'An Economic Consequence of 1688', *Albion*, 6 (1974), 26 35.

[35] Anon., *Plain Dealing*, p. 11.

[36] Chaudhuri, *Trading World of Asia*, p. 432. Davis estimated that although in 1640 some 80 90 per cent of exports from London were of woollen cloth, by 1700 that figure had been reduced to 47 per cent, while re exports in American and Eastern products commanded 30 per cent of total exports. Davis, 'English Foreign Trade', 150.

[37] Chaudhuri, *Trading World of Asia*, p. 432.

more influential were concerns about the principle, rather than the practice, of monopoly. As Pollexfen argued,

Trade ought not to be stinted and contracted to the Advantage of some few, but diffusive for the incouragement of Industry, and free for all persons to ingage in. Joint Stocks may be a good way to advance some Trading Men, but whether may probably advance the Trade of the Nation, or answer the chief ends designed by Trade should be considered.[38]

The third element of opposition came from potential investors who desired better access to the seemingly lucrative investment opportunities provided by the East India Company.[39] Their anger was prompted by the East India Company's limited capital and the perception that stock was concentrated in the hands of the privileged few, and their demands ranged from an enlargement of the existing capital to the dissolution of the Company and the creation of a new one with a greater capital. The question of why such demands continued even as the wartime losses to ships and cargoes rendered foreign trade unprofitable and halted the payment of dividends is again pertinent and may be answered by the relative dearth of lucrative investment opportunities in the late seventeenth century, a problem that was only partly alleviated by the new joint-stock companies that emerged during the 1690s. With few other outlets for investment available, the long-term potential offered by overseas trading companies remained attractive in spite of the strains that war placed on overall profitability.

While the complaints made by the East India Company's opponents were undoubtedly justified, it is notable that, unlike the smaller joint-stock companies, the East India Company could mobilise opinion in its favour through strong counter-arguments. Besides the general claims that the Company had increased trade, made a contribution to improvements in navigation and 'wrought us into that Fund of Wealth, which serv'd not only to Inrich us in Peace but has enabl'd us to defend our selves ... against the Invasion of a most Powerful Enemy', it was asserted that it was only through a joint-stock company that overseas trade could be managed effectively.[40] In particular, foreign trade necessitated defence

---

[38] J. Pollexfen, A *Discourse of Trade, Coyn and Paper Credit* (London, 1697), p. 125.
[39] Jones, 'London Overseas Merchant Groups', p. 264.
[40] J. Child, *The Great Honour and Advantage of the East India Trade to the Kingdom Asserted* (London, 1697), pp. 4 5. Historians have concurred with the Company's arguments. Ralph Davis, for example, noted that the capital required by the trade to the East was so large that it could not be raised by any means other than a joint stock company. Equally, the necessity of dealing with advanced civilisations in addition to the political and commercial rivalry of European competitors meant that an organised company of some form was essential. R. Davis, *English Overseas Trade, 1500 1700* (London: Macmillan, 1973), p. 43.

against native peoples and European rivals. Josiah Child argued that 'for countries with which his Majesty hath no alliance, nor can have any by reason of their distance, or Barbarity ... where there is a necessity of Maintaining Forces and Forts ... Companies of Merchants are absolutely necessary'.[41] This was not an unreasonable claim. The expense of maintaining defensive infrastructure in Asia was enormous, and by 1698 the Old East India Company estimated its expenditure in this respect to have been approximately one million pounds.[42]

It was also argued that the Company had the experience and facilities that were not available to individuals or other groups. Those operating without the Company's guidance would 'through their own unskilfulness ... pay dear for our native Commodities here, and sell them cheap abroad; and also buy Foreign Commodities dear abroad, and sell them here for less than their cost, to the Ruin of themselves, and Destruction of Trade'.[43] This argument was partly justified by the subsequent history of the New East India Company. The new organisation, despite being well funded and enthusiastically pursued, became just a 'mishmash' of traditional regulated ventures, private voyages and some joint-stock activity.[44] Ultimately, it proved no match for the superior organisation and experience of the Old Company.

Finally, the East India Company characterised the concentration of its stock into the hands of the few as a positive advantage. It was argued that the London management was necessarily controlled by a select group of individuals. In a memorandum to Parliament in 1692 the East India Company claimed that neither 'the Company, nor peradventure, any great business in the world did ever thrive where some one or two men, or very few, did not arrive at so much reputation ... as to be able to moderate the councils of the commonwealth or society'.[45] Again this argument must have found favour with those mentioned above who argued that broadening the shareholder base could result in companies being managed by inexperienced individuals.

Trading companies could, therefore, provide far greater justification for their organisation into a joint-stock than domestic manufacturing firms. Unfortunately for their shareholders, their far more prominent position within the early modern English economy meant that opposition was not just confined to a war of words. The battle over the trading

---

[41] J. Child, *A New Discourse of Trade* (London, 1693), pp. 80 1.

[42] Anon., *The Case of the Governor and Company of Merchants of London Trading to the East Indies* (London, 1698), p. 2 cited in I. B. Watson, *Foundation for Empire: English Private Trade in India, 1659 1760* (New Delhi: Vikas, 1980), p. 22.

[43] Child, *New Discourse*, p. 84.   [44] Lawson, *East India Company*, p. 55.

[45] Quoted in Davies, 'Investment in the Later Seventeenth Century', 297.

companies was fought directly and publicly on two fronts: first, on the trade routes in a 'kind of Civil War'[46] between the interlopers who sought to break or evade a company's monopoly and the companies who sought to maintain their privileges;[47] and secondly on the home front against the sustained opposition of factions within Parliament and the wider mercantile community. This latter battle, particularly as it was fought over the East India Company's charter, was to demonstrate very clearly to public opinion how potentially invidious was the relationship between the moneyed men and the government.[48]

Politics and the moneyed men

Given the nature of the East India Company's monopoly and the perceived importance of its trade it is not surprising that links to the state were strong. Indeed, the Company had cultivated a very close connection to the Crown during the reigns of Charles II and James II, gifting to those monarchs considerable sums of money.[49] Both Charles and James reciprocated by supporting an aggressive commercial policy overseas.[50] But the Glorious Revolution changed the character of the Company's relationship with the state. The East India Company had little influence at the new court and was tarnished by its close associations with previous Stuart kings. Regime change also coincided with the expiry of the Company's charter in 1690 and although William III was reluctant to dissolve the East India Company lest it result in the 'interval and interruption of the trade which might occasion the loss of it to the nation', factions within his Parliaments were determined to force a reorganisation that would ensure the Company's stranglehold on trade to the East was loosened.[51]

[46] Pollexfen, *Discourse of Trade, Coyn*, p. 97.
[47] Although prerogative monopoly had been enforced in 1684 in the case of the East India Company v. Sandys, in 1689 a similar case brought by the Royal African Company against private traders ended in the court ruling against the Company thus limiting the enforce ability of monopoly rights granted by royal patent and opening the way for interlopers to engage in foreign trade. This ruling was confirmed by Parliament in 1693 when it acknowledged that 'it [was] the right of all Englishmen to trade to the East Indies, unless prohibited by act of Parliament'. Cited in Stump, 'Economic Consequence', p. 32.
[48] For an overview of the EIC's position in the 1690s see H. Horwitz, 'The East India Trade, the Politicians and the Constitutions, 1689 1702', *Journal of British Studies*, 17 (1978), 1 18.
[49] Lawson, *East India Company*, p. 44.
[50] Lawson cites the affirmation of the Company's charter and the Navigation Acts of 1661 as proof of these policies. Lawson, *East India Company*, p. 46. Sherman also notes the effectiveness of the East India Company lobby in pushing for favourable commercial policies, particularly during the 1670s and 1680s. A. A. Sherman, 'Pressure from Leadenhall: The East India Company Lobby, 1660 1678', *Business History Review*, 50 (1976), 329 55.
[51] Quoted in Horwitz, 'The East India Trade', 5.

It is notable that the Royal African Company was placed in a similar position at this time.[52] It put up a poor fight; its dire financial condition forced accommodation with interlopers and a campaign in favour of free trade to Africa could not be effectively countered by the Company or its supporters. In 1698 Parliament passed a largely unsatisfactory, but conclusive, measure that freed trade to Africa.[53] The East India Company was in a far stronger position than the Royal African Company. Chaudhuri and Israel note that the Company had an 'inherent strength and entrenched position in the commercial life of the City' and assert that William III was necessarily wary of upsetting an organisation that had command of a large number of heavily armed ships and immense corporate funds.[54] It is also clear that the Company used those funds to good effect in an attempt to reclaim its connection with Crown and state.

Of course, the offering of bribes to prominent members of government was not new. The Company itself had been pursuing such strategies for many years.[55] However, as Table 3.1 demonstrates, the monies paid out during the early 1690s in respect of the Company's charter renewal were considerable and quite beyond anything that had gone before.[56] In the short term, the ploy was successful. The charter was renewed in 1693 with just one major concession: the enlargement of the capital by an additional £744,000. Furthermore, the enlargement was permitted on terms that favoured the Company, and the East India Company's enemies were prevented from gaining too large a shareholding by the distribution of free stock options to encourage subscriptions from sympathetic individuals.[57] But because it failed to widen the circle of investors, the capital enlargement did little to satisfy those who were opposed to the East India Company's monopoly and, when

[52] Interestingly, the Hudson's Bay Company, due to the limited scope of its operations and its small size, did not attract the attention of those who wanted to eliminate monopoly. It was investigated by Parliament in the mid eighteenth century but did not lose its monopoly until 1869. R. Harris, *Industrializing English Law: Entrepreneurship and Business Organization, 1720 1844* (Cambridge University Press, 2000), p. 50.

[53] Davies, *Royal African Company*, pp. 122 35. See also A. M. Carlos and J. B. Kruse, 'The Decline of the Royal African Company: Fringe Firms and the Role of the Charter', *Economic History Review*, 49 (1996), 291 313.

[54] K. N. Chaudhuri and J. I. Israel, 'The English and Dutch East India Companies and the Glorious Revolution of 1688 9', in J. Israel, ed., *The Anglo Dutch Moment: Essays on the Glorious Revolution and its World Impact* (Cambridge University Press, 1991), p. 436.

[55] Sherman, 'Pressure from Leadenhall', 337.

[56] Modern analyses of the Company's fight to renew its charter in 1693 are surprisingly few. For a brief overview of events see Lawson, *East India Company*, pp. 51 7. A more detailed if rather dated account can be found in W. W. Hunter, *A History of British India*, 2 vols. (London and New York: Longmans, 1899 1900).

[57] The options protected the new shareholders against falls in the value of the stock and compensated them for the fact that the existing stock was trading below par at the time of

Table 3.1 *Monies paid out in the East India Company's special service*

Year	£	s	d
1688	1,284	13	6
1689	2,096	2	2
1690	3,056	3	8
1691	11,372	15	0
1692	4,659	15	4
1693	80,468	16	8
1694	4,075	6	3
Total	107,013	12	7

Source: JHC, vol. XI, p. 267.

details of the bribes paid were exposed in 1695, the battle over the Company's position intensified.[58]

The consequences of the revelation of the Company's corrupt practices were far-reaching. The scandal revealed to the public the nature of the relationship between the East India Company and the government. John Evelyn reported in his diary 'an extraordinary Clamor' over the matter.[59] The evidence given to Parliament by Thomas Cooke (the deputy governor of the Company and supposedly the chief architect of the attempt to 'buy' the charter) was followed with great attention and published in a number of pamphlets.[60] Several prominent members of the ministry were greatly embarrassed by Cooke's revelations, which contributed to the downfall of the government in October 1695 and the consequent election of a new House of Commons that was far more hostile to the Company. It was this Parliament that agreed to the establishment of the New East India Company in 1698, an act that might easily have destroyed the Old Company.[61]

Yet, far from being a conclusive move, the creation of the New East India Company merely exacerbated the antagonism between the rival

the enlargement. A total of £65,267 10s stock was covered in this way. The options were distributed, probably without the initial knowledge of the Court of Directors, by Sir Thomas Cooke and Sir Basil Firebrace. IOR, B/40, 26 Oct. 1694.

[58] The bribes paid by the EIC were exposed as part of a wider investigation into corruption in politics.

[59] Evelyn, *Diary of John Evelyn*, vol. V, p. 209.

[60] Anon., *A Collection of the Debates and Proceedings in Parliament In 1694 and 1695. Upon the Inquiry into the Late Briberies and Corrupt Practices* (London, 1695); Anon., *The Examinations and Informations upon Oath, of Sir Thomas Cooke, And Several other Persons* (London, 1695).

[61] Horwitz, 'The East India Trade', 7.

factions seeking control of trade to the East. The Old Company retained the right to continue trading and took advantage of the structure of the New Company to become its largest shareholder.[62] From this position of strength the Old Company continued to dominate trade to the East, effectively excluding its rival and ensuring that the only reasonable method of resolving the conflict was through a merger of the two companies. While negotiations to effect the merger proceeded, the issue of trade to the East remained high on the political agenda and once again emerged to dominate the political process during the General Election of 1700/01. During the election campaign it was openly acknowledged that both factions sought to place their own men in Parliament. Indeed, the pertinent question for voters considering the merits of their potential representative was 'not as it ought to be, Is he a Man of Sense, of Religion, of Honesty and Estate? But What Company is he for, the New, or the Old?'[63] In particular, the scale of the New Company's campaign was remarkable. Walcott notes that only two New Company directors sat in the Parliament that was dissolved in 1700, while twelve stood for election in 1701 along with a further twenty candidates who were obviously also New Company men.[64] The campaign also created a great deal of resentment among contemporaries. Undoubtedly, Defoe spoke for many when he accused the two East India Companies of behaving 'as if the Interest of either Company were to be Nam'd in the Day with the *Protestant Religion and the publick Peace*, or as if they, who are fit to be Representatives of the People ... should not be capable of deciding the petty Controversy in Trade between two Rival Companies'.[65]

Ultimately, the outcome of the election was not a triumph for the New Company. Whig forces did not gain a majority in the new House of Commons and thus there was no protection for the New Company candidates against a Tory backlash that was both swift and severe.

---

[62] The New EIC was incorporated as a 'general society'. All those subscribing to the loan had a right to trade to India and could also join their respective rights and trade on a joint stock if they so desired. Scott, *Constitution and Finance*, vol. II, p. 165.

[63] D. Defoe, *The Freeholders Plea Against Stock Jobbing Elections of Parliament Men* (London, 1701), pp. 7 8.

[64] R. Walcott, 'The East India Interest in the General Election of 1700 1701', *English Historical Review*, 71 (1956), 231 2. See also C. Jones, '"A Fresh Division Lately Grown Up Amongst Us": Party Strife, Aristocratic Investment in the Old and New East India Companies and the Vote in the House of Lords on 23 February 1700', *Historical Research*, 68 (1995), 302 17.

[65] Defoe, *Freeholders Plea*, p. 7. For similar sentiments see Anon., *The True Picture of an Ancient Tory* (London, 1702), p. 43; Anon., *A Letter From a Lawyer of the Inner Temple, To His Friend in the Country Concerning the East India Stock and the Project of Uniting the New and Old Companies* (London, 1698), p. 7.

During the months that followed, ten New Company MPs lost their seats amidst accusations of bribery and corruption.[66] But for contemporary observers the initial message of the election campaign held: politics had the potential to become the tool of the moneyed men and elections could be jobbed like stock with seats in the House being sold to the highest bidder.

This message was demonstrated even more effectively by the nation's new dependence on the public funds. As Dickson pointed out, it was alleged that by establishing a dependent relationship between the public creditors and the factions in Parliament who supported it, the national debt had met 'not an economic need ... but a political need'.[67] Davenant's *Modern Whig* was equally explicit:

'Tis true, we have run the Nation over Head and Ears in debt by our Fonds, and new Devices, but mark what a Dependence upon our Nobel Friends, this way of raising Money has occasion'd. Who is it sticks to 'em but those who are concern'd in Tallies and the new Stocks?[68]

Of course, those who supported the new funds were keen to assert this factor as a benefit to the state. Michael Godfrey listed among the Bank of England's advantages, the fact that 'like the other public funds, [it tied] the people faster to the government'.[69] Nevertheless, many feared the consequences of the nation's reliance upon long-term funding and were particularly wary about the new relationship between the state and its creditors. The chief object of their anxiety was an emerging class of men who, as had been amply demonstrated by the battle over trade to the East, could use their connections within the new machinery of public credit to place themselves in positions of power and in positions of hidden influence. The founding of the Bank of England in 1694 exacerbated such concerns.

For many contemporary observers the Bank of England represented the forming of the 'moneyed men' into a cohesive group whose wealth presented a challenge to the existing social elite and whose direct connections to government seemed to give them the power to influence policy decisions. The origins and status of many of the Bank of England's first directors intensified such fears. Drawn largely from the mercantile community and mainly Whig in political affiliation, many were also Huguenot in origin and some had Dutch connections. The establishment of the Bank of England was, therefore, a powerful

---

[66] Walcott, 'East India Interest', 239.   [67] Dickson, *Financial Revolution*, p. 17.
[68] C. Davenant, *The True Picture of a Modern Whig* (London, 1701), p. 26.
[69] M. Godfrey, *A Short Account of the Bank of England* (London, 1695), p. 2.

symbol of the overthrow of a monarch and the rise of Parliament. It also
represented the move away from an agrarian society in which power and
stability was vested in land, to a society that gave power to those in
possession of intangible and inherently unstable forms of wealth. As
such, one observer noted that 'the Effect of [the Bank] will be the
impoverishing all Ranks and Degrees of People in the Kingdom, save
those alone that are immediately interested and concerned in it'.[70] Most
affected, it was alleged, were the gentry and the nobility who,
already burdened by high taxes, feared that the Bank would contribute
to further falls in the value of land and rents.[71] Equally it was argued,
not without some justification, that the taxes exacted from the landed
interest paid dividends and annuities to the public creditors. The author
of *Angliae Tutamen* asserted:

the great Dividends the *Bank* has already made, and is preparing to make ... tell all
the World in honest *English*, that one Part of the Nation preys upon t'other; the
mighty Gains that have arisen to them, since their Establishment, being no less
than Twenty *per Cent.* must be a Loss somewhere, for 'tis all within our selves ...
We are all of one Nation, and if we could extract Profits from Foreigners 'twould
do well, but from one another, enriches not the Publick one jot.[72]

The Bank of England, therefore, seemed to epitomise the worst aspects of
the new forms of finance. It contributed to the undermining of the social
and political order and placed unearned wealth in the hands of the
undeserving speculator.

As shown in the previous chapter, ill feeling did not just manifest
itself in print. Just as the East India Company's critics expressed their
dissatisfaction through the establishment of a rival company, so too did
those opposed to the Bank of England. Moreover, there can be little
doubt that the intention of those in Parliament who supported the rival
Land Bank was to replace the Bank of England.[73] The Land Bank
proposed in 1696 was to have a much broader appeal, particularly to
the country gentleman. It was to be less London-oriented, have provincial outlets and to make extensive provision for low-cost mortgages.[74]

---

[70] Anon., *Some Considerations*, p. 9.
[71] Anon., *A Proposal for a Subscription to Raise One Hundred Thousand Pounds, For Circulating the Credit of a Land Bank* (London, 1695?). For similar sentiments see J. Briscoe, *The Freehold Estates of England, or England itself the best Fund or Security* (London, 1695); Briscoe, *Discourse on the Late Funds*; D. Thomas, *Propositions for General Land Banks* (London, 1695?).
[72] Anon., *Angliae Tutamen*, p. 7.   [73] Rubini, 'Battle for the Banks', 697.
[74] Plans for a Land Bank to provide low cost mortgages for hard hit small land owners had long been in existence but, without the backing of Parliament, they had attracted few investors. See Rubini, 'Battle for the Banks', 687 703.

The Land Bank was also to lend the government £2,564,000, raised from subscribers in specie, at 7 per cent interest, thus making a larger initial contribution than the Bank of England, at a lower cost. In fact, it was only the Land Bank's failure to attract support that ensured the Bank of England retained its position within the economy and its close links to Parliament.

For those brave enough to trust their capital to the new financial market, the contemporary debate represented more than just an expression of prejudice against an unfamiliar financial system. The debate had the power to affect policy and thus directly impact upon the potential of investments. The practical consequences of this were made clear in the removal of the Royal African Company's monopoly and in the establishment of rivals to the Bank of England and the East India Company, actions that fundamentally altered the nature and value of an investment in those companies. The social and political distrust of the joint-stock company, therefore, constituted a key risk for investors, and one that was almost impossible to manage.

Controlling the market

A final, but no less important, concern for investors was the regular call for measures to be taken to control the financial market. Somewhat surprisingly, given that it was often represented as anarchic, the financial market of the early 1690s did not emerge into a regulatory vacuum. An increase in the numbers and activities of brokers following the Restoration had prompted the City of London to pass an Act of Common Council in 1673, which aimed to prevent 'usurious contracts, false Chevelance, and other crafty deceits' by limiting the number of brokers to 100 Englishmen, 12 from the French and Dutch churches and 6 aliens. All admitted brokers were to pay a £20 fee and were required to carry a silver medal and copies of their admission papers as proof of their status. Anyone employing an unlicensed broker could be fined £5 for each offence.[75]

The regulations, together with the oversight of a committee appointed by the City, were evidently sufficient prior to 1691. In February of that year the Committee for Regulating Brokers reported that individuals had from time to time been fined for acting as brokers without a licence

[75] L. K. Davison, 'Public Policy in an Age of Economic Expansion: The Search for Commercial Accountability, 1690 1750', unpublished PhD thesis (Harvard University, 1990), p. 134.

but obviously saw no need for tighter controls.[76] However, by the end of 1691 the Court of Aldermen was facing a more pressing problem. Numerous complaints had been received about the proliferation of unlicensed stockbrokers and, specifically, about the fees they were charging.[77] Attempts to impose tighter controls on the market were clearly ineffectual. In February 1692 the City authorities met again to consider the problem, and the Court of Aldermen was discussing the same complaints in May 1693. With the City authorities seemingly powerless to restrict the practices of brokers and stock-jobbers, attempts began to force the passing of parliamentary legislation.

The main aim of those who wanted to impose restrictions on the market was simple: to control speculation by limiting the activities of stock-jobbers and slowing the turnover of stock.[78] Thus, it was suggested that no stock should be sold unless the owner could prove that they had possessed it for a reasonable period of time, that certain times should be appointed for the exchange of stock and that transfers should incur additional and prohibitive costs. By these measures it was argued 'the extravagant and unaccountable Methods of Brokers, Stock-jobbers, and Others, will in great measure be Restrain'd; the Government supply'd with a Considerable Summ of Money Yearly; the Fair Buyer and Seller at all times Accommodated; and the Tradesmen more at Leisure to follow their several Trades'.[79] Nevertheless, the passing of legislation against the market was not straightforward. A bill introduced in 1694 'for preventing of frauds and abuses in buying and selling of parts and shares in joint stocks' was not passed, nor was another introduced during the 1695–96 session of Parliament.[80]

The reasons why it was so difficult to introduce legislation to control the market were several. First, the new financial market was a grey area for legislators. There was little foundation for them to build upon and the dealings of stock-jobbers were ill understood, making them, as Davison argues, difficult to regulate.[81] Secondly, there was, quite naturally, some opposition to legislation. Recognising that regulation of the market would increase costs, decrease liquidity and had the power

---

[76] London Metropolitan Archives, COL/CA/01/01/099, fos. 350 1. The committee members were Thomas Stampe, John Houblon and William Gore.

[77] LMA, COL/CA/01/01/100.

[78] See, for example, Anon., *Proposal for Putting some Stop to ... Stock Jobbing*; D. Defoe, *The Villainy of Stock Jobbers Detected* (London, 1701), pp. 24 5.

[79] Anon., *Proposal for Putting some Stop to ... Stock Jobbing*.

[80] For a detailed analysis of attempts to legislate against the financial market during the 1690s see Davison, 'Public Policy', pp. 134 62.

[81] Ibid., pp. 254 60.

to render derivative instruments illegal, some contemporaries offered very reasonably framed arguments against the passing of restrictive legislation. For example, the attempt in 1694 to introduce legislation prompted a petition from 'several Merchants, on behalf of themselves, and divers other Merchants and Tradesmen in and about the City of London, and elsewhere' who asserted, albeit without providing specific details, that the bill would ruin trade.[82] In 1697, a pamphleteer published a list of the legitimate uses to which time bargains and options had been put during the period of the recoinage. He stated that the economic constraints under which the country had laboured had forced many to sell Bank stock and notes, and shares in other companies. In order to protect themselves during this time of necessity, many had made 'Agreements to receive back the said Stocks and Notes on certain Terms, whereby they know their certain Loss'. Others had retained stock and notes that they would otherwise have disposed of in order to deliver them when called for by such agreements. Moreover, it was alleged that many people had lent money to the government on tallies 'which they would not have done, if they could not [through the use of options and time bargains] have Insured themselves'. Such individuals, the author argued, had broken no laws and to enact legislation voiding all such contracts would result in 'Properties [being] destroyed, and many Families [being] utterly ruined'.[83]

Thirdly, and most importantly, once the mechanics of government debt became dependent upon the maintenance of liquidity within the financial market, the framing of legislation became more and more problematic. Defoe summed up the problem when in 1719 he reported the opinion of one stock-jobber thus:

if the Government takes Credit, their Funds should come to Market; and while there is a Market we will buy and sell; there is no effectual way in the World, says he, to suppress us but this, *viz.* That the Government should first pay all the publick Debts, redeem all the Funds, and dissolve all the Charters, *viz.* Bank, South Sea, and East India, and buy nothing upon Trust, and then, says he, they need not hang the Stock Jobbers, for they will be apt to hang themselves.[84]

---

[82] *JHC*, vol. XI, p. 116, p. 123.

[83] Anon., *Reasons Humbly Offered, Against a Clause in the Bill for Regulating Brokers* (London, 1697).

[84] Defoe, *Anatomy of Exchange Alley*, p. 2. The need to protect the circulation of the public funds arises often and consistently in pamphlets arguing against the regulation of the market. In 1733, for example, it was argued that restrictions would lead to a small group controlling the funds, which would force foreign buyers out, lead to a loss of liquidity and ultimately destroy the public funds. Anon., *Some Considerations on Public Credit, and the*

Therefore, in spite of regular calls for restrictive legislation, the government could not move quickly to regulate the financial market. Indeed, when legislation was finally passed in 1697 it was, in fact, linked to the engraftment of the government's short-term debt onto the Bank of England's stock. As noted in the previous chapter, before accepting the engraftment the Bank requested a number of concessions from Parliament. These included the understandable requests that the government might in future be a little more conscientious about the repayment of its debt and that no other bank be permitted during the period of the Bank's charter, but the Bank also took the opportunity to request other concessions. In particular, it was argued that the counterfeiting of Bank bills and notes should be made a felony and that 'no Contract, Bargaine or Agreement [derivative, in other words], made for any Bank Stock to be bought or sold, shall be good or valid in Law or Equity' unless it was registered and transferred within a certain number of days.[85] Thus, it was the Bank's desire to protect the value of its assets that resulted in the enactment of restrictive legislation against the financial market. The wording of the preamble to the Act makes the connection clear:

And whereas divers Brokers and Stock Jobbers, or pretended Brokers, have lately set up and carried on most unjust Practices and Designs, in Selling and Discounting of Talleys, Bank Stock, Bank Bills, Shares and Interests in Joint Stocks, and other Matters and Things, and have, and do, unlawfully Combined and Confederated themselves together, to Raise and fall from time to time the Value of such Talleys, Bank Stock and Bank Bills.[86]

A further reflection of the Act's concern with the value of assets rather than the actions of individuals is the fact that the legislation did little to limit the alleged transgressions of the stock-jobbers. In fact, the Act merely reconfirmed many of the restrictions against brokers introduced by the 1673 Act of Common Council mentioned above. It restricted the number of sworn brokers allowed to operate in the City to one hundred. This included brokers of all commodities and not just financial brokers, as is sometimes suggested.[87] Every person acting as a broker had to provide references to prove their 'Ability, Honesty

Nature of its Circulation in the Funds, Occasioned by the Bill now depending in the House, to prevent the pernicious Practice of Stock jobbing (London, 1733) cited in Davison, 'Public Policy', p. 225.
[85] Bank Archives, G7/1, 4 Jan. 1697.
[86] Quoted in Morgan and Thomas, *Stock Exchange*, p. 23.
[87] See, for example, Banner, *Securities Regulation*, p. 39; Dale, *First Crash*, p. 33. A pamphlet published in 1708 estimated that of the 100 sworn brokers, more than half dealt in goods, 16 were chiefly occupied in negotiating bills of exchange, and only around 25 dealt predominantly in equity and debt. Davison, 'Public Policy', p. 177.

and good name' and provide £500 as a good behaviour bond. Brokers were also obliged by the Act to keep a record of their transactions and were disallowed from dealing in any financial instrument, including tallies, bills and joint-stocks, for their own account. Any individual found acting without authorisation was to be fined £500 and pilloried.[88]

Interestingly, the term broker was not used in any surviving stock ledger or transfer books before 1698, thus the effectiveness of the legislation can be traced. After 1698 the title can only be found in the Bank of England's books – a further indication that legislation was enacted under pressure from this institution. Only thirty-one individuals described themselves as a 'broker' in the Bank's transfer books and stock ledgers between early 1698 and the end of 1702. And only twenty-four of those were registered as sworn brokers with the City authorities indicating that, although the legislation prohibited it, some brokers continued to act without official permission.[89]

An attempt to control the use of derivatives was no more effectual. The register set up by the Bank to record such transactions contains only 150 entries, thus it was certainly not capturing all transactions.[90] As Dickson asserted, subsequent attempts to regulate the market in the early eighteenth century were also ineffective.[91] The market adapted techniques to circumvent legislation, attempts to separate jobbing and broking functions failed and, as all subsequent legislatures have discovered, regulations cannot prevent sharp and unexpected movements in share prices. The failure of restrictive legislation was, however, not just a result of the market's resilience, it was also a consequence of a lack of political will and the recognition that although the financial market was undesirable and seemingly dangerous, it was also essential to the smooth operation of the public funds.

Summary

The debate stimulated by the evolution of the financial market represented investment in equity and debt instruments as dangerous and dishonest. Stock-jobbers and brokers were regarded as deceitful individuals, and the joint-stock company as detrimental to the process of

[88] London Metropolitan Archives, Rules to be observed in the Admittance of Brokers, COL/BR/09/006.
[89] See LMA, An alphabetical list of 100 brokers admitted by the Court of Aldermen, COL/BR/03/01/009; IOR, L/AG/14/3/2 6.
[90] Bank Archives, Register Book of contracts in Bank stock, AC27/283.
[91] Dickson, *Financial Revolution*, p. 519.

funding trade and industry. Attitudes were hardened by the political machinations of the East India Company and the obvious connections established by the public funds between the new moneyed interest and the state.

Critics were not always justified in their attacks. In many respects stock-jobbers became convenient scapegoats to explain the inevitable failures of a market that was operating under difficult economic and political circumstances. The dominant representation of the market as dangerous and dishonest did, however, influence the opinions and attitudes of investors. Undoubtedly, some were convinced that fortunes were to be made and that unscrupulous actions would be rewarded. The debate made others more cautious in their approach and privileged the state's debt, which could seemingly provide assurances to the inexperienced investor. It is also probable that a debate that questioned the security and, importantly, the morality of the financial market dissuaded many more from committing their capital to the new opportunities.

Thus, arguments over the nature of the joint-stock company did not just shape attitudes towards the financial market. It had practical and political repercussions and consequently necessitated the close attention of those who placed their capital in joint-stock companies. The political threat levelled against their investments had to be factored into the choices that people made and, as will be argued in later chapters, encouraged in some investors a very active form of stockholding.

4   The development of a financial press

Those who were not deterred by the apparent dangers of early modern investment needed to seek out a more balanced analysis of its potential risks and rewards. Moreover, the communication of investment information was an essential part of the creation of a financial market. The economist Robert Shiller has even gone so far as to suggest a direct connection between the advent of the news media and the rise of financial speculation. Shiller argues that the news media rather than just reporting market events become a part of those events and are consequently 'essential vehicles' for the spread of excitement and interest in the markets.[1] With regard to the advent of the financial market in the 1690s, this argument is, on some levels, a convincing one. London's market emerged at a time when the English news media was starting to undergo a rapid expansion, most particularly following the lapsing of the Licensing Act in 1695.[2] Nevertheless, the connection between the rise of the news media and the spread of information and excitement about the financial market may not be as strong as Shiller suggests. Indeed, before such a connection can be made, the type and utility of the information available to early modern investors must be established and issues of cost, speed of distribution and, most importantly, accuracy must be addressed. The purpose of this chapter, therefore, is to examine the three types of printed information available to investors in the 1690s – the newspaper, the price current and didactic works, such as merchants' manuals – and ask how the information presented in those media helped to inform the decisions made by early modern investors.

---

[1] R. J. Shiller, *Irrational Exuberance* (Princeton, N. J. and Oxford: Princeton University Press, 2000), p. 71.

[2] The Licensing Act had been intended to prevent the publication of seditious and heretical writings but by 1695 had outlived its usefulness and was acknowledged to have 'in no wise answered the end for which it was made'. Quoted in J. Sutherland, *The Restoration Newspaper and its Development* (Cambridge University Press, 1986), p. 25.

Newspapers

Perhaps as a consequence of the turbulent events of the seventeenth century, the English public of the time had a 'nearly pathological interest' in news.[3] It was an interest that extended throughout society. One commentator noted: 'from the Lord to the fiddler, all are grown states-men'.[4] Literacy levels in late seventeenth- and early eighteenth-century England confirm an increasing ability to utilise printed information. Cressy estimates that by the beginning of the eighteenth century, 45 per cent of men and 25 per cent of women in England were literate.[5] London, in particular, boasted a literate populace. Earle's study of Londoners who gave evidence in Church courts indicates that, among deponents born after 1660, 93 per cent of men and 59.4 per cent of women could sign their names.[6]

Given that a signature may stand as a proxy for literacy, early English investors also appear to have been well educated. An examination of the Bank of England's transfer books for the first eight years of its existence reveals that only nineteen of those who bought or sold shares during this time could not sign their name. They formed less than 1 per cent of the total number of investors in the Bank of England and were involved in significantly less than 1 per cent of the total number of transactions.[7] Records for the East India, Royal African and Hudson's Bay Companies are incomplete and less extensive but an examination of the surviving transfer books of those companies reveals no illiterate stockholders.[8] Those who invested in the newly established financial market were, therefore, among the better educated and, arguably, better informed of England's populace.

[3] J. Raymond, 'The Newspaper, Public Opinion, and the Public Sphere in the Seventeenth Century', in J. Raymond, ed., *News, Newspapers and Society in Early Modern Britain* (London: F. Cass, 1999), p. 109.

[4] Anon., *Crackfart & Tony; or the Knave and the Fool: in a Dialogue over a Dish of Coffee* ([London?], 1680) quoted in S. Pincus, '"Coffee Politicians Does Create": Coffeehouses and Restoration Political Culture', *Journal of Modern History*, 67 (1995), 807.

[5] D. Cressy, *Literacy and the Social Order: Reading and Writing in Tudor and Stuart England* (Cambridge University Press, 1980), p. 176.

[6] P. Earle, *A City Full of People: Men and Women of London, 1650 1750* (London: Methuen, 1994), p. 37.

[7] Bank Archives, AC28/32233; AC28/1513 22. The social status of those investors seems broadly consistent with their illiteracy. There were eleven women   eight widows, two spinsters and one married woman   a clothier, a cooper, a coachman, a joiner, a lighterman, a waterman, a merchant taylor and one who described himself as a gentleman.

[8] India Office Records, Old East India Company, Transfer Books, L/AG/14/3/2 6; National Archives, Public Record Office, Royal African Company, Transfer Books, Stock Journals and Stock Ledgers, T70/187 190; National Archives, Public Record Office, Hudson's Bay Company Archives, Transfer Books, BH 1/465, A 43/1 2.

Nevertheless, the investing public's desire for news and their receptiveness to the printed medium cannot prove the utility of English newspapers as a vehicle for disseminating economic and financial information. Early newspapers were restricted in their scope. Until 1695 the *London Gazette* was England's sole licensed newspaper and the news it contained was controlled and prepared by the government.[9] A single sheet newspaper, the *Gazette* devoted its front and sometimes much of its back page to foreign news. Domestic news was generally allotted a limited amount of space in between the foreign news and advertisements for books, medicines and pictures, and requests for information about lost or stolen dogs, horses and servants. The newspapers that appeared immediately after 1695 – most notably *Flying Post*, *Post Boy* and *Post Man* – were similar in focus and content.

Among the domestic news published in the *Gazette* and other newspapers, there were relatively few reports concerning financial and economic matters. It is perhaps reasonable to argue that there was little consciousness among newspapermen of the need for such information, nor was there an understanding of what information would have been of use or interest to investors. Thus, although events and occurrences relevant to the progress of the financial market were advertised and sometimes reported, contradictions were also evident. The Linen Company's sale of 10,000 pieces of white linen in November 1692 was advertised in the *Gazette*; the accompanying rise in stock price was not mentioned.[10] The progress of the subscription to the Bank of England in June and July 1694 was followed closely; events affecting the Bank thereafter were often ignored.[11]

Even when relevant news was reported, it was not accompanied by analysis of the type that can be found in today's financial press. For example, in March 1699 the *Post Man* noted that 'Seven Members of the old East India Company, and as many of the English Company meet this morning, for the first time, in order to treat for a union of the two Companies.'[12] But the *Post Man* was merely stating fact; it gave no indication of what outcome might be expected from the meeting, or what effect an agreement to merge would have on share prices. It was left to the polemicists to speculate upon such things. One such was not optimistic about the prospects for a merger since, he argued, the

---

[9] For a brief history of the *Gazette* see P. M. Handover, *A History of the London Gazette, 1665 1965* (London: HMSO, 1965); P. Fraser, *The Intelligence of the Secretaries of State and their Monopoly of Licensed News, 1660 1688* (Cambridge University Press, 1956).

[10] *London Gazette*, 13 17 Oct. 1692.   [11] Ibid., Jun. Jul. 1694.

[12] *Post Man*, 21 23 Mar. 1699.

New Company, which was 'fresh and young [would not] desire to be in a manner joyn'd in Wedlock with a poor, rotten, painted and scandalous old Whore'.[13]

Similarly, the type of domestic news that might have provided a background for the assessment of value, particularly of the National Debt, was limited since, in reality, the lapsing of the Licensing Act in 1695 had ushered in few real changes. The freedom it offered was merely the freedom to 'publish and be damned'.[14] Newspapermen and publishers continued to be arrested, tried and convicted, imprisoned, fined and pilloried for publishing news that was offensive to the government of the day. Thus, there was certainly no criticism of policy of the type that was expressed privately or in anonymous publications. During the recoinage crisis, for instance, Edmund Bohun complained in a private letter: '[t]he whole blame falles on the Commons of England and very much they are descried by the Lowerr rank of Men who before were the Great admirers of them: the rest think now as before and have met only with what was expected from them'.[15] Reporting in the newspapers was far more guarded. For the most part papers confined themselves to optimistic announcements of the amount of money recently coined. When problems with the process were highlighted, the ills of the recoinage were blamed on individuals or 'evil' stock-jobbers. In May 1696 the *Post Boy* reported that Mr Fells, the goldsmith, had been arrested for refusing to pay his notes in anything other than clipped sixpences.[16] Some months later the *Post Man* asserted, "tis hoped some expedient may be found to put an end to that cursed Trade of Stock-jobbing, which has caused of late more disturbance than the recoining'.[17]

Foreign news, which during times of war was of the utmost importance to investors, was more detailed and more widely reported. Moreover some newspapermen showed themselves to be conscious of its impact on the market. In September 1697 the *Post Boy* reported:

On the 11th early in the morning we received the agreeable News of the Conclusion of the Peace. ... Upon notice of this News the Bells were rung in all parts of this City, the great Guns were fired round the Tower, and at night we had

[13] Anon., *Letter from a Lawyer*, p. 7.
[14] G. C. Gibbs, 'Government and the English Press, 1695 to the Middle of the Eighteenth Century', in A. C. Duke and C. A. Tamse, eds., *Too Mighty to be Free: Censorship and the Press in Britain and the Netherlands* (Zutphen: De Walburg Pers, 1987), p. 87.
[15] BL, Add. MS 5540, fo. 64, Edmund Bohun to John Cary, 31 Jul. 1696 quoted in C. Brooks, 'Taxation, Finance and Public Opinion, 1688 1714', unpublished PhD thesis (University of Cambridge, 1971), p. 22.
[16] *Post Boy*, 7 9 May 1696.   [17] *Post Man*, 14 17 Oct. 1696.

Bonefires and Illuminations, with other Demonstrations of Joy suitable to the occasion: In a word, it has already such Effect on affairs, that the Bank Stock advanced 10 per Cent the first day.[18]

Yet, foreign news was also limited by a number of factors. It was dependent on the arrival of the foreign mail, which was often delayed by poor weather or contrary winds. Indeed, in August 1692 Charles Hatton complained to Sir Charles Lyttelton, 'We have had noe intelligence this fortnight w[hat] was become of o[ur] great fleet and all our transport ships.'[19] Moreover, since there were no daily newspapers until 1703, the circulation of printed news was slow, particularly if the arrival of the foreign post did not coincide with a publication day.

The accuracy of the reporting in newspapers was also questionable. Gibbs asserts that the *Gazette* was 'put together hastily by people who were not professional journalists' and notes that accuracy and content suffered as a result.[20] One contemporary commentator alleged that the *Gazette*'s 'Design was rather to entertain and amuse, than to inform his Reader... for he makes no Difficulty to conceal, displace, and perplex Things at Discretion'.[21] While such inaccuracies were not necessarily the result of deliberate manipulation of the news, it is notable that inconvenient news could be, and was, ignored.[22] As such, printed foreign news was necessarily superseded by other networks of information.

Indeed, the 'discerning and wise' demanded a large volume of news from a variety of sources.[23] Undoubtedly, they would have read newspapers. Some might also have subscribed to manuscript newsletters, which were still popular in the late seventeenth century. Newsletters offered a better balance of foreign and domestic news, were less subject to censorship and more accurate than newspapers.[24] Yet, they were also limited in

---

[18] *Post Boy*, 16 Sep. 1697.

[19] E. M. Thompson, ed., *The Correspondence of the Family of Hatton being chiefly addressed to Christopher First Viscount Hatton A.D. 1601 1704*, 2 vols. (London: Camden Society, 1878), vol. II, p. 183.

[20] Gibbs, 'Government and the English Press', p. 99.

[21] Anon., 'Remarks upon the LONDON GAZETTE, relating to the Streights Fleet, and the Battle of Landen in Flanders', in J. Somers, ed., *A Collection of Scarce and Valuable Tracts*, 16 vols. (London, 1748 52), vol. XI, p. 217.

[22] De Beer notes particularly the omission of Louis XIV's proclamation of the Old Pretender as king of England in 1701. E. S. De Beer, 'The English Newspapers from 1695 1702', in R. Hatton and J. S. Bromley, eds., *William III and Louis XIV* (Liverpool University Press, 1968), p. 119 n. 8.

[23] I. Atherton, 'The Itch Grown a Disease: Manuscript Transmission of News in the Seventeenth Century', in Raymond, *News, Newspapers and Society*, p. 45.

[24] Ibid., p. 40.

circulation, more expensive[25] and, since the post was controlled by the government and considered a useful source of intelligence, manuscript newsletters were subject to delay or destruction at the hands of the Post Office.[26] Therefore, the majority of people in the late seventeenth century would have heard, rather than read the news and, as will be emphasised in the following chapter, given the volatile nature of the financial market, the active investor must have *chosen* to hear, rather than read, the news at the heart of the market where proximity could facilitate swift action, if required.

While the foreign and domestic news reported in the English news-papers may have been of limited use to active investors, papers did function as a valuable means of advertising financial services and products. The *London Gazette* naturally gave full coverage to the developments in public credit. The advertisement for the Million Adventure occupied the first two columns of the paper in two editions in April 1694 and the paper turned over its first column to an announcement of the procedures for taking subscriptions for the Bank of England in early June 1694.[27]

Other companies also used the advertising power of the press. The launch of the Royal African Company in 1671 was accompanied by a four-page subscription announcement detailing the Company's constitution and carrying a half-page illustration of the Company's seal. Perhaps due to this advertising campaign the Royal African Company had little difficulty attracting the £100,000 called for at this time.[28] In 1695, the projectors of the Million Bank placed an unobtrusive, but detailed, advertisement for their scheme in Houghton's *Collection for Improvement*.[29] Companies also used the press to publicise meetings of their General Courts and inform their investors about other items of relevance. In late 1697, for example, the trustees of the Land Bank advertised a change of address in the *Post Boy* announcing that 'if any Person have any Demands from the said Bank' they should come to Mr Springfield's, the apothecary at the Three Golden Anchors against Salisbury Court where the Bank would 'meet every Monday, at Three in the afternoon'.[30]

Lotteries and other projects were constantly advertised in the news-papers of the day. During 1695 and in 1698 and 1699 lottery schemes

---

[25] Snyder suggests that the cost of subscription to manuscript newsletters was between £3 and £5 a year. H. L. Snyder, 'Newsletters in England, 1689 1715 with Special Reference to John Dyer A Byway in the History of England', in D. H. Bond and W. R. McLeod, eds., *Newsletters to Newspapers: Eighteenth Century Journalism* (Morgantown: West Virginia University Press, 1977), p. 8.

[26] Ibid., p. 9.   [27] *London Gazette*, 19 23 Apr., 23 26 Apr. 1694; 7 11 Jun. 1694.

[28] K. Newman, 'Financial Advertising Past and Present', *Three Banks Review*, 140 (1983), 47.

[29] Houghton, *Collection for Improvement*, 12 Apr. 1695.   [30] *Post Boy*, 5 7 Oct. 1697.

occupied nearly all the allotted advertising space in some newspapers. Many advertisements were brief, giving minimal details but directing interested parties to coffee houses or taverns where further information and tickets could be obtained. Some advertisements were detailed. Perhaps being in greater need of revenue, John Houghton was more flexible about the allocation of column inches to his advertisers. The Royal Academies' explanation of their lottery occupied nearly two columns of his paper and on another occasion the projectors of 'A Proposal For the Raising of Two Millions of Money' took out a full page advertisement.[31] Perhaps most fascinating was a question that was 'planted' in the *Athenian Mercury* concerning the potential of the Unparallel'd Adventure. The 'correspondent' wrote,

A friend of mine in the Country to whom I have been formerly obliged has sent me 20 l. to put into any of the Lotteries that I shall think fit, I am no competent judge therein and would willingly put it into the most advantageous, therefore I earnestly desire your advice therein.[32]

A detailed reply suggested that the Million Adventure being finished, the best chance of winning a prize was offered by an alternative lottery, the Unparallel'd Adventure, because 'you are sure for 21 pound to have three Prizes, which at least is 15 pound'.[33] The issue was raised again a few weeks later and received an equally positive reply.[34] Yet, when challenged about their championing of the Unparallel'd Adventure, the Athenian Society claimed that 'we knew nothing of the matter till 'twas publisht, we suppose the Undertaker made and answer'd his own question' and bribed the printer to include it in the issue.[35] Given that two questions on the matter had been published and no rebuttal issued until a challenge was made, the Athenian Society's denial can be questioned. However, if the *Mercury* can be taken at its word, it was an ingenious piece of advertising on the part of the projectors of the Unparallel'd Adventure.

With the advent of the public funds and, in particular, the emergence of a secondary market in Million Adventure tickets, brokers began to advertise their services. One posted a brief notice in Houghton's *Collection for Improvement* stating that it was possible to buy and sell lottery tickets 'at the Mercury-Office at the Trinity-House in Finch-Lane, London, every Day from One a Clock to Four in the Afternoon: Attendance being given those Three Hours only'.[36] Mr Temple, a sworn broker, invited potential clients wishing to trade in foreign money, 'Checquer' debt or bills, or

[31] Houghton, *Collection for Improvement*, 22 Feb. 1695; 25 Jan. 1695.
[32] *Athenian Mercury*, 23 Mar. 1695.   [33] Ibid.   [34] Ibid., 9 Apr. 1695.
[35] Ibid., 24 Sep. 1695.   [36] Houghton, *Collection for Improvement*, passim.

wanting to sell, buy, lend or borrow various stocks to his office 'at Jack's Coffee-house at the North East corner of the Exchange'.[37] These advertisements not only give an insight into the range of services offered by early modern brokers but also, in a scattered market that as yet had no official home, demonstrate the necessity of advertising them.

This type of information was not only presented in the newspapers. Despite the ephemeral nature of such publications, sufficient handbills and pamphlets survive to indicate that London teemed with printed information of interest to investors. The numbers of winning lottery tickets were published regularly, as were advertisements for the schemes themselves.[38] Thomas Neale, for example, issued a number of handbills that explained the details of his lotteries and at least one that sought to discredit his opposition.[39] The projectors of the Honourable Undertaking provided a handbill that gave details of the prizes on offer and a list of more than 120 outlets where tickets could be purchased.[40] Proposals for new projects were printed and distributed so that they might gain support and interest.[41] Petitions calling for the regulation of brokers and for the resumption of annuity payments were disseminated for the same reason.[42] Lists of stockholders in various companies were regularly published to facilitate decision-making during election of directors. The lists doubled as an electoral roll and candidate roster.[43] Handbills were also produced to inform shareholders of other items of importance or interest.[44]

[37] *Post Man*, 12 16 Aug. 1701.
[38] See, for example, Anon., *A list of the Fortunate Adventurers in the Mine Adventure* (London, 1699).
[39] T. Neale, *A Profitable Adventure to the Fortunate* (London, 1693); *The Profitable Adventure to the Fortunate* (London, 1694); *The Profitable Adventure to the Fortunate … Having been reported in Town, and Mentioned in Several News Letters to be Stopt* (London, 1694); *The Second Drawing of the Blank Tickets of the Million Adventure* (London, 1695); *A Second Profitable Adventure to the Fortunate* (London, 1696).
[40] Anon., *Honourable Undertaking*.
[41] See, for example, Anon., *Proposal for Raising Two Millions*; Anon., *A Proposal to Raise a Million of Money by Credit on a Publick Bank* (London, 1694?).
[42] See for example, Anon., *Reasons Humbly Offered*; Anon., *Proposal for Putting some Stop to … Stock Jobbing*; Anon., *Case of the Adventurers in the Million Lottery*.
[43] Parkinson, 'Stock Market in the 1690s', p. 97. For examples of such lists see: Anon., *A List of the Names of all the Partners in the Lead Mines of Bwlchyr Eskir Hir, in the County of Cardigan* (London, 1695); Anon., *The Names of 51 Persons chosen the 10th of September 1695… for a Committee to consider of proper Methods for Settling and Establishing a National Land Bank* (London, 1695); Anon., *List of the Names of All the Adventurers in the Stock of the Honourable East India Company* (London, 1697).
[44] See, for example, Anon., *At a General Court of the Adventurers for the general joynt stock to the East Indies* (London, 1693): a handbill giving details of the new subscription; Anon., *At a General Court of the Adventurers in the general joynt stock to the East Indies* (London, 1694): a handbill giving details of the regulation of private trade by commanders, officers and seamen of the Company's ships.

Interestingly, copies of the Acts of Parliament relating to the establishment of the public funds were also distributed. They served to inform
investors and the wider public of the details and structure of the funds and
of the taxes appropriated for the payment of interest. It was for this
purpose that John Locke sent copies of the Bank of England's charter
and the Commission for Taking Subscriptions to a correspondent in late
June 1694.[45] Such documents also must have served, in the eyes of some
investors, as a type of contract between the creditor and the state. Thomas
Bowrey, a London merchant and an active investor during the early
1690s, retained a number of these publications.[46] Thomas Sandes wrote
to Cornelius Huys on the subject of the Million Lottery, 'y^t you may bee
sure you have right don you in all things & y^t you may better understand
ye whole business of said lottery wee have doe here inclosed send you
abbreviation of ye act of Parlement concerning ye same'.[47]

Thus, although it can be argued that the press provided little news to
investors that would not have been supplanted by rumour, gossip and the
more rapid dissemination of information through London's coffee houses
and the Royal Exchange, by the end of the seventeenth century the financial market generated a great deal of printed information. Handbills and
newspapers were undoubtedly of some use to those seeking to make new
investments and maintain existing ones. But, this type of information
supplied fact rather than analysis. Those seeking help to make a decision
about which of the many schemes and projects offered the greatest potential reward must have looked elsewhere, perhaps beginning with a study
of the price of securities.

Price lists

The price of a security can reveal much to an investor. If current price is
considered in the context of other relevant economic, political and financial information, a judgement can be made about whether a stock is cheap
or expensive relative to current conditions and in comparison with other
similar companies and institutions. A series of prices offers additional data
about trends and the volatility of the market. This advantage was noted

[45] J. Locke, *The Correspondence of John Locke*, edited by E. S. de Beer, 8 vols. (Oxford:
   Clarendon Press, 1979), vol. V, p. 81.
[46] Guildhall Library, London, Papers of Thomas Bowrey, MS 3041/9, iii. Bowrey noted as
   being in his library, 'Act on Beer & Annuity of 14 p. C., 1692'; 'Act. Excise on Salt & Beer
   & for ye Lottery 1694'; 'Act Tonage on Ships & Excise on Beer & for ye Bank, 1694', and
   'Act on Salt for E. India Co:, 1698'.
[47] 'Sandes to Cornelius Huys', 17 Apr. 1694. Bank of England Archives, Letter Book of John
   Browne and Thomas Sandes, M7/3.

by early modern publishers. John Houghton stated in his *Collection for Improvement of Husbandry and Trade*, 'Whoever compares this with the former, will see the Rise and Fall of Markets'.[48] Once an investment has been made, price becomes an essential component of the assessment of its value and the collection of prices is part of the continuous process of observation and re-evaluation that culminates in a decision to either retain or liquidate the investment. Thus, it may be argued that regularly published, and retained, price currents potentially offered valuable information to the early modern investor.

Even before the stock-market boom of the early 1690s share prices were being published in two commodity price currents: *The Prices of Merchandise in London*, which, at the end of the seventeenth century, was published by Robert Woolley, and *Whiston's Merchants Weekly Remembrancer, of the Present-Money-Prices of their Goods Ashoar in London*.[49] From around 1680, both papers published the prices of the East India, Royal African and Hudson's Bay Companies but, somewhat surprisingly, there appears to have been no demand for the publication of the prices of the smaller joint-stock companies that emerged in the early 1690s. Neither paper expanded their price lists to encompass those stocks. The latest surviving copy of *The Prices of Merchandise in London*, which dates from 1696, shows that only the price of Bank of England stock had been added to Woolley's list.[50] Similarly, by November 1694 Whiston had made no additions to his list of share prices.[51]

The earliest known response to the stock-market boom came from John Houghton who began publication of his *Collection for Improvement of Husbandry and Trade* in March 1692.[52] However, although reference is often made to Houghton's contribution to the furtherance of knowledge

[48] Houghton, *Collection for Improvement*, passim.
[49] For further on the history of European price currents see J. J. McCusker, *European Bills of Entry and Marine Lists: Early Commercial Publications and the Origins of the Business Press* (Cambridge, Mass.: Harvard University Library, 1985); J. J. McCusker, 'The Business Press in England before 1775', *The Library*, 8 (1986), 205 31; J. J. McCusker and C. Gravesteijn, *The Beginnings of Commercial and Financial Journalism: The Commodity Price Currents, Exchange Rate Currents, and Money Currents of Early Modern Europe* (Amsterdam: Neha, 1991); L. Neal, 'The Rise of a Financial Press: London and Amsterdam, 1681 1810', *Business History*, 30 (1988), 163 78.
[50] *The Prices of Merchandise in London*, 12 Feb. 1696 in National Archives, Public Record Office, C104/128/68, Papers of Matthias Giesque and Co.
[51] *Whiston's Merchants Weekly Remembrancer, of the Present Money Prices of their Goods Ashoar in London*, 19 Nov. 1694 in NA, PRO, C104/128/68.
[52] Houghton's first periodical, *A Collection of Letters for the Improvement of Husbandry and Trade*, was published between 1681 and 1684. Its successor, *A Collection for Improvement of Husbandry and Trade*, was published between March 1692 and 1703 with a six month break in the latter part of 1692.

about the financial market,[53] his aim was actually far broader. For the very reasonable price of 2d per issue, Houghton's paper provided an essay on a topic he deemed to be of interest to his readers, a limited domestic commodity price list, bills of mortality and, at various times, details of the arrivals and departures of ships, foreign news and advertisements.[54] Houghton also included, from his first publication, a list of share prices. He explained his reasons for doing so thus:

Altho they that live at *London*, may, every Noon and Night on Working days go to Garraway's Coffee House, and see what *Prices* the *Actions* bear of most *Companies* trading in *Joynt Stocks*, yet for those whose Occasions permit not there to see, they may be satisfi'd *once a Week* how it is.[55]

From the first, Houghton's list of stocks went beyond those published by Whiston and Woolley. He published eight stock prices: the East India, Royal African and Hudson's Bay Companies, the Paper Company, Linen Company, Copper Company, Glass Company and the Company for Recovering Treasure from Wrecks off Broadhaven.[56] By 20 April 1692, Houghton had expanded the number of prices given to thirteen and in the following week to fourteen.[57] He also very occasionally provided extra snippets of information, noting in one instance, 'I am informed that Mr. Neale and Mr. Tyzanckes Wrecks in America, managed by Mr. Blake in Finch-Lane, are at Five Pounds each.'[58] On 11 May 1694 Houghton expanded his list of stocks to approximately sixty. He continued to provide prices for a limited number but stated that 'those that desire the Values of [the remainder] to be Published may have them on very reasonable Terms'.[59]

In addition to an expanded list of stock prices, during 1694 Houghton published a series of essays on the nature of the financial market and began to include in his paper exchange rates and an account of the total monies loaned to the Exchequer, which showed the amount of money advanced and the sum thus far repaid on various funds.[60] Given the government's questionable creditworthiness at this time, this last set of data was of particular value to investors in government debt, whether their interest

---

[53] P. Mirowski, 'The Rise (and Retreat) of a Market: English Joint Stock Shares in the Eighteenth Century', *Journal of Economic History*, 41 (1981), 564; Neal, *Rise of Financial Capitalism*, pp. 22 3; Dale, *First Crash*, p. 26.

[54] The price was reduced in 1693 to 1d per issue.

[55] Houghton, *Collection for Improvement*, 6 Apr. 1692.   [56] Ibid., 30 Mar. 1692.

[57] Ibid., 20 Apr. 1692; 27 Apr. 1692.   [58] Ibid., 22 Sep. 1693.

[59] Ibid., 11 May 1694.

[60] Whiston adopted this practice from around mid 1697, also including, at that time, information on the amount of plate brought into the Exchequer and coined. *Whiston's*, 14 Jun. 1697 in NA, PRO, C104/128/68.

was in the new long-term expedients of lotteries, annuities and the Bank of England, or in tallies and short-term loans.

Houghton's reasons for expanding the amount of financial information offered at this particular time are unclear. By mid-1694 the stock-market boom was over. Interest in many of the smaller joint-stock companies of the period had evaporated and the prices of the East India, Royal African and Hudson's Bay Company shares were at a low and appeared to be heading lower. Nor was Houghton offering a specific response to the creation of the public funds. He did make brief mention of the Million Adventure in one of his essays, but when listing 'The Advantages of Stocks' in July 1694 made no reference to the Bank of England.[61] Thus, Houghton's provision of additional financial information was a natural extension of his larger project to clarify 'some Misteries in Trade, and to rectify Men's Judgments', rather than a response to the market's demands for printed financial data.[62]

Nevertheless, the advent of the public funds did eventually create a greater need for printed financial information. *Proctor's Price Current*, which commenced publication in October 1694, while in most respects 'an unimaginative copy of Whiston',[63] included detailed financial information. For a price of 20s per annum Proctor published commodity prices, the course of the exchange in Amsterdam, London and at the Bank, the price of gold and silver and the prices of the East India, Royal African and Hudson's Bay Companies and Bank stock along with prices for blank and benefit Million Adventure tickets, the Orphan's Fund, Orphan's Bank and the Million Bank. Like Houghton, Proctor published details of funds paid into and out of the Exchequer. Furthermore, Proctor gave prominence to financial information, placing it at the top of the first column of his first page. Thus, it seems that he was catering for a readership that was concerned as much with financial matters as with the price of commodities.

Yet, it was not until John Castaing began to publish *The Course of the Exchange, and Other Things* in late 1697 that the London market had its first dedicated financial price current. Castaing, a financial broker of Huguenot origin, was already a presence in the market. As early as 1695 he was advertising his services in Houghton's *Collection for Improvement*.[64] Castaing's *Course of the Exchange* was a bi-weekly, single-column paper and, at a cost of a mere 10s per annum, was cheaper than its rivals. It listed

[61] Houghton, *Collection for Improvement*, 20 Jul. 1694.   [62] Ibid., 8 Jun. 1694.
[63] J. M. Price, 'Notes on Some London Price Currents, 1667 1715', *Economic History Review*, 7 (1954), 247.
[64] Houghton, *Collection for Improvement*, passim.

London exchange rates and details of Exchequer funds. Castaing also listed daily stock prices for the Old East India Company, the New East India Company from 9 September 1698, the Royal African Company, the Orphan's Bank and Million Adventure tickets. Castaing also occasionally quoted prices for single interest payments on Million Adventure tickets and posted other notices of interest to his readers. For example, he noted when the transfer books were closed for the payments of dividends, and made announcements when funds were available to pay interest on lottery tickets.

Castaing, in common with the publishers of all the above-mentioned papers, offered a potentially valuable service to investors. Nonetheless, the age and accuracy of the data presented must have affected its utility. It is probable that, with the exception of Houghton's, prices were collected on the day of publication.[65] McCusker and Gravesteijn suggest that, for the regularly published currents, a clerk would have been employed to collect the data from brokers and compile and prepare the information for printing. The production of price currents, which followed the same form for each edition, took only a few hours and thus data collected at the Royal Exchange in the afternoon could be ready for distribution that same evening.[66]

But, in spite of the relative ease with which price lists could be prepared, with the exception of Castaing's *Course of the Exchange*, papers were distributed weekly. Circulation figures, where available, also indicate that price information was aged before it reached the investor. Glaisyer estimates the print run of Houghton's *Collection for Improvement* to have been in the hundreds, and stamp duty paid on *Proctor's Price Current* in the early eighteenth century suggests that between sixty and seventy copies of that paper were produced each week for domestic distribution.[67] Such limited print runs confirm that most readers perused papers in coffee houses. Printed price data might, therefore, have been a week old before it reached some readers.

Judging the accuracy of published price data ideally requires an independent source for comparison. Between 1692 and 1693 Charles Blunt's customers traded regularly in Linen and Glass Company stock and thus, as may be seen in Figures 4.1 and 4.2, a price series can be created to facilitate comparison with Houghton's published prices. Blunt ceased

[65] Between 16 June 1693 and 22 January 1697, Houghton stated that prices published on Fridays were collected on Wednesdays.

[66] McCusker and Gravesteijn, *Beginnings of Financial Journalism*, p. 296.

[67] N. Glaisyer, 'The Culture of Commerce in England, 1660 1720', unpublished PhD thesis (University of Cambridge, 1999), p. 197; McCusker and Gravesteijn, *Beginnings of Financial Journalism*, p. 297. No duty was payable on papers sent overseas.

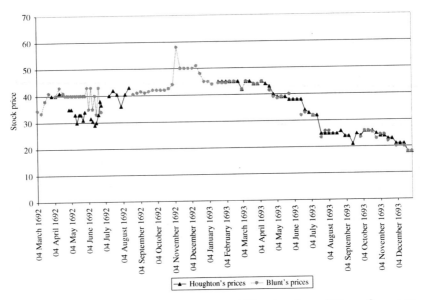

4.1 Comparison of Houghton's and Blunt's prices of Linen Company
stock, 1692 1693
Source: Houghton, *Collection for Improvement*; NA, PRO, C114/165.

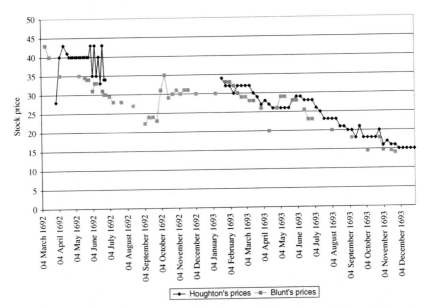

4.2 Comparison of Houghton's and Blunt's prices of Glass Company
stock, 1692 1693
Source: Houghton, *Collection for Improvement*; NA, PRO, C114/165.

trading in 1695 and his low trading volumes in 1694 and 1695 prevent meaningful comparisons, thus there is no consistent method of confirming the accuracy of Houghton's prices between 1694 and 1698. However, Houghton's data was broadly consistent with that recorded in the surviving copies of Whiston's and Proctor's price currents, with the exception of the period of the recoinage from late 1696 to mid-1697 when prices diverged, sometimes significantly. This is not surprising, price currents of this period carried frequent reminders that the shortage of coin and the variable price of guineas made accurate prices impossible to establish, but it must indicate that price data published during this period should be regarded as inconsistent and inaccurate.

In the period after 1698 Houghton was obtaining his prices from Castaing's paper.[68] McCusker and Gravesteijn cite several contemporary sources which suggest that the *Course of the Exchange* was considered to be authoritative and Houghton's decision to use Castaing's prices must confirm that it was a respected source of information.[69] However, while Houghton represented his prices as being collected on Fridays (the day of publication), he was in fact publishing data from Castaing's Tuesday edition, and sometimes from the preceding Friday. Thus, a comparison between Houghton's and Castaing's prices on the same publication day can offer an interesting insight into whether old data rapidly became obsolete. The data presented in Figure 4.3 also highlights the occasions when Houghton failed to update his prices.

Figure 4.1, particularly, and to a lesser extent Figure 4.2 show a relatively close correlation between Houghton's and Blunt's prices.[70] This correlation is also evident in other stock prices compiled from the two sources. It may be confidently asserted, therefore, that Houghton was, for the most part, publishing market prices at this time. Indeed, two factors indicate that Blunt may have supplied prices for publication in the *Collection for Improvement*. First, Houghton was one of Blunt's clients and the two had a relatively close association in 1692 and 1693, during which time Houghton used the broker's services on twenty-five occasions.[71] Secondly, the price of Estcourt's Lead Mine shares – a company managed by some of Blunt's associates and in which Houghton was also a shareholder – was published in the *Collection* between April and August 1694.[72] This was very unusual since Houghton did not generally publish the prices of such companies. Whether or not Blunt was Houghton's

---

[68] Neal, 'Financial Press', 168.
[69] McCusker and Gravesteijn, *Beginnings of Financial Journalism*, pp. 315 16, 346 n. 106.
[70] Also see Appendix 2.   [71] NA, PRO, C114/165.
[72] Houghton, *Collection for Improvement*, 6 Apr. 3 Aug. 1694.

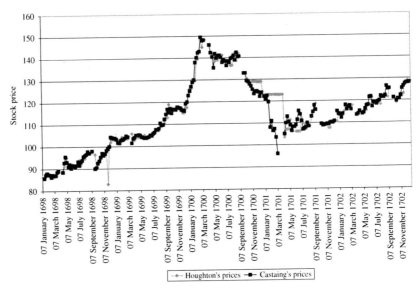

4.3 Comparison of Houghton's and Castaing's prices of Bank of England stock, 1698 1702
Source: Houghton, *Collection for Improvement*; J. Castaing, *The Course of the Exchange, and Other Things* derived from the European State Finance Database, dataset\neal\coe1700.rtf.

correspondent, it would seem that the prices published in 1692 and 1693, notwithstanding the occasional printing error and some periods when prices were not regularly updated, were relatively accurate.

The comparison of Houghton's and Castaing's prices presented in Figure 4.3 demonstrates that between early 1698 and early 1700, when the market was relatively subdued, differences in prices were negligible, again with the exception of the occasional printing error. Thus, Houghton's older data still provided his readers with reasonably accurate information about price level and the volatility of the market. But, as the market became more volatile, prices began to diverge. The divergence was most marked during the period from the end of 1700 to early 1701. Since this was a period of intense antagonism between the Old and New East India Companies, culminating in a proxy battle between the Old Company and the Bank, which was a supporter of the New Company, Houghton's failure to produce up-to-date prices is both inexplicable and concerning. It also amply illustrates the shortcomings of printed price data.

Nevertheless, in spite of the problems of ensuring accuracy, limited circulation, infrequency of publication and the relatively slow speed of distribution, price currents were useful for some investors. Even for the active investor, who would have sought up-to-date price information in Jonathan's or Garraway's or at the Royal Exchange, price currents provided a variety of additional information relating to London's financial market and to the international economic environment. The regular publication of prices and the sequential numbering of price currents also implies that the lists were being retained by some individuals who may have built up a series of data about the market that could have been used to establish trends and to learn from the experiences of others.

Price currents also served the purpose of informing those with little or no access to London's market. Indeed, publications of this nature originated in the practice of providing overseas correspondents with relevant information, and those lists that related more specifically to the new financial market continued to be produced chiefly for the convenience of merchants who wished to keep their correspondents acquainted with the London market.[73] Castaing, for example, published his paper on Tuesdays and Fridays to coincide with the sending of the foreign mail. Only Houghton directed his paper to a predominantly English audience, while still noting that 'these Papers go weekly to Amsterdam'.[74]

For the inexperienced investor such publications provided knowledge of current price allowing them to approach the market with a degree of confidence and to confirm data from other sources.[75] Price currents were also of use to the passive investor, who would have been content with older information as long as it was perceived to be relatively reliable.[76] Indeed, publishers like Proctor and Castaing were probably encouraged by the increasing number of relatively inactive public and private creditors created by the establishment of the Bank of England and the Million Bank and through the secondary market in Million Adventure tickets. Further to this, it is notable that a number of newspapers had begun to publish share prices by the end of the 1690s. *The New State of Europe: Or a True Account of Publick Transactions and Learning* published the prices of the main joint-stock company shares collected at three o'clock each day, as well as the price of shares and blank lottery tickets in the Mine Adventure.[77] From late 1697 the *Post Man* included a short paragraph in

---

[73] F. Braudel, *Civilization and Capitalism 15th 18th Century*, vol. II: *The Wheels of Commerce* (London: Collins, 1982), pp. 409 10; Neal, 'Financial Press', 168; W. D. Smith, 'The Function of Commercial Centres in the Modernization of European Capitalism: Amsterdam as an Information Exchange in the Seventeenth Century', *The Journal of Economic History*, 44 (1984), 992.

[74] Houghton, *Collection for Improvement*, 11 Aug. 1693.

[75] Neal, 'Financial Press', 164.   [76] Ibid., 163.

[77] *The New State of Europe: Or a True Account of Publick Transactions and Learning*, passim.

its collection of London news detailing some of the major joint-stock companies, as did the *Post Boy* from mid-1698.[78] Thus, although the only way to be confident about price levels was to approach the market directly, it is reasonable to suggest that by the beginning of the eighteenth century printed price data was being produced in response to the needs of the infrequent or passive investor.

Guides to the financial market

Just as price currents could not replace personal interaction with the market, direct observation and experience also provided the best education for the early modern investor. Nevertheless, information relevant to the financial market was also contained in some of the didactic and other texts of the period. In particular, although there were no specific guides to the operation of the financial market of the type that Thomas Mortimer was to provide in 1761 when he published *Every Man His Own Broker*,[79] the beginnings of publications that sought to order and explain the new and complex financial world can be observed.

In great part the issues raised by the new financial market were addressed from a negative perspective. As noted in the previous chapter, there was an outpouring of literature during the late seventeenth and early eighteenth centuries that questioned whether the joint-stock company was the most appropriate form of economic organisation for the pursuit of trade and manufacturing, and condemned the actions of stock-jobbers and speculators. This literature seldom provided detached analysis, yet it did serve to inform debate and stimulate discussion about how the market worked. Thus, although the main aim of the anonymous author of one pamphlet was to criticise the actions of stock-jobbers, the text included a detailed analysis of the purpose of refusals and the methods used by stock-jobbers to manipulate the price of certain stocks.[80] Defoe's *Essay Upon Projects* and the *Villainy of Stock-Jobbers Detected* similarly laid the

---

[78] *Post Man*, passim; *Post Boy*, passim.
[79] First published in 1761, *Every Man His Own Broker* went through nine editions; the last was published in 1782. Dickson, *Financial Revolution*, p. 506. Perhaps the definitive guide of this period was Joseph de la Vega's *Confusion de Confusiones* published in Amsterdam in 1688. However, de la Vega's readership was the Sephardi community in Amsterdam and he wrote in literary Spanish, a form highly unsuited to translation. There is no indication that *Confusion de Confusiones* was translated into English and disseminated in London and thus it is unlikely to have influenced English investors. J. I. Israel, 'The Amsterdam Stock Exchange and the English Revolution of 1688', *Tijdschrift voor Geschiedenis*, 103 (1990), 419; J. L. Cardoso, 'Confusion de Confusiones: Ethics and Options on Seventeenth Century Stock Exchange Markets', *Financial History Review*, 9 (2002), 123.
[80] Anon., *Plain Dealing*, p. 4.

operation of the financial market bare and encouraged a wider under-standing of its vices and virtues. T. Saunders in *Fortunatus's Looking-Glass* may have set out to highlight the moral hazards of lotteries and question the honesty of their promoters but, in doing so, he listed all the schemes available at the time of going to press along with the salient details of each project, thus undoubtedly encouraging among some of his readers a critical comparison of the odds associated with each scheme.[81] Even plays like Shadwell's *The Volunteers* familiarised a wider audience with the language of the market and the antics of stock-jobbers.[82]

Such texts were, of course, read by few and were not intended to address the problems of those who used the financial market. However, questions put to the *Athenian Mercury*, which 'let the English public speak for itself', do provide insights into the concerns and interests of some early modern investors.[83] In general, enquirers echoed the worries of writers like Defoe and Saunders. There were no questions regarding investment techniques or the value of assets, but much interest in the moral pro-blems raised by the new forms of finance. On 7 April 1691 a correspondent enquired '[w]hether they are not Enemies to the Government, that lay Wagers that Mons is, or will be taken by the French King'. To which he received the reply that the individuals making such bets should consider whether they want to win or lose. ''Tis Nonsense to pretend the last, and if they say the first, they silently confess the Resolution of the Question must bear an Affirmative.'[84] Another question was put by an investor who was 'considerably concerned' in East India and Royal African Company stock and who could 'now dispose of his Interest at greater Rates, than he is assured they are really worth'. He enquired 'whether in Conscience he may dispose of them, and thereby impose upon the ignorant buyer, who is wholly guided by other Men's Actions', and received by way of a reply a Bible verse: 1 Thessalonians 4:6, 'Let no man go-beyond, or defraud his Brother in any Matter, because the Lord is the Avenger of all such'!'[85]

The lotteries caused the most consternation among readers of the *Athenian Mercury*, stimulating a number of questions particularly in late 1694 and early 1695. In December 1694, for example, a correspondent enquired whether lotteries were, in good conscience, warrantable given

[81] Saunders, *Fortunatus's Looking Glass*.   [82] Shadwell, *The Volunteers*, pp. 239 40.
[83] C. J. Sommerville, *The News Revolution in England: Cultural Dynamics of Daily Information* (Oxford University Press, 1996), p. 103. For further on the type of questions put to the *Athenian Mercury* see H. Berry, *Gender, Society and Print Culture in Late Stuart England: The Cultural World of the Athenian Mercury* (Aldershot: Ashgate, 2003); G. D. MacEwen, *The Oracle of the Coffee House: John Dunston's Athenian Mercury* (San Marino, Calif.: Huntington University Library, 1972).
[84] *Athenian Mercury*, 7 Apr. 1691.   [85] Ibid., vol. 2, no. 24, 1691.

that 'Divine Providence' controlled the disposal of lots. The *Mercury* replied that it believed 'the thing Wicked in it self' and went on to note that men must one day account for their stewardship of their time, money and reputation whereas speculation in a lottery could hardly be said to be an action for the glory of God.[86] In spite of this, the paper was prepared to make an exception for the Million Adventure since it was necessary for the defence of the nation.[87]

This concern with moral issues was, in part, a reflection of the stance taken by the members of the Athenian Society.[88] However, it is interesting to note that the only comprehensive analysis of the nature of the financial market published during the 1690s also commenced by giving due consideration to the moral concerns of its readers. In June and July 1694 John Houghton published a series of seven essays on the subject of the new financial market.[89] In the first essay of the series, however, Houghton rather disingenuously stressed his own lack of involvement in joint-stocks and devoted considerable space to defending the trade in shares to his audience.[90] He stated:

Some abuses may probably have been committed by Traders therein; but must we presently thereupon run down all with a full cry that so deal therein? May we not with as much Justice and Reason cry out against all mankind as Devils, because many are guilty of Diabolical Actions? ... I know many worthy Persons of great Honour and Probity, who deal in Stocks, that do abominate the least unjust Action, and would not for the World have an ill gotten Penny among the rest of their Estates.[91]

In his other essays, Houghton turned to more practical matters. His guide to the market was written in plain language, with an obvious concern for the difficulties that some of his readers may have had in understanding the complexities of finance. Indeed, Houghton was clearly aiming his discussion at those who knew little of the market for he cautioned them 'to be very *wary*, for there are many *cunning Artists* among [the stock-jobbers]'.[92] That his readership numbered among them many with little practical experience of the financial market is also suggested by the necessity Houghton had previously found of appending a brief explanation of the nature of shares to his price lists. On several occasions prior to 1694 he printed a notice that explained:

---

[86] Ibid., 16 Dec. 1693.   [87] Ibid., 16 Oct. 1694.
[88] Members of the Athenian Society have been linked to the Reformation of Manners campaign. Berry, *Gender, Society and Print Culture*, p. 34.
[89] Houghton, *Collection for Improvement*, 8 Jun. 20 Jul. 1694.
[90] Ibid., 8 Jun. 1694. We know from Charles Blunt's ledgers that Houghton was actually an active investor in a number of joint stocks. See NA, PRO, C114/165.
[91] Houghton, *Collection for Improvement*, 8 Jun. 1694.   [92] Ibid., 6 Apr. 1692.

Actions signifie *Shares* in *Companies*: For instance, If ten Men raise 10 *l.* a piece to carry on a Trade; each 10 *l.* is called an *Action* or *Share*; if they have hopes of great Gain, they will not sell their *Share* for 10 *l.* If they fear Loss they'l sell for less; and so *Actions* rise and fall, according to hopes or fears ... I find a great many understand not this affair, therefore I write this.[93]

In the essays published in 1694 Houghton expanded upon the subject, giving a brief history of joint-stock companies, explaining their purpose, how the capital was divided and how such companies were managed. Further essays explained the nature of the market and the various instruments traded, including options and time bargains, where to go to buy and sell shares, and the cost of brokerage. Houghton also reproduced standard contracts for transfers, and for puts and refusals. In his last essay, Houghton once again turned to a defence of the joint-stock company, stressing the 'Advantages [that] may accrue to the Nation, tho' the Undertakers get or lose' and suggesting that 'if an Hundred Stocks more arise, we have no reason to be offended'.[94]

Yet, while the clarity and utility of Houghton's essays cannot be faulted, it is very necessary to place his efforts in context. The operation of the financial market formed the subject of Houghton's main essay on just seven occasions between 1692 and 1703. He spent only slightly less time writing about clay and devoted a greater number of issues to writing about chocolate and the uses of cocoa.[95] Thus, Houghton's guide to the financial market was rooted very firmly within his larger project of providing his readership with a history of England's various trades and economic activities. Its purpose was to satisfy the sceptical and inform the curious; it did not provide a manual for the active investor.

On the other hand, as John Brewer asserts, works of this nature were important as ways of ordering knowledge and providing their reader with a framework through which they could view and analyse their world.[96] In this respect, Houghton's guide was just one of a number that emerged over the course of the seventeenth century, and which served to order and legitimise relevant knowledge. Lewes Roberts's *Map of Commerce*, for example, explained the processes by which foreign trade was undertaken and gave a brief outline of the activities of the main trading companies. It also explained the coinage used in various countries, along with their weights, values and exchange rates.[97] Edward Hatton's *Comes Commercii* included sections on mathematical techniques and tables to assist in the calculation of simple and compound interest. It also outlined standard

[93] Ibid., passim.   [94] Ibid., 20 Jul. 1694.
[95] Ibid., 6 Oct. 17 Nov. 1693; 17 Jan. 21 Mar. 1701.
[96] Brewer, *Sinews of Power*, p. 228.   [97] Roberts, *Merchants Map of Commerce*.

practice among merchants and reproduced sample documents intended to assist in the drawing up of legal agreements, such as power of attorney and letters of credit.[98] Hatton's later publication, *The Merchant's Magazine* published in 1701, also contained a section explaining how to approach financial brokers, noted the rules governing their conduct and outlined brokerage costs.[99] *Cocker's English Dictionary* offered definitions for words such as 'annuity' and 'dividend' and provided an appendix of 'the most difficult Terms used in Trade and Merchandize'.[100] It is equally interesting to note how quickly other relevant financial definitions were incorporated into works of this nature. Within ten years of the publication of *Cocker's Dictionary*, Roger North provided definitions of jobbing, stocks and stock-jobbing in the vocabulary appended to his 1714 publication.[101] That he had little good to say about the practice of stock-jobbing is perhaps less important than the obvious necessity of including a definition of such practices.

Little is known about the numeracy of early modern investors. While a signature may stand as a proxy for literacy, no such test of familiarity with mathematical techniques is available.[102] Yet, a certain level of numeracy would have been essential to those seeking to make wise investment decisions: even a basic comparison of opportunities required an understanding of mathematics. It may be confidently asserted, therefore, that works aimed at introducing merchants and others to basic mathematical techniques were of some use to investors. Moreover, their popularity was unquestionable. *Cocker's Arithmetic*, 'suitable to the meanest capacity', went through many editions.[103] Ayres's *Arithmetick* also contained 'Rules made Plain and easie to the meanest Capacities' and was in its sixth edition by 1702.[104] In addition, Stewart suggests that the financial revolution produced a 'hectic market' for public lecturers, mathematicians and instrument makers who sold their technical knowledge to the many who were keen to exploit it.[105]

---

[98] E. Hatton, *Comes Commercii: or the Trader's Companion* (London, 1699). See also E. Hatton, *The Merchant's Magazine or Trades Man's Treasury* (London, 1701); W. Leybourn, *Panarithmologia* (London, 1693).

[99] Hatton, *Merchant's Magazine*, pp. 208 11.

[100] E. Cocker, *Cocker's English Dictionary* (London, 1704), passim.

[101] R. North, *The Gentleman's Accomptant* (London, 1714), passim.

[102] For a discussion of numeracy in early modern England see K. Thomas, 'Numeracy in Early Modern England', *Transactions of the Royal Historical Society*, vol. XXXVII (1987), pp. 103 32.

[103] E. Cocker, *Cocker's Arithmetic: Being a Plain and Familiar Method* (Glasgow, 1687).

[104] J. Ayres, *Arithmetick: A Treatise Designed for the Use and Benefit of Trades Men* (London, 1702).

[105] L. Stewart, *The Rise of Public Science: Rhetoric, Technology and Natural Philosophy in Newtonian Britain, 1660 1750* (Cambridge University Press, 1992), p. 172.

For those who preferred to be given the answers to their mathematical queries, books of interest tables were available. Such tables enabled rapid and consistent calculation and allowed quick comparisons to be made of various investment opportunities.[106] John Castaing produced a compact version measuring 2½ by 4½ inches and obviously designed to accompany its owner on business. The tables contained calculations of interest at 4, 5, 6, 7 and 8 per cent from one day to ninety-two days and three, six, nine and twelve months.[107] Another work, entitled 'Interest in Eptiome', was advertised in the *Post Boy* in August 1698 as having been compiled by Israel Falgate at the Bank of England.[108] Presumably, Falgate's position at the Bank rendered his credentials unimpeachable.

Linked to texts that gave guidance in mathematical techniques were those that assisted merchants and other interested individuals in the preparation of ledgers and accounts.[109] In general such works explained the use of journals, ledgers and day books, and detailed the principles of the double-entry system. It is likely that few individuals maintained their accounts in precisely the manner prescribed. Moreover, Yamey's studies have indicated that merchants seldom balanced their books regularly and rarely made any calculation of profit and loss.[110] However, an ordered understanding of their financial position was necessary for those who sought to diversify their incomes. Drawing up an account allowed a businessman to take stock and encouraged a critical consideration of business and investment strategies. In an environment where risk was ubiquitous such stocktaking was essential.[111]

Determining the utility of such works is always problematic. Glaisyer and Pennell argue, quite reasonably, that didactic texts added very little to the knowledge of real experts in their field.[112] Nonetheless, the variety of relevant titles published during this period and number of editions

---

[106] Brewer, *Sinews of Power*, p. 228.

[107] J. Castaing, *An Interest Book at 4, 5, 6, 7, 8 per C* (London, 1700).

[108] *Post Boy*, 18 20 Aug. 1698.

[109] See, for example, Hatton, *Merchant's Magazine*; J. Hawkins, *Clavis Commercii or the Key of Commerce* (London, 1704); and J. Vernon, *The Compleat Comptinghouse: Or the Young Lad Instructed* (London, 1678), which included sections on plain arithmetic as well as sections explaining the correct method of keeping accounts. It is also interesting to note that a guide to the keeping of household accounts was produced in 1678 for the benefit of women. Anon., *Advice to the Women and Maidens of London* (London, 1678).

[110] B. S. Yamey, 'Scientific Bookkeeping and the Rise of Capitalism', *Economic History Review*, 1 (1949), 99 113; B. S. Yamey, 'Accounting and the Rise of Capitalism: Further Notes on a Theme by Sombart', *Journal of Accounting Research*, 2 (1964), 117 36.

[111] P. W. Hunter, 'Containing the Marvellous: Instructions to Buyers and Sellers', in N. Glaisyer and S. Pennell, eds., *Didactic Literature in England, 1500 1800: Expertise Constructed* (Aldershot: Ashgate, 2003), pp. 174 85.

[112] N. Glaisyer and S. Pennell, 'Introduction', in ibid., p. 10.

produced suggests a demand. Surviving records also indicate that didactic texts could be found in many private collections.[113] In 1711, for example, Thomas Bowrey listed works in his library which included John Hawkins's *Key of Commerce*, *Lex Mercatoria*, a 'Compleat Attorney', 'Mathematicall Magick', English, Dutch and Malay dictionaries, works on English and French grammar and a book that he described as 'Trade by Sʳ J. Child', probably *A New Discourse of Trade*, published in 1693.[114] Of course, possession of such works does not mean that they were well thumbed. Grassby also notes that the size of merchants' libraries should not be overestimated but does conclude that, among merchants, handbooks and economic tracts were popular, and almanacs that included mathematical tables and other information relevant to business were commonplace.[115]

Manuals of this nature may not have been of direct use to those who regularly used the financial market. It is also true that those with an occasional involvement in the financial market learned an equal, if not greater, amount from their own actions, successes and failures, and discussions with brokers and acquaintances. Nevertheless, the ordering of financial knowledge was an essential part of the development of the market and was a reflection of the diversification of business and investment strategies.

Summary

Printed information was a useful learning tool for the early modern investor. It defined the boundaries of the market, ordered relevant knowledge and allowed the inexperienced and occasional investor to approach the market with a degree of confidence. Printed information was also part of a wider learning process, one that sought to inform the public in general about how the financial market functioned and its utility in the economy. Even in the brief period of time under consideration in this study it is possible to see the emergence of financial information as a commodity. Indeed, the amount of printed information available to the early modern investor is quite striking. However, it is equally important to note how little of that information could be put to direct use when making investment decisions. Its sources were too diverse, it was sometimes inaccurate

---

[113] For a fuller discussion of the books owned and used by merchants see R. Grassby, *The Business Community of Seventeenth Century England* (Cambridge University Press, 1995), pp. 350 5; D. J. Hancock, *Citizens of the World: London Merchants and the Integration of the British Atlantic Community, 1735 1785* (Cambridge University Press, 1995), p. 33.

[114] GLL, MS 3041/9, iii. Bowrey also possessed books on chemistry, smithing, carpentry, joinery, bricklaying and glass making, as well as many scriptural works and travel guides.

[115] Grassby, *Business Community*, pp. 354 5.

and its timeliness was less than could be desired. It must also be noted that, since price currents and newspapers circulated chiefly within coffee houses and other meeting places, printed information often served to draw investors into those places and under the influence of brokers and stock-jobbers, rather than freeing them to pursue information independently. Hence, as will be demonstrated in the following chapter, the gathering of financial news and information remained an activity that was necessarily conducted through direct contact with the market.

5   Networks of information

The previous chapter emphasised that while printed information might have been abundant, its utility for the active investor was questionable. The slow speed at which newspapers were printed and circulated meant that many investors would have found it necessary to seek their information from more direct sources and the price list could offer little to the active investor who would have understood that price was meaningless unless it was considered in the context of a company's past history, current performance and prospects for the future. Consequently, to be well informed the investor had to gain access to a complex information network, which may have included newspapers and price currents, but was also created through letters between acquaintances and business contacts, and in face-to-face meetings, most notably via conversations conducted, or overheard, in the Royal Exchange or the coffee houses of London. The aim of this chapter is to investigate how those networks operated to supply financial information to early modern investors. First, it will examine the nature of the physical space in which information circulated. The second section will investigate the extent to which full information was available to early modern investors. The final part of the chapter will concentrate on those who created networks of information and will ask how information spread from the City to all interested parties.

Exchange Alley

In 1688, Joseph de la Vega wrote that three things moved the market in Amsterdam: 'the conditions in India, European politics, and opinion on the stock exchange itself'. But, he cautioned, because of the gambling of speculators, news was often of little value since it was impossible to know how the market would react in any given situation.[1] Undoubtedly, de la Vega was right to assume that it was not easy to predict the impact

---

[1] de la Vega, *Confusion de Confusiones*, p. 9.

of information upon share prices, yet there is still every reason to believe that economic and political news continued to inform the actions of Dutch investors. It is also reasonable to suppose that London's financial market was similarly responsive to news from India and the progress of the political situation in Europe. Furthermore, since the London market was far more diverse than its counterpart in Amsterdam, domestic politics and economic conditions must be thought of as equally important influences on the actions of English investors.

London's financial market was well placed to attract such information. In particular, the City benefited from England's 'exceptional political and economic centralization'.[2] London was the seat of political power and the connections between Westminster and Whitehall and the City were strong. Wealthy London merchants remained the key source of government funds and the Treasury was, at this time, reliant upon the innovation of private individuals in its search for funding solutions. The main moneyed companies, such as the East India Company and the Bank of England, were as much political entities as economic ones. They were dependent on government for the protection of their monopolies, and companies used lobbyists in an attempt to promote their business in Parliament and at Court. In July 1679, for example, John Verney, on behalf of the Royal African Company, spent a day at Windsor where he had 'discourse with ... Sunderland and afterwards with His Majesty'.[3] Even the smaller companies used lobbyists. In 1690 the White Paper Company employed William Sutton of Byfleet in Surrey as an agent to promote a petition requesting the encouragement and better establishment of white paper manufacture.[4] Thus, close connections were built between London's political and financial centres that facilitated the flow of information.

London was also England's major port and the heart of her economy. Trade and manufacturing was concentrated in and around the capital and, as Defoe noted, the provinces were largely dependent 'upon the city of London ... for the consumption of [their] produce'.[5] Goods, services and migrants flowed into London from the provinces bringing with them fresh news and creating further networks of information.[6] Similarly, news

---

[2] R. Porter, *London: A Social History* (London: Hamish Hamilton, 1994), p. 132.
[3] Quoted in Whyman, *Sociability and Power*, p. 74.
[4] For his pains, if the Bill was passed, Sutton was to receive four shares and be admitted as a member to the Company. M. R. Julian, 'English Economic Legislation, 1660 1714', unpublished MPhil dissertation (London School of Economics, 1979), p. 49.
[5] Quoted in Porter, *London*, p. 133.
[6] Wrigley estimates that perhaps one in six adults in England in the period 1650 to 1750 had experience of living in London, thus creating powerful connections between the capital and the provinces. E. A. Wrigley, 'A Simple Model of London's Importance in Changing

from abroad flowed into London through the movement of foreign merchants and overseas traders. Business correspondence and the personal letters of merchants and other individuals added to the influx of information.[7] In the late seventeenth century it was standard practice to include relevant economic and political information, along with the prices of major commodities, in business letters. This type of information, although directed at specific individuals, would have been rapidly disseminated among other interested parties.

Assessing the effectiveness of such networks of information is not easy and undoubtedly experiences varied. Neal and Quinn argue that the networks established by some merchants and bankers were sufficient to allow arbitrage of exchange rate anomalies, indicating that some individuals were able to establish a highly efficient and consistent system of information exchange.[8] Nevertheless, as Samuel Jeake's brief interest in East India Company stock in mid- to late 1694 showed, it was not always so easy to find reliable information. On 27 July 1694 Jeake received notice from his correspondent Thomas Miller that 'East India stock was upon a Critical point, by reason the Dutch had 8 ships arrived; & they bought no news of 2 or 3 of ours which were expected, which if they arrived before Michaelmas, the stock would rise considerably; if not, or if they miscarried it would fall much lower.'[9] Further entries in Jeake's diary clearly demonstrate the rise and fall of the share price as the rumours of the ships' arrival or miscarriage were heard in London. On 20 August 1694 Jeake received a report that East India Company stock 'was fallen to 77 ... upon a Report that 2 ships were miscarried'.[10] On 4 October he received word that there was 'a discourse on the Exchange of one East India Ship being arrived in Ireland & 3 more coming'.[11] Stock rose on this rumour and fell back a little when it could not be confirmed. By mid-November there was news that the ships were in Plymouth, at which East India Company stock rose to 98 but by 26 November the ships still had not arrived in London and stock retreated to 92, at which point Thomas Miller feared that the

English Society and Economy, 1650 1750', in P. Abrams and E. A. Wrigley, eds., *Towns in Societies: Essays in Economic History and Historical Sociology* (Cambridge University Press, 1978), p. 221.

[7] For further discussion of channels of information, particularly with regard to the Amsterdam market, see Smith, 'Amsterdam as an Information Exchange', pp. 990 5.

[8] L. Neal and S. Quinn, 'Networks of Information: Markets and Institutions in the Rise of London as a Financial Centre, 1660 1760', *Financial History Review*, 8 (2001), 7 26; S. Quinn, 'Gold, Silver and the Glorious Revolution: Arbitrage Between Bills of Exchange and Bullion', *Economic History Review*, 49 (1996), 473 90.

[9] Hunter and Gregory, *Astrological Diary*, p. 244.

[10] Ibid.   [11] Ibid., p. 247.

ships might have been lost and took the sensible decision to liquidate Jeake's holdings.[12]

As this example amply illustrates, nothing could be deemed certain until it could be confirmed at first hand. Indeed, de la Vega warned investors that a ship could even sink at harbour and thwart their hopes.[13] Consequently, the more active investor would have found it necessary to maintain a physical presence in London. This was certainly possible for all investors; there were no restrictions on entering the Royal Exchange or any other parts of the City. There is even evidence to suggest that some women were able to gather information in these places. Cowan notes that Hester Pinney, a thriving businesswoman in the early eighteenth century, had few difficulties dealing with the stock-jobbers at Garraway's and Jonathan's and was able to establish and maintain contacts with the West India merchants during visits to coffee houses.[14] Moreover, many women attended lottery draws and art auctions at coffee houses indicating that such places were not closed to them. However, Cowan does concede that coffee houses were no place for a lady who wanted to preserve her respectability.[15]

Most participants in the financial market of the late seventeenth century lived either in or around London, and the majority of investors did travel to the City in order to complete their transactions. With regard to Bank of England stock, for example, in the period between August 1694 and December 1702, 94 per cent of sellers and 98 per cent of purchasers were present to sign the transfer books.[16] Records for the other joint-stock companies are not as complete, but a similar picture is presented by the East India Company's surviving transfer books, with 98 per cent of sellers and 99 per cent of buyers being present at time of transfer.[17]

The main gathering place for those seeking financial information was Exchange Alley and its adjacent lanes and streets, the limits of which, according to one contemporary source, were 'easily surrounded in about a minute and a half'.[18] As Figure 5.1 shows, into this space were crammed

---

[12] Ibid., passim.   [13] de la Vega, *Confusion*, p. 9.

[14] B. W. Cowan, 'The Social Life of Coffee: Commercial Culture and Metropolitan Society in Early Modern England, 1600 1720', unpublished PhD thesis (Princeton University, 2000), p. 389. For further details of Hester Pinney's life and business dealings see P. Sharpe, 'Dealing with Love: The Ambiguous Independence of the Single Woman in Early Modern England', *Gender and History*, 11 (1999), pp. 209 32.

[15] Cowan, 'Social Life of Coffee', p. 387.

[16] Bank Archives, AC28/32233; AC28/1513 22. Those who were not present to sign the transfer books appointed attorneys to act on their behalf.

[17] IOR, L/AG/14/3/2 6.

[18] Quoted in D. Keene, 'The Financial District of the City of London: Continuity and Change, 1300 1871', in H. A. Diedricks and D. Reeder, eds., *Cities of Finance* (Amsterdam: North Holland, 1996), p. 287.

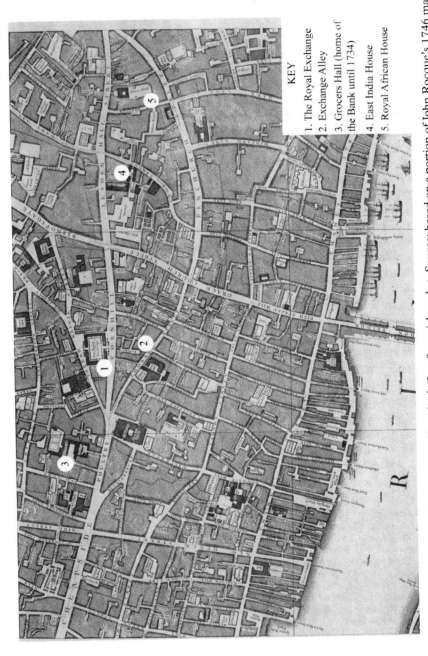

KEY

1. The Royal Exchange
2. Exchange Alley
3. Grocers Hall (home of the Bank until 1734)
4. East India House
5. Royal African House

5.1 Map showing the chief institutions of London's first financial market. Source: based on a portion of John Rocque's 1746 map of the City of London, Westminster and Southwark. Reproduced by permission of Guildhall Library, City of London Corporation.

the chief institutions of the late seventeenth-century financial market, namely the Royal Exchange, Jonathan's and Garraway's coffee houses in Exchange Alley, the Bank of England, East India House and Royal African House. Within these places could be found brokers, stock-jobbers and investors, professional and otherwise, all vying for information. Within the Royal Exchange and in the surrounding areas there were further coffee houses and taverns, the premises of traders, merchants and retailers, and the Post Office. Close by were the complements to the financial market – goldsmith-bankers, scriveners and attorneys. Already this area of London was beginning to have a specialist purpose that, according to Derek Keene, first 'displaced the trade in material goods and then drove out the residential population'.[19]

The Royal Exchange was the heart of this space.[20] For the merchant or businessman, whether resident in London or just visiting, the Royal Exchange was the place to gather information, to socialise, to make contacts and to transact business. As the author of the *Exact Dealer* stated in 1688, it was 'the proper place of bargaining, and getting knowledge of what Commodities are bought in, and to be sold; as also the Intelligence of the Prices, and whether the Rate rises or falls'.[21] The Royal Exchange was also the place where official information circulated. Displays of public authority took place there. Miscreant businessmen were pilloried in front of the Exchange at midday, the time at which commercial activity was at its height.[22] Government and other notices were posted there and hung 'as thick round the Pillars of each Walk, as Bells about the Legs of a *Morrice-Dancer*'.[23] Official announcements also echoed through the building.[24] In addition, the Royal Exchange was the home of the infant stock exchange. However, as noted in Chapter 3, the noise and the nature of the business rapidly turned it into a nuisance and the brokers removed to Exchange Alley in 1698.

The information circulating in the Royal Exchange was supplemented by that generated in the network of coffee houses and taverns located in its immediate vicinity. These public spaces were places of entertainment and refreshment but also furnished the venue for public gatherings, auctions

[19] Ibid., p. 288.
[20] For an evocative description of the Royal Exchange see N. Glaisyer, *The Culture of Commerce in England, 1660 1720* (Woodbridge: Boydell and Brewer, 2006), pp. 27 68.
[21] J. H[ill], *The Exact Dealer: Being an Useful Companion for all Traders* (London, 1688), p. 4, quoted in Glaisyer, *Culture of Commerce*, p. 30.
[22] M. Harris, 'Exchanging Information: Print and Business at the Royal Exchange in the Late Seventeenth Century', in A. Saunders, ed., *The Royal Exchange* (London: Guardian Royal Exchange, 1997) p. 188.
[23] Ned Ward cited in Saunders, *The Royal Exchange*, p. 189.   [24] Ibid.

and lottery draws, and effectively provided office space for all manner of businessmen, merchants and traders. In such places the investor could, for the price of a cup of coffee, peruse a large selection of printed material: domestic and foreign news sheets, journals and bulletins, price currents, auction notices and advertisements.[25] The most important information was, however, communicated verbally. Indeed, the debate encouraged by the atmosphere of the coffee houses was an important part of the assessment of the market value. Dickson saw the constant reappraisal and reassessment of value on the floor of Jonathan's as an essential aspect of the market and one that provided security, as government debt became a commodity that was firmly based upon public discussion and evaluation.[26] It may also be argued that the information to be found in these places was sometimes more useful than that available through official channels. Hence, in 1693 the Governor and Committee of the Hudson's Bay Company awarded the sum of £3 to 'Mr Loyd the Coffee Man [in gratitude] for his Intelligence of the Comp[ies] Shipps'.[27]

It has been suggested that coffee houses were places where new investors could learn about the market from experienced brokers and stock-jobbers. Keene notes the use of coffee houses as venues for philosophical and mechanical demonstrations, claiming this as proof of their legitimacy as places of learning and information exchange.[28] Carlos, Key and Dupree also identify a direct flow of information from brokers and stock-jobbers to inexperienced investors. They suggest that there was 'knowledge and ability on the one side and learning by individuals on the other'.[29] However, such statements should not be accepted without question. In an unregulated market the well-informed have powerful incentives to obstruct or divert information flows and contemporary commentators wrote often of the duplicitous nature of brokers and stock-jobbers, never of their altruistic tendencies.

Meetings of the shareholders of the various joint-stock companies provided more formal venues for the exchange of financial information. Such meetings were regular but, when business was proceeding well, they were not frequent. During the period under consideration, the Bank of

---

[25] B. Lillywhite, *London Coffee Houses: A Reference Book of Coffee Houses of the Seventeenth, Eighteenth and Nineteenth Centuries* (London: George Allen and Unwin, 1963), p. 20.

[26] Dickson, *Financial Revolution*, p. 515.

[27] Quoted in McCusker, *European Bills of Entry*, p. 55.

[28] D. Keene, 'The Setting of the Royal Exchange: Continuity and Change in the Financial District of the City of London, 1300 1871', in Saunders, *Royal Exchange*, p. 260. See also D. Outram, *The Enlightenment* (Cambridge University Press, 1995), pp. 14 30; A. Ellis, *The Penny Universities: A History of the Coffee Houses* (London: Secker and Warburg, 1956).

[29] Carlos *et al.*, 'Learning and Stock Market Institutions', 342.

England's Court of Proprietors met quarterly with an additional meeting for the election of directors, as did the Court of the New East India Company. The Courts of the Old East India, Royal African and Hudson's Bay Companies met annually for the election of directors and so that a statement of the company's financial condition could be presented to the shareholders. However, in all cases additional meetings were called as and when necessary, and during troubled periods in a company's existence shareholders met often. For instance, the Bank of England's shareholders met twelve times between January and March 1697 to discuss the government's demands for further loans.[30] Similarly, the Old East India Company's General Court met seventeen times between May and July 1698 to discuss the threat posed by the New Company.[31]

It is impossible to be exact about the numbers in attendance at such meetings. The Bank did keep lists of the attendees at its General Courts in the period between 1694 and 1697 but each list usually included the names of only a certain number of shareholders and then the list was concluded with the phrase 'and others of the generality'.[32] Although it is unclear how many 'others' attended, the lists do indicate that, in general, between 5 and 15 per cent of those eligible to vote turned out. However, crucial meetings attracted many more people. The meeting that took place on 4 January 1697 to discuss a further loan to the government attracted more than 200 shareholders, around a quarter of those eligible to vote.[33]

The Old East India Company did not keep a register of attendees at its General Courts but on several occasions at meetings regarding the New Company 'a very numerous appearance of the Generality' was recorded.[34] The Royal African and Hudson's Bay companies' meetings were often rather poorly attended but any threats to either company's stability or profitability could encourage a higher attendance, as could the hint of scandal. In December 1692 fifty-four individuals, about a quarter of all shareholders, attended a meeting to discuss the resignation of the Royal African Company's treasurer, Robert Williamson, who had confessed to 'borrowing' the Company's money.[35]

---

[30] Bank Archives, G7/1, passim.   [31] IOR, B/41, passim.
[32] Bank Archives, G7/1, passim.
[33] This finding is echoed by a later study of attendance at the East India Company's general courts which indicates that on average around 8 to 10 per cent of those entitled to attend went routinely to Court debates and about double that number attended on important occasions. H. V. Bowen, 'The "Little Parliament": the General Court of the East India Company, 1750 1784', *The Historical Journal*, 34 (1991), 863.
[34] IOR, B/41, May Jul. 1698.
[35] Royal African Company General Court Minute Book, 20 Dec. 1692, NA, PRO, T70/10.

The presentation of information at such meetings was formalised. In some cases meetings were convened merely to confirm that the company's affairs were in good order. Often when a company was awaiting a decision from Parliament or a response to a petition, meetings were convened to notify shareholders that no new information was forthcoming. However, at such meetings proprietors were in a position to question the directors of companies and the General Courts would have provided the perfect opportunity for like-minded stockholders to meet and establish further networks of information. There is also evidence to suggest that Courts were preceded by other gatherings of shareholders. For instance, with reference to the prospect of a dividend being paid by the Bank, Samuel Jeake wrote to his wife Elizabeth in October 1697, 'To morrow we have a General Court at ye Bank & I find most of ye members are for it', indicating that the potential dividend had already been much discussed in the City.[36]

It is finally worth noting that, in the cases of the trading companies, auctions of goods provided the shareholders with further opportunities for the gathering of relevant information. Indeed, the East India Company held 197 sales of goods during the period under consideration, while the General Court met on only 131 occasions.[37] Auctions not only allowed direct observation of the quality of the Company's wares and the prices achieved by those goods but also allowed those interested in a company's prospects to meet, and may have provided further occasions for the questioning of directors. The frequency, or infrequency, of the auctions also said much about a company's present condition and future prospects.

As the foregoing discussion suggests, although investors seem to have met and congregated in Exchange Alley and its immediate environs, there was not necessarily a centralised place where financial information could be sought and found. Similarly, there does not appear to have been one place in which a market in all joint-stock and debt products was created by open outcry. In fact there is evidence to suggest that markets existed in a variety of places: the Exchange, coffee houses, Grocers Hall – the home of the Bank of England during this period, and East India House. The East India Company was even prepared to send its transfer book to shareholders' homes, if requested. In September 1695, Mr Thorowgood of the Company took the transfer book to Mrs Boon at her home since, being 'indisposed', she could not attend at East India House. In May 1696 Mr Thorowgood took the transfer book to Wanstead for the convenience of Sir Josiah Child, and in May 1698 he was ordered to take the book to

[36] 'Samuel Jeake to Elizabeth Jeake', 21 Oct. 1697, ESRO, Jeake Papers, FRE 5315.
[37] IOR, B/39 B/41; B43 B/44.

the Lord Mayor of London.[38] Clearly for those who were too sick or too important to face the hustle and bustle of Exchange Alley, the market would come to them.

An incident recorded in Thomas Bowrey's surviving papers as a result of a dispute over the sale of Linen Company stock gives further insight into the process of negotiating a trade. When asked to describe the events preceding the dispute Richard Sweet stated 'that on Munday morning being y[e] 15th of this Inst. June Mr Henry Million, Senior, came to his house, & told him that he understood this deponent was Employed to goe to Mr Tho[s] Bowrey of Wapping & treat with him about his Four shares in y[e] Linen Manufacture'.[39] This description highlights two points of interest. First, the negotiation of this trade clearly took place away from the main sphere of the market. The implication is that Sweet waited upon Bowrey at his home or perhaps in a coffee house in Wapping. Secondly, the agreement to trade appears to have been the result of a process of negotiation, rather than an acceptance of the price offered by a seller or market maker. Perhaps this should not be viewed as surprising; Muldrew notes that almost all transactions during the early modern period went through a bargaining process before being agreed.[40] Nevertheless, it does seem unlikely that a process of negotiation was common to all share transactions during this period. The prices recorded in Charles Blunt's ledgers showed very little intraday variation implying that once a price had been set by the successful conclusion of a trade, that price provided the benchmark for further trades on that day, at least among Blunt's clients and contacts.[41] Even so, it is reasonable to suggest that even for those investors located close to the centre of the City, the process of finding a market in a particular stock and agreeing upon a price at which to trade was not a straightforward one.

It also seems probable that the provincial investor and those on the outskirts of London would only have moved into the City to conduct their business if they could not do so close to home. For the passive investor convenience was undoubtedly a greater concern than price, particularly in a market where, for long periods of time, some stocks were relatively stable. In August 1697, for instance, John Hill, a cooper from Southwark, sold £385 Bank of England stock to Edward Wade and £100 Bank stock to Thomas Sodon; both Wade and Sodon were also coopers and also from Southwark, suggesting that this deal was not agreed in Exchange

---

[38] IOR, B/41, 27 Sep. 1695; 1 May 1696; 16 May 1698.   [39] GLL, MS 3041/5 fos. 2 3.
[40] C. Muldrew, *The Economy of Obligation: The Culture of Credit and Social Relations in Early Modern England* (Basingstoke: Macmillan, 1998), p. 42.
[41] See NA, PRO, C114/165.

Alley.[42] Additionally, the East India Company's transfer books show a number of trades executed in 1691 in the county of Essex between John Morley, a butcher from Little Maplestead, Edward Ingram a gentleman from Halstead and John Barnard, a draper from Coggleshall.[43] These villages stand in relatively close proximity to one another and it is probable that the counterparties knew of each other's interest in East India Company stock and resolved to trade among themselves in order to avoid the need for a journey to the City.[44]

These examples should not be taken as evidence of separately functioning regional markets. A close examination of the Bank of England's transfer books shows that 66 per cent of buyers and 76 per cent of sellers who resided outside of the City transacted with a counterparty who gave an address within the City.[45] It is also possible that where a transaction involved both a buyer and a seller who were resident outside the City contact was still made within the environs of Exchange Alley. Notably, only around 11 per cent of buyers and sellers living in Westminster traded with a counterparty who was also resident in that part of London.[46] Smaller populations of investors made finding a suitable counterparty even more difficult. Thus, among investors living in the north of England, only one transaction was conducted between parties living in the same area. In November 1701 Jane Hussey, a spinster of Caythorp in Lincolnshire, sold £100 Bank stock to Anne Hussey, also a spinster and probably Jane's sister.[47] Yet, despite the understandable difficulties that the provincial investor would have faced in finding someone to trade with in his or her immediate locality, it is clear that the City did not command a monopoly of the trade in joint-stocks or government debt.

Noise and confusion

Those who traded away from Exchange Alley sacrificed the price advantage that a larger market with a greater number of actors would have offered. In part investors were prepared to make that sacrifice because of a lack of trust in financial information and an understandable inability to comprehend price movements. Their wariness was intensified by the nature of the market. When brokers and stock-jobbers met, the result was noise and confusion. The financial market encouraged 'uninterrupted,

---

[42] Bank Archives, AC28/1514, 10 Aug. 1697.   [43] IOR, L/AG/14/3/2.
[44] In order to facilitate the exchange of stock, a transfer document was drawn up by the two parties, independently witnessed, and sent to the EIC. The Company then pasted the document into the transfer book.
[45] Bank Archives, AC28/32233, AC28/1513 22.   [46] Ibid.
[47] Bank Archives, AC28/1519, 3 Nov. 1701.

simultaneous, overlapping, rude, quick talk',[48] which made the information conveyed difficult to follow and assimilate. Contemporary plays sometimes depicted the antics of stock-jobbers and can give some idea of the way that information was presented to early modern investors. The following is from a scene set in Jonathan's coffee house during the South Sea Bubble:

5th Brok:	Hoop Petticoat, Bubble
2d Brok:	Your Price for Hoop Petticoat?
5th Brok:	Forty per Cent.
2d Brok:	I'll give it, let me have all it covers.
5th Brok:	You shall have it Sir, to a Hair
6th Brok:	Flying Ships who Buys?
Sev. Brok:	We all Buy how d'ye Sell?
6th Brok:	One Hundred Per Cent.
Sev. Brok:	There's Earnest.

New Cryers run a-cross the end of the room in great haste, tumbling over one another.

1st News Cr:	News from France, Spain, and Italy.
2d News Cr:	Great News from Rome An Account of the Deaths and last Wills and Testament of the Pope, and all his Cardinals.
3d News Cr:	Great News! Good News from the North! The Czar of Muscovy a Dying at his Capital of Petersburg. (The Stock Jobbers buy and talk merrily together.)[49]

Although the market was often quiet, allowing negotiations to be conducted at a relaxed pace, at times when unexpected news broke prices would have changed quickly. On such occasions and within a scattered market it would have been extremely difficult for the inexperienced investor to keep track of price movements.

The language of the market added to the sense of bewilderment. The language used by brokers and stock-jobbers was new and complex. They used nicknames to describe stocks and shorthand forms to describe activities. One historian speculates that such language must have sounded like 'baffling incantations chanted by a strange new sect practising its mysterious rites'.[50] For Defoe the language of the market was not just baffling, it was designed to perpetuate fraud against the ordinary citizen, to *'Fiddle them out of their Money,* by the strange and unheard of Engines

---

[48] A. Preda, 'In the Enchanted Grove: Financial Conversations and the Marketplace in England and France in the 18th Century', *Journal of Historical Sociology,* 14 (2001), 285.

[49] T. Bickerton, *Exchange Alley: Or, the Stock Jobber turn'd Gentleman: with the Humours of Our Modern Projectors* (London, 1720), pp. 23 6 quoted in Preda, 'The Enchanted Grove', p. 292. See also S. Centlivre, *A Bold Stroke for a Wife* (London: Edward Arnold, 1969), pp. 54 8.

[50] W. A. Speck, 'Conflict in Society' in Holmes, *Britain after the Glorious Revolution,* p. 136.

of *Interests, Discounts, Transfers, Tallies, Debentures, Shares, Projects*, and the *Devil and all* of Figures and hard Names'.[51] Before investors could engage fully in the process of gathering information, therefore, they had to master the complexities of the language of the market and learn to keep pace with the rapid changes that occurred. It should, however, be understood that for the speculator the sounds of the market could have been very revealing. Excited babble, angry shouting, and hushed conversations all hinted at deals to be done or secrets to be kept. For any individual coming to the market regularly the first thing to do would have been to listen to its sounds.

Investors who did learn to understand the workings of the market faced numerous other obstacles in their search for reliable information. Information about the general state of the English economy could not easily be found. Certainly, the late seventeenth century was a time of increasing interest in the gathering of information about the economy. The constraints of war particularly encouraged the gathering of economic data with a view to increasing the efficiency of tax assessment and collection. Nevertheless, according to Brewer, the new science of political arithmetic promised more than it delivered. The work of political arithmeticians lacked rigour and discrimination. Their findings were often inaccurate and consequently provided little that could have been used by investors seeking a broad view of the economy.[52]

The quality of information produced by joint-stock companies was similarly questionable. There was a culture of secrecy within some companies. The East India Company was notable in this regard. At times when the Company was experiencing difficulties or was in the process of complex negotiations, it insisted that its directors keep the details of their meetings secret. In February 1690, for example, after 'long and serious Debates' regarding the sending of an ambassador to sue for peace in India and the petitioning of Parliament for the renewal of the Company's charter, it was 'Resolved that this dayes Debate be kept secret'.[53] But there are indications that such practices were both long-standing and common among joint-stock companies. The Hudson's Bay Company concealed evidence of private sales of furs and swore its Committee and General Court to secrecy over the matter.[54] Willan's study of the Russia Company

[51] Defoe, *Villainy of Stock Jobbers*, p. 22.
[52] Brewer, *Sinews of Power*, p. 224. For somewhat more sympathetic views of the work of political arithmeticians see P. Buck, 'People who Counted: Political Arithmetic in the Eighteenth Century', *Isis*, 73 (1982), 28 45 and J. Hoppit, 'Political Arithmetic in Eighteenth Century England', *Economic History Review*, 49 (1996), 516 40.
[53] IOR, B/39, 10 Feb. 1690.
[54] Parkinson, 'London Stock Market', p. 148. Secrecy was necessary because private sales had been outlawed by the charter renewal of 1690.

also found evidence of concealment of relevant facts. In 1597 Robert Dove, one of the oldest members of the Company wrote to Lord Burghley 'when Mr Merrick our agent in Russia hath to certify of any matter that he thinks not meet to be written to the Company generally, he writes the same privately to me to emparte with such of them as I think best'.[55] Such secrecy would have been considered at the time to be perfectly legitimate. Indeed, for the Russia Company the combination of commerce and diplomacy made secrecy essential. Similarly, during the 1690s the East India Company's reticence stemmed from a desire not to give further ammunition to those who sought to remove its monopoly. Nevertheless, the concealment of pertinent facts did not facilitate the decision-making processes of those who held stock or planned to purchase it in the future.

Even when companies did publish pertinent information it was not necessarily to be relied upon. Errors in financial planning were unavoidable given the facilities and knowledge available to early modern company directors.[56] Companies commonly overstretched their resources, failed to make adequate provision for unforeseen circumstances and overestimated their potential revenues. Overseas trading companies faced a myriad of problems when seeking information from foreign outposts. With reference to the East India Company, Chaudhuri noted that natural disasters and unforeseen circumstances could extend the 16-month period taken for ships to complete the round trip from London to Asia. Also badly worded or poorly structured letters hampered understanding, particularly those that made obscure references: 'as if because they know these things, it necessarily follows that we must also'. Moreover, when information was received, the sheer volume made analysis and timely action difficult.[57] All these factors would have made it impossible to provide a reasoned analysis of future profitability.

Nor was there much agreement about how assets should be valued. Hence in 1696 when the East India Company presented a valuation of its net assets to the House of Lords, its calculations were challenged on almost every point. The Company's valuation of £1,224,502 was adjusted by the Lords to a mere £217,721.[58] Contemporary commentators seemed to agree with the lower estimate. One suggested that the East India Company's stock 'in India, upon the Sea, and at Home, is of no real Value, and hardly sufficient to pay their Debts'.[59] Ned Ward asserted

---

[55] Willan, *Early History of the Russia Company*, p. 23.
[56] Scott, *Constitution and Finance*, vol. I, p. 353.
[57] Chaudhuri, *Trading World of Asia*, pp. 74 7.
[58] Scott, *Constitution and Finance*, vol. II, p. 163.
[59] Anon., *Letter from a Lawyer*, p. 7.

that 'Were a schedule of their effects scored on one side and their Indian debts scored on the other, it is believed more bad debts would arise upon the reverse than are due to tradesmen from all the persons of quality in town.'[60]

As a result of such problems, few potential investors would have regarded the value of a company's assets as a key determinant of stock price. Indeed, in 1681 Sir Josiah Child complained:

when we tell gentlemen, or others, they may buy [East India Company] stock, and come into the Company when they please: they presently reply, they know that, but then they must also pay 280 *l*. for 100 *l*. And when we say the intrinsic value is worth so much; which is as true as 2 and 2 makes 4, yet it is not so soon demonstrated to their apprehensions, notwithstanding it is no hard task to make out.[61]

As a further example, in January 1695 the Royal African Company stated to its shareholders that the stock of the Company and its profits amounted to £248,099 11s 1d thus indicating, by the Company's own calculation, that the stock should have been valued at around £40.[62] At that time, Royal African Company stock was actually trading at a price of £24 and it continued its slow decline thereafter, suggesting that investors took little notice of information that contradicted their long-term view of a company's potential.[63]

Some commentators were puzzled by the gap between market prices and estimated intrinsic value. Daniel Defoe commented that East India Company stock had been:

sold from 300 *l*. per cent. to 37 *l*. per cent. from thence with fluxes and refluxes, as frequent as the tides, it has been up at 150 *l*. per cent. again; during all which differences, it would puzzle a very good artist to prove, that their real stock (if they have any) set loss and gain together, can have varied above 10 per cent. upon the whole.[64]

But those closer to the market were more insightful about the reasons for such price fluctuations. In 1691 one pamphleteer listed the fundamental factors that should have depressed the price of the stock in the main trading companies. He noted that the East India, Royal African and Hudson's Bay Companies were suffering as a result of 'war with private traders ... greater risks, higher freight and new duties, [and] ... taxes, etc.' but asserted that it was not those factors that governed prices, rather 'they rise and fall as the humours of the buyers increase or abate'.[65] John

---

[60] E. Ward, *The London Spy*, edited by P. Hyland (Michigan: Colleagues Press, 1993), p. 21.
[61] J. Child, *A Treatise Concerning the East India Trade* (London, 1681), p. 11.
[62] PRO, T70/101, 8 Jan. 1695 NA.   [63] Houghton, *Collection for Improvement*, passim.
[64] Defoe, *Villainy of Stock Jobbers*, p. 5.   [65] Anon., *Plain Dealing*, p. 3.

Houghton, too, argued that stock prices very often reacted 'according to hopes or fears', suggesting that early modern investors had a very keen awareness that market psychology was an important consideration when making investment decisions.[66]

Market psychology was also used by those who preyed upon the hopes and fears of investors by spreading false information. This was a considerable problem since the financial market of the late seventeenth century encompassed no authority to regulate the dissemination of data. As such, those who spread misinformation went unpunished and deliberate attempts to deceive investors were frequent. The most famous incident of this period concerned the siege of the town of Mons. During early 1691 the town of Mons was besieged by Louis XIV's armies. It fell to the French on 29 March 1691, but on 31 March a man dressed as a Dutch officer rode through London crying out that William III had relieved the town. It was alleged that this was a deliberate deception to allow those who had gambled on the relief of the town to call in their 'winnings' before the real outcome of the siege was made known.[67] Nor was this the only incidence of such manipulation. Defoe alleged that 'Stock-Jobbing Brokers' could govern the number of buyers and sellers active in the market and make the prices of stock 'dance attendance on their designs, and rise and fall as they please, without any regard to the Intrinsick worth of the Stock'.[68]

Such incidents ensured that the information provided by brokers and stock-jobbers was widely distrusted, yet investors were also forced to question the veracity of official information. A relevant example is offered by Israel who cites a letter written by an Englishman in Amsterdam to a fellow countryman who was a member of the international diplomatic community at The Hague. He wrote,

There are here some Actionists in the [Dutch] East India Company who, knowing of the honour I have to be known to your Excellency these many years, doe by me propose a handsome gratification if you think fitt to give them the first and best intelligence of things so farre as they may be usefull to give an influence to their way of trade: this I presume to propose daring to think that, as Your Honour would not expose the mysteries and main secrets of the state, so, on the other side, I am bold to thinke that such a correspondency prudently and cunningly managed in this city would be able to doe the King [of England] a great deale of service by making these men to hazard their stocks and ruine themselves.[69]

[66] Houghton, *Collection for Improvement*, passim. Houghton's analysis of the factors that affected asset prices has been confirmed by modern psychologists who have concluded that the emotions that determine risk taking are indeed hope and fear. Shefrin, *Beyond Greed and Fear*, p. 3.
[67] J. Childs, 'Fortunes of War', *History Today*, 53 (2003), 51 5.
[68] Defoe, *Villainy of Stock Jobbers*, p. 5.
[69] Quoted in Israel, 'Amsterdam Stock Exchange', 415 16.

It is not easy to find evidence of such deliberate official misinformation, but there are suggestions that the practice existed. Samuel Jeake wrote in May 1699 of a report of the King of Spain's death that was 'not much credited as coming from the French Ambassador'.[70] In a letter to John Ellis dated 14 August 1688 it was noted that

Last week arrived from the East Indies one Dr St Johns, who has been there for some years as Judge of the Admiralty for the East India Company. He is said to give an account of affairs in those parts, that is quite different from what was published in the Gazette, and not at all comfortable for the nation, at least for those concerned in the same bottom with the Company.[71]

Trust in official sources of information was, therefore, likely to have been very limited.

Thus, early modern investors faced many barriers that would have prevented them gaining full information about the prospects for any stock or debt product. Information circulated in an extended market, lines of communication remained slow and news from both official and unofficial sources was subject to manipulation. Furthermore, the presentation of information during this period was problematic. The new language of the market was complex, making it difficult for inexperienced investors to understand the choices offered to them. Problems in assimilating information would have been compounded by the fact that the data available to investors could not have encompassed all pertinent information. Few joint-stock companies could have made precise predictions about future profits, accounts were seldom made public and the uncertain nature of the political and economic situation in the 1690s made it impossible to make accurate business projections.

Creating networks of information

The need to overcome these barriers ensured that few active investors would have been able to remain passive recipients of news.[72] Indeed, the difficulties of accessing and verifying information led some individuals to create their own networks of information. Sir Henry Furnese seems to have been particularly adept in this respect, 'establishing a kind of Reuter's service on a private scale'.[73] Josiah and Francis Child instituted similar measures. Most notably, they apparently established a private express service from the south of Ireland that gave them early news

---

[70] 'Samuel Jeake to Elizabeth Jeake', May 1699, ESRO, Jeake Papers, FRE 5331.
[71] Ellis, *Ellis Correspondence*, vol. II, p. 119.   [72] Israel, 'Amsterdam Stock Exchange', 414.
[73] C. Duguid, *The Story of the Stock Exchange* (London, 1901), p. 36.

about the arrival of East India Company ships.[74] Creating networks of this
kind naturally required a significant amount of money and influence.
However, the above-mentioned individuals had a formidable reputation
in the financial market, suggesting that their efforts were worthwhile.[75]

Other investors operated in a more limited sphere, but dedicated com-
parable resources to the search for information. For example, John Verney
began his working day 'at the Exchange at eight o'clock precisely, and
thence ... to two or three merchants' houses, and before ten I must be
at [the] custom-house to attend the Commissioners'.[76] Along the route of
Verney's daily walk were the premises of the Royal African Company and
East India House. Verney also visited Lombard Street, where goldsmiths
and scriveners had their businesses, Exchange Alley and Jonathan's and
Garraway's coffee houses, and frequently wandered along Cheapside,
with its many retail outlets, to the book sellers in St Paul's Churchyard.
Verney's walks were not aimless meanderings. He worked hard to obtain
relevant data and clearly studied that data. Whyman particularly notes
that he kept coded lists of ships, captains and cargoes.[77] On the other
hand, his walks were not just taken for the purpose of finding news relevant
to his business; they also had a social purpose. Like most merchants of the
time Verney relied heavily on social networks of information and his
friendships could also influence his investment decisions. His friendship
with Sir Gabriel Roberts, for example, brought him new opportunities for
profit and Verney clearly followed Roberts's lead when selecting investment strategies.[78] Verney's networks of information also extended out-
wards as he communicated the news that he gathered to his own family
and friends.

As Samuel Jeake's preparations for the purchase of East India stock
in 1694 suggest, provincial investors faced different costs. In order to keep
himself informed about price movements and prospects for the stock,
Jeake was forced to rely upon letters from his business associate and friend
Thomas Miller. Miller's letters from London generally arrived in Rye two
days after they were sent,[79] which meant that any information was already
old news when it reached Jeake. When Jeake did finally decide to purchase
stock, these postal delays proved detrimental to his profits. His letter,
dated 28 July 1694, instructing Miller to buy East India stock at 70 arrived

[74] Scott, *Constitution and Finance*, vol. I, p. 358.
[75] Even in 1719 Defoe referred to Sir Josiah Child as the 'Original of Stock Jobbing' and
suggested that 'every Man's Eye when he came to Market, was upon the Brokers, who
acted for Sir *Josiah*; [asking the question] Does Sir *Josiah* Sell or Buy?' Defoe, *Anatomy of
Exchange Alley*, p. 14.
[76] Quoted in Whyman, *Sociability and Power*, p. 73.   [77] Ibid.
[78] Ibid., pp. 71 2.   [79] Hunter and Gregory, *Astrological Diary*, passim.

too late, and by the time Miller replied on 2 August the stock had already risen to 76; a further instruction to buy at 77 was no more successful, and it was not until 10 September that Miller confirmed that the stock had been purchased at a price of 80, a full ten points higher than Jeake's original target.[80]

During subsequent periods of investment activity Jeake took up residence in London, excusing his extended absence to his wife by writing, 'You know ye greatest of our concerns are now here, if they were not I should not stay from you.'[81] During his time in London, Jeake established a number of contacts in the financial market. He attended the Bank of England's General Court on a number of occasions, met with brokers and attended a meeting of the holders of Million Lottery tickets.[82] Jeake also passed the information he gathered on to his wife and to other friends and relations in Rye, thus creating his own networks of information.[83] However, while the establishment of these networks may have facilitated profitable trading in shares and debt, there were other costs to be considered. The necessity of leaving his wife Elizabeth to control business in Rye caused several problems. Money was lost when Elizabeth accepted the wrong price for guineas and on several occasions opportunities in Jeake's main business were lost through his absence from Rye.[84] Full information could, therefore, be costly for the early modern investor.

For those with less time to establish networks of information a broker could offer a dual service: first by imparting up-to-date information and advice and, secondly, by arranging contact with a suitable counterparty for each transaction. Thomas Mortimer, writing in 1761, asserted that this process could, and should, have been circumvented since it was easy for an investor to seek out his own counterparty,[85] but in the less liquid market of the 1690s this may not have been a simple process. Thomas Bowrey clearly found it necessary to use brokers to complete his transactions; his surviving papers include a number of brokerage receipts. Indeed, during 1695 Bowrey paid brokerage to seven different brokers, with the total cost of the seventeen trades conducted in that year being nearly £20.[86] The fact that Bowrey used a number of different brokers may suggest that these individuals were specialising in a particular stock or instrument, but in a developing market such diversity is more likely to be

[80] Ibid., pp. 244 6.   [81] ESRO, Jeake Papers, FRE 5318.
[82] Ibid., FRE 5309; 5307; 5303; 5315.   [83] Ibid., passim.   [84] Ibid., FRE 5315; 5305.
[85] T. Mortimer, *Every Man His Own Broker: or A Guide to Exchange Alley* (London, 1761), pp. xi xv.
[86] GLL, MS 3041/5, ii, fos. 4 17, 22, 24 6.

indicative of the difficulties of accessing information and the problems of finding other investors with whom to trade.

The clearest information about the activities of brokers during London's first stock-market boom comes from Charles Blunt's surviving ledgers. Over a four-year period, between January 1692 and August 1695, Blunt served as intermediary for 156 individuals in relation to just under 1,500 trades in the shares of 23 different companies. It is interesting to note that Blunt was acting almost solely as an intermediary. He appeared as the counterparty in only six of the trades listed in his ledgers. During 1692, his busiest year, Blunt acted as an intermediary for 105 clients. Some traded with Blunt only once, Sir Thomas Estcourt traded through Blunt 115 times, but most of Blunt's clients dealt through him sporadically.[87]

This sporadic activity was, in great part, a result of the nature of the market. As will be seen in the following chapters, few participants traded actively and those who did were Blunt's fellow professionals. The cost of brokerage was also prohibitive. As a general rule, Thomas Bowrey paid five shillings for each £100 nominal stock traded, although the cost of more complex trades, such as time bargains or refusals, seems to have been variable.[88] Blunt charged 10s per share, or per £100 nominal in Bank, East India, Royal African and Hudson's Bay Company stock on any type of transaction and thus, for some of his clients, his services became quite costly.[89] In 1692 the average yearly brokerage bill among Blunt's clients was £14 17s; Sir Thomas Estcourt paid £251 in that year.[90]

The question of whether a broker's services were worth such a high cost is difficult to answer. It is evident that Blunt offered a good service to his clients since he was able to attract the business of some of the most prominent stock-jobbers of the period.[91] He also acted as broker to both parties to the trade in around one-third of the transactions recorded in his ledgers, suggesting that he had very good contacts in the market and was not reliant on other brokers to supply counterparties for his clients. Moreover, Blunt did not offer discounted rates to his loyal customers, in spite of the fact that some of them accumulated large annual bills. Thus he was confident of his value to his clients and evidently did not fear that they would be lured away by cheaper competitors.

It should not be doubted that, for some, establishing a close relationship with a broker could pay dividends. Blunt's clients were offered just such a golden opportunity in February 1693 when he acted as broker in the initial offering of shares in 'Certain Lead Mines and Stocks vested in

---

[87] NA, PRO, C114/165.   [88] GLL, MS 3041/5 ii, passim.   [89] NA, PRO, C114/165.
[90] Ibid.   [91] See Table 7.3, pp. 167 68.

John Lethieullier Esq., and others', more popularly known as Estcourt's Lead Mine. The initial price of the shares was £10 in February 1693 but by mid-1694 the price was being quoted by Houghton at £150.[92] Those who retained their stock realised a significant profit. It is also significant that of the twenty-two individuals listed in Blunt's ledgers as being among the initial subscribers to the mine, only four were not already regular clients.[93] Clearly, therefore, Blunt's loyal customers were offered first refusal of this lucrative opportunity.

Nevertheless, the relationship between client and broker is a complex one. The broker's loyalties are divided between the profit margins of his clients and his own desire to make money, and a broker bringing together two clients must run the risk of being accused of favouring one over the other, particularly when the outcome of a transaction is adverse. Illustrative of this dilemma is the fact that many of Blunt's clients who subscribed to Estcourt's Lead Mine were soon afterwards duped into selling options that gave away their rights to further participation in a rising market.

Given the uncertainties of dealing with brokers and the expense of paying brokerage, most investors would only have used a broker when a counterparty was not forthcoming by other means or when it was necessary to purchase information. Indeed, many of the deals recorded by Blunt were option trades, time bargains or loans backed by stock, indicating that the intermediation of a broker was found to be most useful in circumstances where the trade was complex or required negotiation.[94] It is also notable that East India Company stock and Bank stock featured barely at all in Blunt's ledgers. These much more actively traded stocks must have allowed most investors to make their own arrangements. An analysis of Blunt's profits in the period between 1692 and 1695 is also enlightening. During 1692 Blunt was paid £1,866 in brokerage, and in 1693 he received £2,329 but gross income dropped considerably in 1694 and 1695 when he was paid just £490 and £79 respectively.[95] Clearly, therefore, during the stock-market boom of the early 1690s the broker was an invaluable resource but the advent of the more easily accessible public funds and the decline of the private joint-stock company must have resulted in the decline or failure of many brokerage businesses.

---

[92] NA, PRO, C114/165; Houghton, *Collection for Improvement.*
[93] NA, PRO, C114/165.
[94] The majority of the option trades recorded in the Bank's archives were also conducted by a broker. Bank Archives, AC27/383.
[95] NA, PRO, C114/165.

Most of those who dealt with Blunt were active investors but a broker might also have been useful to the passive investor for whom maintaining a presence in the City would have been costly and difficult. Blunt numbered several women among his clients, including Mary Crawley and Sarah Wind, both of whom traded very infrequently in Linen Company stock.[96] However, given the arcane language of the market and the general distrust of speculators and stock-jobbers, it may be suggested that the passive or inexperienced investor would have eschewed the advice of market professionals in favour of seeking the counsel of friends, relations or, perhaps, an acquaintance with a connection to the market. Partial confirmation of this may be found in the Bank of England's transfer books, which record many occasions on which family members traded together. On 19 December 1699, for example, Charles Killigrew and Colonel Robert Killigrew both sold £500 Bank of England stock.[97] In March 1700 Dame Jane Smith and her daughters Jane and Sarah, all of Isleworth in Middlesex, sold a total of £1,200 Bank stock between them.[98] Frances and Grace Barnham, both spinsters from Maidstone in Kent, were among the original subscribers to the Bank of England and in March 1700 both made the decision to liquidate their holdings.[99] It would seem, in these cases, that the decision to buy and sell stock was a result of deliberation within the family.

Those acting as attorneys for individuals were often friends or relations, rather than professional brokers. Certainly professionals were instructed. Dame Mary Ashe placed her affairs in the hands of Joseph Wilson, a London goldsmith, and Dame Rebecca Atkins used the services of Phesaunt Crisp, a broker. However, Alice Spencer, a spinster resident in Hertfordshire, appointed her brother John as attorney; he acted for Alice on many occasions. Captain Henry Robinson, Commander of His Majesty's ship *Hampton Court*, put power of attorney in the hands of his wife, as did Peter Causton, a minor stock-jobber.[100] Samuel Jeake on extended visits to London in 1697 and 1699 acted for his mother-in-law and for other business associates and acquaintances in Rye and, in turn, regularly placed his own affairs in the hands of his 'loving friend' Thomas Miller.[101]

Whether networks of information were created through market professionals or friends and family there was, due to the necessity of finding someone to trust, a tendency to form relationships with the providers of

[96] Ibid.   [97] Bank Archives, AC28/1517, 2 May 1699.
[98] Ibid., AC28/1516, 5 Mar. 1700.   [99] Bank Archives, M1/1; AC28/1513, 1 Mar. 1700.
[100] Bank Archives, AC28/1513, passim.
[101] ESRO, Jeake Papers, FRE 5305, 5309, 5310, 5321; FRE 5253.

news. In some instances the very close connections developed in the financial market of the 1690s were an advantage for investors. Blunt's favoured clients were offered a golden opportunity that was unavailable to the investing public at large. However, the existence of such close social bonds within a market is also highly problematic. To ensure perfect competition, markets should be impersonal. Given the nature of the information that circulated in the early modern market and the frequent accusations of malfeasance made by contemporary commentators, it is reasonable to suggest that the social networks favoured at this time allowed, and even encouraged, the manipulation of share prices.

Summary

When creating networks of information three factors were important for the early modern investor: accessibility, trust and cost. While it is certain that all were able to access the London market, the difficulties associated with travelling to London, the barriers raised by the complex language of the market and the general distrust of brokers and stock-jobbers would have meant that many investors preferred to gather market information from friends, relatives and trusted associates. For those who chose to engage with the market more actively, information proved costly in monetary terms, and as well as in terms of time and commitment. Full information was restricted to those willing and able to make a full-time commitment to the market or those, like Sir Henry Furnese, with the resources to create their own information networks. This created a two-tiered market in which 'insiders' commanded superior access to information and thus were perhaps in a position to manipulate the market to their own ends. 'Outsiders' had to be content with acting on older, less reliable information, which must have sometimes detrimentally affected their ability to take advantage of new opportunities and often restricted their investment choices.

6   The investors

Given the very many difficulties faced by investors attempting to obtain financial information, it is reasonable to assume that investment activity was concentrated among the few who were either resident in the City or were able to afford the costs incurred when searching for relevant data. This assumption concurs with some historians' representations of the type of individuals who were willing to commit their capital to the new financial market. Cain and Hopkins, for example, described those with an involvement in the public funds as having been 'substantial bankers, merchants and landowners' most of whom lived or had a residence in London or the South East.[1] Even Dickson, who acknowledged the involvement of a wider section of society, still asserted that the public funds relied heavily upon the expertise and capital of the 'London *bourgeoisie*' and only incidentally on other classes of the community.[2] The aim of this chapter is to test those assumptions. An examination will be made of those who were involved in the capital market in 1688. The expansion of that market through the emergence of a variety of new investment opportunities will then be examined in order to quantify the number of investors who became involved in the financial market during the 1690s, and to define their social status and place of residence. Finally, an estimate of the total number of investors involved in the financial market during this period will be presented.

Facts and fiction

In the first place, however, it is necessary to discuss several issues that hinder a complete analysis of the number and type of investors involved in the financial market in the late seventeenth century. The most important issue to consider is the problem of determining the ownership of stock.

[1] P.J. Cain and A.G. Hopkins, *British Imperialism, 1688 2000* (Harlow: Longman, 2002), p. 73.
[2] Dickson, *Financial Revolution*, p. 260.

Dickson noted that ownership of public debt and equities as formally recorded in stock ledgers may be a 'fiction' due to trusts, nominee holdings and other such devices.[3] There is some evidence to suggest that this may have been so. The Bank of England's records for the period under consideration contain more than 300 transactions where stock was bought or sold by a trustee. Overall, however, those transactions involved just 162 individuals and represented a mere 2 per cent of total transactions in this period, suggesting that the use of such devices should not be exaggerated.[4] Moreover, full details of those transactions were recorded in the transfer books and there was seemingly no attempt to conceal their nature.

Examination of the stated purpose of transactions in trust also confirms Dickson's assumption that their use was not a conspiracy to obscure actual ownership.[5] Trusts were used most frequently for the benefit of those who were not in a position to manage their own affairs. Thus, in 1699, Gideon Lauberraine purchased £100 in trust for both Jaconnia and Seger Staats whose residence in Haarlem in Holland prevented them from making their own purchases.[6] Also in that year, Francis Woolley bought £100 in trust for Henry Lawrence, a minor whose father, Richard Lawrence, was recently deceased.[7] From the Bank's records it would seem that very few transactions in trust were used for other purposes. One, however, is worth noting. In December 1700, John Ward and William Burkitt purchased £200 Bank stock in trust for 'the Preacher of the Tuesday lecture in the ... town of Dedham for the time being in Perpetual Succession & to his only use and benefit'.[8] This was undoubtedly a rather novel method of showing appreciation for the town's preacher but was an interesting demonstration of how rapidly the Bank became viewed as the guardian of safe investments.

It is, of course, possible that some trust transactions went unrecorded or that stock was purchased by groups of individuals but only registered in one name. Whyman's studies highlight a number of instances where investments were registered in another's name and she noted that women, in particular, hid assets from their husbands or male guardians in an attempt to maintain a degree of financial independence.[9] The broker Charles Blunt also noted among his accounts several stockholdings held in the names of family members and business associates.[10] Nevertheless, since no stock certificates were issued at this time, stock ledgers and

---

[3] Ibid., p. 251.
[4] Bank Archives, AC28/32233; AC28/1513 22. Dickson also offers a number of examples to support this assumption. Dickson, *Financial Revolution*, p. 252.
[5] Dickson, *Financial Revolution*, p. 253.   [6] Bank Archives, AC28/1517, 11 May 1699.
[7] Ibid., 12 May 1699.   [8] Ibid., AC28/1518, 14 Dec. 1700.
[9] Whyman, *Sociability and Power*, p. 76.   [10] NA, PRO, C114/164, passim.

transfer books formed the only legally binding record of ownership. To allow an asset to be registered in another's name without any indication of joint ownership or trusteeship was, therefore, to take a significant risk.[11]

The risks involved are highlighted by the great care that was taken, most particularly by the Bank of England, to ensure that the information given in the transfer books and stock ledgers was an accurate reflection of ownership. Where groups of individuals were involved in a transaction that fact was acknowledged and all parties to the transaction signed the transfer book. Hence, when John Bryan, a grocer, and his wife, and John Frazell, a victualler, and his wife, sold £100 Bank stock in November 1696 all four were present to sign the transfer book and even the illiterate Jane Frazell made her mark.[12] The Bank of England also required trustees to return stock formally to its owner, when necessary. In February 1702, for example, Captain George Byng transferred to Wolfran Cornwall £1,100 Bank stock that Byng had previously held in trust for Cornwall's use.[13] There was no overt reason for this transaction to have passed through the transfer books other than as a formal record of the relinquishing of the trusteeship.

Companies also went to great lengths to ensure that transfers were undertaken only by the legal owners of the stock or their appointees. During the Bank's very early years wives were taken to one side by Thomas Mercer, the chief accountant, and asked to confirm that their transfer was voluntary.[14] One can only imagine that, with the husband's watchful presence on the other side of the banking hall, few women would have dared to protest that their transaction had been forced. Nevertheless, such an enquiry did afford a semblance of protection to married women.[15] The accounts of minors were also protected. On one occasion Gertrude Carew, because she was a minor, was asked to seek permission from the Court of Directors before her sale of £500 Bank stock could be completed.[16] The East India Company was also conscientious with regard to the transfer of stock. As noted above, the Company was willing to take the transfer book to the homes of the sick or elderly in order to allow proper

---

[11] Dickson noted that foreign investors, who it was alleged by contemporary commentators often used trustees to conceal their activity in English joint stock companies, would have been particularly vulnerable to unscrupulous trustees since they would have operated outside the jurisdiction of the English courts. Dickson, *Financial Revolution*, p. 253.

[12] Bank Archives, AC28/1514, 14 Oct. 1697.   [13] Ibid., AC28/1519, 4 Feb. 1702.

[14] Ibid., AC28/32233, passim.

[15] Since stock was defined as personal estate, married women could in theory retain control of their holdings. In reality, it appears that few women in this period did so.

[16] Bank Archives, AC28/1516, 28 Aug. 1699. Permission was granted and as a result of this case new procedures were instituted to ensure that counterparties were warned that they were trading with a minor and could then proceed at their own risk.

registration of a sale or purchase. Thus, although it remains important to note that the data presented below may be affected by concealed owner-ship or stock held in trust, it is not likely that such accounts will have a significant impact upon interpretation of the structure of ownership of securities.

Another issue to be considered is that of defining the geographical location of investors. Specific addresses were not often recorded in the transfer books, thus it is impossible always to be precise about the location of investors. In particular, many shareholders recorded their addresses merely as 'London'. In the instances where specific addresses can be established for those investors it is clear that 'London' referred to an address within the City, thus it has been assumed that this was generally the case. It is also possible that some investors were resident outside the capital but retained a London address for business or other purposes. However, since there is no reliable method of identifying such individuals, the address noted in the transfer books or stock ledgers is assumed to have been the primary place of residence.

Defining the socio-economic status of investors during the early mod-ern period is also problematic. Occupation or social status was often listed in transfer books or stock ledgers and this offers a method of grouping and identifying investors.[17] However, such labels must be used cautiously for a number of reasons.[18] First, occupations concerned with production and distribution were not specialised in this period, thus distinctions made between manufacturing and retailing may be regarded as some-what artificial. Moreover, an individual who defined himself as a linen draper may have been a small shopkeeper or alternatively may have commanded a much larger trade. There is unfortunately no consistent method of determining the size or value of business commanded by such

---

[17] It should be noted that occupation or status was listed with name and address as a further method of identifying investors. The Bank of England, having a large population of shareholders, was very consistent in its recording of occupations. Other companies, having a much smaller number of shareholders, were far less concerned with providing additional means of identification. Thus, occupations were seldom recorded in the Royal African Company's transfer books, although an exception was made for the three John Smiths who held stock: a silkman, a scrivener and a merchant.

[18] For a further discussion of these issues see W. A. Armstrong, 'The Use of Information about Occupation', in E. A. Wrigley, ed., *Nineteenth Century Society: Essays in the Use of Quantitative Methods for the Study of Social Data* (Cambridge University Press, 1972), pp. 191 253; Clark, *Betting on Lives*; P. J. Corfield, 'Class by Name and Number in Eighteenth Century Britain', *History*, 72 (1987), 38 61; H. Horwitz, '"The Mess of the Middle Class" Revisited: The Case of the "Big Bourgeoisie" of Augustan London', *Continuity and Change*, 2 (1987), 263 96; J. Hoppit, *Risk and Failure in English Business, 1700 1800* (Cambridge University Press, 1987), pp. 56 7.

individuals. Thus, some status groups may disguise large variations in wealth and rank.

Secondly, individual circumstances changed over time and sometimes investors were inconsistent when giving details of their status or occupation. Thomas Bowrey, for example, titled himself a merchant in his marriage contract in 1691, gave his occupation as mariner when dealing in Bank of England stock between 1695 and 1698, and described himself as a gentleman in dealings in later life.[19] Charles Blunt also varied his status, sometimes describing himself as an upholder (or upholsterer) and at other times describing himself as a gentleman.[20]

Thirdly, the title 'gentleman' was beginning to lose its traditional implication of gentle birth and idle living at this time.[21] Indeed, as Thomas Bowrey's adoption of the term implied, it was a title that was increasingly being used by professional men and wealthy merchants. There is, therefore, no simple way of identifying a rentier class. It should also be noted that during this period the distinction between rentier and professional or entrepreneur was blurred, with many individuals obtaining a living from a variety of income sources. For example, Charles Blunt combined the business of broking with a variety of fixed income investments, and an interest in property, in addition to a continuing interest in the upholstery business that had provided his living prior to the advent of the financial market.

A final problem in this regard was specific to the financial market, and concerns the difficulties associated with identifying those who were acting as brokers. Before early 1698 the term 'broker' was not used in financial records, and between 1698 and 1702 the term can only be found being applied in the Bank's transfer books. Moreover, as noted in Chapter 3, the legislation limiting the number of brokers and forcing them to register their occupation was not always strictly adhered to. Therefore, it is impossible to identify consistently all those acting as brokers. Additionally, it should be understood that a 'professional' interest in the market may have been transient or, as often seems to be the case, was interspersed with other economic activity. Jeffrey Stanes, for example, described his occupation as watchmaker but his level of activity within the financial market suggested that he was also both a broker and a stock-jobber.

Clearly, therefore, the socio-economic titles used by individuals at this time potentially disguise a rather more complex picture. Certain individuals, like Jeffrey Stanes and Charles Blunt, placed themselves somewhat

---

[19] GLL, MS 3041/9, i; Bank Archives, AC28/32233; AC28/1513 17.
[20] NA, PRO, C114/165; Bank Archives, AC28/32233; AC28/1513 22.
[21] Corfield, 'Class in Britain', 43.

arbitrarily into categories that did not necessarily accurately reflect their status or economic behaviour. Nevertheless, since there is no consistent method of identifying those who should perhaps belong to alternative status groups, all listed occupations remain as they appear in the original source.[22] The occupational labels used in the following discussion, therefore, should be viewed as revealing how individuals viewed themselves and their rank in society, rather than representing rigid socio-economic groupings. Nevertheless, notwithstanding the above-mentioned examples, there was overall a high degree of consistency in the way investors described their status or occupation. Those, like Jeffrey Stanes, with a seemingly concealed professional interest in the financial market were relatively few, and their levels of activity and impact on the market will be addressed below. Thus, this chapter will provide a far more detailed picture of the social status and economic background of those involved in the early financial market than has hitherto been available.

The expansion of the stock market

Before 1688 there were no more than fifteen joint-stock companies in England, most of which operated with a limited capital. As we have seen, prior to the stock-market boom of the early 1690s facilities for trading in stock were unsophisticated, the stock market was not yet organised nor centred upon a known place or area and, as such, stock changed hands infrequently.[23] Moreover, as Table 6.1 shows, even those stocks that were more actively traded still remained in relatively few hands.

It may also be assumed that some investors retained interests in more than one company. Transfer books and stock ledgers survive for the Royal African, Hudson's Bay and East India Companies allowing this assumption to be tested in those cases. In 1688, thirty-five of those who held stock in the Royal African Company and four of those who held stock in the Hudson's Bay Company also held stock in the East India Company. Only three individuals held stock in all three companies: Stephen Evance, William Des Bouverie and Nicholas Heyward.[24] Davies's analysis of the

---

[22] Exceptions have been made in the very few cases where the occupation for an individual was omitted in the original source, but can be inferred from other records.

[23] Davies, 'Investment in the Later Seventeenth Century', 295.

[24] IOR, H/1; NA, PRO, T70/187; NA, PRO, BH 1/465. Owing to the vagaries of late seventeenth century spelling and the failure to record social status in all cases, it is not always possible to be certain whether the same individuals were investing in more than one company. Only instances where a match can be determined with some certainty are recorded here. It is, therefore, possible that the actual figure was higher but not to any significant degree.

Table 6.1 *Main joint-stock companies of the period prior to 1688*

Company	Date established	Date at which capital/no. of shareholders recorded	Nominal capital (£s)	No. of shareholders
East India	1601	1688	739,782	511
Royal African	1672	1688	111,100	203
Hudson's Bay	1668	1672	10,500	32
White Paper	1686	1686	20,000	
Royal Lustring	1688	1692	60,000	134

Sources: IOR, L/AG/1/10/2, pp. 204 11; Davies, 'Investment in the Later Seventeenth Century', 296; Scott, *Constitution and Finance*, vol. III, pp. 471 5.

market in 1675 drew similar conclusions. At that time, one quarter of those involved in the Royal African Company were also concerned in the East India Company and no investors held shares in all three concerns. Thus, as Davies concluded, it is likely that those with little to invest concentrated on one stock, while the larger investor, instead of spreading his investment evenly, placed the bulk of his capital in his favoured stock with a small or medium-sized 'saving bet on the outsider'.[25] Nevertheless, it is clear that, although the impact of such investors was less than may have been expected, the very limited opportunities for investment were further restricted by shareholders whose interests extended across a number of companies.

Moreover, as the following analysis of holdings in the East India Company demonstrates, many shareholders accumulated large amounts of stock, thus further restricting the diversity of the financial market. Table 6.2 shows that, in 1688, 17 per cent of shareholders (87 individuals) commanded 64 per cent of the Company's capital. Indeed, the top ten investors held 23.44 per cent of the stock, and the largest shareholder at that time, Sir Josiah Child, held £50,000 stock, 6.75 per cent of the total nominal capital.[26] Interestingly, the circulation of East India Company stock in 1688 was further restricted by the fact that £35,768 was held by deceased investors.[27] Their accounts were either dormant or were held in trust for the benefit of heirs and thus were unlikely to be liquidated. Overall, therefore, this analysis indicates that contemporary complaints

[25] Davies, 'Investment in the Later Seventeenth Century', 297.
[26] The top ten investors were Sir Edward Des Bouverie, £10,615; Sir Nathanial Herne, deceased, £10,838; Richard Hutchinson, senior, £11,250; Joseph Herne, £12,333; Dame Mary Ashe, £13,500; Sir James Edwards, £14,000; Thomas Cooke, £15,000; Sir Jeremy Sambrooke, £17,850; Sir John Moore, £18,009; and Sir Josiah Child, £50,000.
[27] IOR, L/AG/1/10/2.

Table 6.2 *Investment in East India Company stock, 1688*

Amount of stockholding	No. of investors	Total amount of stock held by group	As percentage of total nominal capital
£100 or less	52	4,590	0.62
£101 £499	127	33,452	4.52
£500	68	34,000	4.60
£501 £999	55	38,466	5.20
£1,000 £1,999	110	131,657	17.80
£2,000	12	24,000	3.24
£2,001 +	87	473,617	64.02
Total	511	739,782	

Source: IOR, L/AG/1/10/2.

about the concentration of East India Company stock into fewer and fewer hands were entirely justified.

Davies also suggested that, before the Glorious Revolution, the majority of stock was in the hands of dominant social groups. With reference to the position of the Royal African Company in 1675, Davies estimated that one-fifth of the stock was owned by aristocrats, courtiers, gentlemen, lawyers and widows and found that much of the remaining stock was in the hands of the more prominent merchants.[28] Thus, Davies concluded that the majority of stock was held by the top layers of City society.[29]

The East India Company undoubtedly attracted a greater diversity of stockholders. The Company did not always record the status of stockholders in its stock ledgers but it is possible to draw some conclusions. The social status of 207 of the 511 individuals who held stock in 1688 can be determined. There were 65 women, more than double the number recorded in 1675.[30] There were 68 individuals who used the title 'esquire', 4 who described themselves as 'gentlemen' and 56 titled men. The 56 titled men held between them £215,187 stock, 29 per cent of the Company's capital. The other individuals for whom a status can be determined included a clerk, a farrier, a leatherseller, 9 physicians, a scrivener, a skinner and 2 merchants.[31] Overall, therefore, this analysis supports Davies's conclusion that the East India Company was beginning to attract an increasing number of investors from outside the business community

---

[28] Davies, 'Investment in the Later Seventeenth Century', 299.   [29] Ibid.
[30] IOR, L/AG/1/10/2; Davies, 'Investment in the Later Seventeenth Century', 300.
[31] IOR, L/AG/1/10/2.

but 'the bulk of the capital was probably throughout the [seventeenth] century in the hands of City men'.[32]

Thus, it is certain that the establishment of a great number of new companies during the early 1690s created much needed new opportunities for investment. However, it remains important to note that although the number of companies increased, like their pre-Glorious Revolution counterparts, those new concerns also operated with very limited capital and consequently few shareholders. For example, the Linen Company, established in 1690, initially issued only 340 shares.[33] The Company of Glass-Makers of London had only 120 shareholders when it was established in 1691.[34] Records for Estcourt's Lead Mine are incomplete but the transfer book shows that only 103 individuals were active in this stock between 1693 and 1695.[35]

Furthermore, given that, as noted above, a number of shareholders were active in more than one company, it must be questioned whether these opportunities were taken up by fresh capital provided by new investors or by capital provided by those with an established connection to the financial market. Since most of the stock ledgers and transfer books of the joint-stock companies set up during the early 1690s have not survived, the evidence is rather limited. However, Charles Blunt's ledgers can provide some indication of the type of individual who was active in the smaller joint-stock companies. Blunt also recorded minimal details of three initial subscriptions (for Estcourt's Lead Mine, the Orphan's Bank and for a company described in the ledgers as 'Engine'),[36] which can give some insight into the type of interest that new companies attracted. Of the 156 individuals who traded through Charles Blunt between 1692 and 1695 twenty-two (or 14 per cent) were already shareholders in either the East India Company, Royal African Company or Hudson's Bay Company in 1688. With regard to the initial subscriptions undertaken by Blunt's clients, out of a total of twenty-five transactions, only four were made by individuals who were not already actively involved in the financial market.[37] This evidence, although very limited, suggests that the new opportunities that

[32] Davies, 'Investment in the Later Seventeenth Century', 300.
[33] Scott, *Constitution and Finance*, vol. III, pp. 474 5.   [34] Ibid.
[35] NA, PRO, C114/165.
[36] Probably Captain Poyntz's engine for draining land and clearing obstructions. Poyntz's Engine was advertised in the *Collection for Improvement* in mid 1693. It was noted that anyone interested in investing in his invention could meet him 'at Exchange time, at the Marine Coffee House in Birchin Lane'. Houghton, *Collection for Improvement*, 4 Aug. 1693; Scott, *Constitution and Finance*, vol. II, p. 482.
[37] NA, PRO, C114/165.

emerged in the early 1690s did encourage new investors into the market *but* established connections remained important.

More detailed evidence to support this assumption can be found in the East India Company's capital enlargement of 1693. An additional £744,000 stock was offered at par in November of that year in order to comply with the stipulations of the new charter. The issue was over-subscribed. In spite of the fact that the existing stock was trading below par and no individual was permitted to subscribe more than £10,000, a total of £1,220,341 13s 5d was offered to the Company. According to con-temporary reports, half of the new capital offered to the Company came from new adventurers and the remainder from existing shareholders.[38] However, it must be noted that the Company encouraged favoured individuals to subscribe by offering them free options to protect against potential losses on the new stock. Thus, although the general enthusiasm with which the issue was received illustrates the interest in the East India Company as an investment opportunity, the Company retained and uti-lised the ability to determine who received stock and, as such, the capital enlargement in 1693 did little to diversify shareholdings. An examination of those who held East India Company stock in 1696 (see Table 6.3) demonstrates that little had changed in terms of the overall distribution of shares compared to 1688 (see Table 6.2 above). In 1696 the East India Company's stock was still concentrated in the hands of larger shareholders. Indeed, 15 per cent of shareholders held nearly 70 per cent of the stock. The top ten shareholders held between them £251,607, nearly 16 per cent of the stock.[39] In addition, £92,535 stock was still tied up in the Company's trust as a result of Sir Thomas Cooke's previous corrupt share dealings and a total of £71,000 (4.5 per cent of the total capital) remained in the accounts of deceased investors.

With regard to the social status of investors, there were some changes between 1688 and 1696, although it must be acknowledged that the status of proportionally fewer East India Company shareholders can be identi-fied in 1696. The status of only 390 out of 1,196 shareholders was recorded. Of those, 173 were women, a significant increase in numbers since 1688. However, in 1696 women represented only just over 14 per cent of invest-ors as opposed to 12.7 per cent in 1688 and commanded a slightly smaller percentage of the total capital, 5.88 per cent as opposed to 6.35 per cent in 1688. In 1696, there were 100 men who titled themselves 'esquire', one

---

[38] Scott, *Constitution and Finance*, vol. II, p. 159.

[39] Those ten investors were Richard Hutchinson, senior, £19,304; Dame Emma Child, £20,000; Sir Benjamin Bathurst, £20,121; Sir Peter Parravicine, £23,000; Alvaro Da Costa, £24,306; Sir Josiah Child, £26,777; Peter Henriques, Jun., £27,375; Sir William Langhorne, £28,691; Sir Jeremy Sambrooke, £29,446 and Sir John Moore £32,587.

Table 6.3 *Investment in East India Company stock, 1696*

Amount of stockholding	No. of investors	Total amount of stock held by group	As percentage of total nominal capital
£100 or less	209	13,879	0.88
£101 £499	408	103,297	6.56
£500	61	30,500	1.94
£501 £999	143	98,406	6.25
£1,000 £1,999	193	244,748	15.54
£2,000	13	26,000	1.65
£2,001 +	169	1,057,778	67.18
Totals	1,196	1,574,608	

Source: IOR, List of holders of stock, 1696, H/2 fos. 94 144.

gentleman and sixty-seven titled men among the Company's shareholders. The titled men held a total of £302,352 stock. This sum represented 19 per cent of the total capital, a reduction since 1688, but still a significant proportion.[40] A far greater selection of other occupations were recorded in 1696, most being of the middling sort.[41] However, the implication that this represented an increased diversity of shareholders must be tempered by the acknowledgement that a greater population of investors required additional means of identifying individuals. Thus, the recording of diverse occupations may very well have just been the result of diligent bookkeeping.

Indeed, an examination of Charles Blunt's clients indicates that new investment opportunities continued to be taken up chiefly by merchants and others with established connections to the City. The social status of 61 of Blunt's 156 clients can be determined. Twelve of his clients titled themselves 'esquire', there were five gentlemen and four titled men. In addition, twelve merchants, three goldsmiths and three scriveners can be identified. Those thirty-nine individuals conducted nearly 57 per cent of the recorded transactions but it should be noted that the total was dominated by John Blunt, a scrivener and Charles's cousin, who traded a total of 301 times between 1692 and 1695, and Sir Thomas Estcourt who traded 182 times. Together Blunt and Estcourt transacted 23 per cent of Blunt's business.[42] Blunt's other clients represented a cross section of society and

[40] IOR, H/2, pp. 94 144.
[41] Occupations noted in 1696 were a brewer, a clerk, a clothworker, a confectioner, a distiller, seventeen doctors, three drapers, two goldsmiths, a grocer, two haberdashers, an innholder, two leathersellers, a mercer, seven merchants, two packers, one salter, two scriveners, a silkman, a skinner and a vintner.
[42] NA, PRO, C114/165.

included four women, an apothecary (John Houghton), a captain, a colonel, a dyer, an excise officer, a glass grinder, a grocer, a haberdasher, a jeweller, five linen drapers, a mercer, an upholder, a vintner and a watchmaker.[43]

The recorded place of residence of those who were involved in the financial market offers further evidence to support the assumption that the investor base was limited in the early 1690s. Charles Blunt recorded the addresses of about one-third of his clients, all of whom resided in London.[44] The addresses of many of Blunt's remaining clients can be implied from other sources revealing that the majority resided in London, mostly within the Square Mile. Similarly, all shareholders active in Estcourt's Lead Mine who gave an address also resided in London.[45] Evidence from the larger joint-stock companies is limited since often they failed to record the addresses of their shareholders. However, of the 1,086 trades conducted in East India Company stock between June and September 1691, 95 per cent involved one or both parties who were resident in London.[46] Clearly, therefore, few outside London and its immediate environs were either able or willing to take up the new investment opportunities.

Thus, neither the stock-market boom of the early 1690s, nor the East India Company's capital enlargement in 1693 fully enabled the extension and diversification of the investor base. However, the advent of the public funds did introduce a generation of new investors to the financial market. The Million Adventure, for example, had widespread appeal. As its promoter Thomas Neale argued, 'many Thousands who only have small sums, and cannot now bring them into the Publick, [were encouraged] to engage themselves in this Fund'.[47] Two factors ensured that the other forms of public debt also encouraged a wider participation. In the first place, the funds offered substantial opportunities for investment that were not dominated by pre-existing vested interests. The Bank's capital, for example, was to be raised by a subscription that was open to all, 'Natives and Foreigners, Bodies Politick and Corporate'.[48] Moreover, the maximum initial investment was £10,000. Thus, as can be seen in Table 6.4, although 41 per cent of the total nominal capital was held in the hands of just 95 investors, the middle ranks of investors, those who held between £500 and £1,999 stock were more important to the Bank than to the East India Company. Furthermore, only twelve individuals subscribed the maximum £10,000 and thus the top twelve investors commanded just 10 per cent of the stock. Nor did any of those individuals accumulate significant quantities of stock in subsequent years. Indeed, by the end of

[43] Ibid.   [44] Ibid.   [45] Ibid.   [46] IOR, L/AG/ 14/3/2.
[47] Neale, The Profitable Adventure.   [48] Quoted in Giuseppi, Bank of England, p. 12.

Table 6.4 *Initial investment in Bank of England stock, 1694*

Amount of stockholding	No. of investors	Total amount of stock held by group	As percentage of total nominal capital
£100 or less	200	19,500	1.63
£101 £499	251	60,400	5.03
£500	368	184,000	15.33
£501 £999	61	40,050	3.34
£1,000 £1,999	197	211,100	17.59
£2,000	96	192,000	16.00
£2,001 +	95	492,950	41.08
Totals	1,268	1,200,000	

Source: Bank Archives, M1/1.

1697, four investors had liquidated their holdings entirely and only four had increased their holdings.[49]

The second factor that increased the diversity of the public creditors was the form and structure of the debt. As shown in Chapter 2, the public funds, because they were guaranteed by Act of Parliament, seemed to provide assurances to new investors. Thus, they were initially viewed as safe investments and this encouraged a wide participation. Table 6.5 demonstrates this point with regard to the Bank of England. Certainly, the upper echelons of City society commanded a good deal of the Bank's initial capital. Taken together, titled aristocrats and those who described themselves as either gentleman, esquire or merchant subscribed nearly 70 per cent of the initial £1,200,000. However, this group contained more than 600 individuals and since some committed as little as £100 or even £50, a wide variety in rank is implied. Also, no group was dominant in terms of number of investors and there were representatives from a diverse range of occupations, from Henry James, the Master of Queens' College, Cambridge who subscribed £400, and James Atkinson who described himself as a mathematician and committed £100, to Joseph Duglis, a barber who invested £100, and Thomas Smith, a chemist who made an investment of just £25.[50]

[49] The twelve and the value of their holdings in December 1697 were: King William and Mary, jointly, none; James de la Bretonnière, Esq., none; William Brownlowe, Esq., £10,000; Abraham Houblon, merchant, £11,900; Sir John Houblon, £13,225; Thomas Howard, Esq., £9,000; Matthew Humberstone, Esq., £10,000; Sir Theodore Janssen, £10,000; Thomas Mulson, Esq., none; Anthony Parsons, Esq., none; William, Earl of Portland, £19,750; Sir William Scawen, £16,075. Dickson, *Financial Revolution*, p. 257.
[50] Bank Archives, M1/1.

Table 6.5 *Social status/occupation of original subscribers to the Bank of England*[a]

	No. of subscribers	Percentage of total	Total amount subscribed	Percentage of total	Highest amount subscribed	Lowest amount subscribed
Titled aristocrats	63	4.97	176,500	14.71	10,000	500
Gentlemen	168	13.25	91,000	7.58	8,000	100
Esquires	190	14.98	301,200	25.10	10,000	100
Professionals	113	8.91	65,475	5.46	5,000	25
Merchants	201	15.85	257,000	21.42	10,000	50
Finance	9	0.71	2,500	0.21	500	100
Retailing	148	11.67	74,450	6.20	4,400	100
Manufacture	99	7.81	54,050	4.50	4,000	50
Transport	7	0.55	2,700	0.23	600	100
Agriculture	2	0.16	200	0.02	100	100
Building	6	0.47	5,800	0.48	4,000	100
Domestic service	9	0.71	3,500	0.29	1,000	100
Women	153	12.07	71,975	6.00	5,000	50
Corporate	0	0.00	0	0.00	0	0
Unknown	100	7.89	93,650	7.80	6,500	100
Totals	1,268		1,200,000			

Source: Bank Archives, M1/1.

[a] Appendix 5 provides a list of all occupations occurring in each sector in all the records used in this study.

Furthermore, comparison with the lists of those holding shares in other joint-stock enterprises suggests that the Bank drew in capital from investors new to the market. Around 45 per cent of the proprietors of Estcourt's Lead Mine also became holders of Bank stock between 1694 and 1702; the figures for the East India Company, Royal African Company and Hudson's Bay Company were approximately 30, 33 and 35 per cent respectively.[51] Even assuming that there was no overlap of investors between the trading companies, these figures imply that only around 650 of the Bank's original shareholders had prior experience of investment in a major joint-stock enterprise.

It is, however, notable that, as demonstrated in Table 6.6, the majority of the Bank's initial shareholders were still drawn from London or the surrounding areas. In part, this may have been due to the speed with which the Bank's initial subscription was taken up. The books opened on 21 June 1694 and the entire amount was subscribed by 2 July 1694, leaving little time for provincial or foreign investors to raise the funds and make the arrangements necessary for subscription. Nevertheless, activity in Bank stock remained concentrated among those who claimed to be resident in the South East. During 1695, 95 per cent of buyers and 94 per cent of sellers noted that their place of residence was in London or the surrounding areas; in 1698 the figures were 94 and 97 per cent respectively, and in 1702, 95 and 94 per cent.[52]

Table 6.6 also clearly demonstrates that there were few investors domiciled abroad among the Bank's original subscribers.[53] Similar observations have been made about the other forms of early English public

---

[51] NA, PRO, C114/165; NA, PRO, T70/187 98; NA, PRO, BH 1/465. Refer to n. 24 above.

[52] Bank Archives, AC28/32233; AC28/1513 22.

[53] There were a number of foreign names among the original subscribers to the Bank of England. These included many investors who were clearly of Dutch and Huguenot origin but who gave addresses in England. However, Clapham noted that 'most of these foreign names are of men either by law or in effect English'. Clapham, *Bank of England*, vol. I, p. 278. Crouzet concurred with this assessment and, in particular, suggested that the Huguenot and Walloon contribution to the Bank of England should not be exaggerated. F. Crouzet, 'The Huguenots and the English Financial Revolution', in P. Higonnet, D. S. Landes and H. Rosovsky, eds., *Favorites of Fortune: Technology, Growth and Economic Development since the Industrial Revolution* (Cambridge, Mass.: Harvard University Press, 1991), pp. 221 66; F. Crouzet, 'Walloons, Huguenots and the Bank of England', *Proceedings of the Huguenot Society*, vol. XXV (1990), pp. 167 78. Clapham has also noted that while there were not a significant number of Jewish subscribers to the Bank of England, by the early eighteenth century, Jewish names were well represented among the group of shareholders who held £2,000 or more stock. Clapham, *Bank of England*, vol. I, p. 279. See also J. Giuseppi, 'Sephardi Jews and the Early Years of the Bank of England', *Jewish Historical Society of England Transactions*, vol. XIX (1955 59), pp. 53 63.

Table 6.6 *Place of residence of subscribers to the Bank of England, 1694*

Place of residence	Number of subscribers	As percentage of total
London (square mile)	694	54.73
Westminster or Whitehall	189	14.91
South East	208	16.40
South West	33	2.60
East Anglia	10	0.79
Midlands	25	1.97
North of England	5	0.39
Wales	0	0.00
Scotland	0	0.00
Ireland	4	0.32
Netherlands	19	1.50
Foreign (other)	4	0.32
Unknown	77	6.07

Source: Bank Archives, M1/1.

debt. Dickson noted that there were very few foreign names among the subscribers to the tontine of 1693.[54] Thus, despite the assertions of contemporaries, it may be concluded that foreign investors were not initially confident about the prospects for the English public debt.[55] However, foreign investment in the public funds did increase during the early eighteenth century and, according to Dickson, had become significant by 1750.[56] But, during the 1690s foreign investors were few and for the most part investment in the Bank remained chiefly in the hands of those resident in the South East of England.

In spite of this, the social composition of the shareholders continued to diversify, assisted most notably in this period by the capital enlargement in 1697, which allowed government creditors to exchange their short-term debt or tallies for Bank stock. As Table 6.7 indicates, the new capital, while still deriving largely from merchants and the more elite groups, was

[54] Dickson, *Financial Revolution*, pp. 305 6.
[55] John Briscoe, for example, noted that there were 'very considerable Sums ... remitted from Foreign Parts, and paid in by Foreigners' to the Million Act in 1693. Briscoe, *Discourse on the Late Funds*, p. 23 quoted in Dickson, *Financial Revolution*, p. 304.
[56] Dickson, *Financial Revolution*, chapter 12. For further on the amount and type of foreign investment in the public debt during the eighteenth century see C. Wilson, 'Anglo Dutch Investment in Britain in the Seventeenth to Nineteenth Centuries', in Credit Communal de Belgique, *Le Dette Publique aux XVIIIe et XIXe Siècles* (Brussels: Credit Communal de Belgique, 1980); A. C. Carter, *Getting, Spending and Investing in Early Modern Times: Essays on Dutch, English and Huguenot Economic History* (Assen: Van Gorcum, 1975); E. W. Monter, 'Swiss Investment in England, 1697 1720', *Revue Internationale d'Histoire de la Banque*, 2 (1969), 285 98.

Table 6.7 *Social status/occupation of subscribers to the Bank of England, 1697*

Social status/occupation	No. of subscribers	Percentage of total	Total amount subscribed	Percentage of total	Highest amount subscribed	Lowest amount subscribed
Titled aristocrats	32	3.02	92,869	9.28	20,725	155
Gentlemen	91	8.58	80,871	8.08	5,000	125
Esquires	76	7.16	112,551	11.24	14,200	100
Professionals	47	4.43	23,963	2.39	4,025	125
Merchants	190	17.91	248,424	24.81	11,420	125
Finance	15	1.41	24,337	2.43	16,110	125
Retailing	158	14.89	152,540	15.24	12,165	125
Manufacture	134	12.63	89,658	8.96	5,625	62
Transport	36	3.39	24,590	2.46	3,375	125
Agriculture	0	0.00	0	0.00	0	0
Building	9	0.85	5,765	0.58	2,941	70
Domestic service	3	0.28	592	0.06	330	125
Women	46	4.34	27,439	2.74	2,940	125
Corporate	2	0.19	11,750	1.17	11,250	500
Unknown	222	20.92	105,822	10.57	10,050	35
Totals	1,061		1,001,171			

Source: Bank Archives, M1/6–9.

Table 6.8 *Investment in Bank stock in December 1697*

Amount of stockholding	No. of investors	Total amount of stock held by group	As percentage of total capital
£100 or less	226	21,028	0.96
£101 £499	693	174,133	7.91
£500	340	170,000	7.72
£501 £999	274	188,472	8.56
£1,000 £1,999	348	427,900	19.44
£2,000	43	86,000	3.91
£2,001 +	251	1,133,638	51.50
Totals	2175	2,201,171	

Source: Bank Archives, Dividend Books, AC27/581.

also a result of increased contributions from retailers, manufacturers and those in the transport sector. Those who subscribed their tallies to the Bank in 1697 included John Wells, an illiterate waterman from Plaistow who committed a total of £625, Benjamin Masters, a mariner from Southwark who invested £284, and Martha Tomson, a mealwoman from Horsley Down in Surrey who subscribed £250. None had any previous involvement in Bank stock and all retained their holdings into 1698. Masters even bought a further £200 stock in September 1697.[57] The list of new investors with similar profiles is extensive. Thus, at a time when the Bank was highly vulnerable, this capital enlargement, in effect, enforced a widening of its investor base and thus enforced a widening of its support.

It is also notable that, during the period under consideration here, Bank of England stock did not become concentrated among larger shareholders in the same way as East India Company stock. As Table 6.8 demonstrates, the middle ranks of investors remained important holders of Bank stock and the top ten investors held just 7.05 per cent of the stock, in contrast to the nearly 16 per cent of East India Company stock held by the top ten investors in 1696.[58]

Inadequate records make it impossible to give a full account of the social status and size of holdings of those involved in other aspects of

[57] Bank of England Archives, Bank Stock Subscription Books, 1697, M1/6 9; Bank Archives, AC28/1515 17.
[58] The top ten investors in Bank stock were Sir William Gore, £20,725; the Earl of Portland, £19,750; James Bateman, £17,595; Sir Theodore Jansenn, £17,200; Sir William Scawen, £16,075; George Doddington, £14,600; Sir John Houblon, £13,225; Gilbert Heathcote, £12,285; Abraham Houblon, £11,900; Sir Henry Furnese, £11,875. Bank Archives, AC27/581.

the public funds. However, some assumptions can be made about those who purchased Million Adventure tickets. Indeed, an examination of Samuel Jeake's actions and connections in this regard adequately demonstrates how interest in this lottery was widespread. Jeake was informed of the opportunities to be had from investment in the Million Adventure when visiting London in early 1694. On his return to Rye he convinced his mother-in-law Barbara Hartshorne to purchase tickets and also persuaded 'several of the Town of Rye to put in 20 Tickets in partnership'.[59] The Million Adventure was Jeake's first foray into the financial market and it led to his decision to invest in annuities, the Bank of England and the East India Company. Barbara Hartshorne also followed her son-in-law into government annuities and the Bank of England and it is possible that others among Jeake's associates followed suit.

Jeake's actions also highlight the use of syndicates in lottery schemes. Syndicates were a popular way of investing in lottery tickets not only because they allowed those who could not afford a whole ticket to become involved in the lotteries, but also because they allowed groups of individuals to spread their risk over a range of numbers. For these reasons many official ticket sellers and other moneyed men also purchased large numbers of tickets in order to split them and sell off portions.[60] Narcissus Luttrell's record of the prize-winners in the Million Adventure demonstrates that the use of syndicates was widespread and also indicates that tickets were purchased by a wide variety of individuals. Luttrell noted that the £1,000 main prize in this lottery went to four French Protestants, one £500 prize went to a silk throwster, another to Mr Gibbs, a stone cutter, with three partners, and another to a partnership of Mr Proctor, a stationer, and Mr Skinner, a hosier.[61] The diversity of the recorded prize-winners confirms that the desire to take advantage of the opportunities offered by the lottery was certainly not confined to a small number of merchants and the London bourgeoisie.

The establishment of the Company of Mine Adventurers also illustrates how lottery schemes could function to extend participation in the financial market. In 1694 there were just fifty-nine holders of stock in the Lead Mines of Bwlchyr Eskir Hir in the County of Cardigan.[62] The mine, although rich, was subject to flooding and in need of a great deal of investment. The company yielded little profit between 1694 and 1698, at which time Sir Humphrey Mackworth offered the Company's shareholders the chance

[59] Hunter and Gregory, *Astrological Diary*, pp. 232 8.
[60] Dickson, *Financial Revolution*, p. 497.
[61] Luttrell, *Brief Relation*, vol. III, pp. 384, 390, 393, 394.
[62] Anon., *List of … all the Partners in the Lead Mines of Bwlchyr Eskir Hir*.

to exchange their shares for bonds yielding 6 per cent and the opportunity to participate in a lottery that would yield shares in a new company. The scheme proved very popular but it also contained more than an element of fraud. Mackworth diverted funds from the Company into his own accounts and when the lottery was drawn, it was apparent that he and his friends had received many of the prize shares.[63] It is likely, therefore, that the original shareholders made a poor exchange, many of them merely swapping the unlimited potential profit of their shares for bonds that would pay no more than a 6 per cent return. However, a published list of the names of stockholders in 1700 shows that by that time there were more than 600 investors in the venture.[64] Thus, although fraudulent, the lottery did achieve a significant extension of the investor base.[65]

Lottery schemes seldom offered tradable securities as prizes. Nevertheless, the proliferation of private lottery schemes that occurred in the mid-1690s does demonstrate the widespread interest in the new forms of finance. As the foregoing discussion has implied, the opportunities created by the advent of an active stock market had been available to only a very few. However, the stock market had rapidly become the subject of popular interest. By 1693 the antics of stock-jobbers were being presented on the stage in Shadwell's *The Volunteers* and while such individuals were the subject of much criticism, the desire to share in their good fortune was undoubtedly strong. Given that the only difference noted between gaming, gambling and stock-jobbing was that stock-jobbing was the least desirable activity,[66] lotteries seemingly provided the wider public with just such an opportunity.

It is only necessary to look at the spread of the lotteries to see how far a desire for involvement in such investment opportunities had permeated through society.[67] Those who passed judgement in satirical verse

---

[63] Scott, *Constitution and Finance*, vol. II, p. 447. Also see Anon., *List of the Fortunate Adventurers in the Mine Adventure*, which shows that of the sixty four shares drawn on 18 March 1699 Mackworth received four shares for himself, and a further four in partnership with Thomas Minshull, and Bulkeley Mackworth Esq. received two shares.

[64] Anon., *List of all the Adventurers in the Mine Adventure*.

[65] Scott notes that although the project was riddled with fraud, share prices remained steady into the early eighteenth century and blank lottery tickets continued to be traded. By 1707, however, the Company's fraudulent practices and the shortcomings of the mine were exposed. After an investigation by Parliament the Company was restructured and limped on into the late eighteenth century when it was amalgamated with the undertaking that held the charter for the Mineral and Battery Works. For a detailed history of the Company see Scott, *Constitution and Finance*, vol. II, pp. 443 58.

[66] Anon, *Plain Dealing*, p. 6. For similar sentiments see Saunders, *Fortunatus's Looking Glass*, p. 1.

[67] In the Netherlands, too, lotteries encouraged people from 'all kinds of conditions and ranks ... to procure as many tickets as they could'. Schama, *Embarrassment of Riches*, p. 309.

Table 6.9 *Details of selected private lotteries*

Year	Lottery	Main prize	Price of tickets	No. of tickets offered for sale
1693	Undertaking Profitable to the Fortunate	£3,000	10s	50,000
1694	Profitable Adventure to the Fortunate	£4,000	20s	50,000
1694	Double Chance lottery	£5,000	20s	50,000
1695	Good Luck to the Fortunate	£1,000	20s	40,000
1695	The Unparallel'd Adventure	£1,000	20s	21,000
1698	The Honourable Undertaking	£500	12d	90,000
1698	The Ladies Invention	£1,000	6d	500,000
1698	The Wheel of Fortune	£1,000	1d	1,650,000
1698	The Honest Proposal	£1,000	2s	40,000
1699	The Fortunate Chance	£1,000	3d	800,000
1699	The New Wheel of Fortune	£2,000	2d	950,000
Total				4,241,000

Sources: London Gazette, 1693 94; Houghton, Collection for Improvement, 1693 99; Post Boy, 1695 99; Post Man, 1695 99.

commented consistently on the social mix of the crowds who watched the lottery draws, noting that they comprised the highest and the lowest, all with the same dream of winning the main prize. The anonymous author of one pamphlet wrote of 'Ermine and Vermine, Rags and Scarlets, / Promiscuous all, both Lords and Varlets'.[68] And, as Table 6.9 demonstrates, very many lottery tickets were offered for sale at this time, some priced as low as a penny a ticket, suggesting an extremely widespread interest in such schemes.

Additionally, many promoters of the smaller lotteries that followed on from the success of the Million Adventure offered their tickets for sale through a wide distribution network that included a number of provincial towns. The organisers of the Fortunate Chance lottery, for example, placed books of tickets 'in most of the Noted Towns in England'.[69] Equally, Thomas Neale's second 'Profitable Adventure' listed, in addition to twenty-two London sellers, a total of ten provincial towns where tickets could be bought. They ranged from Newcastle in the north east of England to Chester in the north west and Exeter and Bristol in the south west.[70] Many provincial towns also set up their own lotteries. Epsom advertised a

[68] Anon., *Diluvium Lachrymarum: A Review of the Fortunate and Unfortunate Adventurers* (London, 1694), p. 3; for further examples of the type of adventurer represented by contemporary commentators see Anon., *Elegaick Essay*; Anon., *Characters of Gentlemen that have put into the Ladies Invention* (London, 1695).
[69] *Post Boy*, 18 21 Feb. 1699. [70] *London Gazette*, Jul. and Aug. 1694, passim.

lottery in 1695 and placed 40,000 tickets on sale at a cost of five shillings each. The first prize was £200.[71] The 'City of Chichester' held a lottery in the same year, as did Colchester in 1699.[72] Many provincial areas offered prizes in lots of land, with the York lottery in 1699 offering as its main prize the city's largest, best and most convenient inn.[73] Thus, while many of those who invested in equity and debt instruments during the 1690s belonged to the elites of seventeenth-century society and were chiefly resident in the South East, the widespread interest in lottery schemes suggests a geographically and socially diverse participation in the financial revolution.

Counting the investors

Incomplete records make it impossible to present a precise account of the total numbers of those involved in the financial revolution. But some assumptions can be made about the numbers of those involved in the main instruments of the public funds and the major joint-stock companies. Basing his estimate on an examination of the subscriptions to the tontine loan and life annuities of 1693 and the Bank of England in 1694, Dickson concluded that public creditors in this period numbered around 5,000.[74] However, owing to a gap in the record of the tontine loan Dickson was forced to make an estimate of the overlap between the subscribers to these two funds. His conclusion of an 8 per cent overlap is questionable given the far higher correlation between the Bank's proprietors and proprietors in other stocks.[75] As noted above, the overlap between stockholders in the main trading companies and those public creditors who held Bank of England stock was around one-third. This must lead to the conclusion that far fewer public creditors were created by combined expedients of the Bank, the tontine and the sale of annuities. A closer estimate would be around 4,000 individuals holding either annuities or Bank stock or both in late 1694, although the number of the Bank's proprietors did increase over the period under consideration, rising from 1,268 in 1694 to more than 1,900 in 1702, principally as a result of the capital enlargement of 1697. Additionally, in 1698 shares in the New East India Company were taken up by more than 1,400 individuals.[76] Furthermore, Dickson completely disregarded the large numbers of

[71] *Post Boy*, 4 6 Jul. 1695.
[72] *Post Boy*, 3 5 Oct. 1695; *Flying Post*, 30 Mar. 1 Apr. 1699.
[73] *Flying Post*, 26 28 Jan. 1699.   [74] Dickson, *Financial Revolution*, p. 254.   [75] Ibid.
[76] Bank of England Archives, Dividend Books, AC27/581 2; India Office Records, New East India Company, Subscription Book, A/1/54.

individuals who purchased and held Million Adventure tickets. The issue of 100,000 lottery tickets at £10 each and the widespread purchase of tickets by syndicates allowed investors of more limited means access to the public funds, and undoubtedly created substantial numbers of new public creditors. Thus, by 1698 the number of those holding some form of government debt was significantly greater than 5,000.

As noted above, many private joint-stock companies had a very small number of proprietors and, of course, many of those companies had either disappeared or ceased to be actively traded by 1698. Thus, while there may have been several thousand private shareholders involved in the financial market in the early 1690s, by the beginning of the eighteenth century that figure was very much reduced. Indeed, given the overlap noted above, it is likely that the proprietorship of the private joint-stock companies would have added no more than 1,500 to the total number of those involved in the financial market at this time. Overall, therefore, there were around 4,000–5,000 investors involved in the major elements of the public funds and the main joint-stock companies but many thousands more on the periphery retaining Million Adventure tickets.

This represented a very significant increase in the number of investors since 1688, when there were no more than 1,000 individuals holding actively traded stock (see Table 6.1). It must also be asserted that the figures presented here represent snapshots of the numbers of investors at given points in the year, usually when dividend lists were compiled. Thus, investors who held their stock for only a short time or were not holders of stock at the time when lists were compiled are excluded from this assessment. It is interesting to note that between 1694 and 1702, while the total number of holders of Bank stock did not generally exceed 2,000 at any one time, the records show that 16,214 transactions took place among more than 3,800 individuals.[77] It is nevertheless necessary to note that these figures still represented a very small proportion of England's overall population, which was estimated to be approximately 5,000,000 at the end of the seventeenth century.[78] Indeed, even among Londoners, the proportion of those involved in the financial market was very small.[79]

[77] Bank Archives, AC28/32233; AC28/1513 22. Similarly, Carlos, Key and Dupree show that during the first thirty years of the Royal African Company's history there were 4,424 transactions among 1,200 different investors despite the fact that at any one point stock was generally held by around 200 people. Carlos et al., 'Learning and Stock Market Institutions', 325.

[78] Hoppit, Land of Liberty?, p. 52; Holmes, Making of a Great Power, pp. 44 8.

[79] The population of London has been estimated to have been approximately 575,000 by the end of the seventeenth century. Wrigley, 'Simple Model', p. 215; V. J. Harding, 'The Population of London, 1550 1750: A Review of the Published Evidence', London Journal, 15 (1990), 111 28.

And, as will be shown in the next chapter, among this small population of investors, there were few who were actively involved in the financial market. A large number of investors in the major stocks were inactive and the vast majority of active investors traded very infrequently. In fact, the stock market of the 1690s was dominated by twenty or so extremely active individuals, a fact that raises important questions about the nature and effectiveness of that market.

Conclusion

The assumption of a small market is largely borne out by the evidence presented here. Analysis of the market in the early 1690s also supports Dickson's assertion of the dominance of the 'London *bourgeoisie*'. Furthermore, throughout the period under review it was possible for an extremely small number of active investors to dominate trading activity. Nevertheless, it is clear that the advent of the public funds offered new opportunities to a diverse range of investors. In particular, the Million Adventure encouraged many thousands to subscribe to the public funds. It is also necessary to notice those who were on the periphery of the new financial market. Those who played the many lotteries that abounded during the 1690s were emulating their richer counterparts who traded in equities and debt instruments. Indeed, the motives of the two groups were not dissimilar. They shared a desire to experience the excitement and share in the new-found wealth that was potentially offered by the new financial market. Thus, while the financial market may have been dominated by a relatively small number of stock-jobbers, few in England were beyond the reach of the interest and excitement generated by the new forms of finance.

7   Stock-jobbing the market

John Houghton defined stock-jobbers as those who aimed to 'sell to one, and buy of another different Shares of the same Stock for different prices, and so make Advantages'.[1] In other words, stock-jobbers traded with a view to realising short-term profit rather than long-term investment income. Consequently, in the eyes of most contemporaries, stock-jobbers performed no useful function within the economy and, as such, they were generally held in low esteem. Ned Ward's critique was detailed and typical:

[The stock jobber] is a compound of knave, fool, shopkeeper, merchant, and gentleman. His whole business is tricking. When he cheats another he's a knave; when he suffers himself to be outwitted he's a fool. He most commonly keeps a visible trade going, and with whatsoever he gets in his shop he makes himself a domestic merchant upon Change by turning stock adventurer ... He's a kind of speculum wherein you may behold the passions of mankind and the vanity of human life. Today he laughs, tomorrow he grins; is the third day mad, and always labours under those twin passions, hope and fear, rising one day, and falling the next, like mercury in a weather glass ... He's a man whose great ambition is to ride over others, in order to which, he resolves to win the horse, or lose the saddle.[2]

This chapter will look beyond such descriptions. It will show that stock-jobbers were generally astute businessmen, that their actions were essential to the maintenance of liquidity in the early financial market and that while they had the power to manipulate the share price of smaller companies, their adverse influence did not usually extend to larger joint-stocks.

Who were the stock-jobbers

Although many in late seventeenth-century England regarded all those involved in the financial market as deceitful and immoral, stock-jobbers, as defined by John Houghton, were relatively few in number. Indeed, while there were approximately 1,500 holders of Bank of England shares during 1695, only twenty people traded more than twenty times during

---

[1] Houghton, *Collection for Improvement*, 13 Jul. 1694.   [2] Ward, *London Spy*, p. 298.

Table 7.1 *Bank of England stockholders grouped by their level of activity,*
1695 and 1700

	1695		1700	
Level of activity	No. of investors	No. of transactions	No. of investors	No. of transactions
Inactive	c. 750	0	c. 380	0
Trading once a year	354	354	715	715
Trading 2 5 times	277	807	588	1,579
Trading 6 10 times	69	510	127	950
Trading 11 20 times	27	394	69	1,032
Trading 21 50 times	17	428	17	466
Trading 51 + times	3	249	7	1326

Source: Bank Archives, AC28/3233; AC28/1513 15; AC28/1517 19.

the year. More than half the holders of Bank shares did not trade at all
and, as Table 7.1 shows, 85 per cent of those who did traded fewer than
five times during 1695. The pattern was similar in 1700, a year that saw a
great deal of activity in the financial market and particularly in Bank stock.
During that year the proportion of active investors was greater; Bank stock
was held by approximately 1,900 individuals and 1,523 were active. But
once again, around 85 per cent of active individuals traded less than five
times, just twenty-four people traded more than twenty times and activity
was actually dominated in that year by just one man, William Sheppard.[3]
Sheppard, a goldsmith, was the recorded purchaser on 275 transactions
and the seller on 368 transactions. Thus, he was involved in more than
21 per cent of all transactions conducted in that year.[4] This was not typical
of activity in Bank stock but it does demonstrate the ease with which one
person could dominate activity within a particular company.

The East India Company's transfer books do not survive in sufficient
numbers to permit a meaningful examination of trading activity in that
company. However, as Table 7.2 shows, the domination of a few investors
was similarly evident in the smaller joint-stock companies. It is clear,
therefore, that in a market that encompassed thousands of transactions a

[3] Ann Carlos and Larry Neal's study of activity in Bank of England stock during 1720
reached very similar conclusions. Carlos and Neal found that 58 per cent of all sellers and
purchasers entered the market only once during the year and that just fifteen individuals
traded more than thirty times during the year. Carlos and Neal, 'Micro Foundations of the
Early London Capital Market', 511 12.
[4] Bank Archives, AC28/3233; AC28/1513 22.

Table 7.2 *Traders in Estcourt's Lead Mine and Hudson's Bay Company stock grouped by their level of activity, 1693*

	Estcourt's Lead Mine		Hudson's Bay Company	
Level of activity	No. of investors	No. of transactions	No. of investors	No. of transactions
Trading once a year	27	27	26	26
Trading 2 5 times	33	89	32	90
Trading 6 10 times	1	8	2	17
Trading 11 20 times	5	74	2	37

Source: PRO, C114/165; NA, PRO, BH 1/465.

year, there were no more than a few dozen individuals who traded often enough to deserve the title stock-jobber.

Contemporary opinion held that such men (there were no female stock-jobbers during the 1690s) emerged from the lower orders of society. Daniel Defoe compiled 'a black List of 57 persons, who within this ten years past have rais'd themselves to vast Estates, most of them from mechanick and some from broken and desperate Fortunes'.[5] Charles Davenant's fictional stock-jobber Tom Double claimed to have secured a fortune of £50,000 in spite of not having 'Shoes to my Feet' fourteen years earlier.[6] Some historians have followed this lead, depicting the early financial market as a 'riot of social fluidity'.[7] And this was partly true. From the mid-1690s there was a growing social diversity among investors. This is neatly illustrated by a transaction that took place in January 1700 when John Warren, a carpenter from London sold £500 Bank stock to John, Lord Lawarr.[8] Yet, although the financial market of the 1690s might have allowed a carpenter to trade with a lord on equal terms, there remains little evidence to suggest that men like Warren could make money stock-jobbing. Indeed, tales of men without means making great fortunes were probably more a reflection of the unease with which the financial market was regarded than an expression of the realities of trading in the late seventeenth century.

All evidence indicates that during the 1690s it was necessary to have money in order to make money in the financial market. As we shall see below, large movements in share prices were rare, thus substantial holdings would have been needed to create good regular profits. The jobber with only £100 to invest would have waited a long time to make his

---

[5] Defoe, *Villainy of Stock Jobbers*, p. 26.   [6] Davenant, *Modern Whig*, p. 15.
[7] Stewart, *Rise of Public Science*, p. 144.   [8] Bank Archives, AC28/1517, 9 Jan. 1700.

fortune. And, in spite of the increasing affluence of London society at the end of the seventeenth century, Lindert's analysis of the values of early modern personal estates suggests that those with large sums to commit to the financial market must have come from the upper echelons of the higher-status groups.[9] Moreover, as Brewer argues of a later period, it is probable that the real money was to be made in public finance rather than in the stock market,[10] and public finance during the late seventeenth century carried great risks, often necessitated a substantial initial capital outlay, and required established personal connections with government or its friends and an existing reputation in the City.[11]

Even where there were opportunities for making money from the financial market without a high initial capital outlay being required, connections and reputation were important. For example, trading in derivatives could be accomplished relatively cheaply but required the negotiation of complex contracts. Those without reputation and personal contacts would have had some difficulty in negotiating such agreements. And Charles Blunt's brokerage business, which as we have seen offered him a substantial income for no capital outlay and little risk, was successful chiefly because of the constant patronage of Sir Thomas Estcourt and John Blunt.

A further indication of the difficulties of making a living from trading in shares was that, as Ned Ward quite rightly suggested, the typical stock-jobber was not concerned solely with the financial market. Most had other occupations and only jobbed sporadically. Indeed, we find very few stock-jobbers appearing in the transfer books week after week and year after year. The 'other lives' of the successful jobber are important for other reasons too. First, they indicate that, even for the stock-jobber, maintaining a good reputation was important at least in some aspect of their lives. For someone like Gabriel Glover, who stock-jobbed as well as carrying on business as a linen draper, acquiring a reputation for dishonesty in one aspect of his working life must have detrimentally affected other elements of his business. Thus, although many contemporaries imagined that stock-jobbers were constantly chasing opportunities to defraud investors, in reality it is probable that most were as careful of their reputation for honesty and creditworthiness as all other businessmen

---

[9] P. H. Lindert, 'Unequal English Wealth since 1670', *Journal of Political Economy*, 94 (1986), 1136.

[10] Brewer, *Sinews of Power*, p. 209.

[11] For the careers of some prominent public financiers see C. Clay, *Public Finance and Private Wealth: The Career of Sir Stephen Fox, 1627 1716* (Oxford: Clarendon Press, 1978) and G. O. Nichols, 'Intermediaries and the Development of English Government Borrowing: The Case of Sir John James and Major Robert Huntington', *Business History*, 29 (1987), 27 46.

and women of the early modern period. Secondly, the other occupations noted show us that the successful stock-jobber generally already possessed skills and knowledge relevant to active share trading.

Some jobbers, of course, had a background in finance and thus active trading in equity and debt instruments was a natural progression of their existing business and a new opportunity to exploit their skills. The most prominent stock-jobber of the period, for example, was the gold-smith, William Sheppard. The son of a Berkshire yeoman, Sheppard had been apprenticed to the prominent goldsmith John Sweetapple in 1678. Sweetapple had a long-standing involvement in share-trading so undoubtedly Sheppard gained experience watching and perhaps acting for his master. After completing his apprenticeship, Sheppard set up in business for himself and in 1690 began to take on his own apprentices.[12] By the beginning of the stock-market boom, therefore, Sheppard was already an active trader in shares and well placed to become the dominant presence in London's first financial market.

Merchants, particularly those whose business was adversely affected by the Nine Years' War, also found it easy to adapt to the demands of the new financial market.[13] As we have seen, relevant financial information circu-lated in and around the Royal Exchange, hence in spaces and networks that were familiar to them. Equally, managing the uncertainty caused by natural disasters and political realignments, understanding exchange rate and credit risk and making judgements about investment potential was already part of the merchant's daily life.[14] It is hardly surprising, therefore, to find that between 1694 and 1702 more than 20 per cent of sales and purchases in Bank of England stock were conducted by those describing themselves as merchants.[15] The surviving East India Company transfer books also commonly show between 35 and 45 per cent of sales and purchases being conducted by merchants.[16] And as Table 7.3 shows, some merchants also became very active stock-jobbers.

Although many jobbers came from the financial and mercantile com-munities, it is also possible to identify individuals from a variety of other professions whose patterns of investment behaviour indicated that they were stock-jobbing. They included a linen draper, a salter, a gunpowder maker, a watchmaker and a pewterer. Outwardly, the presence of such people among lists of stock-jobbers indicates that it was possible for

[12] Sheppard's first apprentice was his brother, John. Goldsmiths' Company Records, Goldsmiths' Hall, London, Apprenticeship Records, vol. III (1670 90), fo. 81.
[13] For an in depth discussion of merchants' involvement with the financial market see Jones, *War and Economy*.
[14] Grassby, *Business Community*, p. 91.   [15] Bank Archives, AC28/32233; AC28/1513 22.
[16] IOR, L/AG/14/3/2 6.

jobbers without existing relevant skills to be successful. An alternative and perhaps more plausible explanation is that, as Peter Earle suggests, many such occupations had benefited greatly from the growth of inland trade and the commercial revolution of the late seventeenth century.[17] Hence the affluent linen draper or salter might be compared in wealth and knowledge to the average overseas merchant and it is probable that their involvement in the financial market was similarly guided by the skills and experience gained in the course of their everyday occupations.

Thus, the typical stock-jobber was far removed from Davenant's Tom Double. He was likely to have been already affluent, with contacts in the financial world and a good reputation among his fellows and, although stock-jobbing may have been a new departure for him, his success was firmly based on an ability to adapt and utilise existing skills and knowledge.

What did stock-jobbers do?

Table 7.3 shows the range of investment instruments used by the top ten most active stock-jobbers in each of the main joint-stock companies. Each stock-jobber's position in terms of numbers of transactions undertaken is shown by a number; thus, William Sheppard was the most active trader in all four main joint-stock companies. A cross in one of the other columns indicates additional activity in that particular investment opportunity.

Not all stock-jobbers active during the 1690s appear in the table. Positions were calculated by taking the total number of trades over the entire period under consideration (1688–1702 in the case of the East India, Hudson's Bay and Royal African Companies, and 1694–1702 in the case of the Bank of England). Thus, Table 7.3 shows stock-jobbers who were active and achieved a degree of longevity. It excludes others such as the merchant John Hester, who traded Bank stock very enthusiastically during 1696 but was less active in subsequent years, and Jeffrey Stanes, a watch-maker, who was particularly active during 1697 across a range of instruments but did not stock-job consistently over the period.[18] Nevertheless, overall the table does provide a good understanding of the range and type of activity undertaken by the typical stock-jobber during the 1690s.

It is immediately evident that most stock-jobbers were active over a broad range of investment instruments: short-term government debt, annuities, Million Adventure tickets, the shares of the main moneyed companies and, if an individual appeared in Charles Blunt's ledgers

---

[17] Earle, 'Economy of London'.
[18] Bank Archives, AC28/32233; AC28/1513 22, passim.

Table 7.3 *Most prominent stock-jobbers in the main joint-stock companies, 1688–1702*

Surname	First name	Occupation/status	Active in BOE	Tallies in BOE*	Active in EIC	New EIC subscription	Active in RAC	Active in HBC	Blunt's client	Active in Estcourt's Lead Mine	Million Bk cash subs**	Million Bk lottery subs	Million Bk annuity subs
Barrow	Moses	Merchant	3			X							
Bowater	Richard	Mercer					X	X				X	X
Bowles	Phineas	Merchant	6	X	X		4	X	X	X		X	X
Crisp	Phesaunt	Merchant	2		3				X	X			
Cudworth	Samuel	Merchant			X						X		
Dering, Sir	Edward	Knight			X		X	3	X	X			
Des Bouverie	William	Esq.	X		X			5					
Doughty	Edmond	Merchant	X		6		6	X					
Elwick	John	Mercer			X			X	X	X			
English	John	Salter	X		4		10		X				
Evance, Sir	Stephen	Knight			X		X	6					
Genew	William	Esq.			X		X	9					
Glover	Gabriel	Linen draper	X	X	9		X	X	X	X			
Hall	Urban	Merchant	X	X	X		9	X	X	X			X
Hatsell	Laurence	Scrivener			X		2		X		X		
Henriques	Peter, Junior	Merchant	9		10		X						
Hopkins	John	Merchant	5	X	X		X						
Howard	Matthew	Merchant	X	X	X		3	X					
Hudson	Peter	Gunpowder maker			X		X	10	X				
Jansenn, Sir	Theodore	Knight	8	X		X							
Jarvis	George	Merchant	X		8		5				X		
Lancashire	Robert	Merchant	X	X	X		X	7			X		
Levy	Benjamin	Merchant			X		X		X				
Monger	Peter	Goldsmith	4		7		X		X		X		

Table 7.3 (*cont.*)

Surname	First name	Occupation/ status	Active in BOE	Tallies in BOE*	Active in EIC	New EIC subscription	Active in RAC	Active in HBC	Blunt's client	Active in Estcourt's Lead Mine	Million Bk cash subs**	Million Bk lottery subs	Million Bk annuity subs
Nunes	Isaac Fernandes	Merchant	7		X								
Ongley	Samuel	Merchant taylor	X	X	5		X	X				X	X
Perry	John	Esq.	X		X		X	4					
Quessenbrough	Samuel	Pewterer	X		2								
Sheppard	William	Goldsmith	1	X	1	X	1	1	X	X		X	X
Smith	John	Scrivener				X	8	2					
Storey	Samuel	Not known			X	X	7	8	X				
Sweetapple	John	Goldsmith				X							
Torriano	Charles	Merchant	10					X					

Sources: Bank Archives, AC 28/32233; AC28/1513–1522; AC27/382; IOR, L/AG/14/3/2–6; IOR, A/1/54; NA, PRO, T70/187–98; NA, PRO, A43/1–2; NA, PRO, C114/164–5; NA, PRO, C114/16.

*Indicates that the individual subscribed tallies in the Bank of England's engraftment of 1697. A cross in this column, therefore, indicates investment in the Bank of England and holdings of the government's short-term debt.

**It was possible to subscribe to the Million Bank using cash, Million Adventure tickets and annuities. Thus, a subscription in either lottery tickets or annuities implies activity in the Bank itself and in those aspects of government debt.

it implies he had also traded in the shares of many smaller joint-stock companies active during the early 1690s and in derivative instruments. There were some exceptions to the pattern of broad-based activity. Samuel Quessenborough, a pewterer, and John English, a salter, were very active in the East India Company, but had a limited involvement in other stocks. Moses Barrow chiefly traded in Bank shares. But overall there was no appreciable pattern of specialisation.

Establishing the reasons for these patterns of activity is difficult. Because of the distrust that surrounded the early financial market, contemporary writers do not give us a true understanding of what stock-jobbers did. Analysis is further complicated by the imprecise language used during the 1690s. For those contemporaries who analysed the financial market the label 'stock-jobber' encompassed functions and actions that today we would define as either broking, speculating or market making and indeed the term was sometimes applied to those with no more than a passing interest in the market.

Some financial historians have accepted this lack of distinction without question. Carlos, Key and Dupree, for example, attempt to rehabilitate the stock-jobber by suggesting that they were in fact acting as brokers.[19] Morgan and Thomas also argued that there was no distinction between broker and jobber in the early modern financial market.[20] And there is some evidence to support this view. A number of the stock-jobbers listed in Table 7.3 appeared as either broker or attorney in sources that recorded such information. Gabriel Glover, for example, acted for a number of people subscribing to the Million Bank, as did Benjamin Levy.[21] And four of those appearing in the table registered themselves as sworn brokers when new legislation was introduced in 1697.[22] Yet, we should not automatically assume that stock-jobbing was the same as broking. Contemporaries may have used the same label for the two individuals but they certainly saw a distinction between the two functions. Notably, the legislation passed in 1697 made it very clear that brokers were paid a commission for bringing two parties with complementary needs together. Consequently, those who registered as sworn brokers risked prosecution by the City authorities if they were found to be dealing for themselves.[23] Clearly that rule was not always strictly adhered to but it is interesting to

---

[19] Carlos *et al.*, 'Learning and Stock Market Institutions', 340 1.
[20] Morgan and Thomas, *Stock Exchange*, p. 21.
[21] NA, PRO, List of subscriptions to the Million Bank, C114/16, *passim*.
[22] They were Moses Barrow, Phesaunt Crisp, Benjamin Levy and Charles Torriano. London Metropolitan Archives, Index to brokers' bonds, COL/BR/02/074 5; An alphabetical list of 100 brokers admitted by the Court of Aldermen, COL/BR/03/01/009.
[23] LMA, COL/BR/09/006.

note that after 1698 only a few of those who described themselves as brokers in the Bank of England's transfer books traded regularly enough to be also described as stock-jobbers. Equally, Charles Blunt, the one late seventeenth-century broker whose trading behaviour can be examined fully, acted almost exclusively as a middleman. Hence Blunt's name appears very infrequently in company transfer books and ledgers. Moreover, his accounts show him to have been extremely cautious in his approach to personal investment and thus he was unlikely to have been willing to assume even a short-term risk by taking on a customer's position.

Stock-jobbers, therefore, were not just acting as middlemen. Even if their activity was customer-driven at the outset, stock-jobbers accepted the risk of taking on a position without the immediate prospect of off-setting the trade. Because of the gap between purchase and sale, their profits were derived not from brokerage fees but from the differential between bid and offered prices and thus their chief concerns were whether the price at which they bought or sold was sufficient either to yield an immediate profit or to offer protection until the position could be offset, or that a specific transaction made a positive contribution to a longer-term speculative position. In order to accomplish any of these goals, stock-jobbers undoubtedly at times resorted to the exploitation of naïve investors, something that brokers could not have done if they wanted to ensure a long-lasting relationship with their clients. Broking and stock-jobbing, therefore, were not entirely compatible functions.

That stock-jobbing involved speculation in equities and debt instruments is not in dispute. Aside from repeated contemporary accusations of such behaviour, stock ledgers reveal significant and sometimes prolonged accumulations of shares in the accounts of most stock-jobbers and evidence will be presented below to confirm that manipulation of share prices also occurred. Yet, we should also be aware that while there were many opportunities to manipulate stocks or take advantage of pricing anomalies, the practicalities of trading in the early modern market often would have prevented exploitation of those opportunities. In a scattered market jobbers would sometimes have been in the wrong place at an opportune moment. Even for those in the right place, finding an uninformed or naïve investor to exploit would have presented problems. High transaction costs also limited the potential profitability of speculative positions and restricted the ability to hold a position within a moving market.[24]

---

[24] The relatively high cost attached to the transfer of stock during this period should be added to these expenses. Transfers were subject to a stamp duty of 6d from mid 1694 and the Bank of England, at least, charged an administration fee of 5s for each transaction. Bank Archives, G7/1, 15 Dec. 1694.

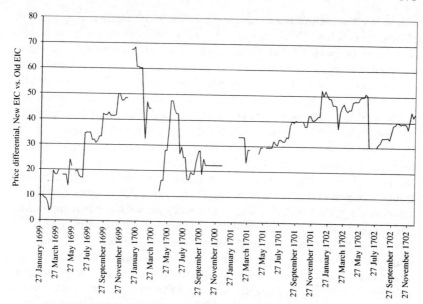

7.1 Spread between New and Old East India Company stock prices, 1699 1702

Source: Houghton, *Collection for Improvement*.

Prices exclude dividends and, as noted in Chapter 4, Houghton's prices for the early part of 1701 must be regarded as inaccurate.

Equally, price spreads were wide, reducing the profitability of any strategy and sometimes necessitating a drawn-out process of negotiation before a deal could be agreed. Moreover, since the use of a broker would often have been necessary, the jobber would have had to chance giving away a strategy with the risk that it might then be communicated to others thus eliminating his price advantage.

Most importantly, arbitrage in this market was almost impossible. There were very few *effective* substitutes for any stocks since most sectors of the economy were insufficiently broad to support more than one or two medium-sized or large enterprises. Even structurally similar enterprises, such as the Million Bank and the Bank of England, and the Old and New East India Companies, failed to provide good foils for one another. Indeed, as Figure 7.1 indicates, the link between the Old and New East India Companies, during the period under review was highly unstable.

The two East India Companies pursued the same business under broadly the same circumstances. They were structurally similar. Although the New

Company was technically a regulated company, members could, and did, choose to combine their trading rights in order to pursue joint ventures. The two companies faced similar risks. And the possibility of a union between the two was raised almost as soon as the New Company was established.[25] There were, of course, factors that stood in the way of a successful conclusion to union negotiations. One commentator noted the prospect that compensation might be demanded of the New Company for the wars against the Mogul empire conducted by the Old Company during the 1680s. He also worried that the New Company might be held responsible for the debts of the Old.[26] Nevertheless, negotiations for a union did proceed throughout the period under review. It is, however, clear that public opinion remained unconvinced. In particular, Figure 7.1 shows no increase in the stability of the price spread between the two companies and no significant convergence of prices. Thus, no jobber or investor could have sought to manage risk in one company using shares, options or time bargains in the other. And, given that the link between the two most structurally similar enterprises of this period was so volatile, it is questionable whether the arbitrage of any anomalies that occurred in debt or equity securities would have been feasible.[27] Those jobbers who sought to make profits out of other people's naïvety, inertia or lack of information were, therefore, seldom taking hedged, controllable risk.

In spite of contemporary fears, therefore, the practicalities of trading in the early modern market limited the damage that could be done by the duplicitous stock-jobber. Furthermore, with the benefit of hindsight, it is possible to argue that stock-jobbing activity in fact benefited the market because it added liquidity and served as a rudimentary market-making function. As Grossman and Miller explain, the market-making function is a necessary one because of 'imperfect synchronization'.[28] In other words market-making is necessary because buyers and sellers do not arrive in the market at the same time. A seller, for example, might arrive in the market willing to sell at the prevailing price but, in the absence of market-makers, would be forced to wait until potential buyers had learned of the offer, had a chance to come to the market and had located the potential seller. Such a delay naturally carries the risk that in the intervening period the price

---

[25] The New Company signalled its willingness to enter into a union as early as 27 January 1699. IOR, B/42, 27 Jan. 1699.

[26] Anon., *Letter From a Lawyer*, p. 7.

[27] It has been argued that, even in modern markets, arbitrage carries too many risks to function effectively to restore equilibrium in financial markets. See, for example, A. Shleifer and R. W. Vishny, 'The Limits of Arbitrage', *The Journal of Finance*, 52 (1997), 35 55.

[28] S. J. Grossman and M. H. Miller, 'Liquidity and Market Structure', *The Journal of Finance*, 43 (1988), 617.

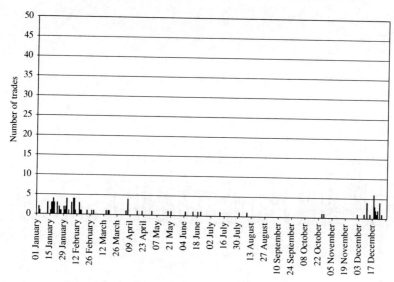

7.2 Estcourt's Lead Mine stock, daily volume, 1694
Source: NA, PRO, C114/165.

might shift.[29] Furthermore, widespread and frequent synchronisation problems will inevitably drive investors away from the market.

Lack of synchronicity was a particular problem for London's first investors for two reasons. First, there was no regular gathering together of interested individuals in any one place. As indicated in Chapter 5, it is likely that the financial market existed in pockets in the various coffee houses of London, notably Jonathan's and Garraway's; in Grocers Hall where the Bank had its home; in the Royal Exchange, even after the brokers left in 1698; in people's homes; and in provincial meeting places. There was, therefore, no one place where an investor could go to be sure of meeting with a suitable counterparty. Even in the busiest periods, prior to transfer books being closed for the election of directors, trade would not have justified such a market nor encouraged one to develop.

Secondly, because many companies operated with only a limited capital and few shareholders, investors would often have found there to be no obvious market in a particular stock. Samuel Jeake, for example, recorded in his diary that having requested his associate Thomas Miller to sell Royal Lustring Company shares in June 1699, he was informed that his order

---

[29] Ibid., 617 18.

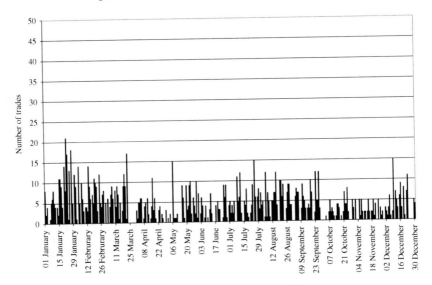

7.3 Bank of England stock, daily volume, 1695
Source: Bank Archives, AC28/32233; AC28/1513 15.

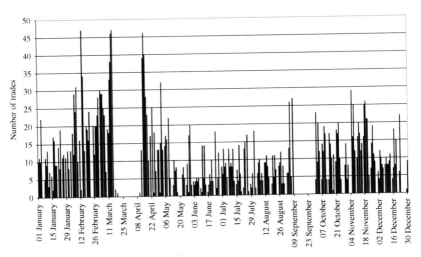

7.4 Bank of England stock, daily volume, 1700
Source: Bank Archives, AC28/1518 20.

could not be filled, 'there being no buyers at all'.[30] And as Figure 7.2 (depicting the level of trade in Estcourt's Lead Mine shares) illustrates, not only was daily activity in some stocks minimal but there were many days and sometimes weeks during which no trading occurred.[31]

Analysis of activity in Bank of England stock provides a stark contrast with Estcourt's Lead Mine stock, but even here a limited daily turnover of shares was evident. The highest number of transactions in Bank stock recorded on any one day was sixty-one on 11 March 1701, the day before the closure of the books for the election of directors and the payment of dividends. This was, however, highly unusual. In 1700, the peak trading year for the period under consideration, the average number of trades in Bank stock was a mere twelve per day. Thus, as Figures 7.3 and 7.4 illustrate, turnover in the busiest and most widely supported joint-stock of this period can at best be described as steady.

It is clear, therefore, that the functioning of London's first stock market would have been enhanced by the presence of market-makers. Without them, the few investors who came each day to the market with genuine requirements would have struggled to complete their transactions in a timely and cost-efficient manner with the inevitable consequence being a loss of investor confidence. That said, it is unlikely that stocks like Estcourt's Lead Mine or the Blue Paper Company consistently attracted the interest of market-makers. This factor undoubtedly contributed to their eventual demise as tradable commodities. In the larger stocks, however, a somewhat different picture emerges. The observable steady turnover of shares and indeed the ultimate survival of companies like the Bank of England and East India Company as tradable entities confirms a greater efficiency in trading that must suggest a level of market-making activity. Equally, grouping together the activity of the most prominent stock-jobbers demonstrates that they commanded a significant proportion of trade in shares. For example, as Table 7.4 shows, in 1700 the activity of the seven most prominent jobbers in Bank stock sometimes constituted as much as one-third of the monthly turnover in stock. Clearly, therefore, the activity of stock-jobbers, whether intentionally or otherwise, had the power to fill the gaps in the market.

---

[30] Hunter and Gregory, *Astrological Diary*, p. 259.

[31] Although Scott estimated that up to one hundred joint stock companies had been established in England by 1695, Houghton listed no more than sixty traded companies in his *Collection for Improvement*, and Blunt's ledgers recorded activity in only twenty three companies in the years between 1692 and 1695. Scott, *Constitution and Finance*, vol. I, p. 327; Houghton, *Collection for Improvement*, passim; NA, PRO, C114/165.

Table 7.4 Number of transactions in Bank stock conducted each month of 1700 by the seven most prominent stock-jobbers

	January	February	March	April	May	June	July	August	September	October	November	December	
William Sheppard	31	60	59	55	50	30	60	44	34	73	115	32	643
Phesaunt Crisp	7	32	9	22	15	9	10	13	7	40	17	16	197
Benjamin Levy	4	12	9	10	8	12	18	14	6	12	47	31	183
Moses Barrow	10	27	13	15	8	0	1	1	0	3	22	2	102
Alexander Gawne	0	23	18	8	1	4	3	10	0	5	13	0	85
Isaac Fernandes Nunes	2	6	7	5	9	1	9	3	6	5	4	2	59
Peter Henriques	2	8	1	5	7	2	6	4	3	12	5	2	57
Totals	56	168	116	120	98	58	107	89	56	150	223	85	1326
As percentage of total turnover	11.16	19.95	14.57	20.41	21.03	21.97	27.02	24.59	33.73	25.42	31.23	22.25	21.85

Source: Bank Archives, AC28/1518–20.

On the other hand, with so few jobbers operating in the market the benefits of their presence was limited to relieving synchronisation problems. There was certainly not enough activity to create an open outcry market and it is most unlikely that there was sufficient competition to close bid/ask spreads. Indeed, we should doubt whether early modern jobbers were even willing to offer two-way prices. For most jobbers, knowledge of a potential counterparty's intention and thus the opportunity to skew the price to reflect their own interests would have been essential to protect the potential profitability of the trade.

In spite of the condemnation heaped upon them, therefore, the activity of stock-jobbers was of benefit to the equity and debt markets. In particular, as noted in Chapter 2, without the liquidity of the financial market the entire edifice of public credit would have crumbled. Nevertheless, and in spite of the difficulties of trading in such an immature and restricted market, stock-jobbers were not there for altruistic reasons and there is no question that some were well placed to reap high rewards from the financial market. In particular, their superior knowledge and position as providers of liquidity undoubtedly allowed them sometimes to take advantage of other investors. Moreover, although the argument cannot be substantiated owing to the limited price data available for this period, it is reasonable to suggest that, for some stock-jobbers, their very presence in the market would have created opportunities to create profits. For example, Figure 7.5 presents a graphical depiction of William Sheppard's trading activity in 1700 which shows him to have been active in Bank stock nearly every trading day that year. At the same time Sheppard was active in other shares and was a broker of government debt.[32] Given the level of his activity he must have been almost constantly at the Royal Exchange or in the coffee houses of Exchange Alley. Thus, he was well known to regular investors and, in all likelihood, those who knew of his reputation observed and followed his actions and views. Such influence might have allowed men like Sheppard to determine the direction of the market and create a very profitable enterprise.

On the other hand, the high profile of Sheppard's business exposed him to attack and by 1702 his business had been destroyed by the financial market he had dominated in previous years. As will be discussed further in the following section, Sheppard was apparently bankrupted by the squabbles between the Old East India Company and the New, which he supported. The precise circumstances are not known but Luttrell recorded in his diary in February 1701, 'Mr Shepherd, a noted banker in Lumbard

---

[32] F. G. H. Price, *A Handbook of London Bankers with Some Account of the Early Goldsmiths* (London: Leadenhall Press, 1890 91), p. 150.

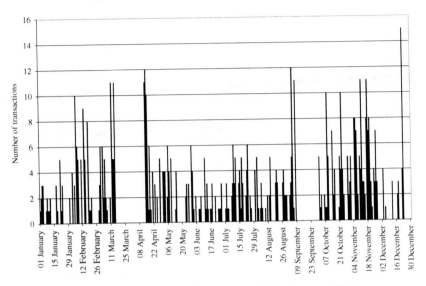

7.5 William Sheppard's daily turnover in Bank stock, 1700
Source: Bank Archives, AC28/1517 19.

Street, having great summs of money drawn upon him occasion'd by the fall of the publick stocks, was forc'd to stop payment at present.'[33] In November 1702 it was announced in the *Gazette* that William Sheppard and his partners, Joseph Bragg and John Sheppard, had been declared bankrupt.[34]

Could stock-jobbers manipulate the market?

Few contemporaries would have regretted the demise of Sheppard's business. The useful function performed by stock-jobbers, although acknowledged by some, was little appreciated by most observers of the market. As we have already seen, they focused instead on the seeming willingness of stock-jobbers to use their privileged position as providers of liquidity to manipulate share prices and dupe inexperienced investors. One of the chief aims of this chapter is to show that stock-jobbers did not always deserve that reputation. Nevertheless, the immaturity of the financial market and particularly its lack of liquidity must have offered opportunities to the unscrupulous and it would be naïve to argue that all stock-jobbers resisted the temptation to make money by whatever means they could.

[33] Luttrell, *Brief Relation*, vol. V, p. 14.   [34] *London Gazette*, 30 Nov. 1702.

Indeed, confirmation that temptation was acted upon is provided by the history of Estcourt's Lead Mine.

The author of *Angliae Tutamen* offered a detailed assessment of the way that mining interests were manipulated. He alleged that those who floated such projects:

[P]retend a mighty Vein of Gold, Silver, or Copper, to be discover'd in a Piece of Ground of their knowledge, then they agree with the Lord, or Patentees, for a small Yearly Rent, or a Part reserv'd (about a Fifteenth) to him, or them, to grant them a Lease for Twenty one Years to dig that Land; which they immediately fall to, and give out 'tis a very rich Mine; then they settle a Company under Articles, divide it into Shares, usually 400, chuse a Committee, a Clerk, and Transfer Book, and pretend to carry on this Work to the Benefit of all the Proprietors.[35]

Estcourt's Lead Mine seems to have been established to a similar pattern. The mine was located in the Halkin district of Flintshire, in North Wales, and was owned by Sir Thomas Grosvenor. In 1692 Grosvenor, disappointed by the local miners' seeming inability to exploit the mine, granted mining rights to his 'cousin and friend' Phineas Bowles, a prominent London broker and stock-jobber, and John Blunt, a scrivener, stock-jobber and Charles Blunt's cousin.[36] Bowles and John Blunt, together with Sir Thomas Estcourt, one of the most celebrated speculators of the age, established a joint-stock company, nominally headed by John Lethieullier, to fund the project. The Company was floated in early 1693, during the later stages of the joint-stock boom. The initial capital value of the Company is not known but a total of 236 £10 shares were taken up by Charles Blunt's clients.[37] Other shares were probably taken up by the main protagonists and perhaps distributed to family and friends or sold privately. An investment of £5,000 was made in the mine suggesting that at least 500 shares had been issued in the initial flotation.[38]

At the time the Company was floated prospects for creating a profitable business were good. Although the precise location of Estcourt's Lead Mine is not known, Edward Llwyd, writing in 1697, noted that the Halkin district was exceptionally rich in lead ore.[39] Moreover, in February 1693 Parliament had passed an Act which freed mine owners to develop their pits and profit from all mineral resources without Crown interference. Previously, base mineral mines that might have contained gold or silver

[35] Anon., *Angliae Tutamen*, p. 18.
[36] N. J. Rhodes, 'The London Lead Company in North Wales, 1693 1792', unpublished PhD thesis (University of Leicester, 1970), pp. 30 1.
[37] NA, PRO, C114/165.   [38] Rhodes, 'London Lead Company', p. 32.
[39] W. Rees, *Industry before the Industrial Revolution*, 2 vols. (Cardiff: University of Wales Press, 1968), vol. II, p. 479.

were subject to the control of the Crown. Recent technical advancements, including the use of gunpowder for blasting and new techniques for smelting and refining lead ore also enhanced the potential of the business.[40]

On the other hand, the Company does seem typical of the type complained of by contemporary critics of the financial market. In particular, the proprietors were all City merchants or moneyed men who, arguably, knew little about mining lead. The movement of the share price also indicates that the Company was ultimately used for speculative purposes. Throughout most of 1693 the share price remained steady at between £8 and £12. In late October and early November of that year prices began to rise, reaching £20 in December 1693. The rise continued in 1694 and in mid-January the price had reached £24–£25. On 22 January stock was trading at £35, and by 26 January 1694 stock was trading at £100.[41] Although no subsequent trades were conducted by Blunt's clients to substantiate the claim, by April 1694 Houghton was quoting the price of Estcourt's Lead Mine stock at £150.[42] In December 1694 and January 1695 there was a further flurry of activity and in early 1695 trading ceased when the Company was amalgamated with the Royal Mines Copper Company.[43]

Using transfer books to study the timing of trading activity can be misleading since there was usually no requirement to register transactions within a certain time. Having agreed upon a trade, the two parties would only meet to sign the transfer book when mutually convenient. Although it is likely that in most cases registration took place within one or two days of the trade being agreed, comparison of Blunt's ledgers with the transfer books of Estcourt's Lead Mines shows some delays of a number of weeks rather than a matter of days. But, bearing this proviso in mind, as Table 7.5 and Figure 7.6 show, a great deal of activity seems to have accompanied and sometimes preceded price movements in Estcourt's Lead Mine shares.

Furthermore, grouping together the activity of the managers of the Company, John Blunt, Phineas Bowles, John Lethieullier and Sir Thomas Estcourt, shows that it was those individuals who dominated share trading during active periods in the Company's history. Blunt, Bowles, Lethieullier and Estcourt all bought shares around the time of the price rises in late 1693 and early 1694, and they all sold heavily in late

---

[40] W. J. Lewis, *Lead Mining in Wales* (Cardiff: University of Wales Press, 1967), p. 9. Burt also argues that mining in this period repaid investment in new technology and organ isation. He suggests that by the early eighteenth century, for the lead industry, the industrial revolution was in full swing. R. Burt, 'Lead Production in England and Wales, 1700 1770', *Economic History Review*, 22 (1969), 249 68.

[41] NA, PRO, C114/165.   [42] Houghton, *Collection for Improvement*, 13 Apr. 1694.

[43] NA, PRO, C114/165; Rhodes, 'London Lead Company', p. 32.

Table 7.5 *Monthly activity in Estcourt's Lead Mine, 1693–1695*

	No. of transactions	No. of shares		No. of transactions	No. of shares
Mar. 93	4	35	Mar. 94	3	20
Apr. 93	3	40	Apr. 94	8	48
May 93	3	27	May 94	3	9
Jun. 93	12	72	Jun. 94	4	18
Jul. 93	8	47	Jul. 94	2	15
Aug. 93	6	32	Aug. 94	1	3
Sep. 93	2	13	Sep. 94	0	0
Oct. 93	29	233	Oct. 94	2	22
Nov. 93	24	161	Nov. 94	0	0
Dec. 93	8	56	Dec. 94	26	489
Jan. 94	32	161	Jan. 95	27	315
Feb. 94	24	205	Feb. 95	3	30

Source: NA, PRO, C114/165.

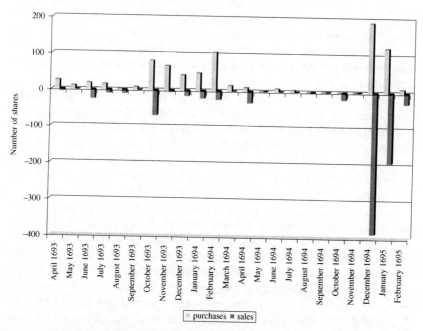

7.6 The activity of John Blunt and associates in Estcourt's Lead Mine stock, 1693 1695
Source: NA, PRO, C114/165.

1694 prior to the Company being amalgamated with the Royal Mines Copper Company.

An account registered in Charles Blunt's ledgers as 'John Blunt and Company' also shows a considerable number of call options in Estcourt's Lead Mine being purchased over the course of 1693 and particularly during October, November and December of that year.[44] Between April and December 1693, John Blunt and Company accumulated call options on a minimum of 282 shares at strike prices of between £10 and £20 and at an average cost of just over two guineas per share for each contract.[45] One anonymous author offered an explanation of the purpose of such actions. He wrote:

[some] having whole stocks or the whole number of shares of a stock in their power, gave or would have given guineas for the refusals [call options] of certain parcels thereof, when they knew the takers could not comply with such contracts but upon terms which they would afterwards please to permit them.[46]

In other words, individuals purchased options despite already being in possession of the majority of the stock of a company. The consequent shortage of tradable shares forced prices higher as the sellers of the options sought to make purchases to cover their positions, at which point the buyers could release their own shares back into the market at a profit and then take a further profit as the same shares were returned to them as a result of the exercise of their options.

Interestingly, the purchase of call options by John Blunt was generally combined with the sale of stock to the option seller. For example, on 16 October 1693 John Blunt and Co. bought a six-month refusal of five shares in Estcourt's Lead Mine from Henry Evans at a strike price of £12 and a cost of 2 guineas per share and, at the same time, sold five shares to Evans at a price of £11.[47] Thus, Evans had a hedged position but could not participate in any future price rises, while Blunt and Co. had eliminated part of their physical position in the stock in order to buy the right to riskless participation in a rising market. Since many, although by no means all, of those investors who sold options to Blunt and Co. in late 1693 were similarly purchasing shares as a hedge, it would seem that Blunt's actions did not conform precisely to the accusations made by contemporary observers that unscrupulous individuals were using the purchase of refusals to corner the market in a particular stock.[48] However, Blunt and Co. were clearly placing themselves in a position to take

---

[44] NA, PRO, C114/165.   [45] Ibid., Account of John Blunt and Co., 1693.
[46] Anon., Plain Dealing, p. 5.   [47] Ibid., 16 Oct. 1693.
[48] Anon., Plain Dealing, p. 4; Houghton, Collection for Improvement, 13 Jul. 1694.

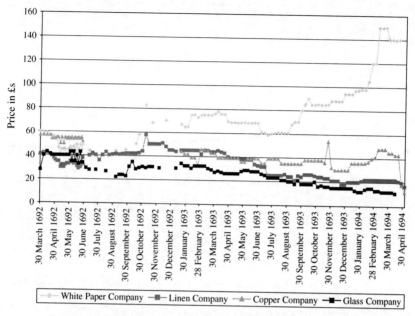

7.7 Prices of White Paper, Linen, Copper and Glass Company stocks, 1692 1694
Source: Houghton, *Collection for Improvement*; NA, PRO, C114/164.

advantage of a large price rise and, given the mine was located in North Wales, it must be assumed they controlled the information presented to the market and could withhold or manipulate the data available to them or, if they so desired, create and disseminate false information. All this they could do without fear of legal censure because, as Defoe asserted, those who manipulated the market risked only their reputation, which was generally already lost, and their souls, 'which trifle is not worth mentioning'.[49] The only reasonable conclusion, therefore, is that the price of Estcourt's Lead Mine stock was manipulated by its managers to their own advantage.

Contemporary observers considered this type of manipulation to be common practice in the market of the 1690s. Nevertheless, John Houghton argued that manipulation was confined to the smaller joint-stock companies, which were inadequately capitalised and easily overwhelmed by 'the Contrivances of a few Men in Confederacy'. Houghton asserted that 'in great Stocks' stock-jobbers found it more difficult to influence share prices.[50] Figures 7.7, 7.8 and 7.9 depicting price

[49] Defoe, *Anatomy of Exchange Alley*, p. 8.
[50] Houghton, *Collection for Improvement*, 6 Jul. 1694.

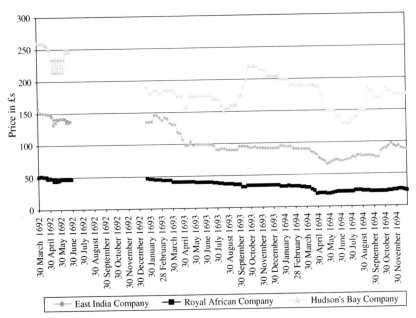

7.8 Prices of East India, Royal African and Hudson's Bay Company stocks, 1692 1694
Source: Houghton, *Collection for Improvement.*

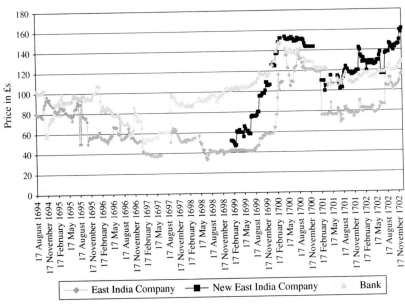

7.9 Prices of Bank of England, Old and New East India Company stocks, 1694 1702
Source: Houghton, *Collection for Improvement*, 1694 98; European State Finance Database, dataset\neal\coe1700s.rtf.

movements in some of the larger joint-stocks substantiate this assumption. They reveal very few instances of large anomalous rises or falls in price.[51] In fact, the charts show a market that operated relatively smoothly and, within sectors, was well integrated. Certainly price movements over the period were significant but there were very few instances of rapid change and price movements were not constantly erratic. Long and sustained alterations in price and trend were the norm and were supported by circumstances in the wider political and economic sphere. Thus, a general decline in prices of shares in the great trading companies during the war years is observable, with the pace of decline becoming marked as the recoinage of 1696/97 added to the country's economic woes. Equally, there was an immediate and significant rally in the prices of all stocks when the Nine Years' War came to an end in September 1697. This was followed by a long-term rise in prices as the public finances were restored and the benefits of peace fed into the wider economy.

The majority of the unusual movements depicted above can be viewed as responses to new information being received by the market. Thus, the rapid rise in prices during November 1692, noted in Figure 7.7, was a result of the unexpected sale of 10,000 pieces of white linen conducted by the Linen Company during that month. The sale caused widespread renewed interest in the Company's fortunes. Yet, all was not as it seemed. Although outwardly successful, the Company was beset by squabbles between its directors who were also, according to MacLeod, guilty of technical and financial incompetence.[52] And it faced the vehement hostility of the woollen industry, factions within which characterised the linen trade as 'despicable' and liable to lead to the decay of England's staple trade.[53] The rapid decline in prices in late November 1692 suggests that some investors were aware of these problems, understood that the Company's apparent productivity was unsustainable and sought to take advantage of the rise in prices to cover or liquidate existing positions. The fact that Charles Blunt's ledgers show a significant level of option trading activity in Linen Company stock during November with a larger than average number of put options (options that protect against falls in

---

[51] It should be noted that a combination of sources have been used in order to achieve a consistent series of prices and obvious printing errors have been smoothed. It must also be acknowledged that, as suggested in Chapter 4, quoted prices were accurate to a degree but could not always be relied upon.
[52] MacLeod '1690s Patents Boom', 564.
[53] Scott, *Constitution and Finance*, vol. III, pp. 93 5. For further details on the development of linen manufacture in England see N. B. Harte, 'The Rise of Protection and the English Linen Trade, 1690 1790', in N. B. Harte and K. G. Ponting, eds., *Textile History and Economic History* (Manchester University Press, 1973), pp. 74 112.

share prices) being traded is further confirmation that the better informed among London's investors were not fooled by the Linen Company's apparent success.[54]

The sharp rise in the price of Bank of England shares in September 1697 was a consequence of the conclusion of the negotiations that ended the Nine Years' War. Samuel Jeake's actions during that month show that this rally was anticipated. In September 1697 Jeake made a speculative purchase of £100 Bank stock at a price of 85½ on the assumption that the market would rise when the peace treaty was finally agreed.[55] His letters to his wife Elizabeth during this time were full of excitement about the prospects for peace and detail how Bank stock rose and fell at the arrival, or failed arrival, of each post from Holland, 'for such is yᵉ humour here up and down every day almost'.[56] Analysis of the type of individual active in Bank stock in September 1697 shows little deviation from the norm. Certainly there was a significant increase in turnover of stock during that month. On average there were 171 trades per month during 1697, whereas in September of that year there were 510 transactions.[57] However, the increased volume was partly a result of the transfer books being closed during the whole of August 1697 for the election of directors, thus creating a build-up of pressure that was relieved as the books reopened in September.[58] Equally, the increase in activity was widespread. No particular individuals were dominant, although Table 7.6 does show merchants to have been major buyers at this time, perhaps indicative of the ease with which they obtained information about the prospects for peace.

Of more interest is the significant rise in Bank and East India Company stock at the beginning of 1700 and the subsequent rapid decline in prices at the beginning of 1701. The rally in the first few months of 1700 was reflective of a more positive economic environment than had been experienced in previous years. The recoinage was complete and credit restored, the harvests of 1699 were good and trade to the East was recovering from its wartime lows.[59] Thus, share prices rose during the early part of the year

---

[54] NA, PRO, C114/165, passim.   [55] ESRO, Jeake Papers, FRE 5303.

[56] Ibid.   [57] Bank Archives, AC28/1514 16.

[58] This election was a result of the negotiations for the engraftment of the tallies. Although the Bank was able to request a number of concessions from the government as a con sequence of its agreeing to engraft the tallies into Bank stock, the government retaliated with a clause which required that not more than two thirds of the Bank's directors could be reappointed at annual elections. This necessitated an election in August 1697. Bank Archives G7/1, 16 Jul. 1697 20 Aug. 1697; Clapham, *Bank of England*, vol. I, p. 50.

[59] J. E. T. Rogers, *The First Nine Years of the Bank of England* (Oxford: Clarendon Press, 1887), pp. 98 9.

Table 7.6 *Activity in Bank stock grouped by the social status/occupation of the investor, September 1697*

	No. of sellers in September	Percentage	No. of sellers in 1697	Percentage	No. of purchasers	Percentage	No. of purchases	Percentage
Titled aristocrats	4	1.47	14	1.87	5	1.77	24	2.85
Gentlemen	24	8.79	78	10.44	26	9.19	100	11.88
Esquires	19	6.96	71	9.50	16	5.65	78	9.26
Professionals	8	2.93	41	5.49	15	5.30	52	6.18
Merchants	79	28.94	222	29.72	102	36.04	250	29.69
Finance	13	4.76	26	3.48	13	4.59	26	3.09
Retailing	78	28.57	151	20.21	66	23.32	160	19.00
Manufacture	23	8.42	72	9.64	19	6.71	68	8.08
Transport	10	3.66	16	2.14	2	0.71	7	0.83
Agriculture	0	0.00	0	0.00	0	0.00	1	0.12
Building	7	2.56	9	1.20	5	1.77	7	0.83
Domestic service	0	0.00	1	0.13	1	0.35	4	0.48
Women	6	2.20	27	3.61	13	4.59	55	6.53
Unknown	2	0.73	18	2.41	0	0.00	10	1.19
Totals	273		746		283		842	

Source: Bank Archives, AC28/1515–16.

encouraging investors into the market. Bank stock reached a peak of 148 in March and both East India Companies staged significant recoveries with Old Company stock reaching a peak of 135 around mid-year and New Company stock hovering around 150.[60] Interestingly, as may be seen in Table 7.7, there is some evidence of investors who might be defined as risk-averse taking profits in the early part of 1700. In particular, a large number of women sold at this time,[61] suggesting that by 1700 the risk-averse investor was relatively well informed about the progress of the main joint-stock companies. Merchants, goldsmiths and brokers purchased more stock than they sold during the first three months of 1700, a contrast with their normally more balanced levels of activity. To a lesser extent the same patterns can be observed in East India Company stock.[62] This suggests that it was indeed those groups who provided liquidity to accommodate the prevailing trends in the larger stocks but offers no confirmation that they led or manipulated the market.

From mid-1700 the political situation, at home and abroad, began to depress prices. The death in July of Princess Anne's only surviving child, the Duke of Gloucester, revived the problem of how to ensure the Protestant succession and the demise of Carlos II of Spain in October brought the problem of the Spanish succession to a head and led to a rapid deterioration in European stability that would ultimately result in war. This unstable situation was compounded by the Parliamentary election of January 1701, which was marked by a bitter struggle for seats between the supporters of the Old and New East India Companies. In addition to this political battle, Defoe alleged that there was a financial attack by the Old Company on the supporters of the New Company, including the Bank of England.[63] In particular, the Old Company were apparently able to collect a large quantity of the notes issued by William Sheppard (noted above as the most prominent stock-jobber of the period and also banker to the New Company) and present them for payment. The New Company and the Bank apparently retaliated by conducting a similar attack against the cash-keepers of the Old East India Company.[64] According to Defoe, the consequences of this battle was that the Old East India Company 'stop[ped the country's] Credit, [broke] our Goldsmiths, [sunk] our Stocks, embarrass[ed] the Bank, and ruine[d] Trade at their Will and Pleasure'.[65]

---

[60] Houghton, *Collection for Improvement*, passim.
[61] Compared to their usual level of activity in the market, as presented in Appendix 3.
[62] IOR, L/AG/14/3/2 6.   [63] Defoe, *Villainy of Stock Jobbers*.
[64] Scott, *Constitution and Finance*, vol. II, pp. 184 5.
[65] Defoe, *Villainy of Stock Jobbers*, p. 16.

Table 7.7 *Activity in Bank stock grouped by the social status/occupation of the investor, January–March 1700*

	No. of sellers	Percentage	No. of sales	Percentage	Average nominal amount (in £s)	No. of purchasers	Percentage	No. of purchases	Percentage	Average nominal amount (in £s)
Titled aristocrats	17	2.84	33	3.08	738	13	3.02	38	3.55	1,098
Gentlemen	82	13.71	121	11.31	441	65	15.08	105	9.81	449
Esquires	68	11.37	146	13.64	744	56	12.99	111	10.37	648
Professionals	44	7.36	66	6.17	472	26	6.03	83	7.76	425
Merchants	136	22.74	216	20.19	560	116	26.91	289	27.01	565
Finance	30	5.02	167	15.61	598	33	7.66	75	21.21	609
Retailing	73	12.21	126	11.78	434	58	13.46	123	11.50	380
Manufacture	52	8.70	76	7.10	344	30	6.96	50	4.67	337
Transport	10	1.67	11	1.03	307	2	0.46	4	0.37	334
Agriculture	0	0.00	0	0.00	0	0	0.00	0	0.00	0
Building	5	0.84	6	0.56	367	1	0.23	2	0.19	400
Domestic service	1	0.17	1	0.09	400	1	0.23	1	0.09	200
Women	71	11.87	86	8.04	373	26	6.03	30	2.08	338
Unknown	9	1.51	15	1.40	740	4	0.93	7	0.65	425
Totals	598		1,070			431		1070		

Source: Bank Archives, AC28/1518–20.

It is clear that Defoe's account can be trusted in at least one respect since it is known that Sheppard experienced financial difficulties and eventually went bankrupt in 1702. Moreover, analysis of those trading Bank stock in February 1701 does reveal that merchants, goldsmiths and brokers sold fairly heavily at that time.

However, activity was not excessive during that month and once again no particular individuals were dominant. Moreover, the accompanying decline in New and Old East India Company share prices during February 1701 would seem to suggest a general panic resulting from the great uncertainty surrounding the economic and political situation of the time. Indeed, it was during January and February 1701 that Louis XIV sent his troops to occupy the 'Barrier Fortresses' in the Spanish Netherlands indicating to all 'well-informed men ... that before long England would once more be at war with France'.[66] As Clapham notes, such scares were apt to produce runs on the Bank.[67] They were also highly likely to destabilise asset prices. Accusations of a deliberate and direct attack on the Bank, therefore, were based only partly in fact. Equally, in spite of the descent into war, both the financial market and the English economy proved relatively resilient throughout the remainder of 1701 and into 1702. Observing the progress of exchange rates Ashton found the crisis to have been over by April 1701.[68] And when war was finally declared in May 1702, the reaction of share prices was measured.

Conclusion

The contemporary perception was that stock-jobbers controlled London's financial market and used their power to gain great estates from other people's misery. This was undoubtedly an exaggeration. Most stock-jobbers had other occupations indicating that they could not make a good living solely from share trading. Those that did make their living from finance had precarious existences. William Sheppard, for example, may have reaped good profits in the short term but was ultimately ruined by his involvement with the financial markets. Equally, it is clear that coordinated groups of speculators could easily take advantage when opportunities for manipulation of the share prices of smaller stocks presented themselves. This undoubtedly had a potentially detrimental effect on the stability of the market and negative consequences for the

---

[66] T. S. Ashton, *Economic Fluctuations in England, 1700 1800* (Oxford: Clarendon Press, 1959), p. 115. See also, Wells and Wills, 'Revolution, Restoration', 435.
[67] Clapham, *Bank of England*, vol. I, p. 62.   [68] Ashton, *Economic Fluctuations*, p. 115.

Table 7.8 Activity in Bank stock grouped by the social status/occupation of the investor, February 1701

	No. of sellers	Percentage	No. of sales	Percentage	Average amount	No. of purchasers	Percentage	No. of purchases	Percentage	Average amount
Titled aristocrats	9	6.92	13	5.49	1,323	11	6.71	17	7.17	1,294
Gentlemen	11	8.46	18	7.59	473	16	9.76	21	8.86	424
Esquires	15	11.54	27	11.39	669	25	15.24	32	13.50	693
Professionals	10	7.69	12	5.06	1,273	12	7.32	16	6.75	853
Merchants	38	29.23	76	32.07	599	39	23.78	53	22.36	574
Finance	18	13.85	60	25.32	635	15	9.15	50	21.10	626
Retailing	11	8.46	13	5.49	477	20	12.20	21	8.86	486
Manufacture	11	8.46	11	4.64	520	10	6.10	11	4.64	380
Transport	0	0.00	0	0.00	0	1	0.61	0	0.00	380
Agriculture	0	0.00	0	0.00	0	0	0.00	1	0.42	350
Building	0	0.00	0	0.00	0	1	0.61	0	0.00	0
Domestic service	1	0.77	1	0.42	100	0	0.00	1	0.42	500
Women	6	4.62	6	2.53	742	13	7.93	13	5.49	0
Unknown	0	0.00	0	0.00	0	1	0.61	1	0.42	423
Totals	130		237			164		237		500

Source: Bank Archives, AC28/1518–21.

investment strategies of less active investors. Nevertheless, the practicalities of trading in the early modern market limited profit-making opportunities and it is quite clear that the reach of the stock-jobber did not
easily extend to the larger joint-stock companies such as the East India
Company and the Bank of England.

8   Investment strategies

Stock-jobbing, as we have seen, involved only a very few investors in London's first financial market. The majority, either because they were not bombarded with information that caused them constantly to reconsider their strategies or because they were focused on securing a long-term investment income rather than short-term capital gains, did not make frequent changes to their investment portfolios. In fact, there was a very high level of inertia among some shareholders. Around half of those who held shares in the East India Company in 1688, for example, were still shareholders in 1699 having weathered one of the most turbulent periods in the Company's history, received no dividends and seen the value of their shares descend from around £300 to around £40.[1] Of those investors who were more active, the quest for capital gains, although undoubtedly important, was not the sole motive for their investment. Their desire to use share ownership as a means of gaining influence within a particular economic or political sphere or even just a sense of loyalty towards the company whose shares they owned meant that they too were not easily swayed by the prospects of gaining quick profits from a speculative enterprise or frightened into liquidating their positions by misinformation and rumour.

The purpose of this chapter is to explain the motives and actions of the quiet majority in London's first financial market. In the following section the risks and rewards of the investment choices available to investors will be analysed. The discussion will then turn to the varied ways in which investors made use of equities and debt instruments. The focus will be on investors whose strategies were predominantly risk-averse but it should be noted that such a definition can only provide a framework for the discussion of behaviour. In reality, the aims of most investors were not static. Investors changed their minds and their use of the market developed. Inevitably, strategies altered as further information came to light, as

---

[1] IOR, L/AG/1/10/2; H/2.

political, economic or even social circumstances changed, and as the investor's confidence increased or decreased. Investment strategies, therefore, were as fluid as the market.

The risks and rewards of investment

The choices open to investors, even prior to the advent of the financial market, were many but land and property had long been the main recourse for those with capital to spare. Grassby suggests that for much of the seventeenth century land was the only safe form of passive investment and in general it provided a secure and regular income.[2] Yet, throughout the seventeenth century the typical yield on land was just 5 or 6 per cent and towards the end of the century falling land values and rents diminished the effectiveness of such investments. The new Land Tax, introduced in 1692, increased costs for landowners especially since it proved impossible to shift the burden of the tax to tenants.[3] Furthermore, any investor wishing to obtain a good income from land was obliged to take an active role in its management. Owners of land or property also incurred maintenance costs, risked a loss of income during periods when tenants could not be found and bore an appreciable risk of default. Thus, land and property continued to be regarded as a stable investment and had a symbolic importance, but during the 1690s higher yields could be found elsewhere.[4]

The risks of investment in trade, whether directly or through bottomry or respondentia loans, naturally increased during the Nine Years' War.[5] But even in times of peace, investment in trade required capital to be committed for long periods of time and carried many dangers. Grassby notes that the weather and temperature impacted upon the availability of commodities, the condition of goods and the speeds at which they reached their destination ports. Markets were highly volatile and could be destroyed by trade barriers, high taxes, adverse exchange rates, changes in fashion, political events or the emergence of competitors.[6] It was little wonder, therefore, that Malynes in *Lex Mercatoria* asserted that 'to be rich and to become

[2] Grassby, *Business Community*, p. 375.
[3] H. J. Habakkuk, 'The Long Term Rate of Interest and the Price of Land in the Seventeenth Century', *Economic History Review*, 5 (1952), 30; H. J. Habakkuk, 'English Landownership, 1680 1740', *Economic History Review*, 10 (1940), 9.
[4] Habakkuk, 'English Landownership', 12.
[5] A bottomry loan was a contract by which money was lent to the owner or owners of a ship for the purpose of funding a voyage. The vessel was bound as security for the loan. If the voyage was successful, then the lender received his money back with interest; if the ship foundered, the money was lost. In the same way, a respondentia loan was secured by the ship's cargo.
[6] Grassby, *Business Community*, pp. 91 2.

poore or to be poore and become rich is a matter inherent to a Merchant's estate'.[7] It is impossible to be precise about the profits earned from trade but Grassby suggests that while fortunes could still be made even in times of war, on average returns from trade over the lifetime of a merchant active during the later seventeenth century ranged between 6 and 12 per cent.[8]

Company or private bonds were suitable for all types of investors. For the risk-averse investor, providing the issuer was of good credit, bonds offered a regular income and the repayment of capital was guaranteed on expiry of the contract. For the merchant or businessman seeking to utilise idle capital, bonds also provided a relatively liquid investment. Private loans or the purchase of bills of exchange offered the possibility of short-term investment and could provide a reasonable return, but carried a greater risk of default and, in this event, recovery costs were high. Similarly, there were many opportunities to lend short term to the government during the 1690s but the state was a poor debtor at this time; its repayments were erratic at best and discounts on its short-term debt were high. On the other hand, loans to corporations, particularly the City of London, and livery companies were more secure and proved popular with investors during the late seventeenth century.[9] The yield on bonds and private lending was ostensibly limited to the statutory maximum rate of 6 per cent but yields varied according to creditworthiness and there were, of course, always ways of circumventing the official rate of interest so that the least worthy debtors would be forced to pay more.[10] Thus, while loans to the City of London commanded only 4 per cent, the government paid 6 per cent in interest and an additional 2 per cent gratuity.[11]

Annuities offered the investor another form of guaranteed income. As we have seen, the yields on government annuities were particularly impressive during the 1690s. Indeed, the life annuities floated in 1693 and 1694 yielded between 10 and 14 per cent depending on the number of lives insured. But, payments were again rather erratic during the 1690s and the overall return on annuities did depend entirely on the longevity of the nominee. The Million Adventure also provided a form of annuity. Blank or non-prize-winning tickets paid £1 a year until 1710; the prize-winning tickets paid between £10 and £1,000 per annum over the same period. As has been demonstrated in previous chapters, this feature

---

[7] Quoted ibid., p. 91.

[8] R. Grassby, 'The Rate of Profit in Seventeenth Century England', *English Historical Review*, 84 (1969), 733.

[9] Davies, *Royal African Company*, p. 51; Grassby, *Business Community*, p. 88.

[10] Grassby argues that the usury laws offered little protection to those considered a poor credit risk. Grassby, *Business Community*, p. 88.

[11] Davies, *Royal African Company*, p. 51; Dickson, *Financial Revolution*, p. 343.

ensured that the lottery tickets became the subject of an active secondary market, which indicates that, in spite of the hiatus in benefit payments between 1695 and 1698, the long-term value of the lottery as an investment product remained high.

The purchase of shares as an investment carried variable risks and offered equally variable rewards. Many of the smaller joint-stock companies floated in the early 1690s must be regarded as speculative assets. Others, notably the Bank of England and the East India Company, could arguably be afforded the status of gilt-edged securities.[12] However, the dividends paid, even on the more secure stocks, were inconsistent particularly during the war years. The East India Company had paid dividends of up to 50 per cent during the 1680s, but made no payments between 1691 and 1700.[13] The Bank paid annual dividends of 10 per cent several times during the 1690s but also paid no dividends between late 1695 and late 1697.[14] Of course, a stock that paid a regular dividend could provide an income and offered the potential for windfall profits from extraordinary dividend payments or capital gains. However, the chief risk of deriving an income through shareholding was the prospect that dividend payments might be suspended without notice. The necessity of liquidating all or part of an investment in order to finance consumption would have been disastrous for those attempting to survive on a fixed capital.[15]

The risks of shareholding were increased by the somewhat ambiguous legal position of shareholders. In an age before the advent of limited liability the exact financial responsibilities of an investor towards a company were not clear.[16] Modern commentators have put forward two arguments to suggest that a form of limited liability was in place.[17] First, Scott asserted

[12] A gilt edged stock is one that is regarded as highly reliable. There was, of course, no real equivalent to this kind of security in the late seventeenth century, but it is possible to argue that EIC stock was regarded in this way in the 1670s and 1680s and that Bank and New East India Company stock were afforded this status from 1698 onwards.

[13] Scott, *Constitution and Finance*, vol. II, p. 179.

[14] Including a 20 per cent bonus paid to stockholders in 1697 in lieu of the final call on the stock. For details of the payments made by the Bank see Scott, *Constitution and Finance*, vol. III, p. 245.

[15] Modern studies argue that investors will not choose to liquidate capital even in cases where this may be done without compromising future income (for example in cases where the capital gains on stock would compensate for a reduction in number of shares held). This is because passive investors do not regard capital and dividends as perfect substitutes. Capital is regarded as sacrosanct, not to be touched in any event. P. L. Bernstein, *Against the Gods: The Remarkable Story of Risk* (New York: Wiley 1998), p. 291; H. M. Shefrin and M. Statman, 'Explaining Investor Preference for Cash Dividends', in Thaler, *Advances in Behavioral Finance*, pp. 393 425.

[16] For a discussion of the legal framework within which early modern companies and corporations existed see Harris, *Industrializing English Law*, chapter 1.

[17] Davies, 'Investment in the Later Seventeenth Century', 293.

that an Act of Parliament passed in 1662 created a type of limited liability. According to Scott, this Act ensured that subscribers to the East India, Royal African and Fishery Companies would not be responsible for company losses above the amount unpaid on their shares.[18] However, Davies contradicted Scott's assertion, noting that the Act referred only to private debts and thus afforded incomplete protection to shareholders. The second argument was that shareholders in companies incorporated by charter enjoyed limited liability as one of the privileges of incorporation.[19] Nevertheless, investors were clearly dubious about such assurances. One pamphleteer warned Bank of England shareholders who held less than £500 stock that they risked being liable for the 'Debts and Damages of the Company contracted by Mismanagement or otherwise', without the benefit of being able to influence decision-making through a vote in the General Court.[20] Moreover, since some companies in the 1690s were established by virtue of a patent, rather than by charter, their shareholders were not protected; although the projectors of the Million Bank, who did not seek a charter for their project, did reassure their subscribers that 'no Person shall be further answerable than his Stock, and that one shall not be answerable for another'.[21]

Davies also noted that some companies retained their right to make calls on their shareholders over and above their liability on unpaid stock. The Royal African Company made such a call in 1705.[22] And companies could make other financial demands on their shareholders. During the credit problems that afflicted the Bank of England in early 1696, the directors informed the General Court that its support was expected. As a result, on 13 May 1696 'every member of the Corporation who [had] any Goldsmiths Notes [was] desired to bring them into the Bank & Change them for Bank Notes'. At the same time a further resolution was passed by the General Court that proprietors would be asked to keep all their cash with, and transact all their business through, the Bank.[23] While such demands were infrequent, risk-averse investors could ill afford to risk any extra burden on their capital.[24]

---

[18] Scott, *Constitution and Finance*, vol. I, p. 270.
[19] H. A. Shannon, 'The Coming of Limited Liability', *Economic History*, 2 (1931), cited in Davies, 'Investment in the Later Seventeenth Century', 293.
[20] Anon., *Observations upon the Constitution of the Company of the Bank of England* (London, 1694), p. 1.
[21] Anon., *An Abstract of the Proposals for the Bank on the Tickets of the Million Adventure* (London, 1695).
[22] Davies, 'Investment in the Later Seventeenth Century', 293.
[23] Bank Archives, G7/1, 13 May 1696.
[24] This assertion is supported by the fact that although women made up only around 10 per cent of stockholders in 1697, 19 per cent of the defaulters on the 20 per cent call of that year were women. Bank Archives, General Ledger, ADM7/1, fos. 331 40.

As the willingness of the General Court to accede to the Bank's above-mentioned demand for support indicated, the rights and responsibilities of shareholding in the early modern period must be given careful consideration when assessing the risks of this type of investment. A shareholder entered into a relationship with a company and it is clear that loyalty was demanded on both sides. In December 1695 when subscriptions were being taken in London for the Darien project, the East India Company required its adventurers to declare that

they neither were, or have been, directly, or indirectly ... concerned in the subscription of any Sum of money, for, or towards the carrying on, of any Joynt Stock of Trade, to the East Indies, by virtue of the Scotch Act, nor had they been any ways concerned in the promoting or procureing of the Same.[25]

Similarly, in 1696, holders of Bank of England shares were prevented from investing in the Land Bank. In this case, as has already been shown, the restriction was more damaging for the Land Bank, but this should not obscure the point that such limits acted as a constraint on the freedom of investors to exercise choice and to diversify their investment portfolios.

Adventurers were also required to use whatever influence they had in a company's favour. Thus, in 1689 when the Royal African Company petitioned Parliament seeking protection against interlopers it requested 'That every Member be desired to make Application to their Freinds [sic] in the Houses and informe them of the Reasonableness of the Thing'.[26] Similarly, at a meeting of the General Court of the Hudson's Bay Company in April 1690 it was requested that any member able to help a petition for the renewal of the Company's charter through the House of Commons should do so.[27] It was, therefore, understood that proprietors would engage actively in the promotion and protection of the company whose stock they owned.

In return for the responsibilities that stockholding conferred, many investors expected to be involved in management decisions. This was possible since joint-stock companies of this period were democratic organisations.[28] The governors and directors of companies were elected

[25] IOR, Court Minutes, B/41, 9 Dec. 1695.
[26] NA, PRO, Royal African Company, General Court Minute Book, 1678 1720, T70/101, 11 Dec. 1689.
[27] NA, PRO, Hudson's Bay Company, A2/1, 3 Apr. 1690.
[28] Pearson has argued that the 'East India Company and the Bank of England represented relatively "despotic" forms of government' in the nineteenth century but this was certainly not true of the Bank of England in the late seventeenth century. In critical periods during the Bank's early years the shareholders were very involved in the decision making pro cesses. It is, however, notable that by 1700, when the Bank was trouble free, meetings of the General Court confined themselves to mundane matters. Thus, what Pearson inter prets as despotism was perhaps the apathy of stakeholders satisfied with the operation and

and although a minimum shareholding was generally required before a proprietor would be entitled to a vote, once that requirement was satisfied no one was excluded, not even women. Indeed, while the political franchise for women in England was not granted until the early twentieth century, some women in the late seventeenth and early eighteenth centuries were exercising their right to influence the decision-making processes of the country's most prominent economic and financial institutions.

Although, as we have already seen, most companies operated under a culture of secrecy, key issues, such as proposed changes to a company's charter, the future direction of the business or perceived threats to profitability, were presented to the proprietors who could signal their assent or disagreement to the directors' proposed actions through their vote. The stockholders could also demand the attention of the directors of a company whenever they deemed it necessary. Thus, a General Court of the Bank of England could be called by any nine proprietors holding £500 or more stock.

It is difficult to quantify how many proprietors regularly exercised their voting rights, but the acquisition of sufficient stock to guarantee a vote was certainly deemed important. When making his initial investment in Bank of England stock Samuel Jeake having committed only £200 but 'understanding that none who subscribed less than £500 could have a Vote by the Charter', resolved to subscribe an additional £300 to ensure that his vote was secured.[29] And it is clear that Jeake used his vote. He attended the Bank's General Courts on numerous occasions and at the end of 1697 he remained in the City to 'use y^t little interest I have' against a further engraftment of tallies on to Bank stock.[30] Many of Jeake's fellow subscribers seem to have been similarly inclined to exercise their voting rights; 64 per cent of the Bank's original subscribers committed a sum of £500 or more.[31] At the election of directors held in July 1697, 458 votes were cast for Samuel Lethieullier suggesting that around one-third of those eligible to vote at this time did so.[32]

The sum of £500 also rapidly became the standard unit of exchange in Bank stock. On average in the years between 1694 and 1702, 34 per cent of transactions were for precisely £500, making it by far the most common unit of transfer.[33] Interestingly, although £500 was the dominant

performance of their interests. R. Pearson, 'Shareholder Democracies? English Stock Companies and the Politics of Corporate Governance during the Industrial Revolution', *English Historical Review*, 117 (2002), 841.

[29] Hunter and Gregory, *Astrological Diary*, p. 241.
[30] Bank Archives, G7/1, passim; ESRO, Jeake Papers, FRE 5319.
[31] Bank Archives, AC27/382. [32] Bank Archives, G7/1, 21 Jul. 1697.
[33] Bank Archives, AC28/32233; AC28/1513 22.

unit of transfer, during the period under consideration the proportion of stockholders holding precisely that amount did not exceed 20 per cent and the prevalence of £500 trades did not increase prior to elections.[34] This indicates that while securing sufficient stock to gain a vote was considered very important, the splitting of holdings of stock into £500 units to be distributed to friends and relations who would then exercise their vote as requested by the original stockholder was not typical at this time.[35]

The very active approach to stock ownership displayed by Samuel Jeake and others was not common to all proprietors. But it may be argued that the dominant view of stockholding in the 1690s was one in which company and proprietor had reciprocal rights and responsibilities and this had the potential to affect investor choice. Since all companies required a minimum level of stock to be held before a vote could be exercised or a directorship taken up, the ability to diversify a portfolio was restricted. If investment capital was limited, investors had to choose between spreading their risk and exercising their right to influence company proceedings. Such considerations might also have prevented investors from disposing of their interests in a particular company during periods when dividends were reduced or stock prices were falling. Furthermore, investors might have been induced to choose to invest in companies with which they imagined their influence to be greater rather than another company with higher profit potential.

Such behaviour had important consequences for the early modern market. In the first place, it conferred a degree of stability since investors would not have liquidated holdings or altered their allegiances with every rumour or shift in market sentiment. In particular, this degree of stability helped to restrict the ability of stock-jobbers to manipulate the prices of the shares of the larger joint-stock companies. Secondly, it would have affected the efficiency of individual investment strategies. The view of investment as the pursuit of rational, self-interested profit maximisation does not allow for relationships of this kind to impact upon the choices investors make.[36] It is assumed that investors should be able to liquidate their holdings at will whenever the occasion called for it but investors in the late seventeenth and early eighteenth centuries were not free in this way.

---

[34] Bank Archives, AC28/32233; AC28/1513 22; AC27/581.

[35] Stock splitting did become common among East India Company shareholders, particularly during the mid eighteenth century. Bowen, 'The "Little Parliament"', 862.

[36] For a further discussion of this issue see M. Granovetter, 'Economic Action and Social Structure: The Problem of Embeddedness', American Journal of Sociology, 91 (1985), 481 510.

Passive investors

The picture of stability or even stagnation within the larger joint-stock companies is reflected in individual levels of trading activity. It was demonstrated in the previous chapter that approximately 85 per cent of those dealing in Bank of England shares traded fewer than five times in a year. Moreover, around one-third of those investors were pursuing risk-averse 'buy and hold' strategies. It is, of course, difficult to be precise about the type of individual pursuing such strategies, nevertheless, it is reasonable to suggest that they would have been reliant upon the income derived from investment for the necessities of life. Women, those whose social status precluded working for a living and those whose working life was over, were typical of this type of investor. The overriding aim for such individuals would have been to gain a regular and reliable income while preserving the integrity of the capital sum. Windfall profits may have been invested more actively or investors may have allocated a certain proportion of funds to riskier endeavours but, in the main, capital was placed in assets that were deemed secure.

Table 8.1, which compares the social status of all those who made just one purchase of Bank stock during 1695 and 1700 with the actions of the entire community of investors, seems to bear out those assumptions. It shows that merchants and those with a professional interest in the financial market were more likely to have been active investors. Gentlemen, professionals, women and to a lesser extent manufacturers were more likely to pursue risk-averse investment strategies.

Although it is difficult to be precise about the background of those describing themselves as 'gentleman', the term was increasingly being adopted by wealthy merchants and other professionals, particularly as they reached a more financially secure period in their lives or as their working lives were coming to an end and a comfortable retirement beckoned. Thomas Bowrey, for example, described himself as a gentleman towards the end of his life after having defined himself as either a merchant or a mariner in previous years.[37] Nicholas Gambier, an apothecary by trade, also adopted the title in 1696 after receiving a substantial inheritance on the death of his father-in-law, James de la Bretonnière.[38] The adoption of a risk-averse investment strategy was natural for those taking a less active interest in business and preparing to pursue a more leisurely lifestyle.

[37] GLL, MS 3041/9 i; Bank Archives, AC28/32233; AC28/1513 17.
[38] Bank Archives, AC28/1513, passim.

The ease with which shares could be liquidated and divided also made them attractive to those preparing towards the end of their life to make provision for their dependants. As the market became more settled in the early eighteenth century, shares or company bonds left in trust could be relied upon to provide an income that might support a widow or dependent children. It is possibly for this reason that professional individuals began to move assets into Bank stock. Clark points out that doctors, lawyers and clergymen had no capital stock to leave to their dependants.[39] It was important to such people to ensure that adequate alternative provision was made. Undoubtedly, other businessmen harboured doubts that their wives or dependants could be trusted to manage the family's affairs after their death. According to one contemporary observer, the merchant assumed that 'if God should call him out of the world while the main of his estate is engaged in trade, he must lose one third of it, through the inexperience and inaptness of his wife to such affairs'.[40] Thus, transferring assets to more secure investments towards the end of one's life protected the integrity of the estate. These assumptions are supported by Earle's assertion that during the 1690s many more businessmen were reaching ages when they needed to place a higher proportion of their assets outside their own immediate business.[41] Greater life expectancy and an ageing affluent population, therefore, increased the demand for outlets for risk-averse investment.

The most prominent difference in Table 8.1 is among female investors. This is not surprising. Lone women were inevitably dependent on income derived from investment and are often viewed as the archetypal risk-averse investor. They have also been noted as being among the most important beneficiaries of the financial revolution,[42] although it is clear that they also retained an interest in more traditional assets. In a study that spanned the period from 1660 to 1730, Earle noted that women owned, or controlled, a sizeable proportion of the London housing stock.[43] And women, by

---

[39] Clark, *Betting on Lives*, p. 168.

[40] Quoted in Habakkuk, 'English Landownership', 11.

[41] P. Earle, *The Making of the English Middle Class: Business, Society and Family Life in London, 1660 1730* (London: Methuen, 1989), pp. 144 5. See also P. Earle, 'Age and Accumulation in the London Business Community, 1665 1720', in N. McKendrick and R.B. Outhwaite, eds., *Business Life and Public Policy: Essays in Honour of D. C. Coleman* (Cambridge University Press, 1986), pp. 38 63.

[42] B.A. Holderness, 'Widows in Pre industrial Society: An Essay Upon Their Economic Functions', in R.M. Smith, ed., *Land, Kinship and Life Cycle* (Cambridge University Press, 1985), p. 437. Sharpe also notes that as the financial market grew more sophisti cated Hester Pinney increasingly invested in 'safer public companies rather than less reliable individuals'. Sharpe 'Dealing with Love', 222.

[43] Earle, *Making of the Middle Class*, pp. 173 4.

Table 8.1 *Comparison of social status/occupation of shareholders making a single purchase of Bank stock with all purchasers, 1695 and 1700*

	1695				1700			
	Number of investors making one purchase	Percentage	All purchasers	Percentage	Number of investors making one purchase	Percentage	All purchasers	Percentage
Titled aristocrats	10	5.95	26	5.11	10	3.44	38	3.88
Gentlemen	32	19.05	78	15.32	60	20.62	149	15.22
Esquires	22	13.10	65	12.77	42	14.43	137	13.99
Professionals	16	9.52	39	7.66	30	10.31	75	7.66
Merchants	24	14.29	150	29.47	42	14.43	240	24.51
Finance	1	0.60	7	1.38	7	2.41	53	5.41
Retailing	21	12.50	71	13.95	34	11.68	133	13.59
Manufacture	12	7.14	24	4.72	22	7.56	71	7.25
Transport	1	0.60	4	0.79	0	0.00	4	0.41
Agriculture	0	0.00	0	0.00	0	0.00	1	0.10
Building	0	0.00	1	0.20	1	0.34	2	0.20
Domestic service	0	0.00	1	0.20	2	0.69	3	0.31
Women	28	16.67	38	7.47	39	13.40	66	6.74
Unknown	1	0.60	5	0.98	2	0.69	7	0.72
Totals	168		509		291		979	

Source: Bank Archives, AC28/32233; AC28/1513; AC28/1518–20.

204   The Origins of English Financial Markets

providing much needed capital, continued to play a key role in the bond and mortgage markets.[44] To a far lesser extent, women had also long been involved in equities. In 1688, for example, sixty-five women held a total of £99,987 East India Company stock, a sum that represented just over 6 per cent of the total capital.[45]

Of course, women were not necessarily risk-averse investors. Lucy Loyd traded in Linen Company, Blue Paper Company and Bank of England shares, undertaking option trades as well as straightforward sales and purchases.[46] Loyd evidently took an active interest in the market, was comfortable dealing with brokers and had an understanding of the more complex aspects of the market. Dame Mary Ashe also traded in Bank and East India Company shares on numerous occasions and was risk-seeking in her approach to investment.[47] In general, however, women required their investments to be safe and secure. It is notable that there were only four women among Charles Blunt's clients, and one of those was acting together with her husband.[48] It is also clear that, during the 1690s, women were responsible for a very limited amount of the overall trading activity in the major joint-stocks. Tables 8.2 and 8.3 show that women consistently accounted for less than 6 per cent of purchases and sales of stock of East India Company and Bank of England stock and often their activity levels in those shares was negligible.

Yet, although women did not actively trade in shares, they did recognise the value of holding stock as a long-term investment. For example, there were 153 women among the original subscribers to the Bank of England; they made up just over 12 per cent of the original subscribers to the Bank.[49] Many retained their holdings for a considerable period of time. Indeed, of the seventy widows who subscribed to the Bank, thirty-six retained their holdings for more than five years.[50] Similarly, of the sixty-five female holders of East India Company stock in 1688, twenty-seven still retained their holdings in 1699.[51]

It should be noted, however, that although shares in the main moneyed companies may have provided a secure investment for widows and spinsters, married women were more vulnerable to losing control of their capital. With regard to Bank stock, husbands invariably countersigned their wife's transactions and married women were clearly not expected to conduct business without their husband's permission. Thus, in 1697

---

[44] Ibid., p. 174.   [45] IOR, H/2 fos. 94 144.
[46] NA, PRO, C114/165; Bank Archives, AC28/32233; AC28/1513 22.
[47] Bank Archives, AC28/32233; AC28/1513 22, passim; IOR L/AG/14/3/2 6.
[48] NA, PRO, C114/165.   [49] Bank Archives, M1/1.
[50] Bank Archives, AC27/382; AC28/32233; AC28/1513 22.   [51] IOR, H/2.

Table 8.2 *Women's activity in East India Company stock*

	No. of female sellers	As percentage of all sellers	No. of sales by women	As percentage of all sales	Average nominal amount (in £s)	No. of female buyers	As percentage of all buyers	No. of purchases by women	As percentage of all purchases	Average nominal amount (in £s)
Jun.–Sep. 1691	7	3.80	14	1.29	446	2	1.08	9	0.83	322
Apr.–Jul. 1694	3	1.65	3	0.55	835	15	5.98	18	3.30	276
Aug.–Dec. 1698	7	3.63	7	1.33	283	2	0.96	2	0.38	219
Jan.–May, Nov, Dec. 1699	4	2.20	4	0.93	663	6	3.97	10	2.33	389
Jan.–Feb. 1700	12	5.97	12	2.62	325	1	0.79	1	0.22	300

Source: IOR, L/AG/14/3/2–6. Observations are partial since many of the East India Company's transfer books from this period have been lost.

Table 8.3 *Women's activity in Bank of England stock*

	No. of female sellers	As percentage of all sellers	No. of sales by women	As percentage of all sales	Average nominal amount (in £s)	No. of female buyers	As percentage of all buyers	No. of purchases by women	As percentage of all purchases	Average nominal amount (in £s)
1694	11	4.80	11	2.98	497	17	7.05	17	4.61	341
1695	20	3.98	31	2.26	282	38	7.47	52	3.79	346
1696	39	8.94	57	4.32	447	31	5.41	47	3.56	424
1697	27	3.61	38	1.90	655	55	6.53	68	3.35	473
1698	53	5.15	70	2.83	360	102	9.07	130	5.26	328
1699	73	7.55	100	4.23	358	86	9.47	115	4.86	357
1700	109	10.02	139	4.58	401	66	6.74	86	2.83	396
1701	54	7.56	65	3.62	439	79	9.65	90	5.01	349
1702	67	9.42	100	6.97	341	87	12.54	96	6.69	461

Source: Bank Archives, AC28/32233; AC28/1513–22.

when Martha Tomson, a married woman, decided to sell stock without her husband's written permission she had to seek approval from Sir James Houblon and Richard Raworth, two of the Bank's directors, before her transfer could be permitted.[52] There was also a consistent pattern of women relinquishing their shareholdings as a result of their marriage. Of the eighty-one transactions in Bank of England stock between 1694 and 1702 conducted by married women, more than 30 per cent were conducted by women disposing of their entire stock. Some wives sold their stock directly to their husbands, as in the case of Judith Dickinson who transferred £325, all her holdings, to her husband William on 9 November 1697.[53] Others sold to strangers but it may be assumed that the proceeds were claimed by their husbands. There was only one transaction conducted by a married woman in the Hudson's Bay Company books during the period under review. It was conducted by a Susannah Dorrill, formerly Susannah Edmanson, widow of John Edmanson. She sold her £700 stock to Nicholas Beeby, who immediately sold it on to Captain Robert Dorrill, Susannah's new husband.[54] Similarly, there was only one married woman recorded in the books of Estcourt's Lead Mine. Elizabeth Lambert, who conducted a number of transactions as a spinster, was recorded as having liquidated her entire stock when she became Elizabeth Hooke.[55] Such instances support Elizabeth Freke's plaintive complaint, made in 1698: 'Mr Frek and my son Frek left mee all alone ... [Mr Freke] haveing before he left me took from mee my thousand pounds given me by my deer father and putt itt in his own name in the East Indy Company ... This I thought very hard usage, butt tis true.'[56] Elizabeth's words may sum up the thoughts of many wives on seeing their secure investments disappear.

   In the longer term the shares of the main moneyed companies and the instruments of the national debt proved to be highly suitable vehicles for risk-averse investors. By the early 1750s, for example, around 25 per cent of the Bank of England's shareholders were women.[57] Their increasing participation was a clear indication of how much progress London's financial market had made in terms of stability and reliability. Yet, during the 1690s there were fewer opportunities to pursue a risk-averse strategy.

[52]   Bank Archives, AC28/1514, 23 Sep. 1697.
[53]   Bank Archives, AC28/1515, 9 Nov. 1697.
[54]   NA, PRO, BH 1/465, 3 Sep. 1696.   [55] NA, PRO, C114/165.
[56]   R. A. Anselment, ed., *The Remembrances of Elizabeth Freke, 1671 1714* (Cambridge University Press, 2001), p. 71.
[57]   Dickson, *Financial Revolution*, p. 298. Figures derived from a sample of stockholders in 1753. For a further discussion of women's increasing commitment and contribution to the public funds see A. M. Carlos and L. Neal, 'Women Investors in Early Capital Markets, 1720 1725', *Financial History Review*, 11 (2004), 197 224.

The market was often volatile, returns on assets, both private and public, remained unpredictable and, most importantly, share ownership was not perceived as a passive activity. In spite of these factors, there were certainly those individuals who cared little for capital gains and merely required that an investment yielded a regular income. Such investors were little concerned with price and were prepared to leave their holdings for a period of years, but very few of them could have felt entirely confident of the reliability of that income.

Merchants, businessmen and part-time speculators

Not all investors had such limited dealings in the new financial market. There were those whose activity was too infrequent for them to be described as stock-jobbers but who did use debt instruments and equities actively and sometimes speculatively. As will be shown below, such investors usually maintained diverse investment portfolios which drew on a mix of traditional and new assets, and their motives and methods were forever shifting with the course of their business. In some instances they might have considered the financial market a good place to lodge idle capital.[58] John Houghton noted that the advantage of investment in joint-stocks was that investors were 'able to command [their capital] whensoever they had occasion, which they found they could more easily do in *Joint-Stock* than in laying out the same in Lands, Houses or Commodities'.[59] It is also likely that as the market became more settled and the prospect of dividends more reliable, shares in the Bank of England particularly were used to supplement income, perhaps providing a stable base for more risky ventures. Equally, it is clear that some individuals were motivated by the seeming prospect of easily obtained capital gains and thus, on occasion, traded speculatively.

Shareholding was also a consequence of social and political motives. Since shares gave access to and influence over a company's decision-making processes, share-ownership may have been particularly desirable for merchants engaged in trade in a particular area. There is not a great deal of available evidence to back such an assumption, but Davies suggested that at least two-thirds of the capital of the Royal African Company was in the hands of businessmen, of whom the majority were overseas traders.[60] Carlos and Stone also noted that within the Hudson's Bay

[58] D.J. Hancock, 'Domestic Bubbling: Eighteenth Century London Merchants and Individual Investment in the Funds', *Economic History Review*, 47 (1994), 696.
[59] Houghton, *Collection for Improvement*, 15 Jun. 1694.
[60] Davies, *Royal African Company*, pp. 69 70.

Company there were a small but significant number of fur traders who both owned shares and became involved in the Company's operation.[61]

It has also been suggested that shareholding sometimes had a broader political significance.[62] In particular, the new moneyed interest has been identified as being mainly Whig in political affiliation. De Krey's study of London politics in the late seventeenth century found that many London Whigs resented their exclusion from the financial opportunities created by England's commercial expansion during the 1670s and 1680s, and looked upon the Glorious Revolution as an opportunity to restructure existing opportunities for investment and create new ones.[63] Their dissatisfaction with the pre-Revolutionary structure of English finance manifested itself through strong support for and involvement in the founding of the Bank of England and the challenge to the East India Company's monopoly that culminated in the establishment of the New Company in 1698. Similarly, Carruthers's study of some of the factors that influenced trading decisions in the early eighteenth century concluded that the financial market was perceived as a vehicle through which political goals could be pursued.[64] However, while the political connections of the major joint-stock companies were clear, as has been argued in earlier chapters, their relations with government were not always cordial. In the unstable environment of the 1690s even the Bank of England was vulnerable to political attack and its political affiliations certainly did not save the New East India Company from being consumed by the Old. Moreover, there is actually very little evidence to suggest that overt political motives should be generally assumed of London's first investors. Both De Krey's and Carruthers's studies were based on limited samples and even Carruthers was forced to conclude that to the professional jobbers, who as we have seen formed the core of the market, political affiliation did not matter.[65]

The uses to which debt and equity securities could be put were exemplified in the investment activities of Samuel Jeake, a merchant from the East Sussex town of Rye.[66] Jeake was first introduced to public finance in 1694 during a visit to London at which time he learned about the Million Adventure and was sufficiently 'animated by the Example of

[61] Carlos and Van Stone, 'Stock Transfer Patterns', 29.
[62] Notably De Krey, *Fractured Society*; Carruthers, *City of Capital*. See also Jones, 'London Overseas Merchant Groups'.
[63] De Krey, *Fractured Society*, p. 134.
[64] Carruthers, *City of Capital*, p. 207.   [65] Ibid., p. 181.
[66] For a fuller discussion of Jeake's investment strategies see A. L. Murphy, 'Dealing with Uncertainty: Managing Personal Investment in the Early English National Debt', *History*, 91 (2006), 200 17.

the Londoners'[67] to want to purchase tickets. Jeake also had strong political motives for supporting the public funds. He was a nonconformist and thus he had a vested interest in supporting a new regime which 'through the mercifull Providence of God, [had delivered him] from the fears of Popery & Persecution'.[68] Furthermore, as a resident of a south coast town, he was in a position to experience at first hand the threat posed by the French. In July 1690 he reported in his diary, '[a] terrible alarm in the Towne of Rye of the Frenches coming to land; they having sent 3 small shallops to sound the depths at coming in to the harbour'.[69] Such experiences undoubtedly increased his willingness to commit funds to the war effort.

Between 1694 and 1699 Jeake had dealings in Million Adventure tickets, Bank of England stock, East India stock and Royal Lustring Company shares.[70] It is also possible that further trades were undertaken, but not recorded in his surviving letters or diaries. His activity in the financial market was sporadic and the bulk of his income between 1694 and his death in 1699 was still derived from his trade in hops, some legal work and moneylending activities.[71] This variety should not be seen as surprising; like every other merchant of the period, Jeake was forced to be adaptable in his approach to business.

In common with many other merchants at this time, Jeake's main motive for diversifying his investments was to compensate for the loss of trade during a time of war. He suggested in his diary that his main aim was to create an income flow at a rate of better than 5 per cent – the yield that he had been receiving from his private moneylending activities.[72] Yet, this essentially passive aim was not always reflected in his actions. Jeake bought annuities and Bank stock for the prospective yield, but also speculated when he had the chance – not always to very good effect.[73] Jeake also failed to take into account all the costs of his involvement in the financial market. His speculations required him to be in London for extended periods of time, consequently his business in Rye suffered while he was pursuing illusory profits in company stocks. He was often forced to borrow in order to fund his adventures in the market, at one point paying 10 per cent for a loan from his mother-in-law, and on another occasion paying 6 per cent for a loan of £100 for a year, 'having no time then spare

[67] Hunter and Gregory, *Astrological Diary*, p. 232.   [68] Ibid., p. 195.
[69] Ibid., p. 204.   [70] Ibid., passim.
[71] East Sussex Record Office, Rye Corporation Archives, RYE/145/11, passim.
[72] Hunter and Gregory, *Astrological Diary*, p. 233.
[73] Notably in East India stock in 1694 when he achieved a profitable outcome and in Bank stock in 1697 when his hesitancy and greed for further profits eroded his returns. Ibid., pp. 244 9; ESRO, Jeake Papers, passim.

to try for it cheaper'.[74] Thus, while Jeake was an astute and well-educated businessman who, on occasion, used the market to good effect, his rational aims could easily be destroyed by his emotional responses to the market.

The Hollis family, father Thomas and sons Thomas junior and John, all cutlers residing in the Minories in London, had a similar level of involvement in the market to Jeake, although less is known about their investments. Their actions can be traced through the Bank of England's transfer books and their timing and activities display sophisticated motives. The family's association with the Bank began in December 1696 when Thomas senior bought £500 stock, an investment sufficient to secure a vote. Over the period under review Thomas made gradual additions to his holdings and his acquisitions ultimately totalled £2,709.[75] His sons, Thomas and John, exchanged tallies for Bank stock during the capital enlargement of 1697. Thomas subscribed £125 at this time and John subscribed £750.[76] At the time, although Bank stock was not performing well, its prospects were still considerably better than those of tallies, thus their subscription should be considered an astute decision. Both sons added to their positions in the following years. They were, however, more reactive in their approach than their father. John liquidated holdings in 1700 and Thomas in 1701. By the eve of the War of Spanish Succession John held only £250 stock and Thomas junior held £175.[77] Their actions in Bank stock seem to contrast well with Samuel Jeake's in that neither father nor sons appear to have engaged in any speculative activity. This indicates a stable approach to investment that was perhaps the result of decisions made in a family setting. The Hollis investments are also interesting because holdings were used to make payments to John Browne, a cutler residing in Sheffield. A total of £600 Bank stock was transferred to John Browne by Thomas junior and John in May and August 1698. Interestingly, John was acting with power of attorney for Browne, seeming to suggest that the transfer of Bank stock was payment for services rendered or goods supplied.[78] For the Hollis family, therefore, shareholding was a source of investment, perhaps providing a retirement fund for Thomas senior, a place to deposit idle capital and a necessary part of their business.

Thomas Bowrey took a far more active approach to investment. Indeed, analysis of his activities might almost have been placed in the previous chapter. Bowrey was born around 1650 and went to India at the age of

[74] Hunter and Gregory, *Astrological Diary*, p. 241.   [75] Bank Archives, AC28/1513 22.
[76] Bank Archives, M1/6 9.   [77] Bank Archives, AC28/1513 22.
[78] Bank Archives, AC28/1513, 18 May 1698; 25 Aug. 1698.

Table 8.4 *Thomas Bowrey's investment activity, 1695*

Month	EIC stock	EIC options	Bank stock	Million Adventure
January		Bgt right to buy £200 EIC	Bgt 500	
February	Bgt 800	Bgt right to buy £900 EIC		Bgt 28 blank tickets
March			Bgt 500	
			Sold 600	
April			Bgt 800	Bgt 7 blank tickets
			Sold 500	
May	Bgt 400		Bgt 700	
			Sold 700	
June	Bgt 600			
July			Bgt £300	
August	Bgt 200		Sold £500	
September			Sold £400	Bgt 29 blank tickets
October	Bgt 300			
November				
December				Bgt 20 blank tickets

Sources: GLL, MS 3041/1, passim; MS 3041/9, iv, passim; Bank Archives, AC27/414; AC27/418.

nineteen as a free merchant. He returned home in 1688, and his marriage to Mary Gardiner in 1691 and the comfortable lifestyle that they pursued suggest that his time in India had left Bowrey a reasonably rich man.[79] Yet, he did not adopt a leisured life. He remained active in business until his death in 1713 and pursued various interests. Bowrey continued to invest in voyages to India and owned property in and around Wapping. He was also an enthusiastic participant in the new financial market. Unfortunately, his papers contain no accounts for the 1690s, but his activities can be partially reconstructed from a number of brokerage receipts and from transfer books and stock ledgers. A number of broker- age bills from the early 1690s reveal activity in East India shares, Royal African Company stock and Linen Company shares. Bowrey also traded options on a number of occasions, committed funds to the state lotteries, and was quick to subscribe to the New East India Company in 1698.[80]

It is possible to reconstruct his activity in shares and debt products in 1695. As Table 8.4 shows, during that year, which was probably his most active, Bowrey traded in East India and Bank stock and bought blank

[79] The Bowreys spent time in Bath and in 1696 Thomas cruised to Holland on a sightseeing tour. GLL, MS 3041/9, iii; R. C. Temple, ed., *The Papers of Thomas Bowrey, 1669 1713* (London: Hakluyt Society, 1927).
[80] GLL, MS 3041/5, passim.

Million Adventure tickets. The purchase of blank lottery tickets was a sensible investment in 1695. The draw for the Million Adventure had already taken place, but blank tickets continued to yield £1 per year until 1710 and the price of tickets after the draw was heavily discounted. Bowrey purchased his tickets at an average price of £7.[81] Thus, he was entitled to expect a reasonable return and for his investment of £588 should have received £84 per year for the following sixteen years, a reasonable yield despite the fact that the principal would not be refunded. Unfortunately, benefit payments on the lottery were interrupted by the poor progress of the war and the government's subsequent credit problems. Thus, Bowrey had to wait until at least 1698 before he saw any return on that particular investment.

Bowrey's trades in Bank stock were rather more interesting. He bought in January when the share price was hovering between 74 and 81, and thus was able to participate in a subsequent rally as the price moved up to around 90 in March 1695. The share price then remained between 90 and 97 for most of the rest of the year, before rising again to 108 in January 1696. Bowrey still retained holdings in early 1696, but just missed the peak of the market, selling out in February at a price of around 85.[82] Bowrey's actions between March and September 1695 are less easy to explain. The relatively stagnant price of stock indicates that jobbing would have provided a poor return. Furthermore, the majority of his counterparties were merchants, many of whom had a regular involvement in the market, thus, Bowrey was not making money from exploiting the ignorance of the occasional investor. It is possible that his activity between March and September was the result of option trading, but there are no surviving option contracts in Bank stock among his papers. Whatever the reason for his trades, it does seem unlikely that they were very profitable.

Bowrey's dogged accumulation of East India Company stock also requires some explanation. Throughout the 1690s the East India Company's share price was vulnerable as a result of systematic attacks on the Company's monopoly and wartime shipping losses. Yet, throughout 1695 Bowrey added to an existing position in East India Company stock through the purchase of shares and options that gave him the right to buy further stock. It is possible that his interest in East India Company stock was a consequence of his trade in Indian goods and possibly stemmed from a desire to influence the ongoing arguments regarding the nature of the Company's monopoly. Many merchants like Bowrey were agitating for the right to greater access to trade to the East Indies and,

[81] GLL, MS3041/9 iv, passim.
[82] Prices quoted in Houghton, *Collection for Improvement*, passim.

as noted above, ownership of shares gave access to and influence over the Company's decision-making processes. Nevertheless, for Bowrey, the political advantages of holding East India Company stock were unlikely to have outweighed the financial costs. At the end of 1695 Bowrey calculated that he had lost £464 18s 9d as a result of his trade in East India stock.[83] He maintained his interest in the Company until at least April 1696, when he had holdings of £1,077 but by 1699 he had no interest in either the East India Company or the Bank of England.[84] Indeed, Bowrey's involvement in the financial market probably came to a halt in early 1696, perhaps as a result of the disappointing returns experienced in 1695. His accounts for the early part of the eighteenth century show that he was once again deriving his living from trade and the sale of imported goods. During this period his involvement in the financial market was relatively limited. He bought and sold East India Bonds in 1707, made a subscription to South Sea stock in 1711 and purchased seventeen tickets in the state lottery of 1710.[85] Bowrey's luck, however, had not improved – all his lottery tickets were blanks!

The cautious moneyed man

Given his experience of the financial market and the contacts he made through his brokerage business, it would not have been surprising to find that Charles Blunt was an active speculator. But his brokerage ledgers and personal accounts tell a different story.[86] Even when the stock-market boom was at its height, Blunt confined his activities to broking rather than stock-jobbing and his personal investment decisions were those of a rather cautious and conservative man. He maintained his upholstery business throughout the stock-market boom and still held goods relating to that business in 1698 suggesting that, in the short term at least, he returned quietly to the business of supplying soft furnishings, putting up and taking down curtain hooks and wall hangings and stuffing feather pillows when the boom was over. Blunt also held a significant amount of idle cash during the later 1690s indicating that he was unwilling to risk the profits of his brokerage business in the market which he supported. Moreover, when Blunt did purchase shares he generally confined his interest to the Bank of England and the Old and New East India Companies.[87]

The reasons for Blunt's lack of interest in the stock market must lie partly in his personality. He was a prudent, some might say parsimonious,

[83] GLL, MS 3041/5, fo. 51.   [84] IOR, H2; Bank Archives, AC27/581 2.
[85] GLL, MS 3041/1, passim.   [86] NA, PRO, Papers of Charles Blunt, C114/164/3.
[87] Ibid., passim.

man who kept careful control of his money. On one occasion he noted in his accounts the sum of sixpence given as a charitable donation to assist wounded soldiers and, on another, he carefully recorded money owed to him by his wife.[88] But his reluctance to invest in shares might also have been born of experience. As a constant observer of the stock market of the early 1690s, Blunt would have known the risks inherent in share trading and understood that with no effective regulatory authority and very little legal sanction against financial fraud, projectors could, and did, set up companies solely with the aim of duping naïve investors. Indeed, Charles had first-hand knowledge of such schemes because he kept the transfer books and owned shares in Estcourt's Lead Mine which, as shown in the previous chapter, was ultimately used for purely speculative purposes by his cousin John Blunt. It should not be supposed that Charles disapproved of his cousin's actions. Indeed, it is probable that he was quite happy to accept the rewards of John's deceit. But perhaps this experience fixed in his mind the need for caution when investing in the stock market of the 1690s.

The result of his prudence was that by the first years of the eighteenth century Blunt had accumulated a considerable fortune and had given up the upholstery business for a quiet life in the country. According to contemporary opinion, this made him quite typical of affluent businessmen in the late seventeenth and early eighteenth century. B. L. de Muralt commented of English merchants in the 1690s, 'No sooner do they acquire wealth, but they quit traffick, and turn country gentlemen.'[89] Defoe also recommended that affluent businessmen should make way for the next generation and with profits of 'say £20,000 he should buy rents, save half his income of £1,000 and thus grow richer'.[90] As can be seen in Table 8.5, the construction of Blunt's investment portfolio in the years between 1703 and 1718 reflects just such a change of lifestyle.

It is immediately apparent that in the years surveyed in Table 8.5 Blunt held no idle cash. That situation was not necessarily typical. In January 1704 he had around £3,000 in the hands of goldsmiths and in January 1712 he had £720 in cash but, for the most part, after 1703 Blunt put all his capital to good use.[91] Equally, far less of his capital was held in goods. Although Blunt held more than 10 per cent of his assets in goods relating to his upholstery business in 1698, the goods and plate recorded after 1703 were always household items. They included his wife's jewellery and an assortment of silver candlesticks, coffee pots, tankards and cutlery. Ever practical, Blunt did not include in his assessment other things of

[88] Ibid.   [89] Quoted in Earle, *Making of the Middle Class*, p. 152.
[90] Ibid.   [91] NA, PRO, C114/164/3, passim.

Table 8.5 *Distribution of Charles Blunt's assets, as a percentage of total*

	1703	1708	1713	1718
Ready money	0	0	0	0
Goods and plate	3.93	2.75	1.80	1.43
Land and property	38.50	34.89	20.08	28.79
Rent	1.32	1.64	2.06	1.08
Private loans	8.44	5.64	3.60	4.91
Shares and dividends	34.83	24.81	49.82	38.00
Fixed income annuities/gov. debt	12.98	30.27	22.64	25.79
Totals	100.00	100.00	100.00	100.00

Source: NA, PRO, C114/164.

value such as furniture, tapestries and linen.[92] It is evident, therefore, that in his mind the items of importance were those on which he could raise money if necessary.

The remainder of Blunt's investment portfolio between 1703 and 1718 continued to reflect his cautious character. It is particularly notable that, in common with all the above-mentioned individuals, Blunt maintained a consistently diverse portfolio of assets. Like many early modern investors, he would have understood that diversification was essential in an economic environment where markets could rapidly contract and the ability to manage risk effectively was limited.[93]

Another indicator of his cautious approach to investment was that Blunt typically held around one-third of his capital in property and land. In fact, by 1718 he had acquired property in Wales (a legacy of his first marriage), Essex, Gloucester, Cambridgeshire and London. His London properties included the freehold of an estate in Lincolns Inn Fields (valued at £2,500) and the forty-year lease of estates in Petty France and St James's Park (valued at £5,000). It is unlikely that his property portfolio yielded a significant income. As Lord Hervey commented in 1707, 'after taxes and repairs allowed [land] never answers above three per cent'.[94] But for a man like Blunt striving to attain gentlemanly status from more humble

---

[92] Ibid.

[93] Diversification of investment portfolios is noted in various studies. See, in particular, Earle, *Making of the Middle Class*; R. Grassby, 'The Personal Wealth of the Business Community in Seventeenth Century England', *Economic History Review*, 23 (1970), 220 34; R. Grassby, 'English Merchant Capitalism in the Late Seventeenth Century', *Past and Present*, 46 (1977), 87 107; Grassby, *Business Community*; Jones, *War and Economy*.

[94] Earle, *Making of the Middle Class*, p. 152.

Table 8.6 *Distribution of investment assets, as a percentage of total*

Type of investment	1665 89	1690 1720
Loans and mortgages	44.40	40.50
Leases	22.20	8.70
Government debt	3.40	12.00
Company stocks and bonds	24.00	35.60
Shipping	6.00	3.20
Totals	100.00	100.00
Number of cases	211	164

Source: Earle, Making of the Middle Class, p. 146.

beginnings, land and property carried a symbolic importance. It was an outward sign of his newly found position in society.

Private lending formed only a very small proportion of Blunt's investments. This marks him as quite different from others of the middling sort in the early eighteenth century. As can be seen in Table 8.6, Peter Earle's analysis of the inventories of Londoners between 1660 and 1720 shows that, on average, loans and mortgages comprised more than 40 per cent of their investments. For Blunt, however, private lending made up less than 10 per cent of his investment portfolio and several of the loans recorded in his accounts were to his family, notably his wife and children.

Blunt preferred to lend to the state. Undoubtedly this decision was due, in part, to the fact that while interest on loans to private individuals was capped by law at 6 per cent until 1714 and 5 per cent thereafter, the state paid between 6.25 and 9 per cent on its debt during the early eighteenth century.[95] But given his cautious character, a willingness to commit so heavily to government debt must also be seen as a demonstration of the significant improvements to state finance that had occurred by the early years of the eighteenth century. Indeed, the experiences of the 1690s had taught the Treasury much about the practicalities of debt issuance, the need to cultivate good relations with the Bank of England and the desirability of maintaining the confidence of foreign and domestic investors.[96] Underpinning these advances was greater political stability under Queen Anne and Sidney Godolphin's competent management of the public finances, which did much to win the confidence of the City.[97]

It is likely that these factors also prompted the growth of Blunt's share portfolio. He had a particular interest in Bank of England stock undoubtedly because its close and now more cooperative ties to government

[95] Dickson, *Financial Revolution*, pp. 60 3.   [96] Ibid., p. 58.   [97] Ibid., pp. 58 9.

provided greater assurances that the state would not renege on debts owed to the Bank. Indeed, the enhanced security of the Bank's income flow from the state meant that its shares had effectively become proxies for government debt. Thus, in 1708 one commentator described the Bank as 'the surest estate, [in which] scarce any money'd man but has a share which he looks upon as his nest egg'.[98]

Although he acquired a significant share portfolio during the first years of the eighteenth century, Blunt was still not an active trader, preferring to pursue passive buy and hold strategies. But, as in the 1690s, he was prepared to take greater risks to invest in the well-proved, if slightly under-handed, business skills of his cousin John. John Blunt had been busy since the 1690s. Under his guidance the Sword Blade Company, in which Charles held shares and a directorship, had been transformed from a manufacturer of weaponry to a land corporation and, in effect, a banking operation. By 1710 John's business dealings and ability to turn a profit had caught the eye of Robert Harley, who had become Chancellor of the Exchequer in the new Tory ministry of that year. Faced with a difficult political situation and urgent financial need resulting from the exigencies of the War of Spanish Succession, Harley turned to the City for solutions. John Blunt and George Caswell, another of the partners of the Sword Blade Bank, proposed a number of schemes which were in effect revitalised versions of the more successful projects of the 1690s. Thus, under John Blunt's guidance a series of lotteries were floated in 1711 and 1712 and, most importantly, in a scheme that was a direct copy of the Bank of England's engraftment of the tallies in 1697, Blunt and partners established a new trading company. The Company, in a debt-for-equity exchange, took over a significant portion of the government's floating debt. Thus was the South Sea Company born.[99] Charles Blunt acted as a receiver of the navy bills and seamen's tickets that were subscribed to the new company, accepted a directorship and received more than £10,000 worth of shares.[100] It is not clear whether he paid full price for those shares, but as Figure 8.1 shows, his association with the South Sea Company certainly formed the basis for a significant increase in his net worth over the next few years.

Between 1711 and 1719 the rising value of South Sea Company shares justified Charles's faith in his cousin's business acumen. From a price of around 66 in September 1711 the shares rose to highs of around 120 in 1718 and 1719.[101] As Figure 8.2 shows, Charles reduced his

[98] Cited in Jones, 'London Merchants', p. 340.
[99] Dickson, *Financial Revolution*, pp. 64 5.
[100] NA, PRO, C114/164/3, account of January 1712.
[101] European State Finance Database, dataset \neal\coe1700s.rtf.

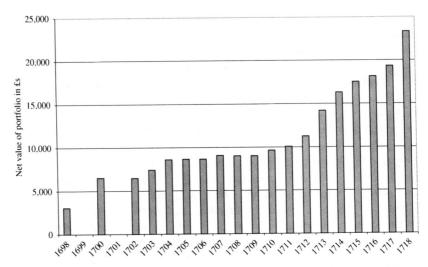

8.1 Value in £s of Charles Blunt's investment portfolio, 1698 1718
Source: NA, PRO, C114/164/3.

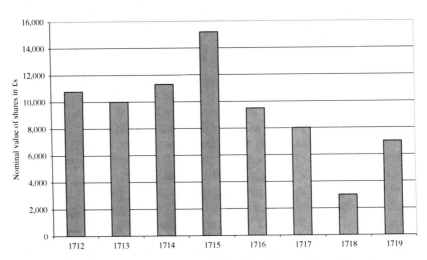

8.2 Nominal value of Charles Blunt's holdings of South Sea Company shares
Source: NA, PRO, C114/164/3.

holdings after 1715 in consequence realising a quite considerable profit. But, ultimately, John Blunt's ambition overreached itself. In 1719 renewed concerns about the level of government debt and the apparent success of John Law's reorganisation of France's financial system encouraged the South Sea Company to propose a scheme that would allow it to convert the whole of the government debt into company shares, excepting those obligations owed to the Bank of England and the East India Company. The scheme quickly captured the public imagination and, as is well known, the South Sea Company's share price rose from just under £100 to around £1,000 in the space of six months.[102] Then, inevitably, the Bubble collapsed just as quickly as investors recognised the insubstantial nature of the promises made by the Company. By October 1720 the share price had slipped back below £200 leaving investors outraged by their losses and missed opportunities.[103]

Charles Blunt undoubtedly profited as share prices rose. It is impossible to know by how much or how deeply embroiled he was in the Company's intrigues but by the end of 1720 one newspaper estimated that he was worth £250,000.[104] If that was true it gave him very little comfort. As the Bubble collapsed angry investors and a humiliated government began to lay the blame for the fiasco at the door of the Company's directors. Perhaps wishing to spare his family the embarrassment of an investigation or perhaps unable to live with the loss of his hard-won riches and status, Charles Blunt slit his own throat.

Between 1692 and 1720 Charles Blunt's relationship with London's financial market progressed from intermediary to investor to insider. For the most part he showed himself to be a cautious man and a smart operator. As a broker he let others take the risks, while he merely took his commission. As an investor he constructed a balanced portfolio of assets that made the most of his knowledge and personal connections. But he was also operating in what was often a dangerous and devious world and ultimately he could not rise above that environment. At his death he, along with all the other directors of the South Sea Company, stood accused of perpetrating a deception that in many people's eyes amounted to treason.

---

[102] Ibid.   [103] Dickson, *Financial Revolution*, pp. 159 60.
[104] Ibid., p. 495 n. 2.

Conclusion

There were no more than fifteen English joint-stock companies in 1685. Their stock was in the hands of around one thousand individuals, many of whom came from the upper echelons of City society, and most of whom lived in London or the surrounding areas. The market in the shares of those companies was limited and unsophisticated. To the disappointment of those who desired involvement in joint-stock investment and who particularly wanted to share in the great profits derived from trade to the East, shares changed hands infrequently. There were no professional market-makers, the term stock-jobber was not in common use and there were few individuals who fulfilled the role of financial broker.

Between 1685 and 1695 that situation was completely altered. Around a hundred new English joint-stock companies were established, a stock market grew up and proved surprisingly capable of supporting the exchange of large amounts of stock, as well as an active derivatives market, and a new class of stock-jobbers and brokers emerged. Thanks to investors like the fictional Mr Hazzard, who believed there was 'more to be got by Stock in a Week, or sometimes in a Day than by any other Business that he ever was acquainted with in a Year', the new stock market boomed. And even those who did not invest found their lives being touched by the advent of the financial market. Indeed, while many were disturbed by the actions of speculators, clearly they could not be ignored. The financial market was soon being represented in popular culture and in 1693 stock-jobbing formed the main sub-plot of Shadwell's play *The Volunteers*. Equally, lottery schemes enticed very many in England to experience the thrill of speculation. In 1698, when Thomas Houghton, the winner of the Wheel of Fortune, purchased his penny lottery ticket he had similar motives and aims to the greatest speculators of the day. Both desired great profits for little outlay and little trouble. The scale of their investment may have differed but, in the public mind, their approach did not.

The speculative boom, although typically short-lived, laid the ground-work for the successful development of England's first funded long-term national debt. Indeed, although the advent of the public funds has been seen by some historians as the driving force behind financial innovation, the government, in its search for a method of funding the Nine Years' War, was in fact responding to developments in the private market and taking advantage of the very great public interest that had been generated by the stock-market boom. But, the public funds did prove to be the most important and enduring of the innova-tions of the 1690s. The advent of a public debt that was accessible and attractive to the ordinary investor was a key development in the history of Britain's financial, political and social development. And in the longer term the new financial system became the cornerstone of Britain's rise to great power status. The innovations of the 1690s, there-fore, are rightly described as a financial revolution.

But London's early financial market also had many flaws. Investors were not always well informed. It is, of course, reasonable to argue that some investors might have considered lack of information to be of little concern. Those with long-term investment aims and faith in the Bank of England's or the East India Company's ability to sustain regular dividend payments would have considered the intermittent receipt of price information sufficient. Nevertheless, it is important to acknowledge that timely and accurate information was seldom available even to the most active of investors. The financial press was in its infancy. Newspapers seldom published relevant economic information. News from abroad could be delayed by adverse winds. Price data was published but it was sometimes inaccurate and it circulated too slowly to be of use to the active investor. There was a culture of secrecy among some joint-stock companies and in an environment where there was no requirement to advertise relevant information and no regularly pub-lished accounts, making a judgement about the current position and future prospects of any enterprise was difficult. Indeed, companies themselves struggled to gain a complete understanding of their financial position.

The information that was available circulated first in the heart of the City, particularly in the Royal Exchange and London's coffee houses. Thus, it circulated in restricted formats and among few people. Moreover, rumour and gossip, deliberately circulated and otherwise, often informed the markets and guided the movement of prices. This book has shown that insiders, those who had regular access to the places where news circulated, gained superior information and were in the best position to take advantage of that information. They could act first and thus reap profits or stem any losses that might have resulted from unexpected news. Those who used the markets regularly had a greater understanding of the failings of market information and thus were able to judge more effectively how the market would react to unexpected news. Potentially, insiders could use their superior knowledge to manipulate the market and it is clear that in some cases they did so. Outsiders had to be content with older, more costly information. They would have experienced difficulties distinguishing fact from rumour and would have struggled to understand the new language of the markets. They might also have found it necessary (as did Samuel Jeake) to devote much time to their investments, perhaps to the detriment of other areas of their economic lives. Such difficulties affected the ability of the infrequent investor to take advantage of potential short-term fluctuations in the market, and impacted upon their long-term decision-making.

The market failed its investors in other ways too. It did not provide effective instrument and company substitutes; thus arbitrage was difficult, if not impossible. Sophisticated hedging instruments – futures and options – were available and were used to the extent of their capabilities but they were not suitable for use by all investors. In particular, the negotiation of contracts was complex, and the use of such instruments required regular attendance at the market and a good flow of information. It is also clear that those who defined the financial market as a dangerous place, particularly for the naïve investor, were correct in many ways. Indeed, although the market was not anarchic, there were no effective restraints on deceitful behaviour and the expected rewards from successful deception could be high. The prices of smaller stocks were, therefore, certainly manipulated and the evidence of Estcourt's Lead Mine suggests that it was the insiders that reaped the rewards of such actions.

In larger stocks, specifically the Bank of England and the East India Company, the process of manipulation was more difficult for several reasons. First, larger stocks tended to have a core of passive investors who, because they were not concerned with capital gains and because they were not in receipt of regular information, did not react to every rumour or fluctuation in price. Secondly, shareholding was not regarded solely as a means of accessing dividends or capital gains. Investors did not always pursue their own aims self-interestedly. Self-interest was tempered by a sense of loyalty to a company that sometimes prevented investors from switching their funds to more profitable assets. These factors created an inherent stability in the main joint-stock companies. Finally, manipulation of a stock requires cooperation and organisation. In an environment where there was little trust, this would have been difficult to achieve on a scale necessary to move the prices of the larger stocks. This analysis is borne out by the price charts produced in Chapter 7, which show a smooth progression of prices and a market that was, for the most part, following long-term trends rather than short-term fluctuations.

Whether or not manipulation was widespread, this did come to be the dominant perception of the financial market at this time. This understanding of the market was compounded by instances of political manipulation by the East India Company, and by the general unease at the extent to which the new financial markets seemed to create an interdependent relationship between the state and the new moneyed men. This had practical implications for the investor. Legislation was threatened, although never fully enacted, that could have damaged liquidity or rendered illegal some of the instruments used by participants at this time. The monopolies of the main trading companies were attacked and even removed during this period, detrimentally affecting the long-term potential of investments. Also, because the joint-stock company was regarded in many quarters as an irritant and a means of speculation rather than a legitimate means of raising capital, the state did not create an environment in which such companies could easily thrive. This particularly affected the new industries established during the early 1690s. Of course, such companies were attacked by speculators and were attempting to operate in an unstable political and economic environment but, equally, the state did not provide the support necessary to protect nascent industry. Indeed, the Commissioners of the Board of Trade, while acknowledging the potential usefulness of new projects, rejected joint-stock financing as a means of funding innovation. The final nails in the coffins of many of the smaller companies came with the introduction of the new public funds, which, with their high and seemingly guaranteed yields, had the short-term effect of crowding out new industry.

The high incidence of failure among the smaller joint-stock companies also indicates the vulnerability of the early financial market. During the 1690s it had to weather economic and political uncertainty, the recoinage, war, the threat of regulation from a heavy-handed state and the antagonism of its critics. The development and survival of an active secondary market in debt and equity securities was, therefore, not inevitable. Indeed, by the beginning of the eighteenth century the scope and extent of London's financial market was much reduced.

Nevertheless, the financial revolution of the 1690s had brought about permanent changes in investment habits and the chief institutions of England's new financial system did endure. Moreover, by the end of our period the future of London's financial market was already taking shape. In the short term, the men who would create the South Sea Bubble had already learned their trade and the enthusiasm for investment and indeed speculation which they exploited had been established. In the longer term the negative perceptions of the market and its participants born in the boom and bust of the 1690s and entrenched by the failure of the South Sea scheme persisted. Notably, speculation continues to attract opprobrium and regulators still seek ways to stifle and control the excesses of the market without inhibiting its economic function.

The learning experiences of early investors also shaped the experiences of those who followed. The investors of the 1690s rapidly learned to manage and exploit risk. Options were used imaginatively and portfolio diversification was a clear priority for many investors. However, just as markets and investors can learn to function efficiently and effectively, they can also learn to function badly, to manipulate prices and to confuse speculation with investment. It was these factors that, during the 1690s, made lottery tickets a sound investment, gambles on the outcomes of sieges a reasonable hedge and the manipulation of the price of joint-stocks an acceptable business strategy, just as in the modern markets acting on insider information is still rife, pyramid schemes are still popular in spite of their well-publicised flaws and those who cannot afford to speculate still buy their weekly lottery ticket. And it remains the case that, observing the success of the lucky few who are first to recognise the potential of a speculative boom or an emerging market, the many who follow are slow to learn that success cannot be replicated time and again. From the stock-market boom of the 1690s to the South Sea Bubble of the 1720s, the dot.com boom of the 1990s and the property boom of the early twenty-first century, investors have fallen prey to 'irrational exuberance'. In some respects, therefore, the functioning of the financial market and behaviour of investors has changed very little in the past three hundred years.

Appendices

Appendix 1 *Annual numbers of share transfers in the main joint-stock companies, 1661–1702*

	East India Company	Royal African Company	Hudson's Bay Company	Bank of England
1661 63[1]	44			
1664 66	57			
1667 69	71			
1670 72	126			
1673 75	152	39	7	
1676 78	131	41	6	
1679 81	172	40	10	
1682 84	780	67	29	
1685 87	537	77	22	
1688	624[2]	101	25	
1689		82	26	
1690		39	50	
1691	3,139	930	149	
1692		491	109	
1693		391	85	
1694	2,426	207	57	369
1695		194	54	1,371
1696		129	22	1,319
1697		195	19	2,056
1698	1,158	734	12	2,471
1699				2,364
1700				3,034
1701				1,795
1702				1,435

Sources: P. Lougheed, 'The East India Company in English Domestic Politics, 1657 1688', unpublished PhD thesis (Oxford University, 1980) cited in Carruthers, *City of Capital*, p. 167; IOR, L/AG/14/3/2 6; NA, PRO, T70/187 98; NA, PRO, BH1/465, A43/1 3; Bank Archives, AC28/32233; 28/1513 22.

225

[1] Table shows average annual transactions for the years, 1661 87.

[2] Few East India Company transfer books survive from the period between 1688 and 1702 and those records encompass no complete years. Thus, the above figures have been calculated by taking an average of the trades conducted in the known periods and multiplying them by 240 the average number of trading days in a year. In 1691, therefore, 1,086 trades were conducted between 4 June and 19 September on 83 trading days an average of 13.08 per day. Multiplying this figure by 240 trading days gives an estimated total for that year of 3,139 trades.

	EIC Houghton	EIC Castaing	New EIC Houghton	RAC Houghton	HBC Houghton	BoE Houghton	BoE Castaing	Linen Co. Houghton	Linen Co. Blunt	Glass Co. Houghton	Glass Co. Blunt
30 Mar. '92	158			51	260			41	40	28	
06 Apr. '92	151			52	260			42	40	40	35
13 Apr. '92	150			51	260			42	41	43	
20 Apr. '92	150			51	258			41	41	41	
23 Apr. '92	149			48	256			40		40	
27 Apr. '92	149			48	256			38		40	
30 Apr. '92	148			49	250			36	35	40	
04 May '92	148			48	250			35	35	40	
07 May '92	145			48	235			35		40	
11 May '92	131			44	215			30	33	40	35
14 May '92	141			48	235			32	30	40	
18 May '92	135			44	215			30	33	40	
21 May '92	141			47	235			32	33	40	34.5
25 May '92	140			45	215			33	31	40	34
28 May '92	141			47	235			33	34	40	34
01 Jun. '92	142			48	215			35		43	
04 Jun. '92	141			47	235			34			
08 Jun. '92	48			48	215			33	31.5	35	31
11 Jun. '92	142			47	235			34	30.5	43	33
15 Jun. '92	135			48	250			31	29	35	33
18 Jun. '92	139			47	245			29	30	40	
22 Jun. '92	135			48	250			30	30	33	
25 Jun. '92	138			47	245			30	33	43	31
27 Jun. '92	137			47	245			32	38	34	30
04 Jul. '92								38	36.5	34	30
11 Jul. '92									40		29.5
											28

Appendix 2 (*cont.*)

	EIC Houghton	EIC Castaing	New EIC Houghton	RAC Houghton	HBC Houghton	BoE Houghton	BoE Castaing	Linen Co. Houghton	Linen Co. Blunt	Glass Co. Houghton	Glass Co. Blunt
18 Jul. '92									42		
25 Jul. '92									40.5		28
01 Aug. '92									36		
08 Aug. '92									40.5		27
15 Aug. '92									43		
22 Aug. '92									40.5		
29 Aug. '92									41		22.25
05 Sep. '92									41.5		24
12 Sep. '92									41		24
19 Sep. '92									41.5		23
26 Sep. '92									42		31
03 Oct. '92									42		35
10 Oct. '92									42		29
17 Oct. '92									42		30
24 Oct. '92									42.5		31
31 Oct. '92									44		30
07 Nov. '92									58		31
14 Nov. '92									50		31
21 Nov. '92									50		
28 Nov. '92									50		30
05 Dec. '92									50		
12 Dec. '92									51		
19 Dec. '92									48		
26 Dec. '92									45		
02 Jan. '93									45		
09 Jan. '93									44		30
16 Jan. '93											

20 Jan. '93	135	47	190	45	44.5	34	33
27 Jan. '93	135	46	180	45	44.5	32	33
03 Feb. '93	135	46	180	45	44.5	32	32
10 Feb. '93	146	45	185	45	45	30	30
17 Feb. '93	146	45	185	45	45	32	29
24 Feb. '93	142	45	180	45		32	29
03 Mar. '93	137	44	180	42	42	32	28
10 Mar. '93	142	44	185	45	45	32	28
17 Mar. '93	140	44	185	45		30	
24 Mar. '93	133	44	185	44	44	29	26
31 Mar. '93	131	41	185	44	44	27	
07 Apr. '93	131	41	180	45	45	28	20
14 Apr. '93	118	41	175	44		27	
21 Apr. '93	117	41	175	43	41.5	26	26
28 Apr. '93	107	41	175	40	39	26	29
05 May '93	98	41	157	39	38.5	26	29
12 May '93	98	41	157	39	39	26	
19 May '93	104	41	175	39		26	
26 May '93	97	41	175	38	40	28	28
02 Jun. '93	99	40	175	38		29	28
09 Jun. '93	99	40	175	38		29	
16 Jun. '93	99	40	175	38	32	28	25.5
23 Jun. '93	99	40	175	34	33	28	23
30 Jun. '93	99	40	175	33		28	23
07 Jul. '93	99	40	175	32	32	26	
14 Jul. '93	99	40	175	32		25	
21 Jul. '93	97	39	170	25	23.5	23	
28 Jul. '93	90	39	170	25	26	23	
04 Aug. '93	90	38	170	25	26	23	
11 Aug. '93	92	38	160	25		23	
18 Aug. '93	92	37	150	25		21	
25 Aug. '93	90	37	155	26		21	20

Appendix 2 (*cont.*)

	EIC Houghton	EIC Castaing	New EIC Houghton	RAC Houghton	HBC Houghton	BoE Houghton	BoE Castaing	Linen Co. Houghton	Linen Co. Blunt	Glass Co. Houghton	Glass Co. Blunt
01 Sep. '93	90			37	155			24		20	
08 Sep. '93	90			37	160			24		20	18
15 Sep. '93	90			36	160			21		18	
22 Sep. '93	90			36	160			25		21	
29 Sep. '93	95			36	175			24	23.5	18	
06 Oct. '93	95			32	175			26	26	18	14.5
13 Oct. '93	95			32	190			26	26	18	
20 Oct. '93	95			34	200			26	25.5	18	
27 Oct. '93	93			34	220			25	23	20	18
03 Nov. '93	93			34	220			24	24.5	16	14.75
10 Nov. '93	94			34	220			24	24.5	17	
17 Nov. '93	92			34	220			23	22	16	14.5
24 Nov. '93	92			34	215			23		16	14
01 Dec. '93	92			34	215			21	20	15	
08 Dec. '93	92			34	215			21		15	
15 Dec. '93	92			34	205			21	20	15	
22 Dec. '93	92			34	205			18	18	15	
29 Dec. '93	92			34	205			18	18	15	
05 Jan. '94	92			34	205			20		15	
12 Jan. '94	92			34	205			20		15	
19 Jan. '94	95			32	200			20		13	
26 Jan. '94	95			32	200			20		12	
02 Feb. '94	94			32	200			21		12	
09 Feb. '94	94			33	200			22		14	
16 Feb. '94	94			32	190			22		15	
23 Feb. '94	91			32	192			22		15	
02 Mar. '94	90			32	190			22		13	

09 Mar. '94	90	32	190		22	13
16 Mar. '94	90	31	190		22	12
23 Mar. '94	90	31	190		22	12
30 Mar. '94	90	30	190		22	12
06 Apr. '94	90	30	190		22	12
13 Apr. '94	85	27	190		22	11
20 Apr. '94	83	25	190		21	
27 Apr. '94	81	20	188		20	
04 May '94	76	21	188		17	
11 May '94	73	21	175		17	
18 May '94	71	21	155		17	
25 May '94	66	20	150		17	
01 Jun. '94	68	20	150		12	
08 Jun. '94	71	21	150		13	
15 Jun. '94	73	22	150		13	
22 Jun. '94	73	23	140		13	
29 Jun. '94	71	23	140		12	
06 Jul. '94	71	23	130		12	
13 Jul. '94	72	23	130		11	
20 Jul. '94	73	23	130		10	
27 Jul. '94	74	23	130		10	
03 Aug. '94	77	23	135		10	
10 Aug. '94	76	25	140		10	
17 Aug. '94	80	25	140	102	9	
24 Aug. '94	79	25	150	102	9	
31 Aug. '94	78	24	150	101	9	
07 Sep. '94	79	24	150	100	9	
14 Sep. '94	79	24	185	100	9	
21 Sep. '94	78	23	180	101	8	
28 Sep. '94	78	23	180	101	8	
05 Oct. '94	76	23	170	101	8	
12 Oct. '94	76	23	170	103	8	

Appendix 2 (*cont.*)

	EIC Houghton	EIC Castaing	New EIC Houghton	RAC Houghton	HBC Houghton	BoE Houghton	BoE Castaing	Linen Co. Houghton	Linen Co. Blunt	Glass Co. Houghton	Glass Co. Blunt
19 Oct. '94	86			23	170	103		∞			
26 Oct. '94	89			23	175	103		∞			
02 Nov. '94	90			23	185	57		∞			
09 Nov. '94	93			24	180	61		∞			
16 Nov. '94	97			24	180	57		∞			
23 Nov. '94	94			25	175	60		∞			
30 Nov. '94	92			25	175	70		∞			
07 Dec. '94	94			26	175	72		∞			
14 Dec. '94	90			26	175	72		∞			
21 Dec. '94	89			25	175	76		∞			
28 Dec. '94	88			24	175	75		∞			
04 Jan. '95	87			24	175	74		∞			
11 Jan. '95	87			23	170	77		∞			
18 Jan. '95	83			23	165	81		∞			
25 Jan. '95	83			22	165	90		∞			
01 Feb. '95	80			22	155	89		∞			
08 Feb. '95	81			22	155	89		∞			
15 Feb. '95	81			22	155	90		∞			
22 Feb. '95	83			22	155	92		∞			
01 Mar. '95	88			22	155	89		∞			
08 Mar. '95	86			22	175	79		∞			
15 Mar. '95	86			21	175	95		∞			
22 Mar. '95	86			21	175	95		∞			
29 Mar. '95	84			20	180	92		∞			
05 Apr. '95	85			20	180	90		∞			
12 Apr. '95	85			20	180	91		∞			
19 Apr. '95	81			20	180	92		∞			

26 Apr. '95	81	20	190	91	8
02 May '95	80	20	200	91	8
10 May '95	79	20	200	91	8
17 May '95	78	20	200	91	8
24 May '95	79	20	200	91	8
31 May '95	79	22	200	92	8
07 Jun. '95	77	22	230	92	8
14 Jun. '95	73	21	230	93	8
21 Jun. '95	78	21	220	97	8
28 Jun. '95	80	22	220	99	8
05 Jul. '95	84	22	215	96	7
12 Jul. '95	85	22	220	97	7
19 Jul. '95	85	22	220	97	7
26 Jul. '95	88	22	220	95	7
02 Aug. '95	91	22	220	97	7
09 Aug. '95	89	22	220	96	7
16 Aug. '95	50	22	220	94	7
23 Aug. '95	89	23	205	95	7
30 Aug. '95	50	23	195	96	7
06 Sep. '95	93	21	195	98	7
13 Sep. '95	77	21	150	97	7
20 Sep. '95	77	21	150	97	7
27 Sep. '95	76	21	105	98	7
04 Oct. '95	75	21	180	93	7
11 Oct. '95	76	21	180	94	7
18 Oct. '95	72	21	190	95	7
25 Oct. '95	50	21	190	95	7
01 Nov. '95	54	21	140	95	7
08 Nov. '95	57	21	140	94	7
15 Nov. '95	56	23	140	94	7
22 Nov. '95	56	23	140	94	7
29 Nov. '95	56	23	130	94	7

Appendix 2 (*cont.*)

	EIC Houghton	EIC Castaing	New EIC Houghton	RAC Houghton	HBC Houghton	BoE Houghton	BoE Castaing	Linen Co. Houghton	Linen Co. Blunt	Glass Co. Houghton	Glass Co. Blunt
06 Dec. '95	57			23	130	97			7		
13 Dec. '95	57			23	130	100			7		
20 Dec. '95	57			18	130	100			7		
27 Dec. '95	57			18	130	100			7		
03 Jan. '96	57			18	130	102			7		
10 Jan. '96	57			18	130	108			7		
17 Jan. '96	59			19	130	107			7		
24 Jan. '96	61			20	125	107			7		
31 Jan. '96	62			20	125	107			7		
07 Feb. '96	57			21	125	93			7		
14 Feb. '96	55			20	120	83			7		
21 Feb. '96	55			20	120	84			7		
28 Feb. '96	55			20	120	88			7		
06 Mar. '96	55			19	120	86			7		
13 Mar. '96	53			19	110	84			7		
20 Mar. '96	53			19	100	82			7		
27 Mar. '96	54			19	100	84			7		
03 Apr. '96	51			19	100	87			7		
10 Apr. '96	53			18	100	85			7		
17 Apr. '96	55			18	100	86			7		
25 Apr. '96	57			17	100	84			7		
02 May '96	56			17	100	84			7		
08 May '96	59			17	100	83			7		
15 May '96	58			17	100	80			7		
22 May '96	67			17	100	79			7		
29 May '96	66			18	105	78			7		
05 Jun. '96	66			18	105	78			7		

12 Jun. '96	66	18	105	78	7
19 Jun. '96	66	18	98	78	7
26 Jun. '96	60	17	98	79	7
03 Jul. '96	60	17	98	79	7
10 Jul. '96	59	17	100	73	7
17 Jul. '96	75	17	100	73	7
24 Jul. '96	55	17	105	75	7
31 Jul. '96	54	17	105	73	7
07 Aug. '96	55	17	105	71	7
14 Aug. '96	55	17	105	70	7
21 Aug. '96	55	17	105	69	7
28 Aug. '96	57	17	105	69	7
04 Sep. '96	57	17	105	69	7
11 Sep. '96	58	17	105	71	7
18 Sep. '96	58	17	105	71	7
25 Sep. '96	65	17	105	70	7
02 Oct. '96	61	17	105	68	7
09 Oct. '96	60	17	105	60	7
16 Oct. '96	56	17	105	60	7
23 Oct. '96	56	17	105	61	7
30 Oct. '96	56	17	105	61	7
06 Nov. '96	55	17	95	64	7
13 Nov. '96	53	17	95	86	7
20 Nov. '96	53	17	95	80	7
27 Nov. '96	52	17	95	81	7
04 Dec. '96	51	17	105	77	7
11 Dec. '96	51	17	105	73	7
18 Dec. '96	52	17	105	73	7
25 Dec. '96	52	17	105	73	7
01 Jan. '97	53	17	105	72	7
08 Jan. '97	53	17	105	73	7
15 Jan. '97	53	16	100	66	5

Appendix 2 (*cont.*)

	EIC Houghton	EIC Castaing	New EIC Houghton	RAC Houghton	HBC Houghton	BoE Houghton	BoE Castaing	Linen Co. Houghton	Linen Co. Blunt	Glass Co. Houghton	Glass Co. Blunt
22 Jan. '97	42			13	80	55		5			
29 Jan. '97	42			13	80	52.5		5			
05 Feb. '97	41			13	80	51		5			
12 Feb. '97	40			13	80	51		5			
19 Feb. '97	40			13	80	55		5			
26 Feb. '97	40			13	80	54.25		5			
05 Mar. '97	40			13	80	54.25		5			
12 Mar. '97	40			13	80	53.25		5			
19 Mar. '97	39			13	80	53		5			
26 Mar. '97	38			13	80	54		5			
02 Apr. '97	38			13	80	54		5			
09 Apr. '97	38			13	80	54		5			
16 Apr. '97	37			13	80	55		5			
23 Apr. '97	37			13	80	56		5			
30 Apr. '97	37			13	80	56		5			
07 May '97	37			13	80	56		5			
14 May '97	37			13	80	56		5			
21 May '97	37			13	80	56		5			
28 May '97	37			13	80	56		5			
04 Jun. '97	38			13	80	61		5			
11 Jun. '97	38			13	80	60.2		5			
18 Jun. '97	38			13	80	60.2		5			
25 Jun. '97	38			13	80	60.2		5			
02 Jul. '97				13	80	60.2		5			
9 Jul. '97				13	80	60.2		5			
16 Jul. '97				13	80	60.2		5			
23 Jul. '97				13	80	60.2		5			

30 Jul. '97							
06 Aug. '97			13	80	60.2		5
13 Aug. '97			13	80	60.2		5
20 Aug. '97			13	80	60.2		5
27 Aug. '97			13	80	60.2		5
03 Sep. '97			13	80	60.2		5
10 Sep. '97	51		13	80	60.2		5
17 Sep. '97	60		13	80	82		5
24 Sep. '97	62		13	105	98		
01 Oct. '97	65		13	105	96		
08 Oct. '97	63		13	120	97.2		
15 Oct. '97	61		13	130	95.2		
22 Oct. '97	64		13	130	95		
29 Oct. '97	63		13	125	93		
05 Nov. '97	59		13	100	91		
12 Nov. '97	57		13	100	90		
19 Nov. '97	55		13	105	88.2		
26 Nov. '97	53		13	120	89		
03 Dec. '97	52		13	130	86.3		
10 Dec. '97	51		13	125	87.3		
17 Dec. '97	51		13	120	90.2		
24 Dec. '97	52		13	120	90.2		
31 Dec. '97			13	115	89		
07 Jan. '98	53			110	86.3		
15 Jan. '98	51	51.75			86	85.75	
22 Jan. '98	52	52.75			86.2	87.25	
28 Jan. '98	54	54.5			87.2	88	
05 Feb. '98	53	52			88.2	87.5	
12 Feb. '98	53	53		100	86.5	87.25	
19 Feb. '98	53	52.75		100	86.5	86.25	
26 Feb. '98	53	53.5		100	86.25	87.25	
05 Mar. '98	53	53.75		100	86.25	87	

Appendix 2 (*cont.*)

	EIC Houghton	EIC Castaing	New EIC Houghton	RAC Houghton	HBC Houghton	BoE Houghton	BoE Castaing	Linen Co. Houghton	Linen Co. Blunt	Glass Co. Houghton	Glass Co. Blunt
12 Mar. '98	54	55			105	87.25	87				
19 Mar. '98	54.75	55.5			110	87	88.5				
25 Mar. '98	55	55			110	89.25	89				
01 Apr. '98	55	55.75			110						
08 Apr. '98					110						
16 Apr. '98					110	91	88.5				
23 Apr. '98		55.5			110	95.5	92.75				
29 Apr. '98		55.5				95	93				
6 May '98	57	53.5				91	91				
13 May '98	51	50.25				91	92				
20 May '98	48.5	49				91.5	90.25				
27 May '98	49	40.75				92.25	91.25				
03 Jun. '98	43	41				91.5	91.5				
10 Jun. '98	42	44				91	90.75				
17 Jun. '98	42.75	38.5				91.25	91.5				
24 Jun. '98	39	36				92	93.25				
01 Jul. '98	35.5	35.25				94	91.5				
08 Jul. '98	33.25	33.75				91.5	93				
15 Jul. '98	33.75	33				94.5	93.75				
22 Jul. '98	38	41				94.5	95.5				
29 Jul. '98	42.75	42				94.5	96				
05 Aug. '98	42.75	42.25				96.75	96.5				
12 Aug. '98	42	41.75				96.75	97.75				
19 Aug. '98	41	41.5		17		97.25	97				
26 Aug. '98	41.25	41.5		17		97.25					
02 Sep. '98	41.5			17		97.25					
09 Sep. '98	41.5	40		17.25			98				

16 Sep. '98	40.25	40		16.75	96.5	90
23 Sep. '98	40.75	38.75		16.5	90	90.5
30 Sep. '98	39.25	39.75		16.5	90.5	92.5
07 Oct. '98	39.75	39.75		15.75	93.5	93.5
14 Oct. '98	40	41		16.25	94.5	95.25
21 Oct. '98	41.25	41.25		16.5	96.5	97
28 Oct. '98	42.75	41.5		16.25	96.75	96
04 Nov. '98	41.5	41.25		16.25	96.25	96.75
11 Nov. '98	41.5	41.75		16.25	97.25	98.25
18 Nov. '98	42	40.25		16	83	99
25 Nov. '98	38	39.5		16	99.75	100
02 Dec. '98	40	39.75		16	102	104.25
09 Dec. '98	40	42.25		16.25	103	104
16 Dec. '98	41	41		16.5	103	103.75
23 Dec. '98	41	41		16.5	103	103.75
30 Dec. '98	41	41		16.5	102.5	103.25
06 Jan. '99	41.25	41.5		16.5	102.5	101.75
13 Jan. '99	41.5	42		16.5	101.5	101.5
20 Jan. '99	42.25	42.5		16.5	104.25	102.75
27 Jan. '99	42.25	41.5		16.5	102.75	103
03 Feb. '99	42	42	52	16.25	103.25	103.25
10 Feb. '99	42.25	42	52	16.25	104	103.75
17 Feb. '99	42	41.75	51.25	16	103.5	104.75
24 Feb. '99	42	42.25	50.75	16	104.5	104.25
02 Mar. '99	43	43.25	49	15		
09 Mar. '99	42.5	42.5	46.75	15.75		
16 Mar. '99	41.5	41.75	47.5	16		
23 Mar. '99	41.75	41.75	61	16	105.75	101.5
30 Mar. '99	42	42	60	16	103	103.5
07 Apr. '99	42.25	42	60	15.75	102.75	104
14 Apr. '99	42	42	62.3	16	104	105
21 Apr. '99	42	41.75	60	16	104	105

Appendix 2 *(cont.)*

	EIC Houghton	EIC Castaing	New EIC Houghton	RAC Houghton	HBC Houghton	BoE Houghton	BoE Castaing	Linen Co. Houghton	Linen Co. Blunt	Glass Co. Houghton	Glass Co. Blunt
28 Apr. '99	42	42	60	16		104	105.25				
05 May '99	42	42	60	16		104	105				
12 May '99	42	42	55.75	16.25		104	104.25				
19 May '99	42	41.75	66	16		104.25	104				
26 May '99	41.75	41.75	63.25	15.75		105	103.75				
02 Jun. '99		42				103.75					
09 Jun. '99	41.75	41.75	61	15.75		103.75	104				
16 Jun. '99	41.75	41.25	61.5	15.75		104.25	104.25				
23 Jun. '99	41.25	41	59	15.75		105.25	105				
30 Jun. '99	41.5	40.5	58.5	15.75		104.75	104.75				
07 Jul. '99	41.5	41.5	58.5	15.75		104.75	105.75				
14 Jul. '99	40.5	40.75	75	15.5		105.75	106.25				
21 Jul. '99	41.5	43	76.25	15.5		107	107.5				
28 Jul. '99	41.5	43	76.25	15.5		107	107.5				
04 Aug. '99	41.5	43	76.25	15.5		107	108				
11 Aug. '99	43.75	45	75.5	15		108.75	110.5				
18 Aug. '99	43.5	45.25	75.5	15		108.75	109.5				
25 Aug. '99	45.5	45.5	76.2	15		109.5	109.75				
01 Sep. '99	45.5	46.25	77	15		110.5	112.25				
08 Sep. '99	46.75	48.5	80	14.75		113	114.5				
15 Sep. '99	46.75	52	80	14.75		113	116.75				
22 Sep. '99	53.25	53.5	95.5	15.5		119	115.25				
29 Sep. '99	53.75	54.5	95.5	15.25		117.5	117				
06 Oct. '99	53.75	53.75	95.5	15.25		117.5	115				
13 Oct. '99	53.75	55.25	96.5	15		116.5	116.5				
20 Oct. '99	56.5	55.5	98	15		116.75	116.75				
27 Oct. '99	56.5	57.25	98	15		116.75	116.5				

03 Nov. '99	56.5	58.5	98	15		116.75	117.75
10 Nov. '99	59	59	100.75	15		118	117.5
17 Nov. '99	59	59.75	109	15		117.5	117.25
24 Nov. '99	59	60	109	15		117.5	116.5
01 Dec. '99	58	58	105.5	15.25		115	116.25
08 Dec. '99	58	57.25	105.5	15.25		115	116
15 Dec. '99	58	59.5	106.5	15		117.5	119.25
22 Dec. '99	58	58.75	106.5	15		117.5	120
29 Dec. '99		58.25				123	
05 Jan. '00	58.5	59.25	126	15		126	125
12 Jan. '00	58.5	59.75	126	15		126	127
19 Jan. '00	59.75	66	128.25	15		130	129
26 Jan. '00	64.5	64.25	125.25	15		129.75	130
02 Feb. '00	64.5	66.5	125.25	15		129.75	138
09 Feb. '00	77	83.5	137.25	18		139.5	140.25
16 Feb. '00	77	87.5	137.25	18		139.5	142.5
23 Feb. '00	93.5	96.5	137.75	19		143	143
01 Mar. '00	116	120	148.5	19		148	149.5
08 Mar. '00	101	102.5	148	19		145	148
15 Mar. '00	108	107	152.5	20		148.25	148.25
22 Mar. '00	108	109	152.5	20		148.25	
29 Mar. '00	109.25	110		23	105		
05 Apr. '00	109.25			23	105		
12 Apr. '00		143		23	105		
19 Apr. '00		137.5		23	105		146
26 Apr. '00	142	140	154	23.25	105	142	142.5
03 May '00	135.5	130	151.75	23.25	105	138.5	140.5
10 May '00	135.5	128	151.75	23.25	105	138.5	135.5
17 May '00	123	117	151	23.25	105	139	142
24 May '00	123	118.75	151	23.25	105	139	140
31 May '00	115.5	110	151.75	23	110	141	141
07 Jun. '00	105	107	152.5	20	110	141.25	140.25

Appendix 2 (*cont.*)

	EIC Houghton	EIC Castaing	New EIC Houghton	RAC Houghton	HBC Houghton	BoE Houghton	BoE Castaing	Linen Co. Houghton	Linen Co. Blunt	Glass Co. Houghton	Glass Co. Blunt
14 Jun. '00	105	109.5	152.5	20	110	141.25	138				
21 Jun. '00	109.5	109.25	153.5	21.25		138.25	139				
28 Jun. '00	109	109.5	151.5	21.25		139	138.5				
05 Jul. '00	109	116.5	151.5	21.25		139	136.5				
12 Jul. '00	122.5	118.5	149.2	21.25		138.75	138.5				
19 Jul. '00	119.75	120	149.2	21.25		137.5	138				
26 Jul. '00	124.5	127.5	149.75	21.25		136.5	139.75				
02 Aug. '00	124.5	135.5	149.75	21.25		136.5	140.25				
09 Aug. '00	135.75	131.5	152.5	24		141.75	141				
16 Aug. '00	134.75	131.75	151.25	23.5		140.25	139				
23 Aug. '00	131.25	131	150.75	23.5		138.75	142.5				
30 Aug. '00	132.25	132.75	151	23.5		142	140.5				
05 Sep. '00	132.25	126.5	151	23.5		142	140.75				
12 Sep. '00	128	127	151.5	24.25							
22 Sep. '00	123.75	125.5	151.5	24.25		133	133				
27 Sep. '00	122.5	121.5	150.5	24.25		132.75	133				
04 Oct. '00	128.5	122	147.2	24.25		130.5	129.5				
11 Oct. '00	119.75	120.25	144.5	23.75		129	129				
18 Oct. '00	121.5	124	143.75	23.5		129	128				
25 Oct. '00	121.5	121.5	143.75	23.5		129	127				
01 Nov. '00	121.5	121.25	143.75	23.5		129	125.5				
08 Nov. '00	121.5	118	143.75	23.5		129	123.5				
15 Nov. '00	121.5	114.75	143.75	23.5		129	124.5				
22 Nov. '00	121.5	118.75	143.75	23.5		129	124.75				
29 Nov. '00	121.5	121.75	143.75	23.5		129	124.25				
06 Dec. '00	121.5	121.75	143.75	23.5		129	124.25				
13 Dec. '00	121.5	119.5	143.75	23.5		129	122.25				

20 Dec. '00	121.5	119.5	143.75	23.5	129	124
27 Dec. '00	119.5		no trans.	no trans.	124.5	122.25
03 Jan. '01	119	117.5	no trans.	no trans.	123	121
10 Jan. '01	119	116	no trans.	no trans.	123	122.5
17 Jan. '01	119	114.25	no trans.	no trans.	123	119.75
24 Jan. '01	119	105.5	no trans.	no trans.	123	108
31 Jan. '01	119	82	no trans.	no trans.	123	111
07 Feb. '01	119	84	no trans.	no trans.	123	106.5
14 Feb. '01	119	79	no trans.	no trans.	123	107.25
21 Feb. '01	76.5	77.5	110	no trans.	123	103.5
28 Feb. '01	76.5	68.5	110	no trans.	123	96
07 Mar. '01	76.5	59	110	no trans.	123	
14 Mar. '01	76.5	65.75	110	no trans.	123	
21 Mar. '01	76.5	75	100	no trans.	123	
28 Mar. '01	76.5	67.75	105	no trans.	123	
04 Apr. '01	76.5		105	no trans.	123	
11 Apr. '01	75.5	80		15.5	103.5	105
18 Apr. '01	78	90.5		18	107	110
25 Apr. '01	78	94.5		18	107	113
02 May '01	78	84.5		18	107	110.5
09 May '01	88	79	115	17	111.5	109
16 May '01	76.5	77	106	16.75	106	106.5
23 May '01	76.5	81.25	106	16.75	106	108.25
30 May '01		80.5			108.25	
06 Jun. '01	76.5	81	106	16.75	106	109
13 Jun. '01	76.5	82	106	16.75	106	111.5
20 Jun. '01	76.5	88	106	16.75	106	115.5
27 Jun. '01	76.5	86.75	106	16.75	106	114
04 Jul. '01	82.5	83.75	114.5	16.5	112.5	111
11 Jul. '01	82	77.75	113	16.5	110	107
18 Jul. '01	78.5	75.5	109	16.5	109.5	107.5
25 Jul. '01	69.25	71.5	102	15	107	108

Appendix 2 (cont.)

	EIC Houghton	EIC Castaing	New EIC Houghton	RAC Houghton	HBC Houghton	BoE Houghton	BoE Castaing	Linen Co. Houghton	Linen Co. Blunt	Glass Co. Houghton	Glass Co. Blunt
01 Aug. '01	76.25	74.75	109	15.25		110.25	110				
08 Aug. '01	71	73	103	15		108.25	108.5				
15 Aug. '01	71	78	103	15		108.25					
22 Aug. '01	79.25	83.5	113	15.25		112.5	113				
29 Aug. '01	83.5	83.5	117	16.5		115	115				
05 Sep. '01	81.5	84	120	16		115.5	118				
12 Sep. '01	84	78.75	124	16.75		118.75	116				
19 Sep. '01	79.5	84	119	16		no trans.					
26 Sep. '01	81		121.25	15.75		no trans.					
03 Oct. '01	78.5	78	118.5	15		no trans.	109.5				
10 Oct. '01	77.75	79	117.75	14.5		109.5	108.75				
17 Oct. '01	77.75	77	117.75	14.5		109.5	109				
24 Oct. '01	77.75	78	117.75	13.5		108.5	109.25				
31 Oct. '01	78	78.5	116	13.75		108.75	109.5				
07 Nov. '01	78	78.25	116	13.75		108.75	109.25				
14 Nov. '01	74.75	75	117	13.5		107.5	110				
21 Nov. '01	74.75	77.25	117	13.5		107.5	110.25				
28 Nov. '01	77.75	78.75	118.25	13.5		109.75	110				
05 Dec. '01	77.75	77.75	118.25	13.5		109.75	110.75				
12 Dec. '01	79	79.5	120	13.25		110.5					
19 Dec. '01	78		120	12.75		110.5					
26 Dec. '01	78	91.5	120	12.75		110.5	115.25				
02 Jan. '02	90.25	90.75	142.5	13.5		114.5	114				
09 Jan. '02	90.5	83	140.5	13.5		114.5	113.75				
16 Jan. '02	83	81	135	12.75		113.25	112.25				
23 Jan. '02	82.75	80.25	133	12.25		113.25	114				

30 Jan. '02					115	
06 Feb. '02	79.25	82.75	128.25	12.25	117	118
13 Feb. '02	83.25	81.5	132.25	12.25	118	116
20 Feb. '02	82.75	82.5	129.25	12.25	118	117
27 Feb. '02	82.75	83.5	129.25	12.25	117	117.75
06 Mar. '02	82.25	80.75	128.5	11.25	117.75	116
13 Mar. '02	82.5	81.5	119.75	11.5	117.75	
20 Mar. '02	82.75	82.75	126.5	11.75	no trans.	
27 Mar. '02	82.5	83	128.5	12	no trans.	
03 Apr. '02	82.25	82.5	129.25	12	113.5	113.5
10 Apr. '02	82.25	83.5	127.25	12	113.5	114
17 Apr. '02	82.5	83.5	126.5	12	114.75	115.25
24 Apr. '02	84.5		129.25		114.75	
01 May '02	84.5	78	129.25	11.75	114.75	114
08 May '02	79.25	78	127	11.25	114	114.5
15 May '02	77.75	79	125.75	11.25	115.25	116.25
22 May '02	78.75	80	126.75	11.25	115.25	117.75
29 May '02	78.75	80.5	126.75	11.25	117.5	118
05 Jun. '02	79.75	81.5	129.25	11	118	121.5
12 Jun. '02	80.25	83.125	130	11	118	121.75
19 Jun. '02	80.25	86	130	11.25	121.25	117.25
26 Jun. '02	83.5	89.5	134.5	12	118.75	119.25
03 Jul. '02	87.75	89	138	12.25	118.25	119
10 Jul. '02	86.5	90.5	116.5	12.5	118.25	118.5
17 Jul. '02	86.5	94.75	116.5	12.5	118.25	119.5
24 Jul. '02	86.5	97.5	116.5		120	
31 Jul. '02	86.5	106	116.5	12.5	118.25	122
07 Aug. '02	105.25	104.25	136.5	15	122	121.5
14 Aug. '02	105.5	103.75	137.5	15	121.25	121.5
21 Aug. '02	104.25	107	138	14.75	121.5	122.25
28 Aug. '02	104.25	113	138	14.75	121.5	126.5
04 Sep. '02	104.25	112	138	14.75	121.5	125.25

Appendix 2 (*cont.*)

	EIC Houghton	EIC Castaing	New EIC Houghton	RAC Houghton	HBC Houghton	BoE Houghton	BoE Castaing	Linen Co. Houghton	Linen Co. Blunt	Glass Co. Houghton	Glass Co. Blunt
11 Sep. '02	112.5	114	146.5	14.5		125.25	125.5				
18 Sep. '02	112.5	109.5	145.75	14		no trans.					
25 Sep. '02	106.5	108.25	142.5	13.75		no trans.					
02 Oct. '02	105.25	106.5	144	13.75		120.5	121.25				
09 Oct. '02	102.75		141.75	13.25		120					
16 Oct. '02	99.75	101.5	139.75	12.5		119	119.75				
23 Oct. '02	104	104	143.75	13		120.25	120.75				
30 Oct. '02	103.5	103.5	142.75	12.75		120.5	120.75				
06 Nov. '02	105.5	106.5	145	13		121.75	122.25				
13 Nov. '02	105.5	107.25	145	13		121.75	125.5				
21 Nov. '02	106.75	108.5	146	13.75		123	126.5				
28 Nov. '02	108.75	109.75	146	14		126.75	127.5				
04 Dec. '02	109.75	112	150	13.5		127.5	128				
11 Dec. '02	115.5	114.25	159.5	14.1		129	128				
18 Dec. '02	115.5	116.25	157.5	14.7		128	128.25				
25 Dec. '02	117.75		161	13.25		128.75					

Sources: Houghton, *Collection for Improvement*; European State Finance Database, dataset \neallcoe1700s.rtf; NA, PRO, C114/165.
Notes: Houghton did not publish the *Collection for Improvement* during the latter half of 1692. During the recoinage crisis, the period from January to September 1697, two prices were quoted by Houghton, one for notes and one for cash. Recorded here is the cash price, the price for notes was consistently higher.

Appendix 3 Activity in Bank of England stock grouped by the social status/occupation of the investor

1694	No. of sellers	Percentage	No. of sales	Percentage	Average nominal amount (in £s)	No. of purchasers	Percentage	No. of purchases	Percentage	Average nominal amount (in £s)
Titled aristocrats	9	3.93	19	5.15	821	19	8.37	34	9.21	897
Gentlemen	28	12.23	31	8.40	455	30	13.22	40	10.84	525
Esquires	41	17.90	64	17.34	837	45	19.82	107	29.00	687
Professionals	16	6.99	20	5.42	380	15	6.61	19	5.15	478
Merchants	70	30.57	141	38.21	520	60	26.43	90	24.39	474
Finance	4	1.75	4	1.08	650	3	1.32	5	1.36	500
Retailing	32	13.97	51	13.82	470	27	12.33	42	11.38	436
Manufacture	10	4.37	14	3.79	300	6	2.64	6	1.63	417
Transport	2	0.87	2	0.54	650	1	0.44	1	0.27	800
Agriculture	0	0.00	0	0.00	0	1	0.44	1	0.27	300
Building	1	0.44	4	1.08	1,000	0	0.00	0	0.00	0
Domestic service	0	0.00	0	0.00	0	0	0.00	0	0.00	0
Women	11	4.80	11	2.98	497	17	7.05	17	4.61	341
Unknown	5	2.18	8	2.17	587	3	1.32	7	1.90	500
Totals	229		369			227		369		

1695	No. of sellers	Percentage	No. of sales	Percentage	Average nominal amount (in £s)	No. of purchasers	Percentage	No. of purchases	Percentage	Average nominal amount (in £s)
Titled aristocrats	23	4.58	83	6.05	876	26	5.11	85	6.20	722
Gentlemen	76	15.14	153	11.16	591	78	15.32	160	11.67	652
Esquires	79	15.74	246	17.94	769	65	12.77	194	14.15	628
Professionals	29	5.78	66	4.81	522	39	7.66	68	4.96	654
Merchants	147	29.28	522	38.07	408	150	29.47	591	43.11	452
Finance	7	1.39	14	1.02	343	7	1.38	11	0.80	455
Retailing	72	14.34	158	11.52	330	71	13.95	139	10.14	409
Manufacture	31	6.18	61	4.45	364	24	4.72	46	3.36	320

	No. of sellers	Percentage	No. of sales	Percentage	Average nominal amount (in £s)	No. of purchasers	Percentage	No. of purchases	Percentage	Average nominal amount (in £s)
Transport	3	0.60	14	1.02	350	4	0.79	15	1.09	353
Agriculture	0	0.00	0	0.00	0	0	0.00	0	0.00	0
Building	0	0.00	0	0.00	0	1	0.20	1	0.07	300
Domestic service	1	0.20	1	0.07	100	1	0.20	1	0.07	1,500
Women	20	3.98	31	2.26	282	38	7.47	52	3.79	346
Unknown	14	2.79	22	1.60	518	5	0.98	8	0.58	375
Totals	502		1,371			509		1,371		

1696	No. of sellers	Percentage	No. of sales	Percentage	Average nominal amount (in £s)	No. of purchasers	Percentage	No. of purchases	Percentage	Average nominal amount (in £s)
Titled aristocrats	22	5.05	76	5.76	908	28	4.89	62	4.70	660
Gentlemen	58	13.30	151	11.45	478	77	13.44	141	10.69	423
Esquires	59	13.53	175	13.27	546	61	10.65	165	12.51	568
Professionals	26	5.96	66	5.00	445	43	7.50	80	6.07	374
Merchants	141	32.34	538	40.79	461	180	31.41	535	40.56	505
Finance	4	0.92	30	2.27	450	6	1.05	28	2.12	554
Retailing	59	13.53	171	12.96	385	95	16.58	186	14.10	431
Manufacture	17	3.90	36	2.73	369	40	6.98	55	4.17	312
Transport	3	0.69	8	0.61	350	2	0.35	2	0.15	250
Agriculture	0	0.00	0	0.00	0	0	0.00	0	0.00	0
Building	0	0.00	0	0.00	0	0	0.00	0	0.00	0
Domestic service	0	0.00	0	0.00	0	3	0.52	4	0.30	250
Women	39	8.94	57	4.32	447	31	5.41	47	3.56	424
Unknown	8	1.83	11	0.83	445	7	1.22	14	1.06	828
Totals	436		1,319			573		1,319		

1697	No. of sellers	Percentage	No. of sales	Percentage	Average nominal amount (in £s)	No. of purchasers	Percentage	No. of purchases	Percentage	Average nominal amount (in £s)
Titled aristocrats	14	1.87	47	2.28	788	24	2.85	63	3.06	638
Gentlemen	78	10.44	168	8.16	434	100	11.88	193	9.38	437

	No. of sellers	Percentage	No. of sales	Percentage	Average nominal amount (in £s)	No. of purchasers	Percentage	No. of purchases	Percentage	Average nominal amount (in £s)
Esquires	71	9.50	179	8.70	620	78	9.26	204	9.91	484
Professionals	41	5.49	55	2.67	399	52	6.18	91	4.42	318
Merchants	222	29.72	781	37.95	423	250	29.69	790	38.39	471
Finance	26	3.48	146	7.09	392	26	3.09	94	4.57	490
Retailing	151	20.21	414	20.12	365	160	19.00	398	19.34	490
Manufacture	72	9.64	141	6.85	362	68	8.08	117	5.69	385
Transport	16	2.14	47	2.28	788	7	0.83	7	0.34	310
Agriculture	0	0.00	0	0.00	0	1	0.12	2	0.10	276
Building	9	1.20	20	0.97	377	7	0.83	13	0.63	200
Domestic service	1	0.13	1	0.05	100	4	0.48	4	0.19	230
Women	27	3.61	38	1.90	655	55	6.53	68	3.35	225
Unknown	18	2.41	18	0.92	564	10	1.19	12	0.63	473
Corporate	1	0.13	1	0.05	564	0	0.00	0	0.00	324
Totals	747		2056		11,250	842		2056		0

1698	No. of sellers	Percentage	No. of sales	Percentage	Average nominal amount (in £s)	No. of purchasers	Percentage	No. of purchases	Percentage	Average nominal amount (in £s)
Titled aristocrats	24	2.33	88	3.56	665	33	2.94	87	3.52	712
Gentlemen	127	12.34	241	9.76	381	162	14.41	251	10.16	388
Esquires	106	10.30	240	9.72	577	143	12.72	372	15.06	514
Professionals	72	7.00	123	4.98	335	105	9.34	183	7.41	336
Merchants	268	26.04	827	33.48	465	235	20.91	696	28.18	483
Finance	31	3.01	206	8.34	420	32	2.85	182	7.37	448
Retailing	192	18.66	432	17.49	345	170	15.12	359	14.53	339
Manufacture	105	10.20	170	6.88	301	98	8.72	159	6.44	293
Transport	16	1.55	26	1.05	217	12	1.07	14	0.57	233
Agriculture	0	0.00	0	0.00	0	2	0.18	2	0.08	150
Building	7	0.68	10	0.40	232	9	0.80	11	0.45	181
Domestic service	4	0.39	5	0.20	280	6	0.53	6	0.24	167

	No. of sellers	Percentage	No. of sales	Percentage	Average nominal amount (in £s)	No. of purchasers	Percentage	No. of purchases	Percentage	Average nominal amount (in £s)
Women	53	5.15	70	2.83	360	102	9.07	130	5.26	328
Unknown	24	2.33	33	1.30	423	15	1.33	19	0.73	239
Corporate	0	0.00	0	0.00	0	0	0.00	0	0.00	0
Totals	1,029		2,471			1,124		2,471		

1699	No. of sellers	Percentage	No. of sales	Percentage	Average nominal amount (in £s)	No. of purchasers	Percentage	No. of purchases	Percentage	Average nominal amount (in £s)
Titled aristocrats	36	3.72	107	4.53	941	29	3.19	73	3.09	674
Gentlemen	128	13.24	245	10.36	425	108	11.89	200	8.46	593
Esquires	110	11.38	254	10.74	630	112	12.33	298	12.61	594
Professionals	75	7.76	150	6.35	452	79	8.70	172	7.28	381
Merchants	222	22.96	573	24.24	524	222	24.45	605	25.59	570
Finance	35	3.62	450	19.04	582	39	4.30	455	19.25	597
Retailing	163	16.86	277	11.72	395	120	13.22	254	10.74	349
Manufacture	102	10.55	166	7.02	378	91	10.02	160	6.77	380
Transport	1	0.10	1	0.04	300	2	0.22	2	0.08	350
Agriculture	0	0.00	0	0.00	0	1	0.11	1	0.04	100
Building	2	0.21	5	0.21	310	8	0.88	10	0.42	245
Domestic service	5	0.52	10	0.42	446	4	0.44	6	0.25	502
Women	73	7.55	100	4.23	358	86	9.47	115	4.86	357
Unknown	15	1.55	26	1.10	699	7	0.77	13	0.55	261
Corporate	0	0.00	0	0.00	0	0	0.00	0	0.00	0
Totals	967		2,364			908		2,364		

1700	No. of sellers	Percentage	No. of sales	Percentage	Average nominal amount (in £s)	No. of purchasers	Percentage	No. of purchases	Percentage	Average nominal amount (in £s)
Titled aristocrats	35	3.22	76	2.50	1,391	38	3.88	124	4.09	974
Gentlemen	164	15.07	279	9.20	512	149	15.22	262	8.64	529
Esquires	131	12.04	336	11.07	742	137	13.99	385	12.69	678

	No. of sellers	Percentage	No. of sales	Percentage	Average nominal amount (in £s)	No. of purchasers	Percentage	No. of purchases	Percentage	Average nominal amount (in £s)
Professionals	86	7.90	192	6.33	487	75	7.66	213	7.02	468
Merchants	242	22.24	677	22.31	717	240	24.51	796	26.24	652
Finance	52	4.78	785	25.87	668	53	5.41	701	23.10	763
Retailing	143	13.14	329	10.84	449	133	13.59	304	10.02	425
Manufacture	85	7.81	167	5.50	424	71	7.25	133	4.38	370
Transport	15	1.38	17	0.56	325	4	0.41	9	0.30	372
Agriculture	1	0.09	1	0.03	100	1	0.10	1	0.03	200
Building	5	0.46	9	0.30	269	2	0.20	4	0.13	200
Domestic service	5	0.46	5	0.16	410	3	0.31	3	0.10	233
Women	109	10.02	139	4.58	401	66	6.74	86	2.83	396
Unknown	14	1.29	21	0.69	538	7	0.72	13	0.43	369
Corporate	1	0.09	1	0.03	500	0	0	0	0.00	0
Totals	1,088		3,034			979		3,034		

1701	No. of sellers	Percentage	No. of sales	Percentage	Average nominal amount (in £s)	No. of purchasers	Percentage	No. of purchases	Percentage	Average nominal amount (in £s)
Titled aristocrats	29	4.06	86	4.79	770	39	4.76	101	5.63	1,029
Gentlemen	87	12.18	190	10.58	485	111	13.55	188	10.47	476
Esquires	98	13.73	212	11.81	625	116	14.16	232	12.92	558
Professionals	50	7.00	80	4.46	558	58	7.08	93	5.18	458
Merchants	185	25.91	508	28.30	605	206	25.15	530	29.53	566
Finance	44	6.16	371	20.67	538	45	5.49	314	17.49	615
Retailing	87	12.18	163	9.08	450	87	10.62	143	7.97	449
Manufacture	57	7.98	88	4.90	420	57	6.96	80	4.46	420
Transport	7	0.98	9	0.50	283	5	0.61	5	0.28	350
Agriculture	2	0.28	2	0.11	350	0	0.00	0	0.00	0
Building	2	0.28	3	0.17	334	3	0.37	3	0.17	367
Domestic service	1	0.14	1	0.06	100	2	0.24	2	0.11	150
Women	54	7.56	65	3.62	439	79	9.65	90	5.01	349

	No. of sellers	Percentage	No. of sales	Percentage	Average nominal amount (in £s)	No. of purchasers	Percentage	No. of purchases	Percentage	Average nominal amount (in £s)
Unknown	11	1.54	17	0.95	563	11	1.34	14	0.78	321
Corporate	0	0.00	0	0.00	0	0	0.00	0	0.00	0
Totals	714		1,795			819		1,795		

1702

	No. of sellers	Percentage	No. of sales	Percentage	Average nominal amount (in £s)	No. of purchasers	Percentage	No. of purchases	Percentage	Average nominal amount (in £s)
Titled aristocrats	34	4.78	94	6.55	740	27	3.89	71	4.95	983
Gentlemen	110	15.47	172	11.99	464	87	12.54	149	10.38	445
Esquires	100	14.06	247	17.21	683	85	12.25	170	11.85	595
Professionals	45	6.33	77	5.37	401	52	7.49	84	5.85	317
Merchants	167	23.49	345	24.04	682	189	27.23	494	34.43	621
Finance	31	4.36	148	10.31	523	30	4.32	136	9.48	544
Retailing	85	11.95	153	10.66	383	78	11.24	137	9.55	439
Manufacture	47	6.61	68	4.74	328	37	5.33	62	4.32	360
Transport	4	0.56	7	0.49	379	7	1.01	14	0.98	357
Agriculture	0	0.00	0	0.00	0	1	0.14	1	0.07	500
Building	4	0.56	5	0.35	252	4	0.58	4	0.28	319
Domestic service	4	0.56	4	0.28	200	2	0.29	2	0.14	394
Women	67	9.42	100	6.97	341	87	12.54	96	6.69	461
Unknown	13	1.83	15	1.05	248	7	1.01	11	0.77	369
Corporate	0	0.00	0	0.00	0	1	0.14	4	0.28	200
Totals	711		1,435			694		1,435		

Source: Bank Archives, AC28/32233; AC28/1513–22.

Appendix 4 *Activity in East India Company stock grouped by the social status/occupation of the investor*

Jun.–Sep. 1691	No. of sellers	Percentage	No. of sales	Percentage	Average nominal amount (in £s)	No. of purchasers	Percentage	No. of purchases	Percentage	Average nominal amount (in £s)
Titled aristocrats	21	11.41	77	7.09	535	22	11.89	65	5.99	490
Gentlemen	14	7.61	19	1.75	284	15	8.11	25	2.30	220
Esquires	26	14.13	55	5.06	395	26	14.05	58	5.34	343
Professionals	12	6.52	71	6.54	222	13	7.03	65	5.99	289
Merchants	57	30.98	267	24.59	258	53	28.65	290	26.70	264
Finance	13	7.07	319	29.37	311	13	7.03	294	27.07	348
Retailing	26	14.13	220	20.26	323	32	17.30	243	22.38	280
Manufacture	6	3.26	40	3.68	211	6	3.24	31	2.85	258
Transport	1	0.54	3	0.28	267	2	1.08	4	0.37	1,369
Agriculture	0	0.00	0	0.00	0	0	0.00	0	0.00	0
Building	0	0.00	0	0.00	0	0	0.00	0	0.00	0
Domestic service	0	0.00	0	0.00	0	0	0.00	0	0.00	0
Women	7	3.80	14	1.29	446	2	1.08	9	0.83	322
Unknown	1	0.54	1	0.09	300	1	0.54	2	0.18	150
Totals	184		1,086			185		1,086		

Apr.–Jul. 1694	No. of sellers	Percentage	No. of sales	Percentage	Average nominal amount (in £s)	No. of purchasers	Percentage	No. of purchases	Percentage	Average nominal amount (in £s)
Titled aristocrats	17	9.34	34	6.23	670	21	8.37	33	6.04	741
Gentlemen	15	8.24	27	4.95	214	19	7.57	28	5.13	506
Esquires	19	10.44	33	6.04	638	27	10.76	47	8.61	574
Professionals	11	6.04	26	4.76	481	14	5.58	21	3.85	370
Merchants	62	34.07	135	24.73	456	100	39.84	210	38.46	500
Finance	14	7.69	151	27.66	625	12	4.78	78	14.29	692
Retailing	30	16.48	109	19.96	523	29	11.55	83	15.20	482
Manufacture	10	5.49	27	4.95	240	9	3.59	22	4.03	228

	No. of sellers	Percentage	No. of sales	Percentage	Average nominal amount (in £s)	No. of purchasers	Percentage	No. of purchases	Percentage	Average nominal amount (in £s)
Transport	1	0.55	3			3	1.20	4	0.73	291
Agriculture	0	0.00	0			0	0.00	0	0.00	0
Building	0	0.00	0			0	0.00	0	0.00	0
Domestic service	0	0.00	0			0	0.00	0	0.00	0
Women	3	1.65			835	15	5.98	18	3.30	276
Unknown	0	0.00	0			2	0.80	2	0.37	286
Totals	182		546			251		546		

Aug.–Dec. 1698

	No. of sellers	Percentage	No. of sales	Percentage	Average nominal amount (in £s)	No. of purchasers	Percentage	No. of purchases	Percentage	Average nominal amount (in £s)
Titled aristocrats	6	3.11	10	1.90	1,025	12	5.77	20	3.80	744
Gentlemen	6	3.11	25	4.75	420	10	4.81	36	6.84	380
Esquires	24	12.44	51	9.70	543	27	12.98	71	13.50	531
Professionals	14	7.25	23	4.37	514	14	6.73	22	4.18	409
Merchants	89	46.11	216	41.06	494	96	46.15	231	43.92	469
Finance	8	4.15	70	13.31	467	10	4.81	34	6.46	675
Retailing	28	14.51	66	12.55	471	26	12.50	58	11.03	440
Manufacture	8	4.15	54	10.27	276	7	3.37	47	8.94	330
Transport	2	1.04	3	0.57	667	4	1.92	5	0.95	500
Agriculture	0	0.00	0	0.00	0	0	0.00	0	0.00	0
Building	0	0.00	0	0.00	0	0	0.00	0	0.00	0
Domestic service	0	0.00	0	0.00	0	0	0.00	0	0.00	0
Women	7	3.63	7	1.33	283	2	0.96	2	0.38	219
Unknown	1	0.52	1	0.19	600	0	0.00	0	0.00	0
Totals	193		526			208		526		

Jan.–May; Nov.–Dec., 1699

	No. of sellers	Percentage	No. of sales	Percentage	Average nominal amount (in £s)	No. of purchasers	Percentage	No. of purchases	Percentage	Average nominal amount (in £s)
Titled aristocrats	8	4.40	12	2.80	834	8	5.30	10	2.33	480
Gentlemen	16	8.79	22	5.13	698	7	4.64	9	2.10	1,587
Esquires	22	12.09	52	12.12	630	19	12.58	42	9.79	597

	No. of sellers	Percentage	No. of sales	Percentage	Average nominal amount (in £s)	No. of purchasers	Percentage	No. of purchases	Percentage	Average nominal amount (in £s)
Professionals	13	7.14	21	4.90	475	7	4.64	13	3.03	765
Merchants	74	40.66	187	43.59	659	69	45.70	195	45.45	678
Finance	12	6.59	52	12.12	725	9	5.96	74	17.25	620
Retailing	22	12.09	37	8.62	440	18	11.92	24	5.59	800
Manufacture	5	2.75	36	8.39	355	5	3.31	49	11.42	288
Transport	1	0.55	1	0.23	1,000	0	0.00	0	0.00	0
Agriculture	0	0.00	0	0.00	0	0	0.00	0	0.00	0
Building	0	0.00	0	0.00	0	1	0.66	1	0.23	300
Domestic service	2	1.10	2	0.47	142	1	0.66	1	0.23	181
Women	4	2.20	4	0.93	663	6	3.97	10	2.33	389
Unknown	3	1.65	3	0.70		1	0.66	1	0.23	511
Totals	182		429		2,817	151		429		

Jan.–Feb. 1700	No. of sellers	Percentage	No. of sales	Percentage	Average nominal amount (in £s)	No. of purchasers	Percentage	No. of purchases	Percentage	Average nominal amount (in £s)
Titled aristocrats	12	5.97	15	3.28	1,152	4	3.17	4	0.87	2,750
Gentlemen	17	8.46	28	6.11	483	7	5.56	13	2.84	1,543
Esquires	15	7.46	27	5.90	942	9	7.14	26	5.68	577
Professionals	10	4.98	12	2.62	486	8	6.35	18	3.93	542
Merchants	85	42.29	207	45.20	667	57	45.24	218	47.60	633
Finance	8	3.98	57	12.45	958	9	7.14	78	17.03	793
Retailing	31	15.42	43	9.39	483	25	19.84	40	8.73	618
Manufacture	8	3.98	54	11.79	409	5	3.97	59	12.88	379
Transport	2	1.00	2	0.44	762	1	0.79	1	0.22	500
Agriculture	0	0.00	0	0.00	0	0	0.00	0	0.00	0
Building	0	0.00	0	0.00	0	0	0.00	0	0.00	0
Domestic service	0	0.00	0	0.00	0	0	0.00	0	0.00	0
Women	12	5.97	12	2.62	325	1	0.79	1	0.22	300
Unknown	1	0.50	1	0.22	500	0	0.00	0	0.00	0
Totals	201		458			126		458		

Source: IOR, L/AG/14/3/2-6.

Appendix 5 *List of occupations included in each socio-economic category*

AGRICULTURE: Farrier, Gamekeeper, Gardener, Grazier, Husbandman, Yeoman.

BUILDING: Bricklayer, Carpenter, Joiner, Mason, Painter, Plumber.

DOMESTIC: Barber, Coachman, Cook, Servant.

MERCHANT: Blackwell Hall Factor, Coal Factor, Cornfactor, Deal Merchant, Factor, Hopmerchant, Keeper of Blackwell Hall, Merchant, Norwich Factor, Timber Merchant, Virginia Merchant.

MANUFACTURE: Anchor Smith, Armourer, Baker, Bevermaker, Biscuit Baker, Blacksmith, Bookbinder, Brassier, Brewer, Broad Weaver, Cabinet Maker, Chocolate Maker, Clockmaker, Clothier, Clothworker, Coach Maker, Collar Maker, Comb Maker, Confectioner, Cooper, Cordwainer, Currier, Cutler, Distiller, Dyer, Embroiderer, Feather Dresser, Felt Maker, Flaxman, Founder, Fringemaker, Gilder, Girdler, Glass Maker, Glover, Gun Maker, Gunpowder Maker, Gunsmith, Hatband Maker, Jeweller, Laceman, Maltster, Milliner, Oilman, Painter Stainer, Pewterer, Printer, Sadler, Sailmaker, Salesman, Scarlet Dyer, Shipwright, Shoe Maker, Silkman, Silk Thrower, Silk Weaver, Skinner, Soap Maker, Sugar Baker, Sugar Refiner, Sword Cutler, Tailor, Tallow Chandler, Template Maker, Tentmaker, Throwster, Tinman, Tinplate Worker, Turner, Upholder, Upholsterer, Watchmaker, Wax Chandler, Weaver, Wheelwright, Wince Cooper, Wire Drawer.

FINANCE: Broker, Goldsmith (NB, the title 'broker' was only used in the Bank of England's transfer books and only after 1698).

PROFESSIONAL: Accountant, Apothecary, Archdeacon, Bachelor of Arts, Bank of England Accountant, Barber Surgeon, Brigadier, Canon, Captain, Cashier of the Bank of England, Chemist, Clerk, College Fellow, Colonel, Commander, Dean, Doctor, Doctor of Divinity, Doctor of Physick, Druggist, Engraver, Major General, Master of Arts, Mathematician, Medical Doctor, Minister, Musician, Notary Public, Physician, Rector, Schoolmaster, Scrivener, Secretary, Solicitor General, Surgeon.

RETAILING: Book Seller, Butcher, Button Seller, Cheesemonger, Corn Chandler, Draper, Feltmonger, Fishmonger, Fruiterer, Glass Seller, Grocer, Haberdasher, Hosier, Indian Gown Seller, Innholder, Ironmonger, Leatherseller, Linen Draper, Mealman/woman, Mercer, Merchant Taylor, Poulterer, Salter, Stationer, Tobacconist, Victualler, Vintner, Woodmonger, Woollen Draper, Wool Seller.

TRANSPORT: Carrier, Lighterman, Mariner, Merchant Seaman, Packer, Warehouse Keeper, Warehouseman, Waterman, Wharfinger.

Bibliography

MANUSCRIPT SOURCES

BANK OF ENGLAND ARCHIVES

Bank stock list of subscribers to capital issues of 1694 and 1697, AC27/382.
Register Book of contracts in Bank stock, 1697 1702, AC27/383.
Stock Ledgers 1694 1702, AC27/413 20.
Dividend Books, 1697 1705, AC27/581 2.
Transfer Books, 1694 1702, AC28/32233, AC28/1513 22.
General Ledgers, 1694 1702, ADM7/1.
Minutes of the Court of Directors, 1694 1702, G4/1 4.
Minutes of the General Court of Proprietors, 1694 1702, G7/1 2.
List of the original subscribers to the Bank of England, 1694, M1/1.
Bank Stock Subscription Books, 1697, M1/6 9.
Court Manuscript Book, M5/448.
Letter Book of John Browne and Thomas Sandes, 1692 96, M7/3.

BRITISH LIBRARY MANUSCRIPTS

Earl of Halifax's Letters on the Land Banks and Finance, 1696 1697, Add. MS 34,355.

BRITISH LIBRARY ORIENTAL AND INDIA OFFICE COLLECTIONS

New East India Company, Subscription Book,1698, A/1/54.
Old East India Company, Court Books, B/39 B/41; B/43 4.
Old East India Company, Lists of holders of stock, 1688 99, H/1 3; L/AG/1/10/2.
Old East India Company, Transfer Books, 1688 1702, L/AG/14/3/2 6.
New East India Company, Transfer Book, 1698 1709, L/AG/14/3/9.

EAST SUSSEX RECORD OFFICE

Frewen Family Archives, Papers of Samuel Jeake, the younger, FRE 5301 33.
Rye Corporation Archives, RYE/145/11.

GOLDSMITHS' COMPANY RECORDS, GOLDSMITHS' HALL, LONDON

Apprenticeship Records, vol. III (1670 90); vol. IV, (1690 1708).

GUILDHALL LIBRARY, LONDON

Papers of Thomas Bowrey, MS 3041/1 11.
Herne Family Papers, MS 6372.

LONDON METROPOLITAN ARCHIVES

Brokers' bonds, COL/BR/02/001 73.
Index to brokers' bonds, COL/BR/02/074 5.
An alphabetical list of 100 brokers admitted by the Court of Aldermen, COL/BR/
    03/01/009.
Committee Reports to the Court of Aldermen, COL/BR/03/02/004.
Resolution of stockbrokers fixing commission for the purchase and sale of various
    stocks, COL/BR/09/003.
Orders of the Court of Aldermen that Brokers shall not enter into Wagers,
    COL/BR/09/004.
Rules to be observed in the Admittance of Brokers, COL/BR/09/006.
Repertories of the Court of Aldermen, 1688 1702, COL/CA/01/01/99 111.

THE NATIONAL ARCHIVES, PUBLIC RECORD OFFICE

Hudson's Bay Company Archives, General Court Minute Book, 1688 1702, BH
    1/19, A 2/1.
Hudson's Bay Company Archives, Transfer Books, 1688 1702, BH 1/465, A 43/1 2.
Papers of Mathias Giesque and Co., C104/128/68.
List of subscriptions to the Million Bank, C114/16.
Papers of Charles Blunt, C114/164 5.
Royal African Company, Court of Assistants Minute Books, 1687 1705,
    T70/82 7.
Royal African Company, General Court Minute Book, 1678 1720, T70/101.
Royal African Company, Transfer Books, Stock Journals and Stock Ledgers,
    1687 1700, T70/187 90.

PUBLISHED PRIMARY SOURCES

Anderson, A., *An Historical and Chronological Deduction of the Origins of Commerce
    from the Earliest Accounts to the Present Time*, 2 vols. (London, 1764).
Anon., *A Casual Discourse about Banks; Between a Brigadier, a Lawyer, a Merchant
    and a Goldsmith* (London, 1695).
Anon., *A Collection of the Debates and Proceedings in Parliament In 1694 and 1695.
    Upon the Inquiry into the Late Briberies and Corrupt Practices* (London, 1695).
Anon., *Advice to the Women and Maidens of London* (London, 1678).
Anon., *A Letter From a Lawyer of the Inner Temple, To His Friend in the Country
    Concerning the East India Stock and the Project of Uniting the New and Old
    Companies* (London, 1698).
Anon., *A Letter to a Friend concerning Credit, and how it may be restor'd to the Bank of
    England* (London, 1697).

Anon., *A List of all the Adventurers in the Mine Adventure, May the first 1700* (London, 1700).

Anon., *A List of the Fortunate Adventurers in the Mine Adventure* (London, 1699).

Anon., *A List of the Names of all the Partners in the Lead Mines of Bwlchyr Eskir Hir, in the County of Cardigan* (London, 1695).

Anon., *An Abstract of the Proposals for the Bank on the Tickets of the Million Adventure* (London, 1695).

Anon., *An Elegaick Essay upon the Decease of the Groom Porter and the Lotteries* (London, 1700).

Anon., *Angliae Tutamen: or the Safety of England* (London, 1695).

Anon., *A particular accompt of the moneys paid into the Receipt of the Exchequer upon the late Million Act* (London, 1694).

Anon., *A plain and easie Way to reduce Guineas* (London, 1695?).

Anon., *A Proposal for a Subscription to Raise One Hundred Thousand Pounds, For Circulating the Credit of a Land Bank* (London, 1695?).

Anon., *A Proposal for Putting some Stop to the Extravagant Humour of Stock Jobbing* (London, 1697).

Anon., *A Proposal for Raising Two Millions of Money* (London, 1695).

Anon., *A Proposal for the Speedy Procuring a Sufficient Quantity of Plate* (London, 1695?).

Anon., *A Proposal Humbly Offer'd ... to raise Two Hundred Thousand Pounds per Annum* (London, 1696?).

Anon., *A Proposal to Raise a Million of Money by Credit on a Publick Bank* (London, 1694?).

Anon., *A Second Discourse about Banks: Between a Brigadier, a Lawyer, a Merchant, and a Goldsmith* (London, 1695?).

Anon., *A Short View Of the Apparent Dangers and Mischiefs From The Bank of England* (London, 1707).

Anon., *At a General Court of the Adventurers for the general joynt stock to the East Indies* (London, 1693).

Anon., *At a General Court of the Adventurers in the general joynt stock to the East Indies* (London, 1694).

Anon., *A Way to Catch the Usurer* (London, 1689).

Anon., *Characters of Gentlemen that have put into the Ladies Invention* (London, 1695).

Anon., *Diluvium Lachrymarum: A Review of the Fortunate and Unfortunate Adventurers* (London, 1694).

Anon., *List of the Names of All the Adventurers in the stock of the Honourable East India Company* (London, 1697).

Anon., *Observations upon the Constitution of the Company of the Bank of England* (London, 1694).

Anon., *Plain Dealing: in a Dialogue between Mr. Johnson and Mr. Wary* (London, 1691).

Anon., *Proposals for National Banks; Whereby The Profits on Usury, tho reduc'd to Three per Cent. Per Annum will supply his Majesty* (London, 1696).

Anon., *Proposals Humbly Offered ... for the Raising of Six Millions of Pounds Sterling* (London, 1696?).

Anon., *Reasons for Encouraging the Bank of England* (London, 1695).

Anon., *Reasons Humbly Offered, Against a Clause in the Bill for Regulating Brokers* (London, 1697).

Anon., *Reasons Humbly Offered Against Altering the Act for Restraining the Number of Brokers* (London, 1708).

Anon., 'Remarks upon the LONDON GAZETTE, relating to the Streights Fleet, and the Battle of Landen in Flanders', in J. Somers (ed.), *A Collection of Scarce and Valuable Tracts*, 16 vols. (London, 1748 52), vol. II, pp. 217 28.

Anon., *Some Considerations Offered against the Continuance of the Bank of England, In a Letter to a Member of the present Parliament* (London, 1694).

Anon., *The Arraignment, Trial, and Condemnation of Squire Lottery, Alias Royal Oak Lottery* (London, 1699).

Anon., *The Case of the Adventurers in the Million Lottery, Humbly Offer'd to the Consideration of the Honourable House of Commons* (London, 1697).

Anon., *The Examinations and Informations upon Oath, of Sir Thomas Cooke, And Several other Persons* (London, 1695).

Anon., *The Honourable Undertaking; or Five Hundred Pounds for One Shilling* (London, 1698).

Anon., *The Names of 51 Persons chosen the 10th of September 1695 ... for a Committee to consider of proper Methods for Settling and Establishing a National Land Bank* (London, 1695).

Anon., *The True Picture of an Ancient Tory* (London, 1702).

Anon., *The Tryal and Condemnation of the Trustees of the Land Bank at Exeter Exchange ... for Murdering the Bank of England at Grocers Hall* (London, 1696).

Anselment, R. A. (ed.), *The Remembrances of Elizabeth Freke, 1671 1714* (Cambridge University Press, 2001).

Ayres, J., *Arithmetick: A Treatise Designed for the Use and Benefit of Trades Men* (London, 1702).

Briscoe, J., *A Discourse on the Late Funds of the Million Act, Lottery Act, and the Bank of England* (London, 1694).

    An Explanatory Dialogue of a Late Treatise, intituled, A Discourse on the late Funds (London, 1694).

    The Freehold Estates of England, or England itself the best Fund or Security (London, 1695?).

Cary, J., *An Essay On The State Of England In Relation to its Trade, its Poor, and its Taxes* (Bristol, 1695).

Castaing, J., *An Interest Book at 4, 5, 6, 7, 8 per C* (London, 1700).

Centlivre, S., *A Bold Stroke for a Wife* (London: Edward Arnold, 1969).

Child, J., *A Treatise Concerning the East India Trade* (London, 1681).

    A Discourse of Trade (London, 1690).

    A New Discourse of Trade (London, 1693).

    The Great Honour and Advantage of the East India trade to the Kingdom, Asserted (London, 1697).

Cocker, E., *Cocker's Arithmetic: Being a Plain and Familiar Method* (Glasgow, 1687).

    Cocker's English Dictionary (London, 1704).

Davenant, C., *An Essay upon Ways and Means of Supplying the War* (London, 1695).

Discourses on the Publick Revenues, And On The Trade of England (London, 1698).

An Essay upon the Balance of Power (London, 1701).

The True Picture of a Modern Whig (London, 1701).

Defoe, D., *An Essay Upon Projects* (London, 1697).

The Freeholders Plea Against Stock Jobbing Elections of Parliament Men (London, 1701).

The Villainy of Stock Jobbers Detected (London, 1701).

An Essay Upon Publick Credit (London, 1710).

The Anatomy of Exchange Alley (London, 1719).

de la Vega, J., *Confusion de Confusiones*. Portions Descriptive of the Amsterdam Stock Exchange Selected and Translated by H. Kellenbenz (Boston, Mass.: Baker Library, 1957).

Ellis, G. (ed.), *The Ellis Correspondence: Letters Written During the Years 1686, 1687, 1688, and addressed to John Ellis, Esq.*, 2 vols. (London, 1829).

Evelyn, J., *The Diary of John Evelyn*, edited by E. S. De Beer, 6 vols. (Oxford: Clarendon Press, 1955).

Godfrey, M., *A Short Account of the Bank of England* (London, 1695).

[Grascome, S.] *An Account of the Proceedings in the House of Commons in Relation to the Recoining the Clipp'd Money* (London, 1696).

Hatton, E., *Comes Commercii: or the Trader's Companion* (London, 1699).

The Merchant's Magazine or Trades Man's Treasury (London, 1701).

Hawkins, J., *Clavis Commercii or the Key of Commerce* (London, 1704).

Hunter, M., and A. Gregory (eds.), *An Astrological Diary of the Seventeenth Century: Samuel Jeake of Rye, 1652 1699* (Oxford University Press, 1988).

Hyde, R. (ed.), *The A to Z of Georgian London* (London: Harry Margary, Lympne Castle in association with Guildhall Library, 1981).

The A to Z of Restoration London (London: Harry Margary, Lympne Castle in association with Guildhall Library, 1992).

Levett, Mayor, Jovis Decimo die Octobris, 1700, *Annoq. Regni Regis Willielmi Tertii Angliae, &c.* [Order that none of the Exchange Brokers do for the future agitate any business in open Alley, 10 October 1700] (London, 1700).

Leybourn, W., *Panarithmologia* (London, 1693).

L. G. and F. P., *Project for the Ready Raising of a Million* (London, 1694).

Locke J., *The Correspondence of John Locke*, edited by E. S. de Beer, 8 vols. (Oxford: Clarendon Press, 1979).

Luttrell, N., *A Brief Historical Relation of State Affairs from September 1678 to April 1714*, 6 vols. (Oxford University Press, 1857).

Malynes, G., *Consuetudo, Vel Lex Mercatoria* (London, 1622).

Mather, C., *Pietas in Patriam: The Life of His Excellency Sir William Phips* (London, 1697).

Mordington, James, Whitelocke, B., and R. Cotton, *A Proposal Humbly Offered ... for Raising a Considerable Sum of Mony Yearly* (London, 1696?).

Mortimer, T., *Every Man His Own Broker: or A Guide to Exchange Alley* (London, 1761).

Neale, T., *A Profitable Adventure to the Fortunate* (London, 1693).

The Profitable Adventure to the Fortunate (London, 1694).

The Profitable Adventure to the Fortunate ... Having been reported in Town, and Mentioned in Several News Letters to be Stopt (London, 1694).

A Further Account of the Proposals ... for Exchanging the Blank Tickets in the Million Adventure (London, 1695).

The Second Drawing of the Blank Tickets of the Million Adventure (London, 1695).

A Second Profitable Adventure to the Fortunate (London, 1696).

North, R., *The Gentleman's Accomptant* (London, 1714).

Paterson, W., *A Brief Account of the Intended Bank of England* (London, 1694).

Pollexfen, J., *A Discourse of Trade, Coyn and Paper Credit* (London, 1697).

Roberts, L., *The Merchants Map of Commerce: wherein the Universal Manner and Matter of Trade is Compendiously Handled* (London, 1676).

Saunders, T., *Fortunatus's Looking Glass, or an Essay Upon Lotteries* (London, 1699).

Settle, E., *Augusta Lachrymans: A Funeral Tear, To the Memory of The Worthy and Honour'd Michael Godfrey, Esq* (London, 1695).

Shadwell, T., *Epsom Wells, and, The Volunteers, or, The Stock Jobbers*, edited by D. M. Walmsley (Boston: D.C. Heath and Co., 1930).

Temple, R. C. (ed.), *The Papers of Thomas Bowrey 1669 1713* (London: Hakluyt Society, 1927).

Thomas, D., *Propositions for General Land Banks* (London, 1695).

Thompson, E. M. (ed.), *The Correspondence of the Family of Hatton being chiefly addressed to Christopher First Viscount Hatton A.D. 1601 1704*, 2 vols. (London: Camden Society, 1878).

Vaughan, R., *For the Perusal of all and every of You* (London, 1695).

Vernon, J., *The Compleat Comptinghouse: Or the Young Lad Instructed* (London, 1678).

Ward, E., *A Hue and Cry After A Man Midwife, Who has Lately Deliver'd the Land Bank of Their Money* (London, 1699).

The London Spy, edited by P. Hyland (Michigan: Colleagues Press, 1993).

NEWSPAPERS AND PERIODICALS

The Athenian Mercury (1691 97).

Castaing, J., *The Course of the Exchange, and Other Things* (London, 1698 1702).

The Flying Post (1693 1702).

The Gentleman's Journal or the Monthly Miscellany (London, 1692 94).

Houghton, J., *A Collection for Improvement of Husbandry and Trade* (London, 1692 1703).

The London Gazette (1688 1702).

The New State of Europe: Or a True Account of Publick Transactions and Learning (1701 02).

The Post Boy (1695 1702).

The Post Man (1695 1702).

Whiston's Merchants Weekly Remembrancer, of the Present Money Prices of their Goods Ashoar in London (1689 96).

Bibliography

263

PARLIAMENTARY PAPERS

Journals of the House of Commons, vols. X, XI.

INTERNET RESOURCES

European State Finance Database, dataset \neal\coe1700s.rtf at http://www.le.ac.
uk/hi/bon/ESFDB/

SECONDARY MATERIAL

Abrahams, D., 'Jew Brokers of the City of London', *Miscellanies (The Jewish Historical Society of England)*, vol. III (1937), pp. 80 93.

Acres, W. M., *The Bank of England from Within, 1694 1900*, 2 vols. (London: Bank of England, 1931).

'Huguenot Directors of the Bank', *Proceedings of the Huguenot Society of London*, vol. XV (1934 37), 238 48.

Alexander, J. M. B., 'The Economic Structure of the City of London at the End of the Seventeenth Century', *Urban History Yearbook* (1989), 47 62.

Anderson, G. M., McCormick, R. E., and R. D. Tollison, 'The Economic Organization of the English East India Company', *Journal of Economic Behaviour and Organization*, 4 (1983), 221 38.

Andréadès, A., *A History of the Bank of England 1640 1903*, 4th edn (London: Cass, 1966).

Appleby, J. O., *Economic Thought and Ideology in Seventeenth Century England* (Princeton University Press, 1978).

Armstrong, W. A., 'The Use of Information about Occupation', in E. A. Wrigley (ed.), *Nineteenth Century Society: Essays in the Use of Quantitative Methods for the Study of Social Data* (Cambridge University Press, 1972).

Ashton, J., *A History of the English Lotteries* (London: Leadenhall Press, 1893).

Ashton, T. S., *Economic Fluctuations in England, 1700 1800* (Oxford: Clarendon Press, 1959).

Bahlman, D. W. R., *The Moral Revolution of 1688* (New Haven: Yale University Press, 1957).

Banner, S., *Anglo American Securities Regulation: Cultural and Political Roots, 1690 1860* (Cambridge University Press, 1998).

Barbour, V., *Capitalism in Amsterdam in the Seventeenth Century* (Ann Arbor: University of Michigan Press, 1950).

Barnes, V. F., 'The Rise of William Phips', *New England Quarterly*, 1 (1928), 271 94.

Baxter, S. B., *The Development of the Treasury, 1660 1702* (London: Longmans, 1957).

Bernstein, P. L., *Against the Gods: The Remarkable Story of Risk* (New York: Wiley, 1998).

Capital Ideas Evolving (New York: Wiley, 2007).

Berry, H. M., *Gender, Society and Print Culture in Late Stuart England: The Cultural World of the Athenian Mercury* (Aldershot: Ashgate, 2003).

Bisschop, W. R., *The Rise of the London Money Market, 1640 1826* (London: Cass, 1968).

Black, F., and M. S. Scholes, 'The Pricing of Options and Corporate Liabilities', *Journal of Political Economy*, 81 (1973), 637 54.

Bond, D. H., and W. R. McLeod (eds.), *Newsletters to Newspapers: Eighteenth Century Journalism* (Morgantown: West Virginia University Press, 1977).

Bonney, R. (ed.), *The Rise of the Fiscal State in Europe, c. 1200 1815* (Oxford University Press, 1999).

Bowen, H. V., 'The "Little Parliament": The General Court of the East India Company, 1750 1784', *Historical Journal*, 34 (1991), 857 72.

'The Bank of England during the Long Eighteenth Century, 1694 1820', in R. Roberts and D. Kynaston (eds.), *The Bank of England: Money, Power and Influence, 1694 1994* (Oxford: Clarendon Press, 1995), pp. 1 18.

Braddick, M. J., *State Formation in Early Modern England c. 1550 1700* (Cambridge University Press, 2000).

Brantlinger, P., *Fictions of State: Culture and Credit in Britain, 1694 1994* (Ithaca, N.Y.: Cornell University Press, 1996).

Braudel, F., *Civilization and Capitalism 15th 18th Century*, vol. II: *The Wheels of Commerce* (London: Collins, 1982).

Brewer, J., *The Sinews of Power: War, Money and the English State, 1688 1783* (London: Unwin Hyman, 1994).

Brewer, J., and S. Staves (eds.), *Early Modern Conceptions of Property* (London: Routledge, 1995).

Brooks, C., 'Public Finance and Political Stability: The Administration of the Land Tax, 1688 1720', *Historical Journal*, 17 (1974), 281 300.

Broz, J. L., and R. S. Grossman, 'Paying for Privilege: The Political Economy of Bank of England Charters, 1694 1844', *Explorations in Economic History*, 41 (2004), 48 72.

Buck, P., 'People who Counted: Political Arithmetic in the Eighteenth Century', *Isis*, 73 (1982), 28 45.

Burn, G., *The Re emergence of Global Finance* (Basingstoke: Palgrave Macmillan, 2006).

Burt, R., 'Lead Production in England and Wales, 1700 1770', *Economic History Review*, 22 (1969), 249 68.

Bywater, M. F., and B. S. Yamey, *Historic Accounting Literature: A Companion Guide* (London: Scolar, 1982).

Cain, P. J., and A. G. Hopkins, *British Imperialism, 1688 2000* (Harlow: Longman, 2002).

Capie, F., 'The Origins and Development of Stable Fiscal and Monetary Institutions in England', in M. D. Bordo and R. Cortes Conde (eds.), *Transferring Wealth and Power from the Old to the New World: Monetary and Fiscal Institutions in the 17th through the 19th Centuries* (Cambridge University Press, 2001), pp. 19 58.

Cardoso, J. L., 'Confusion de Confusiones: Ethics and Options on Seventeenth Century Stock Exchange Markets', *Financial History Review*, 9 (2002), 109 23.

Carlos, A. M., Key, J., and J. L. Dupree, 'Learning and the Creation of Stock Market Institutions: Evidence from the Royal African and Hudson's Bay Companies, 1670 1700', *Journal of Economic History*, 58 (1998), 318 44.

Carlos, A. M., and J. B. Kruse, 'The Decline of the Royal African Company: Fringe Firms and the Role of the Charter', *Economic History Review*, 49 (1996), 291 313.

Carlos, A. M., and L. Neal, 'Women Investors in Early Capital Markets, 1720 1725', *Financial History Review*, 11 (2004), 197 224.

'The Micro Foundations of the Early London Capital Market: Bank of England Shareholders During and After the South Sea Bubble, 1720 1725', *Economic History Review*, 59 (2006), 498 538.

Carlos, A. M., and J. L. Van Stone, 'Stock Transfer Patterns in the Hudson's Bay Company: A Study of the English Capital Market in Operation, 1670 1730', *Business History*, 38 (1995), 15 39.

Carruthers, B. G., *City of Capital, Politics and Markets in the English Financial Revolution* (Princeton University Press, 1996).

Carswell J., *The South Sea Bubble* (Stroud: Alan Sutton, 1993).

Carter, A. C., *Getting, Spending and Investing in Early Modern Times: Essays on Dutch, English and Huguenot Economic History* (Assen: Van Gorcum, 1975).

Cassis, Y., *Capitals of Capital: A History of International Financial Centres* (Cambridge University Press, 2006).

Cawston, G., and A. H. Keane, *The Early Chartered Companies (AD 1296 1858)* (London: Edward Arnold, 1896).

Chancellor, E., *Devil Take the Hindmost: A History of Financial Speculation* (Basingstoke: Macmillan, 1999).

Chandaman, C. D., *The English Public Revenue, 1660 1688* (Oxford: Clarendon Press, 1975).

Chaudhuri, K. N., *The English East India Company: The Study of an Early Joint Stock Company, 1600 1640* (London: Cass, 1965).

The Trading World of Asia and the English East India Company, 1660 1760 (Cambridge University Press, 1978).

Cherry, G. L., 'The Development of the English Free Trade Movement in Parliament, 1689 1702', *Journal of Modern History*, 25 (1953), 103 19.

Childs, J., 'Fortunes of War', *History Today*, 53 (2003), 51 5.

Clapham, J. H., *The Bank of England: A History*, 2 vols. (London: Cambridge University Press, 1945).

Clark, G., 'The Political Foundations of Modern Economic Growth, 1540 1800', *Journal of Interdisciplinary History*, 25 (1996), 563 88.

Betting on Lives: The Culture of Life Insurance in England, 1695 1775 (Manchester University Press, 1999).

Clay, C., *Public Finance and Private Wealth: The Career of Sir Stephen Fox, 1627 1716* (Oxford: Clarendon Press, 1978).

Cohen, J., 'The Element of Lottery in British Government Bonds, 1694 1919', *Economica*, 20 (1953), 237 46.

Coleman, D. C., 'London Scriveners and the Estate Market in the Later Seventeenth Century', *Economic History Review*, 4 (1951), 221 30.

Sir John Banks, Baronet and Businessman: A Study of Business, Politics and Society in Later Stuart England (Oxford: Clarendon Press, 1963).

The Economy of England, 1450 1750 (Oxford University Press, 1977).

'Mercantilism Revisited', *Historical Journal*, 23 (1980), 773 91.

Cootner, P. H. (ed.), *The Random Character of Stock Market Prices* (Cambridge, Mass.: MIT Press, 2000).

Cope, S. R., 'The Stock Exchange Revisited: A New Look at the Market in Securities in London in the Eighteenth Century', *Economica*, 45 (1978), 1 21.

Corfield, P. J., 'Class by Name and Number in Eighteenth Century Britain', *History*, 72 (1987), 38 61.

Cox, J. C., and M. Rubinstein, *Options Markets* (London: Prentice Hall, 1985).

Cressy, D., *Literacy and the Social Order: Reading and Writing in Tudor and Stuart England* (Cambridge University Press, 1980).

Crouzet, F., 'Walloons, Huguenots and the Bank of England', *Proceedings of the Huguenot Society*, vol. XXV (1990), 167 78.

'The Huguenots and the English Financial Revolution', in P. Higonnet, D. S. Landes and H. Rosovsky (eds.), *Favorites of Fortune: Technology, Growth and Economic Development since the Industrial Revolution* (Cambridge, Mass.: Harvard University Press, 1991), pp. 221 66.

Dale, R., *The First Crash: Lessons from the South Sea Bubble* (Princeton, N.J. and Oxford: Princeton University Press, 2004).

Dale, R. S., Johnson, J. E. V., and L. Tang, 'Financial Markets Can Go Mad: Evidence of Irrational Behaviour During the South Sea Bubble', *Economic History Review*, 58 (2005), 233 71.

Davies, K. G., 'Joint Stock Investment in the Later Seventeenth Century', *Economic History Review*, 4 (1952), 283 301.

The Royal African Company (London: Longmans, 1957).

Davis, R., 'English Foreign Trade, 1660 1700', *Economic History Review*, 7 (1954), 150 66.

English Overseas Trade, 1500 1700 (London: Macmillan, 1973).

Deane, P., 'Capital Formation in Britain before the Railway Age', *Economic Development and Cultural Change*, 9 (1961), 352 68.

Deane, P., and W. A. Cole, *British Economic Growth 1688 1959: Trends and Structure* (Cambridge University Press, 1967).

De Beer, E. S., 'The English Newspapers from 1695 1702', in R. Hatton and J. S. Bromley (eds.), *William III and Louis XIV: Essays, 1680 1720 by and for Mark A. Thomson* (Liverpool University Press, 1968), pp. 117 29.

De Krey, G. S., *A Fractured Society: The Politics of London in the First Age of Party, 1688 1715* (Oxford: Clarendon Press, 1985).

De Marchi, N., and P. Harrison, 'Trading "in the Wind" and with Guile: The Troublesome Matter of the Short Selling of Shares in Seventeenth Century Holland', in N. De Marchi and M. Morgan (eds.), *Higgling: Transactors and their Markets in the History of Economics* (Durham, N.C. and London: Duke University Press, 1994), pp. 47 65.

Dickson, P. G. M., *The Financial Revolution in England: A Study in the Development of Public Credit, 1688 1756* (London: Macmillan, 1967).

Diedricks, H. A., and D. Reeder (eds.), *Cities of Finance* (Amsterdam: North Holland, 1996).

Dowling, S. W., *The Exchanges of London* (London: Butterworth, 1929).

Duguid, C., *The Story of the Stock Exchange* (London, 1901).

Earle, P., *The Wreck of the Almiranta: Sir William Phips and the Search for the Hispaniola Treasure* (London: Macmillan, 1979).

The Making of the English Middle Class: Business, Society and Family Life in London, 1660 1730 (London: Methuen, 1989).

A City Full of People: Men and Women of London 1650 1750 (London: Methuen, 1994).

Ekelund, R. B., and R. D. Tollison, *Politicized Economies: Monarchy, Monopoly and Mercantilism* (College Station, Texas: Texas A&M University Press, 1997).

Ellis, A., *The Penny Universities: A History of the Coffee Houses* (London: Secker and Warburg, 1956).

Erickson, A. L., *Women and Property in Early Modern England* (London: Routledge, 1993).

Ewen, C. L., *Lotteries and Sweepstakes: An Historical, Legal and Ethical Survey of their Introduction, Suppression and Re establishment in the British Isles* (London: Heath Cranton, 1932).

Fama, E., 'Efficient Capital Markets: A Review of the Theory and Empirical Work', *The Journal of Finance*, 25 (1970), 383 417.

Foundations of Finance: Portfolio Decisions and Securities Prices (New York: Basic Books, 1976).

Finkelstein, A., *Harmony and the Balance: An Intellectual History of Seventeenth Century English Economic Thought* (Ann Arbor: University of Michigan Press, 2000).

Fox, A., *Oral and Literate Culture in England, 1500 1700* (Oxford: Clarendon Press, 2001).

Francis, J., *Chronicles and Characters of the Stock Exchange* (London: Hindsight, 2001).

Fraser, P., *The Intelligence of the Secretaries of State and their Monopoly of Licensed News, 1660 1688* (Cambridge University Press, 1956).

Fratianni, M., and F. Spinelli, 'Italian City States and Financial Evolution', *European Review of Economic History*, 10 (2006), 257 78.

Fridson, M. S. (ed.), *Extraordinary Popular Delusions and the Madness of Crowds and Confusion de Confusiones* (New York: Wiley, 1996).

Garber, P., *Famous First Bubbles: The Fundamentals of Early Manias* (Cambridge, Mass.: MIT Press, 2000).

Gauci, P., *The Politics of Trade: The Overseas Merchant in State and Society, 1660 1720* (Oxford University Press, 2001).

Gelderblom, O., and J. Jonker, 'Completing a Financial Revolution: The Finance of the Dutch East India Trade and the Rise of the Amsterdam Capital Market, 1595 1612', *Journal of Economic History*, 64 (2004), 641 72.

George, R. H., 'The Treasure Trove of William Phips', *New England Quarterly*, 6 (1933), 294 318.

Gibbs, G. C., 'Government and the English Press, 1695 to the Middle of the Eighteenth Century', in A. C. Duke and C. A. Tamse (eds.), *Too Mighty to be Free: Censorship and the Press in Britain and the Netherlands* (Zutphen: De Walburg Pers, 1987), pp. 87 106.

Gigerenzer, G., et al., *The Empire of Chance: How Probability Changed Science and Everyday Life* (Cambridge University Press, 1989).

Gigerenzer, G., and R. Selten (eds.), *Bounded Rationality: The Adaptive Toolbox* (Cambridge, Mass. and London: MIT Press, 2001).

Gill, D. M., 'The Treasury, 1660 1714', *English Historical Review*, 46 (1931), 600 22.

Giuseppi, J., 'Sephardi Jews and the Early Years of the Bank of England', *Jewish Historical Society of England Transactions*, vol. XIX (1955 59), pp. 53 63.

The Bank of England: A History from its Foundation in 1694 (London: Evans Bros., 1966).

Glaisyer, N., 'Readers, Correspondents and Communities: John Houghton's A Collection for Improvement of Husbandry and Trade (1692 1703)', in A. Shepard and P. Withington (eds.), *Communities in Early Modern England* (Manchester University Press, 2000), pp. 235 51.

'"A due Circulation in the Veins of the Publick": Imagining Credit in Late Seventeenth and Early Eighteenth Century England', *The Eighteenth Century: Theory and Interpretation*, 46 (2005), 277 97.

The Culture of Commerce in England, 1660 1720 (Woodbridge: Boydell and Brewer, 2006).

Glaisyer, N. and S. Pennell (eds.), *Didactic Literature in England, 1500 1800: Expertise Constructed* (Aldershot: Ashgate, 2003).

Goetzmann, W. M., and K. G. Rouwenhorst (eds.), *The Origins of Value: The Financial Innovations that Created Modern Capital Markets* (Oxford University Press, 2005).

Goldgar, A., *Tulipmania: Money, Honor and Knowledge in the Dutch Golden Age* (Chicago and London: University of Chicago Press, 2007).

Granovetter, M., 'Economic Action and Social Structure: The Problem of Embeddedness', *American Journal of Sociology*, 91 (1985), 481 510.

'Economic Institutions as Social Constructions: A Framework for Analysis', *Acta Sociologica*, 35 (1992), 3 11.

Grassby, R., 'The Rate of Profit in Seventeenth Century England', *English Historical Review*, 94 (1969), 721 51.

'The Personal Wealth of the Business Community in Seventeenth Century England', *Economic History Review*, 23 (1970), 220 34.

'English Merchant Capitalism in the Late Seventeenth Century', *Past and Present*, 46 (1977), 87 107.

The Business Community of Seventeenth Century England (Cambridge University Press, 1995).

Griffiths, P., *A Licence to Trade: The History of the English Chartered Companies* (London: E. Benn, 1974).

Grossman, S. J., and M. H. Miller, 'Liquidity and Market Structure', *The Journal of Finance*, 43 (1988), 617 33.

Gwynn, R. D., *Huguenot Heritage: The History and Contribution of the Huguenots in Britain* (London: Routledge and Kegan Paul, 1985).

Habakkuk, H. J., 'English Landownership, 1680 1740', *Economic History Review*, 10 (1940), 2 17.

'The Long Term Rate of Interest and the Price of Land in the Seventeenth Century', *Economic History Review*, 5 (1952), 26 45.

Hacking, I., *The Emergence of Probability: A Philosophical Study of Early Ideas about Probability, Induction and Statistical Inference* (Cambridge University Press, 1975).

Hancock, D. J., 'Domestic Bubbling: Eighteenth Century London Merchants and Individual Investment in the Funds', *Economic History Review*, 47, (1994), 679 702.

  Citizens of the World: London Merchants and the Integration of the British Atlantic Community, 1735 1785 (Cambridge University Press, 1995).

Handover, P. M., *A History of the London Gazette, 1665 1965* (London: HMSO, 1965).

Harding, V. J., 'The Population of London, 1550 1750: A Review of the Published Evidence', *London Journal*, 15 (1990), 111 28.

  'Early Modern London, 1550 1700', *London Journal*, 20 (1995), 34 45.

Harris, R., *Industrializing English Law: Entrepreneurship and Business Organization, 1720 1844* (Cambridge University Press, 2000).

Harrison, P., 'Rational Equity Valuation at the Time of the South Sea Bubble', *History of Political Economy*, 33 (2001), 269 81.

Harte, N. B., 'The Rise of Protection and the English Linen Trade, 1690 1790', in N. B. Harte and K. G. Ponting (eds.), *Textile History and Economic History* (Manchester University Press, 1973), pp. 74 112.

Heim, C. E., and P. Mirowski, 'Interest Rates and Crowding Out During Britain's Industrial Revolution', *Journal of Economic History*, 47 (1987), 117 39.

Hirshleifer, D., 'Investor Psychology and Asset Pricing', *The Journal of Finance*, 56 (2001), 1533 97.

Hoak, D., and M. Feingold, *The World of William and Mary: Anglo Dutch Perspectives on the Revolution of 1688 89* (Stanford University Press, 1996).

Hoare's Bank, *Hoare's Bank: A Record, 1672 1955* (London: Collins, 1955).

Hogarth, R. M., and M. W. Reder (eds.), *Rational Choice: The Contrast Between Economics and Psychology* (Chicago and London: University of Chicago Press, 1987).

Holden, J. M., *The History of Negotiable Instruments in English Law* (London: Athlone Press, 1955).

Holderness, B. A., 'Widows in Pre industrial Society: An Essay Upon Their Economic Functions', in R. M. Smith (ed.), *Land, Kinship and Life Cycle* (Cambridge University Press, 1985), pp. 423 42.

Holmes, G. (ed.), *Britain after the Glorious Revolution, 1689 1714* (London: Macmillan, 1969).

  'Gregory King and the Social Structure of pre industrial England', *Transactions of the Royal Historical Society*, 5th series, vol. XXVII (1977), pp. 41 68.

  The Professions and Social Change in England, 1680 1730 (London: British Academy, 1981).

  The Making of a Great Power: Late Stuart and Early Georgian Britain, 1660 1722 (London and New York: Longman, 1993).

Hoppit, J., *Risk and Failure in English Business, 1700 1800* (Cambridge University Press, 1987).

  'Attitudes to Credit in Britain 1680 1790', *Historical Journal*, 33 (1990), 305 22.

'Political Arithmetic in Eighteenth Century England', *Economic History Review*, 49 (1996), 516 40.

(ed.), *Failed Legislation, 1660 1800 extracted from the Commons and Lords Journals* (London: Hambledon, 1997).

A Land of Liberty? England, 1689 1727 (Oxford: Clarendon Press, 2000).

'The Myths of the South Sea Bubble', *Transactions of the Royal Historical Society*, vol. XII (2002), pp. 141 65.

Horsefield, J. K., *British Monetary Experiments, 1650 1710* (London: G. Bell and Sons, 1960).

'The Stop of the Exchequer Revisited', *Economic History Review*, 35 (1982), 511 28.

Horwitz, H., 'The East India Trade, the Politicians and the Constitutions, 1689 1702', *Journal of British Studies*, 17 (1978), 1 18.

'"The Mess of the Middle Class" Revisited: The Case of the "Big Bourgeoisie" of Augustan London', *Continuity and Change*, 2 (1987), 263 96.

Hunter, W. W., *A History of British India*, 2 vols. (London and New York: Longmans, 1899 1900).

Israel, J., 'The Amsterdam Stock Exchange and the English Revolution of 1688', *Tijdschrift voor Geschiedenis*, 103 (1990), 412 40.

(ed.), *The Anglo Dutch Moment: Essays on the Glorious Revolution and its World Impact* (Cambridge University Press, 1991).

Johnson, R. S., and C. Giaccotto, *Options and Futures: Concepts, Strategies and Applications* (Minneapolis: West Pub. Co., 1995).

Jones, C., '"A Fresh Division Lately Grown Up Amongst Us": Party Strife, Aristocratic Investment in the Old and New East India Companies and the Vote in the House of Lords on 23 February 1700', *Historical Research*, 68 (1995), 302 17.

Jones, D. W., 'London Merchants and the Crisis of the 1690s', in P. Clark and P. Slack (eds.), *Crisis and Order in English Towns, 1500 1700* (London: Routledge, 1972), pp. 311 55.

War and Economy in the Age of William III and Marlborough (Oxford: Blackwell, 1988).

Jones, J. R., *The Revolution of 1688 in England* (London: Weidenfeld and Nicolson, 1972).

Kagel, J. H., and A. E. Roth, *The Handbook of Experimental Economics* (Princeton University Press, 1995).

Kahneman, D., and A. Tversky (eds.), *Choices, Values, and Frames* (Cambridge University Press, 2000).

Karraker, C. H., 'Spanish Treasure, Casual Revenue of the Crown', *Journal of Modern History*, 5 (1933), 301 18.

Kavanagh, T. M., *Enlightenment and the Shadows of Chance: The Novel and the Culture of Gambling in Eighteenth Century France* (Baltimore and London: Johns Hopkins University Press, 1993).

Keay, J., *The Honourable Company: A History of the English East India Company* (London: HarperCollins, 1991).

Kerridge, E., *Trade and Banking in Early Modern England* (Manchester University Press, 1988).

Kindleberger, C. P., *Manias, Panics and Crashes: A History of Financial Crises* (London: Macmillan, 1989).

Lawson, P., *The East India Company: A History* (London and New York: Longman, 1993).

Lees, R. M., 'Parliament and the Proposal for a Council of Trade, 1695 6', *English Historical Review*, 54 (1939), 38 66.

Levi, M., *Of Rule and Revenue* (Berkeley and London: University of California Press, 1988).

Lewis, W. J., *Lead Mining in Wales* (Cardiff: University of Wales Press, 1967).

Li, M. H., *The Great Recoinage of 1696 9* (London: Weidenfeld and Nicolson, 1963).

Lillywhite, B., *London Coffee Houses: A Reference Book of Coffee Houses of the Seventeenth, Eighteenth and Nineteenth Centuries* (London: George Allen and Unwin, 1963).

Lindert, P. H., 'Unequal English Wealth since 1670', *Journal of Political Economy*, 94 (1986), 1127 62.

Macaulay, T. B., *The History of England from the Accession of James the Second*, 8 vols. (London: Dent, 1915).

Macdonald, J., *A Free Nation Deep in Debt: The Financial Roots of Democracy* (Princeton University Press, 2003).

MacEwen, G. D., *The Oracle of the Coffee House: John Dunston's Athenian Mercury* (San Marino, Calif.: Huntington Library, 1972).

Mackay, C., *Extraordinary Popular Delusions and the Madness of Crowds* (Ware: Wordsworth Reference, 1995).

MacLeod, C., 'The 1690s Patents Boom: Invention or Stock Jobbing?', *Economic History Review*, 39 (1986), 549 71.

Inventing the Industrial Revolution: The English Patent System, 1660 1800 (Cambridge University Press, 1988).

Magnusson, L., *Mercantilism: The Shaping of an Economic Language* (London and New York: Routledge, 1994).

McCusker, J. J., *European Bills of Entry and Marine Lists: Early Commercial Publications and the Origins of the Business Press* (Cambridge, Mass.: Harvard University Library, 1985).

'The Business Press in England before 1775', *The Library*, 8 (1986), 205 31.

McCusker, J. J., and C. Gravesteijn, *The Beginnings of Commercial and Financial Journalism: The Commodity Price Currents, Exchange Rate Currents, and Money Currents of Early Modern Europe* (Amsterdam: Neha, 1991).

McFadden, D., 'Rationality for Economists?', *Journal of Risk and Uncertainty*, 19 (1999), 73 105.

McKendrick, N., and R. B. Outhwaite (eds.), *Business Life and Public Policy: Essays in Honour of D. C. Coleman* (Cambridge University Press, 1986).

Merton, R. C., 'Theory of Rational Option Pricing', *The Bell Journal of Economics and Management Science*, 4 (1973), 141 83.

Michie, R., (ed.), *The Development of London as a Financial Centre*, 4 vols. (London: I. B. Tauris, 1998).

The Stock Exchange: A History (Oxford University Press, 1999).

The Global Securities Market: A History (Oxford University Press, 2006).

Mirowski, P., 'The Rise (and Retreat) of a Market: English Joint Stock Shares in the Eighteenth Century', *Journal of Economic History*, 41 (1981), 559 77.

'What Do Markets Do? Efficiency Tests of the Eighteenth Century London Stock Market', *Explorations in Economic History*, 24 (1987), 107 29.

Monter, E. W., 'Swiss Investment in England, 1697 1720', *Revue Internationale d'Histoire de la Banque*, 2 (1969), 285 98.

Morgan, E. V., and W. A. Thomas, *The Stock Exchange: Its History and Functions* (London: Elek, 1969).

Muldrew, C., *The Economy of Obligation: The Culture of Credit and Social Relations in Early Modern England* (Basingstoke: Macmillan, 1998).

Murphy, A. L., 'Lotteries in the 1690s: Investment or Gamble?', *Financial History Review*, 12 (2005), 227 46.

'Dealing with Uncertainty: Managing Personal Investment in the Early English National Debt', *History*, 91 (2006), 200 17.

'"Come vanno i titoli"? Informazione e investimenti a Londra alla fine del XVII secolo', *Quaderni Storici*, 41 (2007), 133 54.

'Trading Options before Black Scholes: A Study of the Market in Late Seventeenth Century London', *Economic History Review*, 62, S1 (2009), 8 30.

Neal, L., 'The Integration and Efficiency of the London and Amsterdam Stock Markets in the Eighteenth Century', *Journal of Economic History*, 47 (1987), 97 115.

'The Rise of a Financial Press: London and Amsterdam, 1681 1810', *Business History*, 30 (1988), 163 78.

The Rise of Financial Capitalism: International Capital Markets in the Age of Reason (Cambridge University Press, 1990).

Neal, L., and S. Quinn, 'Networks of Information: Markets and Institutions in the Rise of London as a Financial Centre, 1660 1760', *Financial History Review*, 8 (2001), 7 26.

Newman, K., 'Financial Advertising Past and Present', *Three Banks Review*, 140 (1983), 46 56.

Nichols, G. O., 'Intermediaries and the Development of English Government Borrowing: The Case of Sir John James and Major Robert Huntington', *Business History*, 29 (1987), 27 46.

North, D. C., and B. R. Weingast, 'Constitutions and Commitment: The Evolution of Institutions Governing Public Choice in Seventeenth Century England', *Journal of Economic History*, 49 (1989), 803 32.

O'Brien, P. K., 'The Political Economy of British Taxation, 1660 1815', *Economic History Review*, 41, (1988), 1 32.

'Fiscal Exceptionalism: Great Britain and its European Rivals from Civil War to Triumph at Trafalgar and Waterloo', London School of Economics Working Paper, 65/01 (2001).

O'Brien, P. K., and P. A. Hunt, 'The Rise of a Fiscal State in England, 1485 1815', *Historical Research*, 66 (1993), 129 76.

O'Brien, P. K., Keene, D., 't Hart, M., and H. van der Wee (eds.), *Urban Achievement in Early Modern Europe* (Cambridge University Press, 2004).

Outram, D., *The Enlightenment* (Cambridge University Press, 1995).

Pearson, R., 'Shareholder Democracies? English Stock Companies and the Politics of Corporate Governance During the Industrial Revolution', *English Historical Review*, 117 (2002), 840 66.

Pincus, S., '"Coffee Politicians Does Create": Coffeehouses and Restoration Political Culture', *Journal of Modern History*, 67 (1995), 807 34.

Plumb, J. H., *The Growth of Political Stability in England, 1675 1725* (London: Macmillan, 1967).

Plummer, A., *The London Weavers' Company, 1600 1970* (London: Routledge and Kegan Paul, 1972).

Pocock, J. G. A., *Virtue, Commerce and History: Essays on Political Thought and History Chiefly in the Eighteenth Century* (Cambridge University Press, 1985).

Poitras, G., *The Early History of Financial Economics, 1478 1776: From Commercial Annuities to Life Annuities and Joint Stocks* (Cheltenham: Edward Elgar, 2000).

Porter, R., *London: A Social History* (London: Hamish Hamilton, 1994).

Preda, A., 'In the Enchanted Grove: Financial Conversations and the Marketplace in England and France in the 18th Century', *Journal of Historical Sociology*, 14 (2001), 276 307.

'The Rise of the Popular Investor: Financial Knowledge and Investing in England and France, 1840 1880', *The Sociological Quarterly*, 42 (2001), 205 32.

Price, F. G. H., *A Handbook of London Bankers with Some Account of the Early Goldsmiths* (London: Leadenhall Press, 1890 91).

Price, J. M., 'Notes on Some London Price Currents, 1667 1715', *Economic History Review*, 7 (1954), 240 50.

Price, R., *British Society, 1680 1880: Dynamism, Containment and Change* (Cambridge University Press, 1999).

Quinn, S., 'Tallies or Reserves? Sir Francis Child's Balance between Capital Reserves and Extending Credit to the Crown, 1685 1695', *Business and Economic History*, 23 (1994), 39 51.

'Balances and Goldsmith Bankers: The Co ordination and Control of Inter banker Debt Clearing in Seventeenth Century London', in D. Mitchell (ed.), *Goldsmiths, Silversmiths and Bankers: Innovation and the Transfer of Skill, 1550 to 1750* (Stroud: Alan Sutton, 1995), pp. 53 76.

'Gold, Silver and the Glorious Revolution: Arbitrage between Bills of Exchange and Bullion', *Economic History Review*, 49 (1996), 473 90.

'The Glorious Revolution's Effect on English Private Finance: A Microhistory, 1680 1705', *Journal of Economic History*, 61 (2001), 593 615.

Raven, J., 'The Abolition of the English State Lotteries', *Historical Journal*, 34 (1991), 371 89.

Raymond, J. (ed.), *News, Newspapers and Society in Early Modern Britain* (London: F. Cass, 1999).

Rees, W., *Industry before the Industrial Revolution*, 2 vols. (Cardiff: University of Wales Press, 1968).

Reith, G., *The Age of Chance: Gambling in Western Culture* (London and New York: Routledge, 1999).

Rich, E. E., *The Hudson's Bay Company*, 3 vols. (London: The Hudson's Bay Record Society, 1961).

Richards, R. D., 'The Exchequer Bill in the History of English Government Finance', *Economic History*, 3 (1934 37), 193 211.

'The Lottery in the History of English Government Finance', *Economic History*, 3 (1934 37), 57 76.

Roberts, C., 'The Constitutional Significance of the Financial Settlement of 1690', *Historical Journal*, 20 (1977), 59 76.

Rogers, J. E. T., *The First Nine Years of the Bank of England* (Oxford: Clarendon Press, 1887).

Rose C., *England in the 1690s: Revolution, Religion and War* (London: Blackwell, 1999).

Roseveare, H., *The Treasury: The Evolution of a British Institution* (London: Allen Lane, 1969).

The Treasury, 1660 1870: The Foundations of Control (London: George Allen and Unwin, 1973).

The Financial Revolution, 1660 1760 (Harlow: Longman, 1991).

Rubini, D., 'Politics and the Battle for the Banks, 1688 1697', *English Historical Review*, 85 (1970), 693 714.

Saunders, A. (ed.), *The Royal Exchange* (London: Guardian Royal Exchange, 1997).

Schama, S., *The Embarrassment of Riches: An Interpretation of Dutch Culture in the Golden Age* (London: Collins, 1987).

Schubert, E. E., 'Innovations, Debts and Bubbles: International Integration of Financial Markets in Western Europe, 1688 1720', *Journal of Economic History*, 48 (1986), 299 306.

Scott, W. R., *The Constitution and Finance of English, Scottish and Irish Joint Stock Companies to 1720*, 3 vols. (London: Cambridge University Press, 1910 12).

Scoville, W. C., 'The Huguenots and the Diffusion of Technology', *Journal of Political Economy*, 60 (1952), 294 311.

Sharpe, P., 'Dealing with Love: The Ambiguous Independence of the Single Woman in Early Modern England', *Gender and History*, 11 (1999), 209 32.

Shefrin, H., *Beyond Greed and Fear: Understanding Behavioral Finance and the Psychology of Investing* (Boston, Mass.: Harvard Business School Press, 2000).

Sherman, A. A., 'Pressure from Leadenhall: The East India Company Lobby, 1660 1678', *Business History Review*, 50 (1976), 329 55.

Shiller, R. J., *Irrational Exuberance* (Princeton, N. J. and Oxford: Princeton University Press, 2000).

Shleifer, A., *Inefficient Markets: An Introduction to Behavioural Finance* (Oxford University Press, 2000).

Shleifer, A., and R. W. Vishny, 'The Limits of Arbitrage', *The Journal of Finance*, 52 (1997), 35 55.

Smelser, N. J., and R. Swedberg (eds.), *The Handbook of Economic Sociology* (Princeton University Press, 1994).

Smith, R. G. E., 'Uncertainty, Information and Investment Decisions', *The Journal of Finance*, 26 (1971), 67 82.

Smith, W. D., 'The Function of Commercial Centres in the Modernization of European Capitalism: Amsterdam as an Information Exchange in the Seventeenth Century', *Journal of Economic History*, 44 (1984), 985 1005.

Somerville, C. J., *The News Revolution in England: Cultural Dynamics of Daily Information* (Oxford University Press, 1996).

Stasavage, D., 'Credible Commitment in Early Modern Europe: North and Weingast Revisited', *Journal of Law, Economics and Organization*, 18 (2002), 155 86.

 Public Debt and the Birth of the Democratic State: France and Great Britain, 1688 1789 (Cambridge University Press, 2003).

 'Partisan Politics and Public Debt: The Importance of the "Whig Supremacy" for Britain's Financial Revolution', *European Review of Economic History*, 11 (2007), 123 53.

Staves, S., *Married Women's Separate Property in England, 1660 1833* (Cambridge, Mass. and London: Harvard University Press, 1990).

Stewart, L., *The Rise of Public Science: Rhetoric, Technology and Natural Philosophy in Newtonian Britain, 1660 1750* (Cambridge University Press, 1992).

Stump, W., 'An Economic Consequence of 1688', *Albion*, 6 (1974), 26 35.

Sussman, N., and Y. Yafeh, 'Institutional Reforms, Financial Development and Sovereign Debt: Britain, 1690 1790', *Journal of Economic History*, 66 (2006), 906 35.

Sutherland, J., *The Restoration Newspaper and its Development* (Cambridge University Press, 1986).

Swan, E. J., *Building the Global Market: A 4000 Year History of Derivatives* (London: Kluwer Law International, 2000).

Temin, P., and H. J. Voth, 'Credit Rationing and Crowding Out During the Industrial Revolution: Evidence from Hoare's Bank, 1702 1862', *Explorations in Economic History*, 42 (2005), 325 48.

 'Banking as an Emerging Technology: Hoare's Bank, 1702 1742', *Financial History Review*, 13 (2006), 149 78.

Thaler, R. (ed.), *Advances in Behavioural Finance* (Princeton University Press, 1993).

't Hart, M., '"The Devil or the Dutch": Holland's Impact on the Financial Revolution in England, 1643 1694', *Parliaments, Estates and Representation*, 11 (1991), 39 52.

Thirsk, J., and J. P. Cooper (eds.), *Seventeenth Century Economic Documents* (Oxford: Clarendon Press, 1972).

Thomas, K., 'Numeracy in Early Modern England', *Transactions of the Royal Historical Society*, 37 (1987), 103 32.

Thompson, J. W., 'Some Economic Factors in the Revocation of the Edict of Nantes', *The American Historical Review*, 14 (1908), 38 50.

Thornton, P., and N. Rothstein, 'The Importance of Huguenots in the London Silk Industry', *Proceedings of the Huguenot Society of London*, vol. XX (1958 64), pp. 60 88.

Tracy, J. D., *A Financial Revolution in the Habsburg Netherlands: Renten and Renteniers in the County of Holland, 1515 1565* (Berkeley: University of California Press, 1985).

 (ed.), *The Rise of Merchant Empires: Long Distance Trade in the Early Modern World, 1350 1750* (Cambridge University Press, 1990).

Walcot, R., 'The East India Interest in the General Election of 1700 1701', *English Historical Review*, 71 (1956), 223 39.

Walker, R. B., 'Advertising in London Newspapers, 1650 1750', *Business History*, 15 (1973), 112 30.

Ward, E. F., *Christopher Monck, the Duke of Albemarle* (London: John Murray, 1915).

Watson, I. B., *Foundation for Empire: English Private Trade in India, 1659 1760* (New Delhi: Vikas, 1980).

Weingast, B. R., 'The Economic Role of Political Institutions: Market Preserving Federalism and Economic Development', *Journal of Law, Economics and Organization*, 11 (1995), 1 31.

'The Political Foundations of Limited Government: Parliament and Sovereign Debt in 17th and 18th Century England', in J. Drobak and J. Nye (eds.), *The Frontiers of the New Institutional Economics* (San Diego and London: Academic Press, 1997), pp. 213 46.

Weir, D. R., 'Tontines, Public Finance, and Revolution in France and England, 1688 1789', *Journal of Economic History*, 49 (1989), 95 124.

Wells, J., and D. Wills, 'Revolution, Restoration, and Debt Repudiation: The Jacobite Threat to England's Institutions and Economic Growth', *Journal of Economic History*, 60 (2000), 418 41.

Whyman, S. E., *Sociability and Power in Late Stuart England: The Cultural Worlds of the Verneys, 1660 1720* (Oxford University Press, 1999).

Willan, T. S., *The Early History of the Russia Company, 1553 1603* (Manchester University Press, 1956).

Williamson, J. G., 'Why was British Growth So Slow During the Industrial Revolution?', *Journal of Economic History*, 44 (1984), 687 712.

Wilson, C., *England's Apprenticeship, 1603 1763* (London: Longman, 1971).

'Anglo Dutch Investment in Britain in the Seventeenth to Nineteenth Centuries', in Credit Communal de Belgique, *Le Dette Publique aux XVIIIe et XIXe Siècles* (Brussels: Credit Communal de Belgique, 1980).

Winch, D., and P. K. O'Brien (eds.), *The Political Economy of British Historical Experience, 1688 1914* (Oxford University Press, 2002).

Wrigley, E. A., 'A Simple Model of London's Importance in Changing English Society and Economy, 1650 1750', in P. Abrams and E. A. Wrigley (eds.), *Towns in Societies: Essays in Economic History and Historical Sociology* (Cambridge University Press, 1978), pp. 215 43.

Yamey, B. S., 'Scientific Bookkeeping and the Rise of Capitalism', *Economic History Review*, 1 (1949), 99 113.

'Accounting and the Rise of Capitalism: Further Notes on a Theme by Sombart', *Journal of Accounting Research*, 2 (1964), 117 36.

UNPUBLISHED THESES AND DISSERTATIONS

Brooks, C., 'Taxation, Finance and Public Opinion, 1688 1714', unpublished PhD thesis (University of Cambridge, 1971).

Coffman, D. D., 'The Fiscal Revolution of the Interregnum: Excise Taxation in the British Isles, 1643 1663', unpublished PhD thesis (University of Pennsylvania, 2008).

Cowan, B. W., 'The Social Life of Coffee: Commercial Culture and Metropolitan Society in Early Modern England, 1600 1720', unpublished PhD thesis (Princeton University, 2000).

Davison, L. K., 'Public Policy in an Age of Economic Expansion: The Search for Commercial Accountability, 1690 1750', unpublished PhD thesis (Harvard University, 1990).

Glaisyer, N., 'The Culture of Commerce in England, 1660 1720', unpublished PhD thesis (University of Cambridge, 1999).

Jones, D. W., 'London Overseas Merchant Groups at the End of the Seventeenth Century and the Moves against the East India Company', unpublished PhD thesis (University of Oxford, 1970).

Julian, M. R., 'English Economic Legislation, 1660 1714', unpublished MPhil dissertation (London School of Economics, 1979).

Murphy, A. L., 'Society, Knowledge and the Behaviour of English Investors, 1688 1702', unpublished PhD thesis (University of Leicester, 2005).

Parkinson, G., 'The London Stock Market in the 1690s', unpublished MPhil dissertation (University of Cambridge, 2006).

Parsons, B., 'The Behaviour of Prices on the London Stock Market in the Early Eighteenth Century', unpublished PhD thesis (University of Chicago, 1974).

Quinn S., 'Banking before the Bank: London's Unregulated Goldsmith Bankers, 1660 1694', unpublished PhD thesis (University of Illinois at Urbana Champaign, 1994).

Rhodes, N. J., 'The London Lead Company in North Wales, 1693 1792', unpublished PhD thesis (University of Leicester, 1970).

Thomas, J. H., 'Thomas Neale, a Seventeenth Century Projector', unpublished PhD thesis (University of Southampton, 1979).

Index

Lightning Source UK Ltd.
Milton Keynes UK
UKOW052244291112

202947UK00009B/247/P